Writing correctly

P9-CJH-956

A Canadian
Writer's
Reference

A Canadian
Writer's
Reference

Seventh Edition

Diana Hacker

Nancy Sommers
Harvard University

Contributing ESL Specialist
Kimberli Huster
Robert Morris University

bedford/st.martin's
Macmillan Learning

Boston | New York

For Bedford/St. Martin's

Vice President, Editorial, Macmillan Learning Humanities: Edwin Hill
Senior Program Director for English: Leasa Burton
Senior Program Manager: Stacey Purviance
Director of Content Development: Jane Knetzger
Executive Editor: Michelle M. Clark
Senior Media Editor: Barbara G. Flanagan
Development Editor: Will Stonefield
Canadian Editor: Dawn Hunter
Editorial Assistant: Aislyn Fredsall
Senior Content Project Manager: Kendra LeFleur
Executive Marketing Manager: Joy Fisher Williams
Marketing Manager: Vivian Garcia
Senior Workflow Project Supervisor: Joe Ford
Production Supervisor: Robin Besofsky
Senior Media Producer: Allison Hart
Copy Editor: Arthur Johnson
Indexer: Ellen Kuhl Repetto
Photo Editor: Angela Boehler
Permissions Editor: Kalina Ingham
Text Design: Claire Seng-Niemoeller
Cover Design: John Callahan
Composition: Lumina Datamatics, Inc.
Printing and Binding: RR Donnelley

Acknowledgments

Stephen J. Gould. Excerpt from "Were Dinosaurs Dumb?" *Natural History*, 87(5): 9–16. Reprinted by permission of Rhonda R. Shearer.
Anne and Jack Rudloe, Excerpt from "Electric Warfare: The Fish That Kill with Thunderbolts," *Smithsonian* 24(5): 95–105. Reprinted by permission of Jack Rudloe.
Betsy Taylor, excerpt from "Big Box Stores are Bad for Main Street," in Masci, D. (1999, November 19). *The Consumer Culture. CQ Researcher*, 9, 1001–1016. Copyright © 1999 by CQ Press, a division of Sage Publications, Inc. Reprinted by permission of SAGE Publications, Inc.

Preface for instructors

Dear Colleagues:

Welcome to the seventh edition of *A Canadian Writer's Reference*. When you assign *A Canadian Writer's Reference*, you send an important message to your students: Writing is worth studying and practising. And you make it easy for students to find answers to their writing questions quickly and efficiently. The more comfortable students become using their handbook, the more confident and successful they become as college and university writers.

As I developed the seventh Canadian edition, I kept one central question in mind: What is the value of owning a handbook? We know that 79 percent of students surveyed by Bedford/St. Martin's say that using a handbook makes them feel more confident as academic writers. Yet we know, too, that students can access free online materials about writing. *How does owning a handbook help students succeed as college or university writers?*

A Canadian Writer's Reference is designed so that students can feel confident in their investment; they find what they need and understand what they find. In the handbook, they receive straightforward, trusted answers to their questions about every aspect of college and university writing, from drafting a thesis statement to formatting a paper. And in LaunchPad, the companion media, students have plenty of opportunities to practise and strengthen their skills. On the open web, students might search for help and receive millions of results, including outdated and questionable information that is more confusing than illuminating. And free websites offer no practice tools that include feedback, scoring, and tracking.

A Canadian Writer's Reference is designed for teachers, too, so that students in their classes are all on the same page, with access to the same trusted advice and to answers to common questions and solutions to specific writing problems. The value of the handbook, as I learn from fellow teachers, is that it provides a common vocabulary, both within the classroom and across a writing program, to meet a college's or university's learning outcomes.

A Canadian Writer's Reference helps students succeed because it breaks down complex tasks and challenging concepts, providing step-by-step instruction, one lesson at a time. Take research, for example, one of the most challenging assignments for first-year writers. The seventh edition uses a "how to" approach — both in the handbook and in LaunchPad — to bring students into the research process, showing them how to ask a research question, enter a research conversation, go beyond a Google search, read and evaluate sources, avoid plagiarism, annotate bibliography entries, and more. The instruction and guidance students need to compose successful academic essays is all in one place, so when they're writing their papers at 2 a.m., they have a trusted source to consult. And in that moment, when a student takes ownership of the writing experience, the handbook becomes *My Canadian Writer's Reference.*

On the first day of class I tell my students, *Everything you need to become a successful writer in any college or university course is in* A Canadian Writer's Reference; *buy it, become friends with it.* With the seventh edition, students have the valuable combination of a print resource and a comprehensive online resource to build their success and confidence as college or university writers and as writers in the world beyond. I am eager to share the new edition with you, confident that you and your students will find value in *A Canadian Writer's Reference.*

Nancy Sommers with student writer Michelle Nguyen. (Photo by Mara Weible)

Nancy Sommers

nancy_sommers@harvard.edu

What's new in this edition?

When students take ownership of their college or university writing experience, and when they have the tools that enable them to do so, they gain confidence — and that confidence brings success, not only in the writing course but in the writing students do for other courses as well. **A Canadian Writer's Reference**, Seventh Edition, and **LaunchPad** together offer postsecondary writers a learning tool that builds confidence. What's most exciting about the seventh edition is our emphasis on help that is **personal, practical**, and **digital**. *A Canadian Writer's Reference* is reimagined as a system that helps students target their needs and see their successes; that offers innovative practice with writing, reading, thinking, and research; and that lives in a familiar, accessible environment.

New in the handbook

- **New ways to navi-gate** bring students to key content quickly. Common student questions about writing, written in plain language, appear on each tab and help students find answers to questions

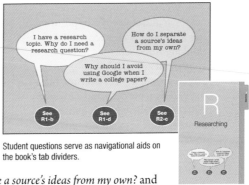

Student questions serve as navigational aids on the book's tab dividers.

such as *How do I separate a source's ideas from my own?* and *What can I do if my writing is too wordy?* Chapter previews, featured in the writing and research sections, direct students to specific help within the chapter.

- **A new *how-to* approach** offers step-by-step instruction that will help students apply writing advice in practical ways and transfer skills to many different kinds of writing assignments. Fourteen new boxes offer the straightforward help that instructors and students want.

NEW **HOW TO** BOXES

- How to solve five common problems with thesis statements, 8
- How to write helpful peer review comments, 21
- How to improve your writing with an editing log, 30
- How to read like a writer, 61
- How to draft an analytical thesis statement, 66
- How to write a summary of a multimodal text, 74
- How to draft a thesis statement for an argument, 90
- How to deliver a speech or presentation, 104
- How to enter a research conversation, 332
- How to go beyond a Google search, 336
- How to avoid plagiarizing from the web, 347
- How to be a responsible research writer, 373
- How to answer the basic question "Who is the author?" 398
- How to cite a source reposted from another source, 418

- **New Writer's Choice** boxes on grammar and style offer opportunities for students to practise critical thinking at the sentence level. A new **rhetorical approach to grammar coverage** emphasizes decision making based on purpose and audience. This approach makes grammar content more teachable by giving instructors flexibility — a way to individualize instruction for students who may need more than a conventional explanation of the rules.

The Writer's Choice box on choosing a point of view appears on page 124.

- **New emphasis on peer review** supports students as they practise the skills they need to collaborate in college and university writing environments and beyond. Thoroughly revised content in section C3 illustrates best practices for peer review.

- **More attention to research** helps students meet important academic requirements. MLA's 2016 guidelines and the *Chicago Manual of Style's* 2017 guidelines inform the research coverage so that students have up-to-date advice and models as well as instruction for conducting responsible research. A new APA-style review of the literature paper shows proper formatting and effective writing.

- **ForeWords for English is custom content made simple.** Developed especially for writing courses, our ForeWords for English program contains a library of the most popular requested content in easy-to-use modules (12–16 pages each) to help you build the best possible text. Choose from modules on time management, CSE style, business writing, sentence templates for academic writing, writing proposals, and more. Of course you can still include original department- or school-specific material as well. Visit **macmillanlearning.com/forewords /composition**.

The following Hacker handbook content is available for custom editions: *Writing in the Disciplines; Resources for Multilingual Writers and ESL; Understanding and Composing Multimodal Projects;* and *Strategies for Online Learners.* And for programs or instructors who prefer a digital-only handbook, a full e-book for *A Canadian Writer's Reference* is available. Contact your publisher's representative for more information.

Now in LaunchPad

As an instructor, you may be looking for new ways to get the most out of your handbook. **LaunchPad** combines innovative practice and assessment tools in a fully customizable course space. LaunchPad allows you to mix our resources with yours, assign easily, and save yourself time. For students, LaunchPad is the space in which they will learn and practise key skills.

- **LearningCurve, exercises, and writing activities**, all of them assignable and most of them autoscored, provide opportunities for students to practise reading, writing, grammar, and research skills. LaunchPad features more than 30 LearningCurve activities and more than 280 exercises. Feedback in the exercises and in the adaptive LearningCurve activities makes the engagement a learning experience. The **gradebook** in LaunchPad, which can integrate with your LMS, allows you to view, track, and report students' progress.
- **Video tools** make it easy to **integrate open-source content** (videos from YouTube and other sources) into your LaunchPad course and allow you to build scorable, trackable response assignments around that content. The video tools allow your class to engage in online discussions about the material, fostering a social environment.
- **Over 140 Grammar Girl podcasts** that delve into key concepts in mechanics, style, and usage. Students can listen to the podcasts at home or on the go as a supplement to the handbook. You can also easily assign the podcasts as homework.

What hasn't changed?

The handbook **covers a lot of ground.** Neither Google nor an OWL can give students the confidence that comes with a coherent reference that covers all the topics they need in a writing course. *A Canadian Writer's Reference* supports students as they compose for different purposes and audiences and in a variety of genres and as they collaborate, revise deeply, conduct research, document sources, format their writing, and edit for clarity.

It's **easy to use and easy to understand.** The handbook's explanations are brief, accessible, and illustrated by examples, most by student writers. The book's many boxes, charts, checklists, and menus are designed to help users find what they need quickly.

It provides **authoritative, trustworthy instruction.** Most writing resources on the web offer *information*, but they don't offer *instruction.* With the seventh edition of *A Canadian Writer's Reference,* students have reference content that has been class-tested by hundreds of thousands of students and instructors. Users who loved the new **Writing Guides** in the sixth edition will be pleased to know they are still here in the seventh.

It is available as an **affordable e-book** from partner vendors that offer mobile-friendly, accessible e-books that match the content of our print books and that provide students with the ability to read, highlight, take notes, and search. Both offline and download options are available. Visit **macmillanlearning.com/ebooks** for more information.

It comes with the **service and support** you have come to expect from Bedford/St. Martin's. We have been in the field of composition with you for more than thirty-five years. We provide professional resources, professional development workshops, training for digital tools, and quick, personal service when you need it.

And, as always, you get more with Bedford/St. Martin's

At Bedford/St. Martin's, providing support to teachers and their students who use our books and digital tools is our top priority. The dynamic Bedford/St. Martin's English Community is now our home for professional resources, including *Bedford Bits*, our popular blog with new ideas for the composition classroom. To connect with our authors and your colleagues, join us at **community.macmillan.com,** where you can download titles from our professional resource series, review projects in the pipeline, sign up for webinars, or start a discussion.

Acknowledgments

I am grateful for the expertise, enthusiasm, and classroom experience that so many individuals brought to the seventh edition.

Reviewers

Elizabeth Acosta, El Paso Community College; Brian Adler, Pasadena City College; Lisa Busonic Avendano, Lincoln Land Community College; Eberly Barnes, University of California, San Diego; Michelle Bean, Rio Hondo College; Jason Beardsley, Santa Monica College; Matt Birkenhauer, Northern Kentucky University; Brett Bodily, North Lake College; Scott Boltwood, Emory & Henry College; Michael Brokos, Johns Hopkins Carey Business School; Merissa Brown, Leeward Community College; Christopher Cain, Towson University; Bryonie Carter, St. Charles Community College; Cheryl Clark, Miami Dade College; Virginia Crisco, California State University, Fresno; Jim Crooks, Shasta College; Amy Peterson Cyr, University of Maine at Augusta; Ann Dean, University of Massachusetts, Lowell; Tom Deans, University of Connecticut; Regina Dilgen, Palm Beach State College; Bonnie Dowd, Montclair State University; Patricia Keefe Durso, Fairleigh Dickinson University; Heather Elko, Eastern Florida State College; Laura Ellis-Lai, Texas State University; David Estrada, Rio Hondo College; Carol-Ann Farkas,

Massachusetts College of Pharmacy and Health Sciences; Karen Forgette, University of Mississippi; Tikenya Foster-Singletary, Spelman College; Elizabeth Fourzan, El Paso Community College; Amy Fugazzi, Northern Kentucky University; Monica Fuglei, Arapahoe Community College; Karen Gocsik, University of California, San Diego; Angela Green, University of Mississippi; Gary Hall, Victoria College; Anna Hall-Zieger, Blinn College; Kathryn Harrington, Community College of Denver; Lynn Hawkins, Daytona State College; Andrea Holliger, Lone Star College; Nancy Kennedy, Edmonds Community College; Amanda Knight, Andrew College; Richard Kraskin, Daytona State College; Elizabeth Kreydatus, Virginia Commonwealth University; Jane Kuenz, University of Southern Maine; Tamara Kuzmenkov, Tacoma Community College; Jessica Labbe, Guilford Technical Community College; Jennifer Laufenberg, Bossier Parish Community College; Bill Leach, Florida Institute of Technology; Can Li, Red River College; Bronwen Llewellyn, Daytona State College; Walter Lowe, Green River Community College; Jennifer Lutman, Colgate University; Marta Magellan, Miami Dade Virtual College; Andrea Mason, Arapahoe Community College; Carola Mattord, Kennesaw State University; John McKinnis, Buffalo State College; Terrence McNulty, Middlesex Community College; Zia Miric, University of Illinois at Urbana-Champaign; Tiffany Mitchell, University of Tennessee at Chattanooga; Dawn Montgomery, University of Alaska Southeast, Ketchikan; Alice Myatt, University of Mississippi; Robin Jean Gray Nicks, University of Tennessee; Barbra Nightingale, Broward College; Michele Ninacs, Buffalo State College; Vicki Pallo, Virginia Commonwealth University; Nancy Pederson, University of Minnesota, Morris; Margaret Price, The Ohio State University; Jeff Pruchnic, Wayne State University; Kristin Redfield, Forsyth Technical Community College; Kristin Reed, Virginia Commonwealth University; Jennifer Rios, Fresno City College; Megan Salter, Middle Georgia State University; Jean Sorensen, Grayson County College; Kathleen Spada, Northern Kentucky University; Lucas A. Street, Augustana College; Jamey Temple, University of the Cumberlands; Kate Tirabassi, Keene State College; Marlea Trevino, Grayson College; Leah Van Vaerenewyck, Lesley University; Heather Blain Vorhies, University of North Carolina at Charlotte; Jennifer Holly Wells, Montclair State University; Richard Williamson, Blinn College; Nancy Wilson, Texas State University; Greg Winston, Husson University; Virginia Wright-Peterson, University of Minnesota at Rochester; Diane Yerka, University of Minnesota at Morris.

Editorial advisers

I was thrilled to have the help of the following individuals, fellow teachers of writing, in shaping a new edition that responds to students' needs, saves teachers time, includes digital options, and reflects current pedagogy and practices:

Heidi Ajrami, Victoria College
C. J. Baker-Schverak, Eastern Florida State College

Elizabeth Haddox, El Paso Community College
Jessica Kidd, University of Alabama
Guy Krueger, University of Mississippi
Tracy Michaels, University of Massachusetts, Lowell
C. Cole Osborne, Guilford Technical Community College
Mauricio Rodríguez, El Paso Community College

Student reviewers

It is always instructive and rewarding to involve students in the development of new content. I thank the following students for reviewing early-stage writing and citation videos: Abigail Dellinger from Forsyth Technical Community College; Angel Carboni, Pal Patel, and Shandice Rowe from Massachusetts College of Pharmacy and Health Sciences; Ron Butts, Katie Hazelwood, and Shaneqia Johnson from Middle Georgia State University; Fernando Alvidrez, Andrea Esparza, Christian Melgarejo, Lorena Pedroza, and Jacob Perez from Rio Hondo College; Seungah Kim, Henry Medelius, Kyle Seifert, and Justine Stoberl from SUNY Buffalo; Elizabeth Johnson from University of South Carolina; and Grant Hovey from Virginia Polytechnic Institute and State University.

Contributors

I thank the following fellow teachers of writing for their smart revisions of important content: Kimberli Huster, ESL specialist at Robert Morris University and Duquesne University, updated the advice for multilingual writers, and Sara McCurry, instructor of English at Shasta College, improved *Teaching with Hacker Handbooks*. I also thank Robert Koch, director of the Center for Writing Excellence at University of North Alabama, for a series of new Writer's Choice boxes. For helping me to think about new content on pronouns and gender, I am deeply grateful to Margaret Price, associate professor of English at The Ohio State University.

Student contributors

Including sample student writing in each edition of the handbook and its media makes the resources more useful for you and your students. I would like to thank these students for letting us adapt their work as models: Ned Bishop, Sophie Harba, Sam Jacobs, Michelle Nguyen, Emilia Sanchez, April Bo Wang, Matt Watson, and Ren Yoshida.

Bedford/St. Martin's

A comprehensive handbook is a collaborative writing project, and it is my pleasure to acknowledge and thank the enormously talented Bedford/St. Martin's editorial team, whose focus on students informs each new feature of *A Canadian Writer's Reference*. Edwin Hill, vice president for humanities editorial, and Leasa Burton, senior program director for English, offer their commitment to and deep knowledge of the field of composition and the ways in which it is changing. Stacey Purviance, senior program manager, brings her creative energy and thoughtful contributions to the handbook. She has brilliantly and generously inspired us to envision new ways to pair print and digital content. Doug Silver, product manager for English, helps us reimagine writers' and teachers' opportunities with digital tools.

Michelle Clark, executive editor, is the editor every author dreams of having — a treasured friend and colleague and an endless source of creativity and clarity. Michelle combines wisdom with patience, imagination with practicality, and hard work with good cheer. Will Stonefield, development editor, has worked to develop new content and models for a Canadian audience; his care and attention is visible throughout the seventh edition. Barbara Flanagan, senior media editor, brings unrivalled expertise in documentation — mastering the 2016 MLA update and the 2017 *Chicago* update — and manages content development for LaunchPad. Mara Weible, senior editor, brings to the project her teacher's sensibility; I thank her for working with student writer April Wang on a new APA-style research essay and for developing the multimodal supplement. Thanks also to Cara Kaufman, associate editor, for developing the ESL supplement and helping us create online writing tutorials, and to Julia Domenicucci, assistant editor, who played a key role with LaunchPad and the citation tutorials. Many thanks to the media production team — Michelle Camisa and Allison Hart — for delivering engaging handbook tools for students in the digital age. Finally, thanks to Toronto-based editor Dawn Hunter, who has updated this edition of *A Canadian Writer's Reference*, adding examples based on Canadian culture and literature throughout the text and ensuring that the text conforms to Canadian conventions.

Practical advice from Bedford colleagues Joy Fisher Williams and Vivian Garcia, who, like me, spend many, many hours on the road and in faculty offices, is always treasured. Many thanks to Kendra LeFleur, senior content project manager, who has produced quality content on a tight schedule — and who expertly managed a redesign of the print book. And thanks to Arthur Johnson, copy editor, for his thoroughness and attention to detail; to Claire Seng-Niemoeller, text designer, who crafted a clean and more accessible seventh edition; and to John Callahan, designer, who has introduced a striking new cover.

Last, but never least, I offer thanks to my own students who, over many years, have shaped my teaching and helped me understand their challenges in becoming college writers. Thanks to my friends and colleagues Jenny Doggett,

Joan Feinberg, Suzanne Lane, Maxine Rodburg, Laura Saltz, and Kerry Walk for sustaining conversations about the teaching of writing. And thanks to my family: to Joshua Alper, an attentive reader of life and literature, for his steadfastness across the drafts; to my parents, Walter and Louise Sommers, who encouraged me to write and set me forth on a career of writing and teaching; to my extended family, Ron, Charles Mary, Alexander, Demian, Devin, Liz, Kate, Sam, Terry, Steve, and Yuval, for their good humour and good cheer; and to Rachel and Curran, Alexandra and Brian, witty and wise beyond measure, always generous with their instruction and inspiration in all things that matter. And to Lailah Dragonfly, my granddaughter, thanks for the joy and sweetness you bring to life.

Nancy Sommers

A Canadian
Writer's
Reference

C

Composing and Revising

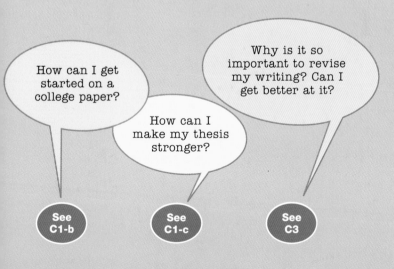

How can I get started on a college paper?

See C1-b

How can I make my thesis stronger?

See C1-c

Why is it so important to revise my writing? Can I get better at it?

See C3

C Composing and Revising

Writing is a process of figuring out what you think, not a matter of recording already developed thoughts. Since it's not possible to think about everything all at once, most experienced writers handle a piece of writing in stages — planning, drafting, revising, and editing. As you discover what you want to say, you'll often find yourself circling back to earlier stages to develop your ideas.

C1 Planning

- Checklist for assessing the writing situation 5
- How to solve five common problems with thesis statements 8
- Sample formal outline 11

C1-a Assess the writing situation.

Begin by taking a look at your writing situation. Consider your subject, your purpose, your audience, available sources of information, and any assignment requirements such as genre, length, document design, and deadlines (see the checklist on p. 5).

Purpose

In many writing situations, part of your challenge will be determining your purpose, or reason for writing. The wording of an assignment may suggest its purpose. If no guidelines are given, you may need to ask yourself, "What is my goal?" or "What do I want to accomplish?" Identify which one or more of the following aims you hope to accomplish.

to inform	to analyze
to explain	to synthesize
to summarize	to propose
to persuade/argue	to call readers to action
to evaluate	to reflect

Audience

Take time to consider readers and their expectations: Who will be reading your draft? What is your relationship to your readers? What information will your audience need to understand your ideas? The choices you make as you write will tell readers who you think they are (novices or experts, for example) and will show respect for your readers' values and perspectives.

 LaunchPad **ACTIVITIES FOR C1**
macmillan learning
7 Exercises, 2 Writing Practice activities

Academic English   What counts as good writing varies from culture to culture. In some situations, you will need to become familiar with the writing styles — such as direct or indirect, personal or impersonal, plain or embellished — that are valued by the culture for which you are writing.

NOTE: When you write an email message to an instructor, a classmate, or a potential employer, respect your audience by using a concise, meaningful subject line; keeping paragraphs brief and focused; proofreading for errors; and paying attention to your tone. Don't write something that you wouldn't feel comfortable saying directly to your reader. Also, if you include someone else's words, let your reader know the source. Finally, avoid forwarding another person's message without permission.

Genre

Pay close attention to the genre, or type of writing, assigned. Each genre is a category of writing meant for a specific purpose and audience — an essay in a writing class, a lab report or research proposal in a biology class, a policy memo in a criminal justice class, or a case study for an education class. Often the genre is assigned, but sometimes the genre is yours to choose. In addition, you may need to decide which delivery format will best help you communicate your purpose and reach readers — for example, traditional written paragraphs, presentation slides, or a podcast for your argument essay. Seeking out examples of writing in the genre in which you are composing is often helpful.

C1-b Explore your subject.

Experiment with one or more techniques for exploring your subject and discovering your purpose: talking and listening, reading and annotating texts, asking questions, brainstorming, freewriting, keeping a journal, blogging. Whatever technique you turn to, the goal is the same: to generate ideas that will lead you to a question or topic that you want to explore further.

Talking and listening

Talking about your ideas can help you develop them before you begin to write them down. By talking and listening to others, you can hear yourself think aloud and also discover what your listeners find interesting, what they are curious about, and where they disagree with you. If you are writing an argument, you can try it out on listeners with other points of view.

Checklist for assessing the writing situation

Subject

- Has the subject been assigned, or are you free to choose your own?
- Why is your subject worth writing about? What questions would you like to explore?
- Do you need to narrow your subject to a more specific topic?

Purpose and audience

- Why are you writing: To inform readers? To persuade them? To call them to action? Some combination of purposes?
- Who are your readers? How well informed are they about the subject?
- Will your readers resist any of your ideas? What objections might you need to anticipate and counter?

Genre

- What genre — type of writing — does your assignment require: A report? A proposal? An analysis of data? An essay?
- What are the expectations of your assigned genre? For instance, what type of evidence is typically used in the genre?
- Does the genre require a specific format or organization?

Sources of information

- Where will your information come from: Reading? Research? Direct observation? Interviews? Questionnaires?
- What type of evidence suits your subject, purpose, audience, and genre?
- What documentation style is required: MLA? APA? CMS?

Length and document design

- Do you have length specifications? If not, what length seems appropriate, given your subject, purpose, audience, and genre?
- What format is required? Do you have guidelines or examples to consult?
- How might visuals help you convey information?

Deadlines

- What are your deadlines? How much time will you need for the various stages of writing, including proofreading and printing or posting the final draft?

Reading and annotating texts

Reading is an important way to deepen your understanding of a topic, learn from the insights and research of others, and expand your perspective. Annotating a text encourages you to read actively — to highlight key concepts, to note possible contradictions in an argument, or to raise questions for further research and investigation. As you annotate, you record your impressions and begin a conversation with a text and its author. See A1-a for a student's annotations on an assigned article.

Asking questions

Asking questions is another productive way to get started on a piece of writing. You might try asking the questions journalists ask themselves: Who? What? When? Where? Why? and How? If you were writing about a negative reaction to a film, for instance, you might want to ask: *Who* objected to the film, and *why*? *What* were the objections, and *when* were they voiced? Such questions will help you discover important facts.

If you are writing in a particular discipline, try to find out which questions its scholars typically explore. Look for clues in assigned readings and class discussions to understand how a discipline's questions help you identify its concerns.

Brainstorming and freewriting

Brainstorming and freewriting are good ways to figure out what you know and what questions you have. Write (in list form or sentence form) whatever comes to mind without pausing to think about word choice, spelling, or even meaning. The goal is to write quickly and freely to discover what questions are on your mind and what directions you might pursue.

Keeping a journal

A journal is a collection of informal, exploratory, or experimental writing. In a journal, often meant for your eyes only, you can take risks. You might free-write, pose questions, comment on an interesting idea from one of your classes, or keep a list of questions that occur to you while reading. You might imagine a conversation between yourself and your readers or stage a debate to understand opposing positions.

Blogging

Although a blog is a type of journal, it is a public writing space rather than a private one. In a blog, you can explore an idea for a paper by writing posts from different angles. Since most blogs have a commenting feature, you can create a conversation by inviting readers to give you feedback in the form of questions, counterarguments, or suggestions for other sources on a topic.

C1-c Draft and revise a working thesis statement.

For many types of writing, you will be able to assert your central idea in a sentence or two. Such a statement, which ordinarily appears in the opening paragraph of your finished essay, is called a *thesis*.

Understanding what makes an effective thesis statement

An effective thesis statement is a central idea that conveys your purpose, or reason for writing, and that requires support. An effective thesis should

- state a position that needs to be explained and supported
- use concrete language
- be appropriate for the length requirements of the assignment, not too broad or too narrow
- stand up to the "So what?" test (see p. 10)

Whether your thesis is an answer to a question you have asked or a resolution of a problem you have identified, it should be a sharply focused statement that announces your position on a debatable topic.

Drafting a working thesis

As you explore your topic, you will begin to see possible ways to focus your material. At this point, try to settle on a *tentative* central idea, or working thesis statement. The more complex your topic, the more your focus may change. As your ideas develop, you'll need to revisit your working thesis to see whether it represents the position you want to take and whether it can be supported by the sources of evidence you have accumulated.

You'll find that the process of answering a question you have posed, resolving a problem you have identified, or taking a position on a debatable topic will focus your thinking and lead you to develop a working thesis. Here, for example, are one student's efforts to pose a question and draft a working thesis for an essay in his ethics course. (See p. 10 for another example of a working thesis.)

QUESTION

Should athletes who enhance their performance through biotechnology be banned from athletic competition?

WORKING THESIS

Athletes who boost their performance through biotechnology should be banned from athletic competition.

Solve five common problems with thesis statements

Revising a working thesis is easier if you have a method or an approach. The following problem/solution approach can help you recognize and solve common thesis problems.

① **Common problem:** The thesis is a statement of fact.

Solution: Enter a debate by posing a question about your topic that has more than one possible answer. For example: Should the polygraph be used by private employers? Your thesis should be your answer to the question.

Working thesis: *The first polygraph was developed by Dr. John Larson in 1921.*

Revised: *Because the polygraph has not been proved reliable, even under controlled conditions, its use by private employers should be banned.*

② **Common problem:** The thesis is a question.

Solution: Take a position on your topic by answering the question you have posed. Your thesis statement should be your answer to the question.

Working thesis: *Did Prime Minister John Diefenbaker make the decision to scrap the Avro Arrow?*

Revised: *Although Prime Minister John Diefenbaker made the announcement that the Avro Arrow would be scrapped, an analysis of the evidence suggests the decision was not his alone.*

③ **Common problem:** The thesis is too broad.

Solution: Focus on a subtopic of your original topic. Once you have chosen a subtopic, take a position in an ongoing debate and pose a question that has more than one answer. For example: Should people be tested for genetic diseases? Your thesis should be your answer to the question.

Working thesis: *Mapping the human genome has many implications for health and science.*

Revised: *Although scientists can now detect genetic predisposition for specific diseases, policymakers should establish clear guidelines about whom to test and under what circumstances.*

4 **Common problem:** The thesis is too narrow.

Solution: Identify challenging questions that readers might ask about your topic. Then pose a question that has more than one answer. For example: Do the risks of genetic testing outweigh its usefulness? Your thesis should be your answer to the question.

Working thesis: *A person who carries a genetic mutation linked to a particular disease might or might not develop that disease.*

Revised: *Though positive results in a genetic test do not guarantee that the disease will develop, such results can cause psychological trauma; genetic testing should therefore be avoided if possible.*

5 **Common problem:** The thesis is vague.

Solution: Focus your thesis with concrete language and clues about where the essay is headed. Pose a question about the topic that has more than one answer. For example: How does the physical structure of Memorial Hall shape the experience of the visitors? Your thesis — your answer to the question — should use specific language.

Working thesis: *Memorial Hall in the Canadian War Museum is an interesting place.*

Revised: *The symbolic use of natural light in the Canadian War Museum's Memorial Hall gives visitors a tangible reminder of the sacrifices soldiers have made.*

This working thesis offers a useful place to start writing — a way to limit the topic and focus a first draft — but it doesn't take into consideration the expectations of readers who will ask "Why?" and "So what?" The student has taken a position — athletes who use performance enhancers should be banned — but he hasn't answered *why* these athletes should be banned. To fully answer his own question, he might push his thinking with the word *because.*

STRONGER WORKING THESIS

Athletes who boost their performance through biotechnology should be banned from competition *because* biotechnology gives them an unfair advantage and disrupts the sense of fair play.

Revising a working thesis

As you move to a clearer, more specific position you want to take, you'll start to see ways to revise your working thesis. You may find that the evidence you collected supports a different thesis; or you may find that your position has changed as you have learned more about your topic.

Revision is ongoing; as your ideas evolve, your working thesis will evolve, too. One effective way to revise a working thesis is to put it to the "So what?" test, asking questions such as "Why would a person want to read an essay with this thesis?" Such questions help you keep audience and purpose in mind as you revise.

Putting your working thesis to the "So what?" test

Use the following questions to help you revise your working thesis.

- Why would readers want to read an essay with this thesis? How would you respond to a reader who hears your thesis and asks "So what?" or "Why does it matter?"
- Will any readers disagree with this thesis? If so, how might you revise in response?
- Is the thesis too obvious? If you cannot come up with an interpretation that opposes your own, consider revising your thesis.
- Can you support your thesis with the evidence available?

C1-d Draft a plan.

Listing and organizing supporting ideas can help you figure out how to develop your thesis. Creating outlines, whether formal or informal, can help you make sure your writing is focused and logical and can help you identify any gaps in your support.

When to use an informal outline

You might want to sketch an informal outline to see how you will support your thesis and to figure out a tentative structure for your ideas. Informal outlines can take many forms. Perhaps the most common is simply the thesis followed by a list of major ideas.

> Working thesis: Animal testing should be banned because it is bad science and doesn't contribute to biomedical advances.
>
> - Most animals don't serve as good models for the human body.
> - Drug therapies can have vastly different effects on different species—92 percent of all drugs shown to be effective in animal tests fail in human trials.
> - Some of the largest biomedical discoveries were made without the use of animal testing.
> - The most effective biomedical research methods—tissue engineering and computer modelling—don't use animals.
> - Animal studies are not scientifically necessary.

If you began by brainstorming a list of ideas, you can turn the list into a rough outline by crossing out some ideas, adding others, and putting the ideas in a logical order.

When to use a formal outline

Early in the writing process, rough outlines have certain advantages: They can be produced quickly, they are obviously tentative, and they can be revised easily. However, a formal outline may be useful later in the writing process, after you have written a rough draft, especially if your topic is complex. A formal outline can help you see whether the parts of your essay work together and whether your essay's structure is logical.

The following formal outline brought order to the research paper that appears in MLA-5b. The student's thesis is an important part of the outline. Everything else in the outline supports the thesis, directly or indirectly.

FORMAL OUTLINE

> Thesis: In the name of public health and safety, state governments have the responsibility to shape health policies and to regulate healthy eating choices, especially since doing so offers a potentially large social benefit for a relatively small cost.

➡

I. Debates surrounding food regulation have a long history in the United States.

   A. The 1906 Pure Food and Drug Act guarantees inspection of meat and dairy products.

   B. Such regulations are considered reasonable because consumers are protected from harm with little cost.

   C. Consumers consider reasonable regulations to be an important government function to stop harmful items from entering the marketplace.

II. Even though food meets safety standards, there is a need for further regulation.

   A. The typical American diet—processed sugars, fats, and refined flours—is damaging over time.

   B. Related health risks are diabetes, cancer, and heart problems.

   C. Passing chronic-disease-related legislation is our single most important public health challenge.

III. Food legislation is not a popular solution for most Americans.

   A. A proposed New York City regulation banning the sale of soft drinks greater than twelve ounces failed in 2012, and in California a proposed soda tax failed in 2011.

   B. Many consumers find such laws to be unreasonable restrictions on freedom of choice.

   C. Opposition to food and beverage regulation is similar to the opposition to early tobacco legislation; the public views the issue as one of personal responsibility.

   D. Counterpoint: Freedom of "choice" is a myth; our choices are heavily influenced by marketing.

IV. The United States has a history of regulations to discourage unhealthy behaviours.

   A. Tobacco-related restrictions faced opposition.

   B. Seat belt laws are a useful analogy.

   C. The public seems to support laws that have a good cost-benefit ratio; the cost of food/beverage regulations is low, and most people agree that the benefits would be high.

V. Americans believe that personal choice is lost when regulations such as taxes and bans are instituted.

   A. Regulations open up the door to excessive control and interfere with cultural and religious traditions.

   B. Counterpoint: Burdens on individual liberty are a reasonable price to pay for large social health benefits.

VI. Public opposition continues to stand in the way of food regulation to promote healthier eating. We must consider whether to allow the costly trend of rising chronic disease to continue in the name of personal choice, or whether we are willing to support the legal changes and public health policies that will reverse that trend.

C2 Drafting

- Strategies for drafting an introduction 14
- Choosing visuals to suit your purpose 16
- Strategies for drafting a conclusion 18

Generally, the introduction to a piece of writing announces the main point; the body develops it, usually in several paragraphs; and the conclusion drives it home. You can begin drafting, however, at any point. If you find it difficult to introduce a paper that you have not yet written, try drafting the body first and saving the introduction for later.

C2-a Draft an introduction.

Your introduction will usually be a paragraph of 50 to 150 words (in a longer paper, it may be more than one paragraph). Perhaps the most common strategy is to open with a few sentences that engage, or hook, the reader and that establish your purpose for writing and your central idea, or *thesis*. (See also C1-c.)

In the following introduction, the thesis is highlighted.

> As the United States industrialized in the nineteenth century, using immigrant labor, social concerns took a backseat to the task of building a prosperous nation. The government did not regulate industries and did not provide an effective safety net for the poor or for those who became sick or injured on the job. Immigrants and the poor did have a few advocates, however. Settlement houses such as Hull-House in Chicago provided information, services, and a place for reform-minded individuals to gather and work to improve the conditions of the urban poor. Alice Hamilton was one of these reformers. Her work at Hull-House spanned twenty-two years, and she later expanded her reform work throughout the nation. Hamilton's efforts helped to improve the lives of immigrants and drew attention and respect to the problems and people that until then had been ignored.
>
> — Laurie McDonough, student

Whether you are writing for a scholarly audience, a professional audience, or a general audience, you cannot assume your readers' interest in the topic. The sentences leading to your thesis should hook readers by sparking their curiosity, drawing them into the world of your essay and giving them a reason to continue reading.

NOTE: Different writing situations call for different introductions. For more examples of effective introductions, see pages 67, 76, and 427.

 LaunchPad
macmillan learning

ACTIVITIES FOR C2

2 Writing Practice activities

Strategies for drafting an introduction

Whether you are composing a traditional essay or a multimodal work such as a slide presentation or a video, the following strategies can provide a hook for your reader:

- Offer a surprising statistic or an unusual fact
- Ask a question
- Introduce a quotation or a bit of dialogue
- Provide historical background
- Define a term or concept
- Propose a problem, contradiction, or dilemma
- Use a vivid example or image
- Develop an analogy
- Relate an anecdote (story)

Academic English   If you come from a culture that prefers an indirect approach in writing, you may feel that asserting a thesis early in an essay sounds unrefined or even rude. In North America, however, readers appreciate a direct approach, which shows that you understand your topic and value your readers' time.

C2-b Draft the body.

The body of your essay develops support for your thesis, so it's important to have at least a working thesis before you start writing. What does your thesis promise readers? What question are you trying to answer? What problem are you trying to solve? What is your position on the topic? Keep asking these questions as you draft the body of your essay.

Asking questions as you draft

You may already have written an introduction that includes your working thesis. If not, as long as you have a draft thesis, you can begin developing the body and return later to the introduction. If your working thesis suggests a plan or if you have sketched a preliminary outline, try to organize your paragraphs accordingly.

Draft the body of your essay by writing at least one paragraph about each supporting point you listed in the planning stage. If you do not have a plan, pause for a few moments and sketch one (see C1-d). As you draft the body, keep asking questions; keep anticipating what your readers may need to know.

At times, however, you might not know what you want to say until you have written a draft. It is possible to begin without a plan — assuming you are prepared to treat your first attempt as a "discovery draft" that you may need to revise, deeply, at a later stage. Whether or not you have a plan when you begin drafting, you can often figure out a workable order for your ideas by stopping each time you start a new paragraph to think about what your readers will need to know to follow your train of thought.

For more detailed help with drafting and developing paragraphs, see C5.

Using sources responsibly: As you draft, keep careful notes about sources you read and consult. (See R2-c.) If you quote, paraphrase, or summarize a source, include a citation, even in your draft. You will save time and avoid plagiarism if you do so.

Adding visuals as you draft

As you draft, you may decide that support for your thesis could come from one or more visuals. Visuals can convey information concisely and powerfully. Graphs and tables, for example, can simplify complex numerical information. Images — including photographs and diagrams — often express ideas vividly. Keep in mind that if you download a visual or use published information to create your own visual, you must credit your source. Also be sure to choose visuals to supplement your writing, not to substitute for it.

While drafting, consider how a visual supports your purpose and how your audience might respond to the visual. For example, in writing about the shift from print to online news, student writer Sam Jacobs used a screen shot of a link embedded in a news article to illustrate a point (see A4-h).

The chart on pages 16–17 describes eight types of visuals and their purposes.

Using sources responsibly: If you create a chart or graph using information from your research, you must cite the source of the information even though the visual is your own. If you download a photograph from the web, you must credit the person or organization that created it, just as you would cite any other source that you use in a college or university paper (see MLA-2, APA-2, or CMS-2, depending on the documentation style you are required to use).

Choosing visuals to suit your purpose

Pie chart

Pie charts compare a part or parts to the whole. Segments of the pie represent percentages of the whole (and always total 100 percent).

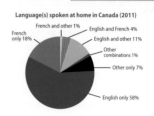

Language(s) spoken at home in Canada (2011)

French and other 1%
French only 18%
English and French 4%
English and other 11%
Other combinations 1%
Other only 7%
English only 58%

Bar graph (or line graph)

Bar graphs highlight trends over a period of time or compare numerical data. Line graphs display the same data as bar graphs; the data are graphed as points, and the points are connected with lines.

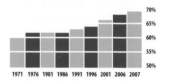

THE PURSUIT OF PROPERTY
Home ownership rates in Canada

70%
65%
60%
55%
50%

1971 1976 1981 1986 1991 1996 2001 2006 2007

Infographic

An infographic presents data in a visually engaging form. The data are usually numerical, as in bar graphs or line graphs, but they are represented by a graphic element rather than bars or lines.

In Canada, about 13% of kids under age 18 live in low-income families.

Table

Tables display numbers and words in columns and rows. They can be used to organize complicated numerical information into an easily understood format.

Sources [top to bottom]: Data for pie chart, bar graph, and infographic from Statistics Canada; data for table from www.postsecondary.org.

Prices of daily doses of AIDS drugs
($US)

Drug	Brazil	Uganda	Côte d'Ivoire	US
3TC (Lamuvidine)	1.86	3.28	2.95	8.70
ddC (Zalcitabine)	0.24	4.17	3.75	8.80
Didanosine	2.04	5.26	3.48	7.25
Efavirenz	6.96	n/a	6.41	13.13
Indinavir	10.32	12.79	9.07	14.93
Nelfinavir	4.14	4.45	4.39	6.47
Nevirapine	5.04	n/a	n/a	8.48
Saquinavir	6.24	7.37	5.52	6.50
Stavudine	0.56	6.19	4.10	9.07
ZDV/3TC	1.44	7.54	n/a	18.78
Zidovudine	1.08	4.34	2.43	10.12

Source: UNAIDS, 2000

Choosing visuals to suit your purpose, *continued*

Photograph

Photographs vividly depict people, scenes, or objects discussed in a text.

Library of Congress, Prints & Photographs Division, Reproduction Number LC-DIG-highsm-04024.

Diagram

Diagrams, useful in scientific and technical writing, concisely illustrate processes, structures, or interactions.

National Institutes of Health.

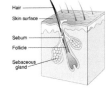

Flowchart

Flowcharts show structures (the hierarchy of employees at a company, for example) or steps in a process and their relation to one another. (See also p. 121 for another example.)

Map

Maps illustrate distances, historical information, or demographics and often use symbols for geographic features and points of interest.

Lynn Hunt et al., *The Making of the West.* Copyright © 2016 by Bedford/ St. Martin's. Reprinted by permission of Bedford/St. Martin's.

C2-c Draft a conclusion.

A conclusion should remind readers of the essay's main idea without repeating it. The concluding paragraph might also remind readers why the main idea matters or what's at stake. Your conclusion should drive your main point home and, perhaps, give readers something more to consider.

To conclude an essay analyzing the shifting roles of women in the military services, one student discusses her topic's implications for society as a whole.

> As the military continues to train women in jobs formerly reserved for men, our understanding of women's roles in society will no doubt continue to change. As news reports of women training for and taking part in combat operations become commonplace, reports of women becoming CEOs, police chiefs, and even president of the United States will cease to surprise us. Or perhaps we have already reached this point.
>
> — Rosa Broderick, student

To make the conclusion memorable and to give a sense of completion, you might bring readers full circle by returning to the thesis or including a detail from the introduction.

Whatever concluding strategy you choose, keep in mind that an effective conclusion is decisive and unapologetic. Avoid introducing completely new ideas at the end of an essay. And because the conclusion is so closely tied to the rest of the essay, be prepared to rewrite it as you revise your draft.

NOTE: For more examples of effective conclusions, see pages 68 and 77–78.

Strategies for drafting a conclusion

In addition to echoing your main idea, a conclusion might do any of the following:

- Briefly summarize your essay's key points
- Propose a course of action
- Offer a recommendation
- Discuss the topic's wider significance or implications
- Redefine a key term or concept
- Pose a question for future study

C3 Reviewing, revising, and editing

Revising is rarely a one-step process. Global matters — thesis, purpose, organization, content, and overall strategy — generally receive attention first because global revisions involve bigger changes, including rewrites of paragraphs or whole sections of a paper. Editing, on the other hand — improvements in sentence structure, word choice, grammar, punctuation, and mechanics — usually comes later. (See C3-b for advice on keeping an editing log.)

Writing multiple drafts allows you to write in stages and strengthen your paper through both revising and editing.

C3-a See revising as a social process.

To revise is to *re-see*, and the comments you receive from your reviewers — instructors, peers, and writing centre tutors — will help you re-see your draft from your readers' point of view. When you ask readers for their comments, revision becomes a social experience, connecting you with the suggestions and insights of readers who help you shape your work in progress.

Feedback gives you perspective on what's working and not working in your draft and keeps the expectations of your readers in mind. Asking readers simple questions such as "Do you understand my main idea?" and "Is my draft organized?" will help you see your draft through readers' eyes.

C3-b Use peer review: Revise with comments.

Peer review gives you the benefit of real readers and an opportunity to see your draft through their eyes. When peers — classmates and fellow students — read your work, they offer feedback, pointing out where they are intrigued or confused. They offer their insights and suggestions, answer your questions, and help you strengthen your draft.

The following guidelines will help you learn from your reviewers' comments and revise successfully.

BE ACTIVE Help reviewers understand your purpose for writing and provide background about why you chose your topic, why it matters to you, and what

 LaunchPad macmillan learning **ACTIVITIES AND MODELS FOR C3**
2 Exercises, 5 Writing Practice activities, 1 Sample student paper

you hope to accomplish in your draft. Tell reviewers your specific concerns so they can provide focused feedback.

LISTEN WITH AN OPEN MIND   After you've worked hard on a draft, you might be surprised to hear reviewers tell you it still needs more development. Don't take criticism personally. Your readers are responding to your essay, not to you. If comments show that a reviewer doesn't understand what you're trying to do, don't be defensive. Instead, consider why your reader is confused, and figure out how to clarify your point. Responding to readers' objections — instead of dismissing them — may strengthen your ideas and make your essay more persuasive. Taking feedback seriously will make you a stronger writer.

WEIGH FEEDBACK CAREFULLY   As you begin revising, you may find yourself sorting through suggestions from many people, including instructors, tutors, and peer reviewers. Sometimes these readers will agree, but often their advice will differ. Your reviewers will probably make more suggestions than you can use, so be strategic. Sort through all the comments you receive with your original goals in mind, and focus on global concerns first (see p. 28) — otherwise, you'll be facing the impossible task of trying to incorporate everyone's advice.

KEEP A REVISION AND EDITING LOG   Make a clear and simple list of the global and sentence-level concerns that keep coming up in most of your reviewers' comments. That list can serve as a starting point each time you revise a paper to help you learn about your strengths and weaknesses as a writer. For more on improving your writing with editing logs, see page 30.

C3-c Use peer review: Give constructive comments.

Peer review allows you to read the work of your classmates and to learn from one another. As you offer advice about how to strengthen a peer's thesis or how to use a visual to convey concise information, you are thinking about the purpose of a thesis and the role of visuals. When you propose a strategy for focusing an introduction or for anticipating a counterargument, you not only help your classmate but also benefit from the process of thinking strategically about revision.

As a peer reviewer, your work is to engage with a writer as a reader. It isn't your job to rewrite, correct, or proofread the work of your peers. It is your job, though, to offer thoughtful, encouraging comments to show peers what they're doing well and how they might build on their strengths.

Write helpful peer review comments

1 **View yourself as a coach, not a judge.** Think of yourself as asking questions and proposing possibilities, not dictating solutions. Help the writer identify the strengths and limitations of a draft. Try phrasing comments this way: "Have you thought about . . . ?" or "How can you help a reader understand this point?"

2 **Pay attention to global issues first.** Focus on the big picture — purpose, thesis, organization, and content — before sentence structure, word choice, and grammar.

3 **Restate the writer's main idea.** As a reader, you can help the writer see whether he or she is expressing points clearly. Can you follow the writer's train of thought? Restate the writer's thesis and main ideas to check your understanding.

4 **Be specific.** Point to specific places in a draft and show your classmate how, why, and where a draft is effective or confusing. Instead of saying "I like your draft," say exactly what you like: "You use a surprising statistic in your introduction, and it really hooks me as a reader." Or instead of offering a generality such as "Your draft doesn't have much support," give a specific suggestion: "Try putting the data from paragraph three into a graph."

Strategies for revising
with comments

Often the comments you'll receive are written as shorthand commands — "Be specific!" — or as questions — "What is your main point?" Such comments don't immediately show you *how* to revise, but they do identify where revision might improve your draft. Ask reviewers to explain their comments if you don't understand them. The following sample comments and revision strategies will help you think about how to apply feedback to your own writing — and where to look for help in *A Canadian Writer's Reference*.

The comment: Unfocused introduction

Understanding the comment When readers point out that your introduction needs to be "focused," the comment often signals that the beginning sentences of your essay are vague, are unconnected to the rest of your essay, and don't establish your purpose for writing.

Strategies for revising

- **Reread your introduction and ask questions.** Are the sentences leading to your thesis specific enough to engage readers and communicate your purpose? Do these sentences lead logically to your thesis? Do they spark your readers' curiosity and offer them a reason to continue reading? (**See C2-a.**)

- **Try engaging readers with a "hook"** in your introduction — a question, a quotation, a vivid example, or a surprising statistic. (**See the chart on p. 14.**)

The comment: Consider opposing viewpoints

Understanding the comment When readers suggest that you "consider opposing viewpoints," the comment often signals that you need to recognize and respond to possible objections to your argument.

Strategies for revising

- **Read more** to learn about the debates surrounding the topic. Understand the various sides of your issue so you can anticipate and counter objections to your argument. (**See R1-a and R1-b.**)

- **Be open-minded.** Although it might seem illogical to introduce opposing arguments, you'll show your knowledge of the topic by recognizing that not everyone draws the same conclusions or holds the same point of view. (**See A4-f.**)

- **Introduce and counter objections** with phrases like these: "Some readers might point out that . . .." or "Critics of this view argue that . . .." (**See p. 95.**)

The comment: *Be specific*

Understanding the comment When readers say that you need to "be specific," the comment often signals that you could strengthen your writing with additional details.

Strategies for revising

- **Reread your topic sentence** to understand the focus of the paragraph. (**See C5-a.**)

- **Ask questions.** Does the paragraph contain claims that need support? Have you provided evidence — specific examples, vivid details and illustrations, statistics and facts — to help readers understand your ideas and find them persuasive? (**See A4-e.**)

- **Interpret your evidence.** Remember that details and examples don't speak for themselves. You will need to show readers how evidence supports your claims. (**See A1-d and MLA-3c.**)

The comment: *Cite your sources*

Understanding the comment When readers point out that you need to "cite your sources," the comment often signals that you need to acknowledge and give proper credit to the contributions of others.

Strategies for revising

- **Reread your sentence and ask questions.** Have you properly acknowledged all contributions — words, ideas, facts, or visuals — that you use as evidence? Have you given credit to the sources you quote, summarize, or paraphrase? Have you made it clear to readers how to locate each source if they want to consult it? (**See MLA-2, APA-2, or CMS-2.**)

- **Ask your instructor** which documentation style you are required to use — MLA, APA, or *Chicago*.

- **Revise** by including an in-text citation for any words, ideas, facts, or visuals that you use as evidence — and by including quotation marks around any language borrowed word-for-word from a source. (**See MLA-2c, APA-2c, or CMS-2c.**)

The following excerpt from an online peer review session shows a peer reviewer offering constructive comments.

EXCERPT FROM AN ONLINE PEER REVIEW SESSION

Juan (peer reviewer): Rachel, your essay makes a great point that credit card companies often hook students on a cycle of spending. But it sounds as if you're blaming students for their spending habits and credit card companies for their deceptive actions. Is this what you want to say?

Peer reviewer restates writer's main point and asks a question to help her clarify her ideas.

Rachel (writer): No, I want to keep the focus on the credit card companies. I didn't realize I was blaming students. What could I change?

Writer takes comment seriously and asks reviewer for specific suggestion.

Juan (reviewer): In paragraphs three and four, you group all students together as if all students have the same bad spending habits. If students are your audience, you'll be insulting them. What reader is motivated to read something that's alienating? What is your purpose for writing this draft?

Peer reviewer points to specific places in the draft and asks questions to help writer focus on audience and purpose.

Rachel (writer): Well . . . It's true that students don't always have good spending habits, but I don't want to blame students. My purpose is to call students to action about the dangers of credit card debt. Any suggestions for narrowing the focus?

Writer is actively engaged with peer reviewer's comments and doesn't take criticism personally.

Juan (reviewer): Most students know about the dangers of credit card debt, but they might not know about specific deceptive practices companies use to lure them. Maybe ask yourself what would surprise your audience about these practices.

Peer reviewer responds as a reader and acts as a coach to suggest possible solutions.

Rachel (writer): Juan, that's a good idea. I'll try it.

Writer thanks reviewer for his help and leaves session with a specific revision strategy.

POST COMMENT

C3-d Highlights of one student's peer review process

Student writer Michelle Nguyen wrote a draft in response to an assignment that asked her to write a brief essay about how one or more specific experiences with writing shaped her as a writer.

Here are the questions Nguyen gave her peer reviewers before they read her draft.

QUESTIONS FROM NGUYEN TO PEER REVIEWERS

Alex, Brian, and Sameera: Thanks for reading my draft. Here are three questions I have about my draft: Is my focus clear? Is there anything that confuses you? What specifically should I cut or add to strengthen my draft?

ROUGH DRAFT WITH PEER COMMENTS

My family used to live in the heart of Hanoi, Vietnam. The neighborhood was small but swamped with crime. Drug addicts scoured the alleys and stole the most mundane things—old clothes, worn slippers, even license plates of motorbikes. Like anyone else in Vietnam in the '90s, we struggled with poverty. There was no entertainment device in our house aside from an 11" black-and-white television. Even then, electricity went off for hours on a weekly basis.

I was particularly close to a Vietnam War veteran. My parents were away a lot, so the old man became like a grandfather to me. He taught me how to ride a bicycle, how to read, how to take care of small pets. He worked sporadically from home, fixing bicycle tires and broken pedals. He was a wrinkly old man who didn't talk much. His vocal cords were damaged during the war, and it caused him pain to speak. In a neighborhood full of screaming babies and angry shop owners and slimy criminals, his home was my quiet haven. I could read and write and think and bond with someone whose worldliness came from his wordlessness.

The tiny house he lived in stood at the far end of our neighborhood. It always smelled of old clothes and forgotten memories. He was a slight man, but his piercing black eyes retained their intensity even after all these years. He must have made one fierce soldier.

"I almost died once," he said, dusting a picture frame. It was one of those rare instances he ever mentioned his life during the war. As he talked, I perched

Alex F: You might want to add a title to focus readers.

Sameera K: I really like your introduction. It's so vivid. Think about adding a photo so readers can relate. What does Hanoi look like?

Brian S: You have great details here to set the scene in Hanoi, but why does it matter that you didn't have an "entertainment device"? Maybe choose the most interesting among all these details.

Brian S: Worldliness came from wordlessness—great phrase! Is this part of your main idea? What is your main idea?

Sameera K: You do a good job of showing us why this Vietnam veteran was important to you, but it seems like this draft is more a story about the man and not about you. What do you want readers to understand about you?

myself on the side of an armchair, rested my head on my tiny hands, and listened intently. I didn't understand much. I just liked hearing his low, humming voice. The concept of war for me was strictly confined to the classroom, and even then, the details of combat were always murky. The teachers just needed us to know that the communist troops enjoyed a glorious victory.

"I was the only survivor of my unit. 20 guys. All dead within a year. Then they let me go," he said. His voice cracked a little and his eyes misted over as he stared at pictures from his combatant past. "We didn't even live long enough to understand what we were fighting for."

He finished the sentence with a drawn-out sigh, a small set of wrinkles gathering at the end of his eyes. Years later, as I thought about his stories, I started to wonder why he referred to his deceased comrades by the collective pronoun "we." It was as if a little bit of him died on the battlefield with them too.

Three years after my family left the neighborhood, I learned that the old man became stricken with cancer. When I came home the next summer, I visited his house and sat by his sickbed. His shoulder-length mop of salt and pepper hair now dwarfed his rail-thin figure. We barely exchanged a word. He just held my hands tightly until my mother called for me to leave, his skeletal fingers leaving a mark on my pale palms. Perhaps he was trying to transmit to me some of his worldliness and his wisdom. Perhaps he was telling me to go out into the world and live the free life he never had.

Some people say that writers are selfish and vain. The truth is, I learned to write because it gave me peace in the much too noisy world of my Vietnamese childhood. In the quiet of the old man's house, I gazed out the window, listened to my thoughts, and wrote them down. It all started with a story about a wrinkly Vietnam War veteran who didn't talk much.

> **Sameera K:** I'm curious to hear more about you and why this man was so important to you. What did he teach you about writing? What did he see in you?

> **Alex F:** This sentence is confusing. Your draft doesn't seem to be about the selfishness or vanity of writers.

> **Brian S:** What does "it" refer to? I think you're trying to say something important about silence and noise and literacy, but I'm not sure what it is.

After reading her draft and considering the feedback from her classmates, Nguyen realized that she had chosen a good direction but that she hadn't focused her draft to meet the expectations of the assignment. Her classmates offered her valuable suggestions about adding a photograph and clarifying her main idea. With her classmates' specific questions and suggestions in mind and their encouragement to see the undeveloped possibilities in her draft, Nguyen developed some goals for revising.

MICHELLE NGUYEN'S REVISION GOALS

- Add a title.
- Revise introduction to set the scene more dramatically. Use Sameera's idea to include a photo of my neighbourhood.
- Make the story my story, not the man's story. Answer Sameera's question: What did the man see in me and I in him? Delete extra material about the old man.
- Answer Brian's question: What is my main idea?
- Follow Brian's suggestion about the connection between word-lessness and worldliness. Make the contrasts sharper between the neighbourhood and the man's house.
- Figure out what main idea I'm trying to communicate. See if there is a possible idea in the various contrasts. The surprise was finding writing in silence, not in the noisy exchange of voices in my neighbourhood.

See pages 32–33 for Nguyen's revised draft.

C3-e Approach global revision in cycles.

Revision is more effective when you approach it in cycles, rather than attempting to change everything all at once. Keep in mind these four common cycles of global revision: engaging the audience, sharpening the focus, improving the organization, and strengthening the content. For a global revision checklist, see page 28.

Engaging the audience

Sometimes a rough draft needs an overhaul because it is directed at no particular audience. A good question to ask yourself and your reviewers is the toughest question a reader might ask: "So what?" If your draft can't pass the "So what?" test (see p. 10), you may need to rethink your entire approach.

Sharpening the focus

A clearly focused draft fixes readers' attention on one central idea and does not stray from that idea. You can sharpen the focus of a draft by clarifying the introduction (especially the thesis) and by deleting any text that is off the point.

Improving the organization

A draft is well organized when its major divisions are logical and easy to follow. To improve the organization of your draft, you may need to take one or more of the following actions: adding or sharpening topic sentences, moving blocks of text, and inserting headings.

Checklist for global revision

Purpose and audience

- Does the draft address a question, a problem, or an issue that readers care about?
- Is the draft appropriate for its audience? Does it address the audience's knowledge of and attitudes toward the subject?

Focus

- Is the thesis clear? Is it prominently placed?
- Does the thesis answer a reader's "So what?" question? (See p. 10.)
- If the draft has no thesis, do you have a good reason for omitting one?

Organization and paragraphing

- Is each paragraph unified around a main point?
- Does each paragraph support and develop the thesis?
- Have you provided enough organizational cues for readers (such as topic sentences or headings)?
- Have you presented ideas in a logical order?

Content

- Is the supporting material relevant and persuasive?
- Which ideas need further development? Have you left your readers with any unanswered questions?
- Are the parts proportioned sensibly? Do major ideas receive enough attention?
- Where might you delete redundant or irrelevant information?

Point of view

- Is the dominant point of view — first person (*I* or *we*), second person (*you*), or third person (*he, she, it, one,* or *they*) — appropriate for your purpose and audience? (See S4-a.)

Strengthening the content

In reviewing the content of a draft, first consider whether your argument is sound. Second, consider whether you should add or delete any text (sentences or paragraphs). If your purpose is to argue a point, consider how persuasively you have supported your point to an intelligent audience. If your purpose is to inform, be sure that you have presented your ideas clearly and with enough detail to meet your readers' expectations.

C3-f Revise and edit sentences.

When you *revise* sentences, you focus on clarity and effectiveness; when you *edit*, you check for correctness. Sentences that are wordy, vague, or rambling may distract readers and make it hard for readers to focus on your purpose or grasp your ideas. Read each sentence slowly to determine if it is as specific and clear as possible. You might find it helpful to read your work aloud and trust your ears to detect awkwardness, wordiness, or a jarring repetition.

What follows is a rough-draft paragraph with a student's edits; the changes solve a variety of sentence-level problems.

> Although some cities have found creative ways to improve access to public transportation for passengers with physical disabilities, ~~and to fund other programs, there have been problems in~~ our city has struggled with ~~due to the need to address~~ budget constraints and competing ~~needs~~ priorities. ~~This~~ The budget crunch has led citizens to question how funds are distributed.~~?~~ For example, last year ~~when~~ city officials voted to use available funds to support ~~had to choose between allocating funds for accessible transportation or allocating funds to~~ after-school programs rather than transportation upgrades.~~, they voted for the after-school programs.~~ It is not clear to some citizens why ~~these~~ after-school programs are more important.

The original paragraph was too wordy, a problem that can be addressed through any number of revisions.

Some of the improvements do not involve choice and must be made in any revision. The hyphen in *after-school programs* is necessary; a noun must be substituted for the pronoun *these* in the last sentence; and the question mark in the second sentence must be changed to a period.

Improve your writing with an editing log

An important aspect of becoming a postsecondary writer is learning how to identify the grammar, punctuation, and spelling errors that you make frequently. You can use an editing log to keep a list of your common errors, anticipate error patterns, and learn the rules needed to correct the errors.

1 When your instructor or tutor returns a draft, review any errors he or she has identified.

2 Note which errors you commonly make. For example, have you seen "run-on sentence" or "need a transition" marked in other drafts?

3 Identify the advice in the handbook that will help you correct the errors.

4 Make an entry in your editing log. A suggested format appears below.

SAMPLE EDITING LOG PAGE

Original Sentence

Athletes who use any type of biotechnology give themselves an unfair

advantage they should be banned from competition.

Edited Sentence

Athletes who use any type of biotechnology give themselves an unfair
     , and
advantage they should be banned from competition.
          ^

Rule or Pattern Applied

To edit a run-on sentence, use a comma and a coordinating conjunction

(*and, but, or*). *A Canadian Writer's Reference*, section G6-a

---

C3-g Proofread the final manuscript.

Proofreading is a special kind of reading: a slow and methodical search for misspellings, typographical mistakes, and missing words or word endings. Such errors can be difficult to spot in your own work because you may read what you intended to write, not what is actually on the page. To fight this tendency, try one or more of the following tips.

PROOFREADING TIPS

- Remove distractions and allow yourself ten to fifteen minutes of pure concentration — without your cell phone.
- Proofread out loud, articulating each word as it is actually written.
- Proofread your sentences in reverse order.
- Proofread hard-copy pages; mistakes can be difficult to catch on-screen.
- Don't rely too heavily on spell checkers and grammar checkers. Before automatically accepting their changes, consider accuracy and appropriateness.
- Ask a volunteer (a friend, roommate, or co-worker) to proofread after you. A second reader may catch something you didn't.

C3-h Sample student revision: Literacy narrative

On pages 25–26, you'll find Michelle Nguyen's first draft, along with the highlights of her peer review process. Comments from reviewers helped Nguyen see her draft through her readers' eyes and develop a revision plan (see p. 27). One reviewer asked: "What is your main idea?" Another reviewer asked: "What do you want readers to understand about you?" As she revised, Nguyen made both global revisions and sentence-level revisions to clarify her main idea and to delete extra material that might distract readers from her story. Nguyen's final draft, "A Place to Begin," starts on page 32.

Michelle Nguyen

Professor Wilson

English 101

22 September 2015

Nguyen formats her final draft using MLA guidelines.

A Place to Begin

I grew up in the heart of Hanoi, Vietnam—Nhà Dầu—a small but busy neighbourhood swamped with crime. Houses, wedged in among cafés and other local businesses (see fig. 1), measured uniformly about 200 square feet, and the walls were so thin that we could hear every heated debate and impassioned disagreement. Drug addicts scoured the vicinity and stole the most mundane things—old clothes, worn slippers, even license plates of motorbikes. It was a neighborhood where dogs howled and kids ran amok and where the earth was always moist and marked with stains. It was the 1990s Vietnam in miniature, with all the turmoil and growing pains of a newly reborn nation.

Nguyen revises her introduction to engage readers with vivid details.

In a city perpetually inundated with screaming children and slimy criminals, I found my place in the home of a Vietnam War veteran. My parents were away a lot, so the old man became like a grandfather to me. He was a slight man who didn't talk much. His vocal cords had been damaged during the war, and it caused him pain to speak. In his quiet home, I could read and write in the presence of someone whose worldliness grew from his wordlessness.

Sentences are revised for clarity and specificity.

Nguyen focuses on one key story in response to reviewers' questions.

His tiny house stood at the far end of our neighbourhood and always smelled of old clothes and forgotten memories. His wall was plastered with pictures from his combatant past, pictures that told his life story when his own voice couldn't. "I almost died once," he said, dusting a picture frame. It was one of those rare instances he ever mentioned his life during the war.

Nguyen's revisions clarify her main idea.

I perched myself on the side of the armchair, rested my head on my tiny hands, and listened intently. I didn't understand much. I just liked hearing his low, raspy voice.

"I was the only survivor of my unit. Twenty guys. All dead within a year. Then they let me go."

Nguyen develops her narrative with dialogue.

He finished the sentence with a drawn-out sigh, a small set of wrinkles gathering at the corner of his eye.

I wanted to hear the details of that story yet was too afraid to ask. But the bits and pieces I did hear, I wrote down in a notebook. I wanted to

Marginal annotations indicate MLA-style formatting and effective writing.

Nguyen 2

Fig. 1. Nhà Dầu neighbourhood in Hanoi (personal photograph by author).

make sure that there were not only photos but also written words to bear witness to the old veteran's existence.

Once, I caught him looking at the jumbled mess of sentences I'd written. I ran to the table and snatched my notebook, my cheeks warmed with a bright tinge of pink. I was embarrassed. But mostly, I was terrified that he'd hate me for stealing his life story and turning it into a collection of words and characters and ambivalent feelings.

"I'm sorry," I muttered, my gaze drilling a hole into the tiled floor.

Quietly, he peeled the notebook from my fingers and placed it back on the table.

In his muted way, with his mouth barely twisted in a smile, he seemed to be granting me permission and encouraging me to keep writing. Maybe he saw a storyteller and a writer in me, a little girl with a pencil and too much free time.

The last time I visited Nhà Dầu was for the veteran's funeral two years ago. It was a cold November afternoon, but the weather didn't dampen the usual tumultuous spirit of the neighborhood. I could hear the jumble of shouting voices and howling dogs, yet it didn't bother me. For a minute I closed my eyes, remembering myself as a little girl with a big pencil, gazing out a window and scribbling words in my first notebook.

Many people think that words emerge from words and from the exchange of voices. Perhaps this is true. But the surprising paradox of writing for me is that I started to write in the presence of silence. It was only in the utter stillness of a Vietnam War veteran's house that I could hear my thoughts for the first time, appreciate language, and find the confidence to put words on a page. With one notebook and a pencil, and with the encouragement of a wordless man to tell his story, I began to write. Sometimes that's all a writer needs, a quiet place to begin.

As her peer reviewers suggested, Nguyen adds a photograph to help readers visualize Hanoi.

Nguyen revises to keep the focus on her story and not the old man's, as her peer reviewers suggested.

Nguyen revises her final two paragraphs, circling back to the scene from the introduction, giving the narrative coherence.

Nguyen revises the final paragraph to show readers the significance of her narrative.

Following a peer reviewer's advice, Nguyen chooses words from her final sentence for her title.

How to write a literacy narrative

A **literacy narrative** allows you to reflect on key reading or writing experiences and to ask: How have my experiences shaped who I am as a reader or writer? A sample literacy narrative begins on page 32.

Key features

- **A well-told narrative** shows readers what happened. Lively details present the sights, sounds, and smells of the world in which the story takes place. Dialogue and action add interest and energy.

- **A main idea or insight** about reading or writing gives a literacy narrative its significance and transforms it from a personal story to one with larger, universal interest.

- **A well-organized narrative,** like all essays, has a beginning, a middle, and an ending and is focused around a thesis or main idea. Narratives can be written in chronological order, in reverse chronological order, or with a series of flashbacks.

- **First-person point of view (*I*)** gives a narrative immediacy and authenticity. Your voice may be serious or humorous, but it should be appropriate for your main idea.

Thinking ahead: Presenting or publishing

You may have some flexibility in how you present or publish your literacy narrative. If you have the opportunity to submit it as a podcast, a video, or another genre, leave time in your schedule for recording or filming. Also, in seeking feedback, ask reviewers to comment on your plans for using sounds or images.

Writing your literacy narrative

1 Explore

What story will you tell? You can't write about every reading or writing experience or every influential person. Find one interesting experience to focus your narrative. Generate ideas with questions such as these:

- What challenges have you confronted as a reader or a writer?
- Who were the people who nurtured (or delayed) your reading or writing development?

- What are your childhood memories of reading or writing?
- What images do you associate with learning to read or write?
- What is significant about the story you want to tell? What larger point do you want readers to take away from your narrative?

❷ Draft

Figure out the best way to tell your story. A narrative isn't a list of "this happened" and then "that happened." It is a focused story with its own logic and order. You don't need to start chronologically. Experiment: What happens if you start in the middle of the story or work in reverse? Try to come up with a tentative organization, and then start to draft.

❸ Revise

Ask reviewers for specific feedback. Here are some questions to guide their comments:

- What main idea do readers take away from your story? Ask them to summarize this idea in one sentence.
- Is the narrative focused around the main idea?
- Are the details vivid? Sufficient? Where might you convey your story more clearly? Would it help to add dialogue? Would visuals deepen the impact of your story?
- Does your introduction bring readers into the world of your story?
- Does your conclusion provide a sense of the story's importance?

C3-i Format the final manuscript.

Use the manuscript format recommended by your instructor or for your academic discipline. For examples of writing in MLA style, see A4-h and MLA-5b. For examples that show APA or CMS formatting, see APA-5b and CMS-5b, respectively.

C4 Preparing a portfolio; reflecting on your writing

- Sample reflective letter 37
- Writing guide: How to write a reflective letter 40

At the end of the semester, your instructor may ask you to submit a portfolio, or collection, of your writing. A writing portfolio often consists of drafts, revisions, and reflections that demonstrate a writer's thinking and learning processes or that showcase the writer's best work.

C4-a Understand the benefits of reflection.

Reflection — the process of stepping back periodically to examine your decisions, preferences, strengths, and challenges as a writer — helps you recognize your growth as a writer and is the backbone of portfolio keeping. When you submit your portfolio for a final evaluation or reading, you may be asked to include a reflective opening statement — a cover letter, an introduction, a preface, a memo, or an essay.

Reflective writing allows you to do the following:

- show that you can identify strengths and weaknesses in your writing
- comment on the progress you've made in the course
- understand your own writing process
- demonstrate that you've made good writing decisions
- comment on how you might use skills developed in your writing course in other courses where writing is assigned

TIP: Save your notes, drafts, and reviewers' comments for possible use in your portfolio. The more you have assembled, the more you have to choose from to represent your best work.

C4-b Student writing: Reflective letter for a portfolio

Student writer Lucy Bonilla was assigned to submit a portfolio at the end of her writing course. She was asked to include three essays from the semester, with drafts, and to write a cover letter in which she reflected on her growth as a writer. On the following pages is Lucy Bonilla's reflective letter. For a guide to writing a reflective letter, see pages 40–41.

LaunchPad macmillan learning   **MODEL FOR C4**
1 Sample student paper

Bonilla 1

9 December 2016

Professor Todd Andersen

Humanities Department

Johnson State College

Dear Professor Andersen,

    This semester has been more challenging than I had anticipated. I have always been a good writer, but I discovered this semester that I had to stretch myself in ways that weren't always comfortable. I learned that if I wanted to reach my readers, I needed to understand that not everyone sees the world the way I do. I needed to work with my peers and write multiple drafts to understand that a first draft is just a place to start. I have chosen three pieces of writing for my portfolio: "Negi and the Other Girl: Nicknames and Identity," "School Choice Is a Bad Choice," and "Flat-footed Advertising." Each shows my growth as a writer in different ways, and the final piece was my favorite assignment of the semester.

    The peer review sessions that our class held in October helped me with my analytical response paper. My group and I chose to write about "Jíbara," by Esmeralda Santiago, for the Identity unit. My first and second drafts were unfocused. I spent my first draft basically retelling the events of the essay. I think I got stuck doing that because the details of Santiago's essay are so interesting—the biting termites, the burning metal, and the *jíbara* songs on the radio—and because I didn't understand the differences between summary and analysis. My real progress came when I decided to focus the essay on one image—the mirror hanging in Santiago's small house, a mirror that was hung too high for her to look into. Finding a focus helped me move from listing the events of the essay to interpreting those events. I thought my peers would love my first draft, but they found it confusing. Some of their comments were hard to take, but their feedback (and all the peer feedback I received this semester) helped me see my words through a reader's eyes.

    While my Identity paper shows my struggle with focus, my next paper shows my struggle with argument. For my argument essay, I wrote about charter schools. My position is that the existence of charter schools weakens the quality of public schools. In my first draft, my lines

---

Reflective writing can take various forms. Bonilla wrote her reflection as a letter.

Reflective writing often calls for first person (*I*).

Bonilla lists the pieces included in her portfolio by title.

Bonilla comments on a specific area of growth.

Even in the reflective document, Bonilla includes elements of good postsecondary writing, such as using transitions.

Bonilla 2

of argument were not in the best order. When I revised, I ended the paper with my most powerful argument: Because they refuse to adopt open enrollment policies and are unwilling to admit students with severe learning or behavior problems, charter schools are elitist. While revising, I also introduced a counterargument in my final draft because our class discussion showed me that many of my peers disagree with me. To persuade them, I needed to address their arguments in favor of charter schools. My essay is stronger because I acknowledged that both the proponents and the opponents of abandoning charters want improved education for America's children. It took me a while to understand that including counterarguments would actually make my argument more convincing, especially to readers who don't already agree with me. Understanding the importance of counterargument helped me with other writing I did in this course, and it will help me in the writing I do for my major, political science.

> Bonilla reflects on how skills from her writing course will carry over to other courses.

Another stretch for me this semester was seeing visuals as texts that are worth more than a five-second response. The final assignment was my favorite because it involved a number of surprises. I wasn't so much surprised by the idea that ads make arguments because I understand that they are designed to persuade consumers. What was surprising was being able to see all the elements of a visual and write about how they work together to convey a clear message. For my essay "Flat-footed Advertising," I chose the EAS Performance Nutrition ad "The New Theory of Evolution for Women." In my summary of the ad, I noted that the woman who follows the EAS program for twelve weeks and "evolves" is compared to modern humans and our evolution from apes as shown in the classic 1966 *March of Progress* illustration (Howell 41). It was these familiar poses of "Nicolle," the woman in the image, that drew me to study this ad.

In my first draft, I made all of the obvious points, looking only literally at the comparison and almost congratulating the company on such a clever use of a classic scientific drawing. Your comments on my draft were a little unsettling because you asked me "So what?"—why would my ideas matter to a reader? You pushed me to consider the ad's assumptions and to question the meaning of the word *evolve*. In my revised essay, I argue that even though Nicolle is portrayed as powerful, satisfied, and "fully evolved," the EAS ad campaign rests on the assumption that

> Bonilla mentions how comments on her draft helped her revise.

Bonilla 3

performance is best measured by physical milestones. In the end, an ad that is meant to pay homage to woman's strength is in fact demeaning. My essay evolved from draft to draft because I allowed my thinking to change and develop as I revised. I've never revised as much as I did with this final assignment. I actually cared about this essay, and I wanted to show my readers why my argument mattered.

      The expectations for college writing are different from those for high school writing. I believe that my portfolio pieces show that I finished this course as a stronger writer. I have learned to take risks in my writing and to use the feedback from you and my peers, and now I know how to acknowledge the points of view of my audience to be more persuasive. I'm glad to have had the chance to write a reflection at the end of the course. I hope you enjoy reading this portfolio and seeing the evolution of my work this semester.

In her conclusion, Bonilla summarizes her growth in the course.

Sincerely,

Lucy Bonilla

Lucy Bonilla

How to write a reflective letter

A **reflective letter** gives you an opportunity to introduce yourself as a writer, to show your progress and key decisions, and to introduce the contents of a portfolio. A sample reflective letter begins on page 37.

Key features

- **First-person perspective (I)** gives a reflective statement its individuality and authenticity. You are the writer; you are introducing your work and explaining your choices.

- **A thoughtful tone** shows you examining and learning from your experiences and evaluating your strengths and limitations as a writer. Your honest assessment of your work shows that you are a trustworthy and sincere interpreter of your progress.

- **A focused opening statement** provides readers with specific details to understand the contents and organization of your portfolio.

- **Acknowledgment** of the assistance you received shows that you are responsible to readers and reviewers.

Thinking ahead: Presenting or publishing

You may have some flexibility in how you present or publish a reflective piece for your portfolio. Some instructors require a formal essay; others may ask for a letter. Still others may invite you to submit an audio file. If you are submitting an e-portfolio, chances are that your instructor will require your reflective statement in digital form. If you're publishing for the web, you may want to insert headings for easier navigation.

Writing your reflective letter

1 **Explore**

Generate ideas by brainstorming responses to questions such as these:

- Which piece of writing is your best entry? What does it illustrate about you as a writer, student, or researcher?

- How do the selections in your portfolio illustrate your strengths or challenges?

- What do you learn about your development when you compare your early drafts with your final drafts?

- What do your drafts reveal about your revision process? Examine in detail the revisions you made to one key piece and the changes you want readers to notice.
- How will you use the skills and experiences from your writing course in future courses?

❷ Draft

Follow the guidelines given for the form of your reflection — an essay, a cover letter, a memo — and focus your reflections to avoid a list-like structure. Experiment with headings and various chronological or thematic groupings. Ask: What have I learned — and how?

❸ Revise

Ask reviewers for specific feedback. Here are some questions to guide their comments:

- What major idea do readers take away from your reflective statement? Can they summarize this idea in one sentence?
- Where in your piece do readers want more reflection and more detailed explanations?
- Is your reflective statement focused and organized?
- Have you used specific passages from drafts, feedback, or other documents from your portfolio to illustrate your reflections?
- Have you explained how you will apply what you learned to future writing assignments?
- What added details might give readers a fuller perspective of your development and your accomplishments as a writer?

C5 Writing paragraphs

- Common transitions 52

A paragraph is a group of sentences that focuses on one main point or example. Except for special-purpose paragraphs, such as introductions and conclusions (see C2-a and C2-c), paragraphs develop and support an essay's main point, or thesis. Aim for paragraphs that are well developed, organized, coherent, and neither too long nor too short for easy reading.

C5-a Focus on a main point.

A paragraph should be unified around a main point. The main point should be clear to readers, and all sentences in the paragraph should relate to it.

Stating the main point in a topic sentence

As readers move into a paragraph, they need to know where they are in relation to the whole essay and what to expect in the sentences to come. A good topic sentence, a one-sentence summary of the paragraph's main point, acts as a signpost pointing in two directions: backward toward the thesis of the essay and forward toward the body of the paragraph. Usually the topic sentence (highlighted in the following example) comes first in the paragraph.

> All living creatures manage some form of communication. The dance patterns of bees in their hive help to point the way to distant flower fields or announce successful foraging. Male stickleback fish regularly swim upside-down to indicate outrage in a courtship contest. Male deer and lemurs mark territorial ownership by rubbing their own body secretions on boundary stones or trees. Everyone has seen a frightened dog put his tail between his legs and run in panic. We, too, use gestures, expressions, postures, and movement to give our words point.
>
> — Olivia Vlahos, *Human Beginnings*

In postsecondary writing, topic sentences are often necessary for advancing or clarifying the lines of an argument or reporting the research in a field. In business writing, topic sentences (along with headings) are essential because readers often scan for information and summary statements. Sometimes the topic sentence is introduced by a transitional sentence linking the paragraph to earlier material, and occasionally the topic sentence is withheld until the end of the paragraph.

 LaunchPad **ACTIVITIES FOR C5**
macmillan learning
4 Exercises, 3 Writing Practice activities, 3 LearningCurve activities

Sticking to the point

Sentences that do not support the topic sentence destroy the unity of a paragraph. If the paragraph is otherwise focused, such sentences can simply be deleted or perhaps moved elsewhere. In the following paragraph describing the inadequate facilities in a high school, the information about the chemistry instructor (highlighted) is off the point.

> As the result of tax cuts, the educational facilities of Tommy Douglas Collegiate have reached an all-time low. Some of the books date back to 1990 and have long since shed their covers. The few computers in working order must share one printer. The lack of lab equipment makes it necessary for four or five students to work at one table, with most watching rather than performing experiments. Also, the chemistry instructor left to have a baby at the beginning of the semester, and most of the students don't like the substitute. As for the furniture, many of the upright chairs have become recliners, and the desk legs are so unbalanced that they play seesaw on the floor.

Sometimes the solution for a disunified paragraph is not as simple as deleting or moving material. Writers often wander into uncharted territory because they cannot think of enough evidence to support a topic sentence. Feeling that it is too soon to break into a new paragraph, they move on to new ideas for which they have not prepared the reader. When this happens, the writer is faced with a choice: Either find more evidence to support the topic sentence or adjust the topic sentence to mesh with the evidence that is available.

C5-b Develop the main point.

Though an occasional short paragraph is fine, particularly if it functions as a transition or emphasizes a point, a series of brief paragraphs suggests inadequate development. How much development is enough? That varies, depending on the writer's purpose and audience.

For example, when health columnist Jane Brody wrote a paragraph attempting to convince readers that it is impossible to lose fat quickly, she knew that she would have to present a great deal of evidence because many dieters want to believe the opposite. She did *not* write only the following.

UNDERDEVELOPED PARAGRAPH

> When you think about it, it's impossible to lose — as many diets suggest — 10 pounds of *fat* in ten days, even on a total fast. Even a moderately active person cannot lose so much weight so fast. A less active person hasn't a prayer.

This three-sentence paragraph is too skimpy to be convincing. But the paragraph that Brody did write (see p. 44) contains enough evidence to convince even skeptical readers.

WELL-DEVELOPED PARAGRAPH

When you think about it, it's impossible to lose — as many . . . diets suggest — 10 pounds of *fat* in ten days, even on a total fast. A pound of body fat represents 3,500 calories. To lose 1 pound of fat, you must expend 3,500 more calories than you consume. Let's say you weigh 170 pounds and, as a moderately active person, you burn 2,500 calories a day. If your diet contains only 1,500 calories, you'd have an energy deficit of 1,000 calories a day. In a week's time that would add up to a 7,000-calorie deficit, or 2 pounds of real fat. In ten days, the accumulated deficit would represent nearly 3 pounds of lost body fat. Even if you ate nothing at all for ten days and maintained your usual level of activity, your caloric deficit would add up to 25,000 calories. . . . At 3,500 calories per pound of fat, that's still only 7 pounds of lost fat.

— Jane Brody, *Jane Brody's Nutrition Book*

C5-c Choose a suitable pattern of organization.

Although paragraphs (and indeed whole essays) may be patterned in any number of ways, certain patterns of organization occur frequently, either alone or in combination:

examples and illustrations (p. 44)   analogy (p. 47)

narration (p. 45)   cause and effect (p. 47)

description (p. 45)   classification and division (p. 48)

process (p. 46)   definition (p. 48)

comparison and contrast (p. 46)

These patterns (sometimes called *methods of development*) have different uses, depending on the writer's subject and purpose.

Examples and illustrations

Examples, perhaps the most common method of development, are appropriate whenever the reader might be tempted to ask, "For example?"

Normally my parents abided scrupulously by "The Budget," but several times a year Dad would dip into his battered black strongbox and splurge on some irrational, totally satisfying luxury. Once he bought over a hundred comic books at a flea market, doled out to us thereafter at the tantalizing rate of two a week. He always got a whole flat of pansies, Mom's favorite flower, for us to give her on Mother's Day. One day a boy stopped at our house selling fifty-cent raffle tickets on a sailboat, and Dad bought every ticket the boy had left — three books' worth.

— Connie Hailey, student

Illustrations are extended examples, frequently presented in story form. When well selected, they can be a vivid and effective means of developing a point.

> Part of [Harriet Tubman's] strategy of conducting was, as in all battlefield operations, the knowledge of how and when to retreat. Numerous allusions have been made to her moves when she suspected that she was in danger. When she feared the party was closely pursued, she would take it for a time on a train southward bound. No one seeing Negroes going in this direction would for an instant suppose them to be fugitives. Once on her return she was at a railroad station. She saw some men reading a poster and she heard one of them reading it aloud. It was a description of her, offering a reward for her capture. She took a southbound train to avert suspicion. At another time when Harriet heard men talking about her, she pretended to read a book which she carried. One man remarked, "This can't be the woman. The one we want can't read or write." Harriet devoutly hoped the book was right side up.
>
> — Earl Conrad, *Harriet Tubman*

Narration

A paragraph of narration tells a story or part of a story. The following paragraph recounts one of the author's experiences in the African wild.

> One evening when I was wading in the shallows of the lake to pass a rocky outcrop, I suddenly stopped dead as I saw the sinuous black body of a snake in the water. It was all of six feet long, and from the slight hood and the dark stripes at the back of the neck I knew it to be a Storm's water cobra — a deadly reptile for the bite of which there was, at that time, no serum. As I stared at it an incoming wave gently deposited part of its body on one of my feet. I remained motionless, not even breathing, until the wave rolled back into the lake, drawing the snake with it. Then I leaped out of the water as fast as I could, my heart hammering.
>
> — Jane Goodall, *In the Shadow of Man*

Description

A descriptive paragraph sketches a portrait of a person, place, or thing by using concrete and specific details that appeal to one or more of the senses — sight, sound, smell, taste, and touch. Consider, for example, the following description of the grasshopper invasions that devastated the midwestern United States in the late 1860s.

> They came like dive bombers out of the west. They came by the millions with the rustle of their wings roaring overhead. They came in waves, like the rolls of the sea, descending with a terrifying speed, breaking now and again like a mighty surf. They came with the force of a williwaw and they formed a huge, ominous, dark brown cloud that eclipsed the sun.

They dipped and touched earth, hitting objects and people like hail-
stones. But they were not hail. These were *live* demons. They popped,
snapped, crackled, and roared. They were dark brown, an inch or longer
in length, plump in the middle and tapered at the ends. They had transparent wings, slender legs, and two black eyes that flashed with a fierce
intelligence.

— Eugene Boe, "Pioneers to Eternity"

Process

A process paragraph is structured in chronological order. A writer may choose
this pattern either to describe how something is made or done or to explain to
readers, step by step, how to do something. The following paragraph explains
how to perform a "roll cast," a popular fly-fishing technique.

Begin by taking up a suitable stance, with one foot slightly in front of
the other and the rod pointing down the line. Then begin a smooth, steady
draw, raising your rod hand to just above shoulder height and lifting the rod
to the 10:30 or 11:00 position. This steady draw allows a loop of line to form
between the rod top and the water. While the line is still moving, raise the
rod slightly, then punch it rapidly forward and down. The rod is now flexed
and under maximum compression, and the line follows its path, bellying
out slightly behind you and coming off the water close to your feet. As you
power the rod down through the 3:00 position, the belly of line will roll
forward. Follow through smoothly so that the line unfolds and straightens
above the water.

— *The Dorling Kindersley Encyclopedia of Fishing*

Comparison and contrast

To compare two subjects is to draw attention to their similarities, although the
word *compare* also has a broader meaning that includes a consideration of differences. To contrast is to focus only on differences.

Whether a paragraph stresses similarities or differences, it may be patterned in one of two ways. The two subjects may be presented one at a time,
as in the following paragraph contrasting Ulysses S. Grant and Robert E. Lee,
two generals on opposite sides in the American Civil War.

So Grant and Lee were in complete contrast, representing two dia-
metrically opposed elements in American life. Grant was the modern man
emerging; beyond him, ready to come on the stage, was the great age of steel
and machinery, of crowded cities and a restless, burgeoning vitality. Lee
might have ridden down from the old age of chivalry, lance in hand, silken
banner fluttering over his head. Each man was the perfect champion of his
cause, drawing both his strengths and his weaknesses from the people he led.

— Bruce Catton, "Grant and Lee: A Study in Contrasts"

Or a paragraph may proceed point by point, treating the two subjects together, one aspect at a time. The following paragraph uses the point-by-point method to contrast speeches given by US presidents Abraham Lincoln in 1860 and Barack Obama in 2008.

> Two men, two speeches. The men, both lawyers, both from Illinois, were seeking the presidency, despite what seemed their crippling connection with extremists. Each was young by modern standards for a president. Abraham Lincoln had turned fifty-one just five days before delivering his speech. Barack Obama was forty-six when he gave his. Their political experience was mainly provincial, in the Illinois legislature for both of them, and they had received little exposure at the national level — two years in the House of Representatives for Lincoln, four years in the Senate for Obama. Yet each was seeking his party's nomination against a New York senator of longer standing and greater prior reputation — Lincoln against Senator William Seward, Obama against Senator Hillary Clinton.
>
> — Garry Wills, "Two Speeches on Race"

Analogy

Analogies draw comparisons between items that appear to have little in common. Writers can use analogies to make something abstract or unfamiliar easier to grasp or to provoke fresh thoughts about a common subject. In the following paragraph, physician Lewis Thomas draws an analogy between the behaviour of ants and that of humans.

> Ants are so much like human beings as to be an embarrassment. They farm fungi, raise aphids as livestock, launch armies into wars, use chemical sprays to alarm and confuse enemies, capture slaves. The families of weaver ants engage in child labor, holding their larvae like shuttles to spin out the thread that sews the leaves together for their fungus gardens. They exchange information ceaselessly. They do everything but watch television.
>
> — Lewis Thomas, "On Societies as Organisms"

Cause and effect

A paragraph may move from cause to effects or from an effect to its causes. The topic sentence in the following paragraph mentions an effect; the rest of the paragraph lists several causes.

> The fantastic water clarity of the Mount Gambier sinkholes results from several factors. The holes are fed from aquifers holding rainwater that fell decades — even centuries — ago, and that has been filtered through miles of limestone. The high level of calcium that limestone adds causes the silty detritus from dead plants and animals to cling together and settle quickly to the bottom. Abundant bottom vegetation in the shallow sinkholes also helps bind the silt. And the rapid turnover of water prohibits stagnation.
>
> — Hillary Hauser, "Exploring a Sunken Realm in Australia"

Classification and division

Classification is the grouping of items into categories according to some consistent principle. The following paragraph classifies species of electric fish.

> Scientists sort electric fishes into three categories. The first comprises the strongly electric species like the marine electric rays or the freshwater African electric catfish and South American electric eel. Known since the dawn of history, these deliver a punch strong enough to stun a human. In recent years, biologists have focused on a second category: weakly electric fish in the South American and African rivers that use tiny voltages for communication and navigation. The third group contains sharks, nonelectric rays, and catfish, which do not emit a field but possess sensors that enable them to detect the minute amounts of electricity that leak out of other organisms.
>
> — Anne and Jack Rudloe, "Electric Warfare: The Fish That Kill with Thunderbolts"

Division takes one item and divides it into parts. As with classification, division should be made according to some consistent principle. The following paragraph describes the components that make up a baseball.

> Like the game itself, a baseball is composed of many layers. One of the delicious joys of childhood is to take apart a baseball and examine the wonders within. You begin by removing the red cotton thread and peeling off the leather cover — which comes from the hide of a Holstein cow and has been tanned, cut, printed, and punched with holes. Beneath the cover is a thin layer of cotton string, followed by several hundred yards of woolen yarn, which makes up the bulk of the ball. Finally, in the middle is a rubber ball, or "pill," which is a little smaller than a golf ball. Slice into the rubber and you'll find the ball's heart — a cork core. The cork is from Portugal, the rubber from southeast Asia, the covers are American, and the balls are assembled in Costa Rica.
>
> — Dan Gutman, *The Way Baseball Works*

Definition

A definition puts a word or concept into a general class and then provides enough details to distinguish it from others in the same class. In the following paragraph, the writer defines *crowdsourcing* as a savvy business practice.

> Despite the jargony name, crowdsourcing is a very real and important business idea. Definitions and terms vary, but the basic idea is to tap into the collective intelligence of the public at large to complete business-related tasks that a company would normally either perform itself or outsource to a third-party provider. Yet free labor is only a narrow

part of crowdsourcing's appeal. More importantly, it enables managers to expand the size of their talent pool while also gaining deeper insight into what customers really want.

— Jennifer Alsever, "What Is Crowdsourcing?"

C5-d Make paragraphs coherent.

When sentences and paragraphs flow from one to another without bumps, gaps, or shifts, they are said to be coherent. Coherence can be improved by strengthening the ties between old information and new.

Linking ideas clearly

Readers expect to learn a paragraph's main point in a topic sentence early in the paragraph. Then, as they move into the body of the paragraph, they expect to encounter specific details, facts, or examples that support the topic sentence — either directly or indirectly.

If a sentence does not support the topic sentence directly, readers expect it to support another sentence in the paragraph and therefore to support the topic sentence indirectly. The following paragraph begins with a topic sentence. The highlighted sentences are direct supports, and the rest of the sentences are indirect supports.

> Though the open-space classroom works for many children, it is not practical for my son, David. First, David is hyperactive. When he was placed in an open-space classroom, he became distracted and confused. He was tempted to watch the movement going on around him instead of concentrating on his own work. Second, David has a tendency to transpose letters and numbers, a tendency that can be overcome only by individual attention from the instructor. In the open classroom, he was moved from teacher to teacher, with each one responsible for a different subject. No single teacher worked with David long enough to diagnose the problem, let alone help him with it. Finally, David is not a highly motivated learner. In the open classroom, he was graded "at his own level," not by criteria for a certain grade. He could receive a B in reading and still be a grade level behind, because he was doing satisfactory work "at his own level."

— Margaret Smith, student

Repeating key words

Repetition of key words is an important technique for gaining coherence. To prevent repetitions from becoming dull, you can use variations of the key word (*hike, hiker, hiking*), pronouns referring to the word (*gamblers . . . they*), and synonyms (*run, spring, race, dash*). In the following paragraph describing plots among indentured servants, historian Richard Hofstadter binds sentences together by repeating the key word *plots* and echoing it with a variety of synonyms (which are highlighted).

> Plots hatched by several servants to run away together occurred mostly in the plantation colonies, and the few recorded servant uprisings were entirely limited to those colonies. Virginia had been forced from its very earliest years to take stringent steps against mutinous plots, and severe punishments for such behavior were recorded. Most servant plots occurred in the seventeenth century: a contemplated uprising was nipped in the bud in York County in 1661; apparently led by some left-wing offshoots of the Great Rebellion, servants plotted an insurrection in Gloucester County in 1663, and four leaders were condemned and executed; some discontented servants apparently joined Bacon's Rebellion in the 1670's. In the 1680's the planters became newly apprehensive of discontent among the servants "owing to their great necessities and want of clothes," and it was feared they would rise up and plunder the storehouses and ships; in 1682 there were plant-cutting riots in which servants and laborers, as well as some planters, took part.
>
> — Richard Hofstadter, *America at 1750*

Using parallel structures

Parallel structures are frequently used within sentences to underscore the similarity of ideas (see S1). They may also be used to bind together a series of sentences expressing similar information. In the following passage describing folk beliefs, anthropologist Margaret Mead presents similar information (highlighted) in parallel grammatical form.

> Actually, almost every day, even in the most sophisticated home, something is likely to happen that evokes the memory of some old folk belief. The salt spills. A knife falls to the floor. Your nose tickles. Then perhaps, with a slightly embarrassed smile, the person who spilled the salt tosses a pinch over his left shoulder. Or someone recites the old rhyme, "Knife falls, gentleman calls." Or as you rub your nose you think, That means a letter. I wonder who's writing?
>
> — Margaret Mead, "New Superstitions for Old"

Maintaining consistency

Coherence suffers whenever a draft shifts confusingly from one point of view to another or from one verb tense to another (see S4). In addition, coherence can suffer when new information is introduced with the subject of each sentence. As a rule, a sentence's subject should echo a subject or an object in the previous sentence.

Providing transitions

Transitions are bridges between what has been read and what is about to be read. Transitions help readers move from sentence to sentence; they also alert readers to more global connections of ideas — those between paragraphs or even larger blocks of text.

SENTENCE-LEVEL TRANSITIONS   Certain words and phrases signal connections between (or within) sentences. Frequently used transitions are included in the chart on page 52.

Skilled writers use transitional expressions with care, making sure, for example, not to use *consequently* when *also* would be more precise. They are also careful to select transitions with an appropriate tone, perhaps preferring *so* to *thus* in an informal piece, *in summary* to *in short* for a scholarly essay.

In the following paragraph, an excerpt from an argument that dinosaurs had the "'right-sized' brains for reptiles of their body size," biologist Stephen Jay Gould uses transitions (highlighted) to guide readers from one idea to the next.

> I don't wish to deny that the flattened, minuscule head of large-bodied Stegosaurus houses little brain from our subjective, top-heavy perspective, but I do wish to assert that we should not expect more of the beast. First of all, large animals have relatively smaller brains than related, small animals. The correlation of brain size with body size among kindred animals (all reptiles, all mammals, for example) is remarkably regular. As we move from small to large animals, from mice to elephants or small lizards to Komodo dragons, brain size increases, but not so fast as body size. In other words, bodies grow faster than brains, and large animals have low ratios of brain weight to body weight. In fact, brains grow only about two-thirds as fast as bodies. Since we have no reason to believe that large animals are consistently stupider than their smaller relatives, we must conclude that large animals require relatively less brain to do as well as smaller animals. If we do not recognize this relationship, we are likely to underestimate the mental power of very large animals, dinosaurs in particular.
>
> — Stephen Jay Gould, "Were Dinosaurs Dumb?"

PARAGRAPH-LEVEL TRANSITIONS   Paragraph-level transitions usually link the *first* sentence of a new paragraph with the *first* sentence of the previous paragraph. In other words, the topic sentences signal global connections.

Look for opportunities to allude to the subject of a previous paragraph (as summed up in its topic sentence) in the topic sentence of the next one. In his essay "Little Green Lies," Jonathan H. Adler uses this strategy in the topic sentences of the following paragraphs, which appear in a passage describing the benefits of plastic packaging.

> Consider aseptic packaging, the synthetic packaging for the "juice boxes" so many children bring to school with their lunch. One criticism of aseptic packaging is that it is nearly impossible to recycle, yet on almost every other count, aseptic packaging is environmentally preferable to the packaging alternatives. Not only do aseptic containers not require refrigeration to keep their contents from spoiling, but their manufacture requires less than one-10th the energy of making glass bottles.
>
> What is true for juice boxes is also true for other forms of synthetic packaging. The use of polystyrene, which is commonly (and mistakenly) referred to as "Styrofoam," can reduce food waste dramatically due to its insulating properties. (Thanks to these properties, polystyrene cups are much preferred over paper for that morning cup of coffee.) Polystyrene also requires significantly fewer resources to produce than its paper counterpart.

Common transitions

TO SHOW ADDITION	and, also, besides, further, furthermore, in addition, moreover, next, too, first, second
TO GIVE EXAMPLES	for example, for instance, to illustrate, in fact, specifically
TO COMPARE	also, similarly, likewise
TO CONTRAST	but, however, on the other hand, in contrast, nevertheless, still, even though, on the contrary, yet, although
TO SUMMARIZE OR CONCLUDE	in other words, in short, in conclusion, to sum up, therefore
TO SHOW TIME	after, as, before, next, during, later, finally, meanwhile, since, then, when, while, immediately
TO SHOW PLACE OR DIRECTION	above, below, beyond, farther on, nearby, opposite, close, to the left
TO INDICATE LOGICAL RELATIONSHIP	if, so, therefore, consequently, thus, as a result, for this reason, because, since

TRANSITIONS BETWEEN BLOCKS OF TEXT   In long essays, you will need to alert readers to connections between blocks of text that are more than one paragraph long. You can do this by inserting transitional sentences or short paragraphs at key points in the essay. Here, for example, is a transitional paragraph from a student research paper. It announces that the first part of the paper has come to a close and the second part is about to begin.

> Although the great apes have demonstrated significant language skills, one central question remains: Can they be taught to use that uniquely human language tool we call grammar, to learn the difference, for instance, between "ape bite human" and "human bite ape"? In other words, can an ape create a sentence?

C5-e If necessary, adjust paragraph length.

Most readers feel comfortable reading paragraphs that range between one hundred and two hundred words. Shorter paragraphs can require too much starting and stopping, and longer ones can strain the reader's attention span. There are exceptions to this guideline, however. Paragraphs longer than two hundred words frequently appear in scholarly writing, where writers explore complex ideas. Paragraphs shorter than one hundred words occur in business writing and on websites, where readers routinely skim for main ideas; in newspapers because of narrow columns; and in informal essays to quicken the pace.

In an essay, the first and last paragraphs will ordinarily be the introduction and the conclusion. These special-purpose paragraphs are likely to be shorter than paragraphs in the body of the essay. Typically, the body paragraphs will follow the essay's outline: one paragraph per point in short essays, several paragraphs per point in longer ones. Some ideas require more development than others, however, so it is best to be flexible. If an idea stretches to a length unreasonable for a paragraph, you should divide the paragraph, even if you have presented comparable points in the essay in single paragraphs.

Paragraph breaks are not always made for strictly logical reasons. Writers use them for all of the following reasons (the list continues on p. 54).

REASONS FOR BEGINNING A NEW PARAGRAPH

- to mark off the introduction and the conclusion
- to signal a shift to a new idea
- to indicate an important shift in time or place
- to emphasize a point (by placing it at the beginning or the end, not in the middle, of a paragraph)
- to highlight a contrast

- to signal a change of speakers (in dialogue)
- to provide readers with a needed pause
- to break up text that looks too dense

Beware of using too many short, choppy paragraphs, however. Readers want to see how your ideas connect, and they become irritated when you break their momentum by forcing them to pause every few sentences. Here are some reasons you might have for combining some of the paragraphs in a rough draft.

REASONS FOR COMBINING PARAGRAPHS
- to clarify the essay's organization
- to connect closely related ideas
- to bind together text that looks too choppy

A

Academic Reading, Writing, and Speaking

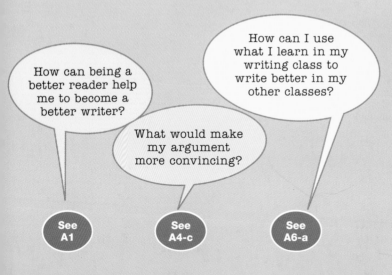

How can being a better reader help me to become a better writer?

See A1

What would make my argument more convincing?

See A4-c

How can I use what I learn in my writing class to write better in my other classes?

See A6-a

Academic Reading, Writing, and Speaking

When you write in college or university, you pose questions, explore ideas, and engage in scholarly debates and conversations. To join in those conversations, you will read and respond to texts, evaluate other people's arguments, and put forth your own ideas.

A1 Reading and writing critically

- Guidelines for active reading 60
- How to read like a writer 61
- Guidelines for writing a summary 64
- How to draft an analytical thesis statement 66

Postsecondary writing requires you to become a critical reader — questioning and conversing with the texts you read. When you read critically, you read with an open, curious mind to understand both what is said and why. And when you write critically, you respond to a text with thoughtful questions and insights, offering your judgment of *how* the parts of a text contribute to its overall effect.

A1-a Read actively.

Reading, like writing, is an active process that happens in steps. Most texts, such as the ones assigned in college or university, don't yield their meaning with one quick reading. Rather, they require you to read and reread to grasp their main points and to comprehend layers of meaning.

When you read actively, you pay attention to details you would miss if you just skimmed a text. First, you read to understand the main ideas. Then you make note of what interests, surprises, or puzzles you. Active readers preview a text, annotate it, and then converse with it.

Previewing a text

Previewing — looking quickly through a text before you read — helps you understand its basic features and structures. A text's title, for example, may reveal an author's purpose; a text's format may reveal what kind of text it is — a book, a report, a memo, and so on. The more you know about a text before you read it, the easier it will be to dig deeper into it.

Annotating a text

Annotating helps you record your responses to a text. As you annotate, you write questions and reactions in the margins of the text or in digital comments. You might circle or underline the author's main points or place question marks or asterisks by the text's thesis or major pieces of evidence. Annotating a text will help you answer the question "What is this text about?"

LaunchPad macmillan learning **ACTIVITIES FOR A1**

6 Writing Practice activities, 1 Sample student paper, 1 LearningCurve activity, 4 Video tutorials

The following example shows how one student, Emilia Sanchez, annotated an article from *CQ Researcher*, a newsletter about social and political issues.

ANNOTATED ARTICLE

Big Box Stores Are (Bad) for Main Street

BETSY TAYLOR

Title gives away Taylor's position.

There is plenty of reason to be concerned about the proliferation of Wal-Marts and other so-called "big box" stores. The question, however, is not whether or not these types of stores create jobs (although several studies claim they produce a net job loss in local communities) or whether they ultimately save consumers money. The real *concern about having a 25-acre slab of concrete with a 100,000 square foot box of stuff land on a town is whether it's good for a community's soul.

Assumes readers are concerned.

* Main point of article. But what does she mean by "community's soul"?

The worst thing about "big boxes" is that they have a tendency to produce Ross Perot's famous "big sucking sound" — sucking the life out of cities and small towns across the country. On the other hand, small businesses are great for a community. They offer more personal service; they won't threaten to pack up and leave town if they don't get tax breaks, free roads and other blandishments; and small-business owners are much more responsive to a customer's needs. (Ever try to complain about bad service or poor quality products to the president of Home Depot?)

Lumps all big boxes together.

"Either/or" argument — Main Street is good, big boxes are bad.

Assumes all small businesses are attentive.

Yet, if big boxes are so bad, why are they so successful? One glaring reason is that (we've become a nation of hyper-consumers,) and the big-box boys know this. Downtown shopping districts comprised of small businesses take some of the efficiency out of overconsumption. There's all that hassle of having to travel from store to store, and having to pull out your credit card so many times. Occasionally, we even find ourselves chatting with the shopkeeper, wandering into a coffee shop to visit with a friend or otherwise wasting precious time that could be spent on acquiring more stuff.

True?

Word choice makes author seem sentimental.

Author's argument seems one-sided and makes assumptions about consumers.

But let's face it — bustling, thriving city centers are fun. They breathe life into a community. They allow cities and towns to stand out from each other. They provide an atmosphere for people to interact with each other that *just cannot be found at Target, or Wal-Mart or Home Depot.

* Shopping at Target to save money — is that bad?

Is it anti-American to be against having a retail giant set up shop in one's community? Some people would say so. On the other hand, if you board up Main Street, what's left of America?

Ends with emotional appeal. Seems too simplistic!

Conversing with a text

Conversing with a text—or responding to a text and its author—helps you move beyond your initial notes to draw conclusions about what you've read. Perhaps you ask additional questions, point out something that doesn't make sense, or explain how the author's points suggest wider implications. As you talk back to a text, you look more closely at how the author works through a topic, and you analyze the author's evidence and conclusions. Conversing takes your notes to the next level. For example, student writer Emilia Sanchez noticed on a first reading that her assigned text closed with an emotional appeal to the reader. On a second reading, she started to question whether that emotional appeal worked or whether it was really too simplistic a way to look at the topic. (See A1-e.)

Many writers use a **double-entry notebook** to converse with a text and its author and to generate ideas. To create one, draw a line down the centre of a notebook page or create a two-column table in a Word or Google document. On the left side, record what the author says; include quotations, sentences, and key terms from the text. On the right side, record your observations and questions. A double-entry notebook allows you to visualize the conversation between you and the author as it develops.

Using sources responsibly: Put quotation marks around words you copy from the text, and keep an accurate record of page numbers for quotations.

Here is an excerpt from student writer Emilia Sanchez's double-entry notebook.

Ideas from the text	My responses
"The question, however, is not whether or not these types of stores create jobs (although several studies claim they produce a net job loss in local communities) or whether they ultimately save consumers money" (1011).	*Why are big-box stores bad if they create jobs or save people money? Taylor dismisses these possibilities without acknowledging their importance. My family needs to save money and needs jobs more than "chatting with the shopkeeper" (1011).*
"The real concern . . . is whether [big-box stores are] good for a community's soul" (1011). "[S]mall businesses are great for a community" (1011).	*Taylor is missing something here. Are all big-box stores bad? Are all small businesses great? Would getting rid of big-box stores save the "soul" of America? Taylor assumes that small businesses are always better for consumers.*

Asking the "So what?" question

As you read and annotate a text, make sure you understand its thesis, or central idea. Ask yourself, "What is the author's thesis?" Then put the author's thesis to the "So what?" test: "Why does this thesis matter? Why does it need to be argued?" Perhaps you'll conclude that the thesis is too obvious and doesn't matter at all—or that it matters so much that you feel the author stopped short and overlooked key details. Or perhaps you'll feel that a reasonable person might draw different conclusions about the issue.

Guidelines for active reading

Preview a written text

- Who is the author? What are the author's credentials?
- What is the author's purpose: To inform? To persuade? To call to action?
- Who is the expected audience?
- When was the text written? Where was it published?
- What kind of text is it: A report? A scholarly article? A letter?

Annotate a written text

- What surprises, puzzles, or intrigues you about the text?
- What question does the text attempt to answer?
- What is the author's thesis, or central idea?
- What type of evidence does the author provide to support the thesis? How persuasive is this evidence?

Converse with a written text

- What are the strengths and limitations of the text?
- Has the author drawn conclusions that you question? Do you have a different interpretation of the evidence?
- Does the text raise questions that it does not answer?
- Does the author consider opposing viewpoints and treat them fairly?

Ask the "So what?" question

- Why does the author's thesis need to be argued, explained, or explored? What's at stake?
- What has the author overlooked in presenting this thesis?

Read like a writer

Reading like a writer helps you identify the techniques writers use so that you can use them, too. To read like a writer is to pay attention to *how* a text is written and *how* it creates an effect on you.

1 Review any notes you've made on a text. What passages do you find effective? What words have you underlined? If you think the text is powerful or well written, commit yourself to figuring out *why* and *how* the text works.

2 Ask *what*, *why*, and *how* questions about the techniques writers use. *What* introductory techniques, for instance, do writers use to hook readers? *Why* and *how* are these techniques effective? *How* do they keep readers reading? As a reader, identify the specific techniques you appreciate so they may become part of your repertoire as a writer.

3 Observe how writers use specific academic writing techniques you want to learn. For instance, if you're interested in learning how writers vary their sentence structure, pay attention to these techniques when you read.

4 Use your experiences as a reader to plan the effect you want to create for your readers. Make deliberate choices to create this effect.

A1-b Outline a text to identify main ideas.

You are probably familiar with using an outline as a planning tool to help you organize your ideas. An outline is a useful tool for reading, too. Outlining a text — identifying its main idea and major parts — can be an important step in your reading process.

As you outline, look closely for a text's thesis statement (main idea) and topic sentences because they serve as important signposts for readers. A thesis statement often appears in the introduction, usually in the first or second paragraph. Topic sentences can be found at the beginning of most body paragraphs, where they announce a shift to a new topic. (See C2-a and C5-a.)

Put the author's thesis and key points in your own words. Here, for example, are the points Emilia Sanchez identified as she prepared to write her analysis of the text printed on page 58. Notice that Sanchez does not simply trace the author's ideas paragraph by paragraph; instead, she sums up the article's central points.

OUTLINE OF "BIG BOX STORES ARE BAD FOR MAIN STREET"

Thesis: Whether or not they take jobs away from a community or offer low prices to consumers, we should be worried about "big-box" stores like Wal-Mart, Target, and Home Depot because they harm communities by taking the life out of downtown shopping districts.

I.   Small businesses are better for cities and towns than big-box stores are.
  A. Small businesses offer personal service; big-box stores do not.
  B. Small businesses don't make demands on community resources as big-box stores do.
  C. Small businesses respond to customer concerns; big-box stores do not.

II. Big-box stores are successful because they cater to consumption at the expense of benefits to the community.
  A. Buying everything in one place is convenient.
  B. Shopping at small businesses may be inefficient, but it provides opportunities for socializing.
  C. Downtown shopping districts give each city or town a special identity.

Conclusion: Although some people say that it's anti-American to oppose big-box stores, actually these stores threaten the communities that make up America by encouraging buying at the expense of the traditional interactions of Main Street.

Reading online

For many assignments, you will be asked to read online sources. It is tempting to skim online texts rather than read them carefully. When you skim a text, you are less likely to remember what you have read and less inclined to reread to grasp layers of meaning.

The following strategies will help you read critically online.

Read slowly. Instead of sweeping your eyes across the screen, slow down the pace of your reading to focus on each sentence.

Avoid multitasking. Close other applications, especially messaging and social media. If you follow a link for background or the definition of a term, return to the text immediately.

Annotate electronically. Use software tools and commenting features to record your thoughts as you read online texts.

Print the text. If you prefer to read and annotate printed texts, print a copy. Record information about the source so that you can find it again, if needed, and cite it properly.

A1-c Summarize to deepen your understanding.

Your goal in summarizing a text is to state the work's main ideas and key points simply, objectively, and accurately in your own words. Writing a summary does not require you to judge the author's ideas; it requires you to *understand* the author's ideas. In summarizing, you condense information, put the author's ideas in your own words, and test your understanding of what the text says. If you have sketched a brief outline of the text (see A1-b), refer to it as you draft your summary.

Following is Emilia Sanchez's summary of the article that is printed on page 58.

In her essay "Big Box Stores Are Bad for Main Street," Betsy Taylor argues that chain stores harm communities by taking the life out of downtown shopping districts. Explaining that a community's "soul" is more important than low prices or consumer convenience, she argues that small businesses are better than stores like Home Depot and Target because they emphasize personal interactions and don't place demands on a community's resources. Taylor asserts that big-box stores are successful because "we've become a nation of hyper-consumers" (1011), although the convenience of shopping in these stores comes at the expense of benefits to the community. She concludes by suggesting that it's not "anti-American" to oppose big-box stores because the damage they inflict on downtown shopping districts extends to America itself.

—Emilia Sanchez, student

Guidelines for writing a summary

- In the first sentence, mention the title of the text, the name of the author, and the author's thesis.
- Maintain a neutral tone; be objective.
- As you present the author's ideas, use the third-person point of view and the present tense: *Taylor argues....* (If you are writing in APA style, see APA-3c.)
- Keep your focus on the text. Don't state the author's ideas as if they were your own.
- Put all or most of your summary in your own words; if you borrow a phrase or a sentence from the text, put it in quotation marks and give the page number in parentheses.
- Limit yourself to presenting the text's key points.

A1-d Analyze to demonstrate your critical thinking.

Whereas a summary most often answers the question of *what* a text says, an analysis looks at *how* a text conveys its main idea. As you read and reread a text — previewing, annotating, and conversing — you are forming a judgment of it.

Balancing summary with analysis

If you have written a summary of a text, you may find it useful to refer to the main points of the summary as you write your analysis. Your readers may or may not be familiar with the text you are analyzing, so you need to summarize the text briefly to help readers understand the basis of your analysis. The following strategies will help you balance summary with analysis.

- Remember that readers are interested in your ideas about the text.
- Pose questions that lead to an interpretation or a judgment of the text rather than to a summary.
- Focus your analysis on the text's thesis and main ideas or some prominent feature of the reading.
- Pay attention to your topic sentences to make sure they signal analysis.

Here is an example of how student writer Emilia Sanchez balances summary with analysis in her essay about Betsy Taylor's article (see p. 58). Before stating her thesis, Sanchez summarizes the article's purpose and central idea.

Summary

[In her essay "Big Box Stores Are Bad for Main Street," Betsy Taylor focuses not on the economic effects of large chain stores but on the effects these stores have on the "soul" of America. She argues that stores like Home Depot, Target, and Wal-Mart are bad for America because they draw people out of downtown shopping districts and cause them to focus on consumption. In contrast, she believes that small businesses are good for America because they provide personal attention, encourage community interaction, and make each city and town unique.] [But

Analysis

Taylor's argument is unconvincing because it is based on sentimentality—on idealized images of a quaint Main Street—rather than on the roles that businesses play in consumers' lives and communities.]

Drafting an analytical thesis statement

An effective thesis statement for analytical writing responds to a question about a text or tries to resolve a problem in the text. Remember that your thesis isn't the same as the text's thesis or main idea. Your thesis presents your judgment of the text's argument.

If Emilia Sanchez had started her analysis of "Big Box Stores Are Bad for Main Street" (p. 58) with this thesis statement, she merely would have repeated the main idea of the article.

INEFFECTIVE THESIS STATEMENT

Big-box stores such as Wal-Mart and Home Depot promote consumerism by offering endless goods at low prices, but they do nothing to promote community.

Instead, Sanchez wrote the following thesis statement, which offers her judgment of Taylor's argument.

EFFECTIVE THESIS STATEMENT

By ignoring the complex economic relationship between large chain stores and their communities, Taylor incorrectly assumes that simply getting rid of big-box stores would have a positive effect on America's communities.

Draft an analytical thesis statement

Analysis begins with asking questions about a text. As you draft your thesis, your questions will help you form a judgment about the text. Let these steps guide you as you develop an analytical thesis statement.

1 **Review your notes to remind yourself of the author's main idea,** supporting evidence, and, if possible, his or her purpose (reason for writing) and audience (intended reader).

2 **Ask *what*, *why*, or *how* questions.** What has the author overlooked or failed to consider? Why might a reasonable person draw a conclusion different from the author's? How does the text complicate or clarify something you've been thinking about or reading about?

3 **Write your thesis as an answer to the questions** you have posed or as the resolution of a problem you have identified in the text. Remember that your thesis isn't the same as the text's thesis. Your thesis presents your judgment of the text.

4 **Test your thesis.** Is your position clear? Is your position debatable? The answer to both questions should be yes.

5 **Revise your thesis.** Why does your position matter? Put your working thesis to the "So what?" test (see p. 59). Consider adding a *because* clause to your thesis (see p. 10).

A1-e Sample student essay: Analysis of an article

Following is Emilia Sanchez's analysis of the article by Betsy Taylor (see p. 58). Sanchez used MLA (Modern Language Association) style to format her paper and cite the source. A guide to writing an analytical essay begins on page 69.

Emilia Sanchez

Professor Goodwin

English 10

20 October 2016

Rethinking Big-Box Stores

In her essay "Big Box Stores Are Bad for Main Street," Betsy Taylor focuses not on the economic effects of large chain stores but on the effects these stores have on the "soul" of America. She argues that stores like Home Depot, Target, and Wal-Mart are bad for America because they draw people out of downtown shopping districts and cause them to focus on consumption. In contrast, she believes that small businesses are good for America because they provide personal attention, encourage community interaction, and make each city and town unique. But Taylor's argument is unconvincing because it is based on sentimentality—on idealized images of a quaint Main Street—rather than on the roles that businesses play in consumers' lives and communities. By ignoring the complex economic relationship between large chain stores and their communities, Taylor incorrectly assumes that simply getting rid of big-box stores would have a positive effect on America's communities.

Taylor's use of colorful language reveals that she has a sentimental view of American society and does not understand economic realities. In her first paragraph, Taylor refers to a big-box store as a "25-acre slab of concrete with a 100,000 square foot box of stuff" that "land[s] on a town," evoking images of a powerful monster crushing the American way of life (1011). But she oversimplifies a complex issue. Taylor does not consider that many downtown business districts failed long before chain stores moved in, when factories and mills closed and workers lost their jobs. In cities with struggling economies, big-box stores can actually provide much-needed jobs. Similarly, while Taylor blames big-box stores for harming local economies by asking for tax breaks, free roads, and other perks, she doesn't acknowledge that these stores also enter into economic partnerships with the surrounding communities by offering financial benefits to schools and hospitals.

> Opening briefly summarizes the article's purpose and thesis.

> Sanchez begins to analyze Taylor's argument.

> Thesis expresses Sanchez's judgment of Taylor's article.

> Signal phrase introduces quotations from the source; Sanchez uses an MLA in-text citation.

> Sanchez identifies and challenges Taylor's assumptions.

Marginal annotations indicate MLA-style formatting and effective writing.

Sanchez 2

Clear topic sentence announces a shift to a new topic.

Taylor's assumption that shopping in small businesses is always better for the customer also seems driven by nostalgia for an old-fashioned Main Street rather than by the facts. While she may be right that many small businesses offer personal service and are responsive to customer complaints, she does not consider that many customers appreciate the service at big-box stores. Just as customer service is better at some small businesses than at others, it is impossible to generalize about service at all big-box stores. For example, customers depend on the lenient return policies and the wide variety of products at stores like Target and Home Depot.

Sanchez refutes Taylor's claim.

Taylor blames big-box stores for encouraging American "hyper-consumerism," but she oversimplifies by equating big-box stores with bad values and small businesses with good values. Like her other points, this claim ignores the economic and social realities of American society today. Big-box stores do not force Americans to buy more. By offering lower prices in a convenient setting, however, they allow consumers to save time and purchase goods they might not be able to afford from small businesses. The existence of more small businesses would not change what most Americans can afford, nor would it reduce their desire to buy affordable merchandise.

Sanchez treats the author fairly.

Conclusion returns to the thesis and shows the wider significance of Sanchez's analysis.

Taylor may be right that some big-box stores have a negative impact on communities and that small businesses offer certain advantages. But she ignores the economic conditions that support big-box stores as well as the fact that Main Street was in decline before the big-box store arrived. Getting rid of big-box stores will not bring back a simpler America populated by thriving, unique Main Streets; in reality, Main Street will not survive if consumers cannot afford to shop there.

Sanchez 3

Work cited page is in MLA style.

Work Cited

Taylor, Betsy. "Big Box Stores Are Bad for Main Street." *CQ Researcher,*
    vol. 9, no. 44, 1999, p. 1011.

How to write an analytical essay

An **analysis** of a text allows you to examine the parts of a text to understand *what* it means and *how* it makes its meaning. Your goal is to offer your judgment of the text and to persuade readers to see it through your analytical perspective. A sample analytical essay begins on page 67.

Key features

- **A careful and critical reading** of a text reveals what the text says, how it works, and what it means. In an analytical essay, you pay attention to the details of the text, especially its thesis and evidence.

- **A thesis that offers a clear judgment** of a text anchors your analysis. Your thesis might be the answer to a question you have posed about the text or the resolution of a problem you have identified in the text.

- **Support for the thesis** comes from evidence in the text. You summarize, paraphrase, and quote passages that support the claims you make about the text.

- **A balance of summary and analysis** helps readers who may not be familiar with the text you are analyzing. Summary answers the question of *what* a text says; an analysis looks at *how* a text makes its point.

Thinking ahead: Presenting and publishing

You may have the opportunity to present or publish your analysis in the form of a multimodal text such as a slide show presentation. Consider how adding images or sound might strengthen your analysis or help you to better reach your audience. (See section A2.)

Writing your analytical essay

1 **Explore**

Generate ideas for your analysis by brainstorming responses to questions such as the following:

- What is the text about?
- What do you find interesting, surprising, or puzzling about this text?
- What is the author's thesis or central idea? Put the author's thesis to the "So what?" test. (See p. 59.)
- What do your annotations of the text reveal about your response to it?

2 **Draft**

- Draft a working thesis to focus your analysis. Remember that your thesis is not the same as the author's thesis. Your thesis presents *your* judgment of the text.

- Draft a plan to organize your paragraphs. Your introductory paragraph will briefly summarize the text and offer your thesis. Your body paragraphs will support your thesis with evidence from the text. Your conclusion will pull together the major points and show the significance of your analysis. (See C1-d.)
- Identify specific words, phrases, and sentences from the text as evidence to support your thesis.

③ Revise

Ask your reviewers to give you specific comments. You can use the following questions to guide their feedback.

- Is the introduction effective and engaging?
- Is summary balanced with analysis?
- Does the thesis offer a clear judgment of the text?
- What objections might other writers pose to your analysis?
- Is the analysis well organized? Are there clear topic sentences and transitions?
- Is there sufficient evidence? Have you analyzed the evidence?
- Have you cited words, phrases, or sentences that are summarized or quoted?

A2 Reading and writing about multimodal texts

In many of your postsecondary classes, you'll have the opportunity to read and write about multimodal texts such as advertisements, maps, videos, or websites. Multimodal texts combine two or more of the following modes: words, static images, moving images, and sound.

Writing about multimodal texts differs from writing about written texts — a video is a different type of text from a report, of course — but there are also similarities. All texts can be approached in a critical way. The strategies and advice offered in A1 for critically reading and writing about texts also apply to multimodal texts.

 LaunchPad macmillan learning   **ACTIVITIES AND MODELS FOR A2**
4 Writing Practice activities, 3 Sample student projects

wwf.org

What will it take before we respect the planet?

Multimodal texts, such as this World Wildlife Fund (WWF) ad, combine modes. Here, words and an image work together to communicate an idea.

A2-a Read actively.

Any multimodal text can be read — that is, carefully approached and examined to understand *what* it says and *how* it communicates its purpose and reaches its audience. When you read a multimodal text, you are reading more than words; you might also be reading a text's design and composition, and perhaps even its pace and volume. Your work as a reader involves understanding the modes — words, images, and sound — separately and then analyzing how the modes work together.

When you read a multimodal text, you'll find it's helpful to preview, annotate, and converse with the text — just as with written texts.

Previewing a multimodal text

Previewing starts when you look at the basic details of a multimodal text and pay attention to first impressions. You ask questions about the text's subject matter and design, its context and creator or composer, and its purpose and intended audience. The more you can gather from a first look, the easier it will be to dig deeper into the meaning of a text.

Annotating a multimodal text

Annotating a text — jotting down observations and questions — helps you read actively to answer the question "What is this text about?" In annotating, you generate ideas by paying close attention to each mode. For example, you might question the choice of music in an audio essay and wonder what this choice implies about the intended audience.

The example on page 73 shows how one student, Ren Yoshida, annotated an advertisement.

Conversing with a multimodal text

Conversing with a text — or responding to a text and its author — helps you move beyond your early notes to form judgments about the text you're examining. You might choose to examine the choice of mode — why the message is conveyed in moving images rather than printed words, for example — or why the background music becomes much louder at one point. You might point out something that is puzzling, contradictory, or provocative about the relationship between two modes.

A2-b Outline to identify main ideas.

Outlining is a useful tool to understand a text that you've been assigned to read. When you outline a multimodal text, you identify its main idea or purpose and sketch a list of its key elements. Because ads, websites and videos may not explicitly state a purpose, you may have to puzzle it out from the details in the work. When you outline, put the text's main ideas and key elements in your own words.

A2-c Summarize to deepen your understanding.

Your goal in summarizing a multimodal text is to state the work's central idea and key points simply, objectively, and accurately, in your own words, and usually in paragraph form. Since a summary must be fairly short, you must make judgments about what is most important. Here is the summary Ren Yoshida drafted as he prepared to write an analysis of the advertisement on page 73.

> The Equal Exchange advertisement is selling the message that together farmers and consumers hold the future of the planet in their hands. At the center of the ad is a farmer whose outstretched hands, full of raw coffee, offer the fruit of her labor and a partnership with consumers. The ad suggests that in a global world producers and consumers are bound together. A cup of coffee is more than just a morning ritual; a cup of coffee is part of an equal exchange that empowers farmers to stay on their land and empowers consumers to do the right thing.
>
> —Ren Yoshida, student

Annotated advertisement

When you choose Equal Exchange fairly traded coffee, tea or chocolate, you join a network that empowers farmers in Latin America, Africa, and Asia to:

- Stay on their land
- Care for the environment
- Farm organically
- Support their family
- Plan for the future

www.equalexchange.coop

Photo: Jesus Choqueheranca de Quevero, Coffee farmer & CEPICAFE Cooperative member, Peru

What is being exchanged?

Why is "fairly traded" so hard to read?

"Empowering" — why in an elegant font? Who is empowering farmers?

"Farmers" in all capital letters — shows strength?

Straightforward design and not much text.

Outstretched hands. Is she giving a gift? Inviting partnership?

Hands: heart-shaped, foregrounded.

Raw coffee beans are red: earthy, natural, warm.

Positive verbs: consumers choose, join, empower; farmers stay, care, farm, support, plan.

How do consumers know their money helps farmers stay on their land?

Write a summary of a multimodal text

1 In the first two sentences, mention the **title of the text and the name of the composer** (or the sponsoring organization or company), and provide some brief information about the context — where the text appeared and when, why, and for whom the text was composed.

2 State the text's **central idea** or message.

3 Maintain a **neutral tone**; be objective.

4 As you present the text's ideas, use the **third-person point of view and the present tense**: *The focus of the ad is. . . . Devaney uses the infographic to argue. . . .* (If you are writing in APA style, see APA-3b.) Limit yourself to presenting the text's major points.

5 Keep your **focus on the text**. Don't state the text's or composer's ideas as if they were your own.

6 Put your **summary in your own words**; if you borrow language from the text, put it in quotation marks and cite the text (see R2-c).

> ## Guidelines for analyzing a multimodal text
>
> The following questions may help you break down and examine a text such as an advertisement, a website, or an infographic.
> - What is your first impression of the text? What details in the text create this response?
> - When and why was the text created? Where did the text appear?
> - What clues suggest the text's intended audience? What assumptions are being made about the audience?
> - What is the thesis, central idea, or message of the text?
> - Does this text tell a story? How would you sum up the story?
> - What modes are used, and why? How do the modes work together?
> - How does the arrangement of sounds or design details help convey the text's meaning or serve its purpose?

A2-d Analyze to demonstrate your critical reading.

Whereas a summary most often answers the question of *what* a text says, an analysis looks at *how* a text conveys its main idea or message. As you read and reread a multimodal text — previewing, annotating, and conversing — you are forming a judgment of it.

An effective thesis statement for analytical writing about a multimodal text responds to a question about the text or tries to resolve a problem in the text. Remember that your thesis isn't the same as the text's thesis or main idea. Your thesis presents your judgment of the text's argument. If you find that your thesis is restating the text's message, turn to your notes to see if the questions you asked earlier in the process can help you revise.

A2-e Sample student writing: Analysis of an advertisement

On the following pages is Ren Yoshida's analysis of the Equal Exchange advertisement that appears on page 73.

Yoshida 1

Ren Yoshida

Professor Marcotte

English 101

4 November 2015

Sometimes a Cup of Coffee Is Just a Cup of Coffee

A farmer, her hardworking hands full of coffee beans, reaches out from an Equal Exchange advertisement ("Empowering"). The hands, in the shape of a heart, offer to consumers the fruit of the farmer's labor. The ad's message is straightforward: in choosing Equal Exchange, consumers become global citizens, partnering with farmers to help save the planet. Suddenly, a cup of coffee is more than just a morning ritual; a cup of coffee is a moral choice that empowers both consumers and farmers. This simple exchange appeals to a consumer's desire to be a good person—to protect the environment and do the right thing. Yet the ad is more complicated than it first seems, and its design raises some logical questions about such an exchange. Although the ad works successfully on an emotional level, it is less successful on a logical level because of its promise for an equal exchange between consumers and farmers.

The focus of the ad is a farmer, Jesus Choqueheranca de Quevero, and, more specifically, her outstretched, cupped hands. Her hands are full of red, raw coffee, her life's work. The ad successfully appeals to consumers' emotions, assuming they will find the farmer's welcoming face and hands, caked with dirt, more appealing than startling statistics about the state of the environment or the number of farmers who lose their land each year. It seems almost rude not to accept the farmer's generous offering since we know her name and, as the ad implies, have the choice to "empower" her. In fact, how can a consumer resist helping the farmer "[c]are for the environment" and "[p]lan for the future," when it is a simple matter of choosing the right coffee? The ad sends the message that our future is a global future in which producers and consumers are bound together.

First impressions play a major role in the success of an advertisement. Consumers are pulled toward a product, or pushed away, by an ad's initial visual and emotional appeal. Here, the intended audience is busy people, so the ad tries to catch viewers' attention and make a strong impression immediately. Yet with a second or third viewing, consumers might start to

The source is cited in the text. No page number is available for the online source.

Yoshida summarizes the content of the ad.

Thesis expresses Yoshida's analysis of the ad.

Details show how the ad appeals to consumers' emotions.

Yoshida interprets details such as the farmer's hands.

Marginal annotations indicate MLA-style formatting and effective writing.

Yoshida 2

ask some logical questions about Equal Exchange before buying their morning
coffee. Although the farmer extends her heart-shaped hands to consumers,
they are not actually buying a cup of coffee or the raw coffee directly from
her. In reality, consumers are buying from Equal Exchange, even if the ad
substitutes the more positive word *choose* for *buy*. Furthermore, consumers
aren't actually empowering the farmer; they are joining "a network that
empowers farmers." The idea of a network makes a simple transaction more
complicated. How do consumers know their money helps farmers "[s]tay on
their land" and "[p]lan for the future" as the ad promises? They don't.

> Yoshida begins
> to challenge the
> logic of the ad.

> Words from
> the ad serve as
> evidence.

    The ad's design elements raise questions about the use of the key terms
equal exchange and *empowering farmers*. The Equal Exchange logo suggests
symmetry and equality, with two red arrows facing each other, but the words
of the logo appear almost like an eye exam poster, with each line decreasing
in font size and clarity. The words *fairly traded* are tiny. Below the logo, the
words *empowering farmers* are presented in contradictory fonts. *Empowering*
is written in a flowing, cursive font, almost the opposite of what might be
considered empowering, whereas *farmers* is written in a plain, sturdy font. The
ad's varying fonts communicate differently and make it hard to know exactly
what is being exchanged and who is becoming empowered.

> Clear topic
> sentence
> announces a shift.

> Summary of the
> ad's key features
> serves Yoshida's
> analysis.

    What is being exchanged? The logic of the ad suggests that consumers
will improve the future by choosing Equal Exchange. The first exchange
is economic: consumers give one thing—dollars—and receive something
in return—a cup of coffee—and the farmer stays on her land. The second
exchange is more complicated because it involves a moral exchange. The ad
suggests that if consumers don't choose "fairly traded" products, farmers
will be forced off their land and the environment destroyed. This exchange,
when put into motion by consumers choosing to purchase products not "fairly
traded," has negative consequences for both consumers and farmers. The
message of the ad is that the actual exchange taking place is not economic
but moral; after all, nothing is being bought, only chosen. Yet the logic of this
exchange quickly falls apart. Consumers aren't empowered to become global
citizens simply by choosing Equal Exchange, and farmers aren't empowered to
plan for the future by consumers' choices. And even if all this empowerment
magically happened, there is nothing equal about such an exchange.

> Yoshida shows
> why his thesis
> matters.

    Advertisements are themselves about empowerment—encouraging
viewers to believe they can become someone or do something by

Yoshida 3

Conclusion includes a detail from the introduction.

identifying, emotionally or logically, with a product. In the Equal Exchange ad, consumers are emotionally persuaded to identify with a farmer whose face is not easily forgotten and whose heart-shaped hands hold a collective future. On a logical level, though, the ad raises questions because

Conclusion returns to Yoshida's thesis.

empowerment, although a good concept to choose, is not easily or equally exchanged. Sometimes a cup of coffee is just a cup of coffee.

Yoshida 4

Work Cited

"Empowering Farmers." Equal Exchange, equalexchange.coop/.
Advertisement. Accessed 14 Oct. 2015.

A3 Reading arguments

- Testing inductive reasoning 81
- Evaluating ethical, logical, and emotional appeals as a reader 84

Many of your postsecondary assignments will ask you to read and write arguments about debatable issues. The questions being debated might be matters of public policy (*Should corporations be allowed to advertise on public school property?*), or they might be scholarly issues (*What role do genes play in determining behaviour?*). On such questions, reasonable people may disagree.

As you read arguments across the disciplines and enter into academic or public policy debates, pay attention to the questions being asked, the evidence being presented, and the various positions being argued. You'll find the critical reading strategies introduced in section A1 — previewing, annotating, and conversing with texts — to be useful as you ask questions about an argument's logic, evidence, and use of appeals.

LaunchPad macmillan learning **ACTIVITIES FOR A3**
2 Exercises, 3 Writing Practice activities, 2 LearningCurve activities

A3-a Distinguish between reasonable and fallacious argumentative tactics.

When you evaluate an argument, look closely at the evidence behind it. Some unreasonable argumentative tactics are known as *logical fallacies*, or errors in logic. Most of the fallacies—such as hasty generalizations and false analogies—are misguided or dishonest uses of legitimate argumentative strategies. The examples in this section suggest when such strategies are reasonable and when they are not.

Generalizing (inductive reasoning)

Writers and thinkers generalize all the time. We look at a sample of data and conclude that data we have not observed will most likely conform to what we have seen. From a spoonful of soup, we conclude just how salty the whole bowl will be.

When we draw a conclusion from an array of facts, we are engaged in inductive reasoning. Such reasoning deals in probability, not certainty. For a conclusion to be highly probable, it must be based on evidence that is sufficient, representative, and relevant. (See the chart on p. 81.)

The fallacy known as *hasty generalization* is a conclusion based on insufficient or unrepresentative evidence.

HASTY GENERALIZATION

In a single year, scores on standardized tests in Ontario's public schools rose by ten points. Therefore, more children than ever are succeeding in Canada's public school systems.

Data from one province do not justify a conclusion about the whole of Canada.

A *stereotype* is a hasty generalization about a group. Here are a few examples.

STEREOTYPES

Women are bad bosses.

Politicians are corrupt.

Children are always curious.

Stereotyping is common because of our human tendency to perceive selectively. We tend to see what we want to see; we notice evidence confirming our already formed opinions and fail to notice evidence to the contrary. For example, if you have concluded that politicians are corrupt, your stereotype will be confirmed by news reports of legislators being indicted—even though every day the media describe public officials serving their communities honestly and well.

> **Academic English** Many hasty generalizations contain words such as *all, ever, always,* and *never,* when qualifiers such as *most, many, usually,* and *seldom* would be more accurate.

Drawing analogies

An analogy points out a similarity between two things that are otherwise different. Analogies can be an effective means of arguing a point. It is not always easy
to draw the line between a reasonable and an unreasonable analogy. At times,
however, an analogy is clearly off base, in which case it is called a *false analogy*.

> **FALSE ANALOGY**
> If we can send a spacecraft to Mars, we should be able to find a cure for the
> common cold.

The writer has falsely assumed that because two things are alike in one
respect, they must be alike in others. Exploring the solar system and finding a cure for the common cold are both scientific challenges, but the problems confronting medical researchers are quite different from those solved
by space scientists.

Tracing causes and effects

Demonstrating a connection between causes and effects is rarely simple. For
example, to explain why a chemistry course has a high failure rate, you would
begin by listing possible causes: inadequate preparation of students, poor
teaching, lack of qualified tutors, and so on. Next you would investigate each
possible cause. Only after investigating possible causes would you be able to
weigh the impact of each cause and suggest appropriate remedies.

Because cause-and-effect reasoning is complex, it is not surprising that
writers oversimplify it. In particular, writers sometimes assume that because
one event follows another, the first is the cause of the second. This common
fallacy is known as *post hoc*, from the Latin *post hoc, ergo propter hoc*, meaning
"after this, therefore because of this."

> **POST HOC FALLACY**
> Since Premier Taptuna took office, unemployment of minority group mem-
> bers in the territory has decreased by 7 percent. Premier Taptuna should be
> applauded for reducing unemployment among minority groups.

Is the governor solely responsible for the decrease? Are there other reasons?
The writer must show that Premier Taptuna's policies are responsible for the
decrease in unemployment; it is not enough to show that the decrease followed
the premier's taking office.

Weighing options

Especially when reasoning about problems and solutions, writers must
weigh options. To be fair, a writer should mention the full range of options,
showing why one is superior to the others or might work well in combination with others.

It is unfair to suggest that only two alternatives exist when in fact there are more. Writers who set up a false choice between their preferred option and one that is clearly unsatisfactory present faulty *either . . . or* logic.

***EITHER . . . OR* FALLACY**

Our current war against drugs has not worked. Either we should legalize drugs or we should turn the drug war over to our armed forces and let them fight it.

Are these the *only* solutions — legalizing drugs and calling out the army? Other options, such as funding for drug abuse prevention programs, are possible.

Testing inductive reasoning

Though inductive reasoning leads to probable and not absolute truth, you can assess a conclusion's likely probability by asking three questions. This chart shows how to apply those questions to a sample conclusion based on a survey.

CONCLUSION	The majority of students on our campus would volunteer at least five hours a week in a community organization if the school provided a placement service for volunteers.
EVIDENCE	In a recent survey, 723 of 1,215 students said they would volunteer at least five hours a week in a community organization if the school provided a placement service for volunteers.

1. Is the evidence sufficient?

   That depends. On a small campus (say, 3,000 students), the pool of students surveyed would be sufficient for market research, but on a large campus (say, 30,000), 1,215 students are only 4 percent of the population. If those 4 percent were known to be truly representative of the other 96 percent, however, even such a small sample would be sufficient (see question 2).

2. Is the evidence representative?

   The evidence is representative if those responding to the survey reflect the characteristics of the entire student population: age, gender, ethnicity, field of study, overall number of extracurricular commitments, and so on. If most of those surveyed are majors in a field like social work, the researchers should question the survey's conclusion.

3. Is the evidence relevant?

   Yes. The results of the survey are directly linked to the conclusion. A survey about the number of hours students work for pay, by contrast, would not be relevant because it would not be about *choosing to volunteer.*

Making assumptions

An assumption is a claim that is taken to be true — without the need of proof. Most arguments are based to some extent on assumptions, since writers rarely have the time and space to prove all the conceivable claims on which an argument is based. For example, someone arguing about the best means of limiting population growth in developing countries might assume that the goal of limiting population growth is worthwhile. For most audiences, there would be no need to articulate this assumption or to defend it.

There is a danger, however, in failing to spell out and prove a claim that is clearly controversial. Consider the following short argument, in which a key claim is missing.

ARGUMENT WITH MISSING CLAIM

Violent crime is increasing. Therefore, we should bring back the death penalty.

The writer seems to be assuming both that the death penalty deters violent criminals and that it is a fair punishment — and that most audiences will agree. These are not reasonable assumptions; the writer will need to state and support both claims.

When a missing claim is an assertion that few would agree with, we say that a writer is guilty of a *non sequitur* (Latin for "it does not follow").

NON SEQUITUR

Christopher gets plenty of sleep; therefore, he will be a successful student in the university's pre-med program.

Does it take more than sleep to be a successful student? The missing claim — that people with good sleep habits always make successful students — would be hard to prove.

Deducing conclusions (deductive reasoning)

When we deduce a conclusion, we put things together, like any good detective. We establish that a general principle is true, that a specific case is an example of that principle, and that therefore a particular conclusion about that case is a certainty.

Deductive reasoning can often be structured in a three-step argument called a *syllogism*. The three steps are the major premise, the minor premise, and the conclusion.

1. Anything that increases radiation in the environment is dangerous to public health. (Major premise)
2. Nuclear reactors increase radiation in the environment. (Minor premise)
3. Therefore, nuclear reactors are dangerous to public health. (Conclusion)

The major premise is a generalization. The minor premise is a specific case. The conclusion follows from applying the generalization to the specific case.

Deductive arguments break down if one of the premises is not true or if the conclusion does not logically follow from the premises. In the following brief argument, the major premise is very likely untrue.

UNTRUE PREMISE

The police do not give speeding tickets to people driving less than eight kilometres per hour over the limit. Dominic is driving ninety-five kilometres miles per hour in a ninety-kilometre-per-hour zone. Therefore, the police will not give Dominic a speeding ticket.

The conclusion is true only if the premises are true. If the police sometimes give tickets for driving less than eight kilometres per hour over the limit, Dominic cannot safely conclude that he will avoid a ticket.

In the following argument, both premises might be true, but the conclusion does not follow logically from them.

CONCLUSION DOES NOT FOLLOW

All members of our club ran in this year's Scotiabank Ottawa Marathon. Jay ran in this year's Scotiabank Ottawa Marathon. Therefore, Jay is a member of our club.

The fact that Jay ran the race is no guarantee that he is a member of the club. Presumably, many runners are nonmembers.

Assuming that both premises are true, the following argument holds up.

CONCLUSION FOLLOWS

All members of our club ran in this year's Scotiabank Ottawa Marathon. Jay is a member of our club. Therefore, Jay ran in this year's Scotiabank Ottawa Marathon.

A3-b Distinguish between legitimate and unfair emotional appeals.

There is nothing wrong with appealing to readers' emotions. After all, many issues worth arguing about have an emotional as well as a logical dimension. Even the Greek logician Aristotle lists *pathos* (emotion) as a legitimate argumentative tactic. For example, in an essay criticizing big-box stores (see p. 58), writer Betsy Taylor has a good reason for tugging at readers' emotions: Her subject is the decline of city and town life. In her conclusion, Taylor appeals to readers' emotions by invoking their national pride.

LEGITIMATE EMOTIONAL APPEAL

Is it anti-American to be against having a retail giant set up shop in one's community? Some people would say so. On the other hand, if you board up Main Street, what's left of America?

Emotional appeals, however, are frequently misused. Many of the arguments we see in the media, for instance, strive to win our sympathy rather than our

Evaluating ethical, logical, and emotional appeals as a reader

Ancient Greek rhetoricians distinguished among three kinds of appeals used to influence readers — ethical, logical, and emotional. As you evaluate arguments, identify these appeals and question their effectiveness. Are they appropriate for the audience and the argument? Are they balanced and legitimate or lopsided and misleading?

Ethical appeals (*ethos*)

Ethical arguments, also known as *credibility arguments*, call upon a writer's character, knowledge, and authority. Ask questions such as the following when you evaluate the ethical appeal of an argument.

- Is the writer informed and trustworthy? How does the writer establish authority?
- Is the writer fair-minded and unbiased? How does the writer establish reasonableness?
- Does the writer use sources knowledgeably and responsibly?
- How does the writer describe the views of others and deal with opposing views?

Logical appeals (*logos*)

Reasonable arguments appeal to readers' sense of logic, rely on evidence, and use inductive and deductive reasoning. Ask questions such as the following to evaluate the logical appeal of an argument.

- Is the evidence sufficient, representative, and relevant?
- Is the reasoning sound?
- Does the argument contain any logical fallacies or unwarranted assumptions?
- Are there any missing or mistaken premises?

Emotional appeals (*pathos*)

Emotional arguments appeal to readers' beliefs and values. Ask questions such as the following to evaluate the emotional appeal of an argument.

- What values or beliefs does the writer address, either directly or indirectly?
- Are the emotional appeals legitimate and fair?
- Does the writer oversimplify or dramatize an issue?
- Do the emotional arguments highlight or shift attention away from the evidence?

intelligent agreement. A TV commercial suggesting that you will be thin and attractive if you drink a certain diet beverage is making a pitch to emotions. So is a political speech that recommends electing a candidate because he is a devoted husband, father, and volunteer firefighter.

The following passage illustrates several types of unfair emotional appeals.

UNFAIR EMOTIONAL APPEALS

This progressive proposal to build a ski resort in the provincial park has been carefully researched by Desjardins, the largest credit union in the province; furthermore, it is favoured by a majority of the local merchants. The only opposition comes from tree huggers who care more about trees than they do about people. One of their leaders was recently arrested for disturbing the peace.

Words with strong positive or negative connotations, such as *progressive* and *tree hugger*, are examples of *biased language*. Attacking the people who hold a belief (environmentalists) rather than refuting their argument is called *ad hominem*, a Latin term meaning "to the man." Associating a prestigious name (Desjardins) with the writer's side is called *transfer*. Claiming that an idea should be accepted because a large number of people (the majority of merchants) are in favour is called the *bandwagon appeal*. Bringing in irrelevant issues (the arrest) is a *red herring*, named after a trick used in fox hunts to mislead the dogs by dragging a smelly fish across the trail.

Advertising makes use of ethical, logical, and emotional appeals to persuade consumers to buy a product or embrace a brand. This Patagonia ad makes an ethical appeal with its copy that invites customers to rethink their purchasing practices.

A3-c Judge how fairly a writer handles opposing views.

The way in which a writer deals with opposing views is telling. Some writers address the arguments of the opposition fairly, conceding points when necessary and countering others, all in a civil spirit. Other writers will do almost anything to win an argument: either ignoring opposing views altogether or misrepresenting such views and attacking their proponents.

Writers build credibility — *ethos* — by addressing opposing arguments fairly. As you read arguments, assess the credibility of your sources by looking at how they deal with views not in agreement with their own.

Describing the views of others

Some writers and speakers deliberately misrepresent the views of others. One way they do this is by setting up a "straw man," a character so weak that he is easily knocked down. The *straw man* fallacy consists of an oversimplification or outright distortion of opposing views. For example, in a debate in British Columbia over attempts to control the cougar population, pro-cougar groups characterized their opponents as trophy hunters bent on shooting harmless cougars. In truth, hunters were only one faction of those who saw a need to control the cougar population.

During Toronto's bid for voting representation, some politicians set up a straw man, as shown in the following example.

> **STRAW MAN FALLACY**
>
> Toronto residents are lobbying for provincehood. Giving a city such as Toronto the status of a province would be unfair.

The straw man wanted provincehood. In fact, most Toronto citizens wanted voting representation in any form, not necessarily through provincehood.

Quoting opposing views

Writers often quote the words of writers who hold opposing views. In general, this is a good idea, for it ensures some level of fairness and accuracy. At times, though, both the fairness and the accuracy are an illusion.

A source may be misrepresented when it is quoted out of context. All quotations are to some extent taken out of context, but a fair writer will explain the context to readers. To select a provocative sentence from a source and to ignore the more moderate sentences surrounding it is both unfair and misleading. Sometimes a writer deliberately distorts a source with ellipsis dots, which tell readers that words have been omitted from the original source. When those words are crucial to an author's meaning, omitting them is obviously unfair. (See P6-c.)

> **ORIGINAL SOURCE**
>
> Johnson's *History of the American West* is riddled with inaccuracies and astonishing in its blatantly racist description of the Indian wars.
>
> —B. R., reviewer

> **MISLEADING QUOTATION**
>
> According to B. R., Johnson's *History of the American West* is "astonishing in its . . . description of the Indian wars."

A4 Writing arguments

- Using ethical, logical, and emotional appeals as a writer 88
- How to draft a thesis statement for an argument 90
- Anticipating and countering opposing arguments 94
- Writing guide: How to write an argument essay 100

Evaluating the arguments of other writers prepares you to construct your own. When you ask questions about the logic and evidence of the arguments you read (see A3), you become more aware of such needs in your own writing. And when you pose objections to arguments, you more readily anticipate and counter objections to your own arguments.

A4-a Identify your purpose and context.

In constructing an argument, you take a stand on a debatable issue. Your purpose is to explain your understanding of the truth about a subject or to propose the best solution to a problem, reasonably and logically, without being combative. Your aim is to persuade your readers to reconsider their positions by offering new reasons to question existing viewpoints.

Academic English   Academic audiences in Canada will expect your writing to be assertive and confident — neither aggressive nor passive. You can create an assertive tone by acknowledging different positions and supporting your ideas with specific evidence.

TOO AGGRESSIVE	Of course only registered organ donors should be eligible for organ transplants. It's selfish and shortsighted to think otherwise.
TOO PASSIVE	I might be wrong, but I think that maybe people should have to register as organ donors if they want to be considered for a transplant.
ASSERTIVE	If only registered organ donors are eligible for transplants, more people will register as donors.

If you are uncertain about the tone of your work, ask for help at your school's writing centre.

 LaunchPad
macmillan learning

ACTIVITIES AND MODELS FOR A4

4 Writing Practice activities, 2 LearningCurve activities, 1 Sample student paper, 4 Video tutorials

It is best to start by informing yourself about the debate or conversation around a subject, sometimes called its *context*. If you are planning to write about the subject of offshore drilling, you might want to read sources that shed light on the social context (the concerns of consumers, the ideas of lawmakers, the proposals of environmentalists) and sources that may inform you about the intellectual context (scientific or theoretical responses by geologists, oceanographers, or economists) in which the debate is played out. Because your readers may be aware of the social and intellectual contexts in which your issue is grounded, you will be at a disadvantage if you are not informed. Conduct some research before preparing your argument. Reading even a few sources will deepen your understanding of the conversation around the issue.

A4-b View your audience as a panel of jurors.

Do not assume that your audience already agrees with you. Instead, envision skeptical readers who, like a panel of jurors, will make up their minds after listening to all sides of the argument. If you are arguing a public policy issue, you

Using ethical, logical, and emotional appeals as a writer

To construct a convincing argument, you must establish your credibility (*ethos*) and appeal to your readers' sense of logic and reason (*logos*) as well as to their values and beliefs (*pathos*).

Ethical appeals (*ethos*)

To accept your argument, a reader must see you as trustworthy, fair, and reasonable. When you acknowledge alternative positions, you build common ground with readers and gain their trust by showing that you are knowledgeable. And when you use sources responsibly and respectfully, you inspire readers' confidence in your judgment.

Logical appeals (*logos*)

To persuade readers, you need to appeal to their sense of logic and sound reasoning. When you provide evidence, you offer readers logical support for your argument. And when you clarify underlying assumptions and avoid logical fallacies, you appeal to readers' desire for reason.

Emotional appeals (*pathos*)

To establish common ground with readers, you need to appeal to their beliefs and values as well as to their minds. When you offer vivid examples, surprising statistics, or compelling visuals, you engage readers in your argument. And when you balance emotional appeals with logical appeals, you highlight the human dimension of an issue to show readers why they should care about your argument.

may want to aim your paper at readers who represent a variety of positions and find common ground among them. In the case of the debate over offshore drilling, for example, imagine a jury that represents those who have a stake in the matter, such as consumers, policymakers, and environmentalists.

At times, you can deliberately narrow your audience. If you are working within a word limit, for example, you might not have the space in which to address the concerns of all interested parties. Or you might be primarily interested in reaching one segment of a general audience, such as consumers. Once you identify a specific audience, it's helpful to think about what kinds of arguments and evidence will appeal to that audience.

A4-c In your introduction, establish credibility and state your position.

When you are constructing an argument, make sure your introduction includes a thesis statement that establishes your position on the issue you have chosen to debate (see also C2-a). In the sentences leading up to the thesis, establish your credibility (*ethos*) with readers by showing that you are knowledgeable and fair-minded. If possible, build common ground with readers who may not at first agree with your views, and show them why they should consider your thesis.

In the following introduction, student Kevin Smith establishes his credibility by introducing both sides of the debate.

Smith shows that he is familiar with the legal issues surrounding school prayer.	Although the US Supreme Court has ruled against prayer in public schools on First Amendment grounds, many people still feel that prayer should be allowed. Such people value prayer as a practice central to their faith and believe that prayer is a way for schools to reinforce moral principles. They also compellingly point out a paradox in the First Amendment itself: at what point does the separation of church and state restrict the freedom of those who wish to practice their religion? What proponents of school prayer fail to realize, however, is that the Supreme Court's decision, although it was made on legal grounds, makes sense on religious grounds as well. Prayer is too important to be trusted to our public schools.	Smith is fair-minded, presenting the views of both sides. Thesis builds common ground.

— Kevin Smith, student

TIP: A good way to test a thesis while drafting and revising is to imagine a counterargument to your argument (see A4-f). If you can't think of an opposing point of view, rewrite your thesis as a debatable statement.

Draft a thesis statement for an argument

1 **Identify the various positions in the debate which you're writing about.** At the heart of a good argument are debate and disagreement. An argumentative thesis takes a clear position on a debatable issue and is supported by evidence. Identify the points in the debate on which there is disagreement. Consider your own questions and thoughts about the topic.

2 **Review any notes you have taken** to clarify your own thoughts about the debate.

3 **Pose a question that has not yet been dealt with sufficiently.** Write this question either in your draft or in your notes to guide your thinking. An open-ended question will make a stronger thesis. If your question can be answered with yes or no, add *why* or *how* to it.

4 **Write your thesis as an answer to your question.** Include the topic, your position, and any language that might preview the organization of your argument or show why you are making the argument.

5 **Test your thesis.** Is your position clear? Is your position debatable? The answer to both questions should be yes.

6 **Revise your thesis.** Why does your position matter? Put your working thesis to the "So what?" test (see p. 59). Consider adding a *because* clause to your thesis (see p. 10).

A4-d Back up your thesis with persuasive lines of argument.

Arguments of any complexity contain lines of argument that, when taken together, might reasonably persuade readers that the thesis has merit. The following, for example, are the main lines of argument that Sam Jacobs used in his paper about the shift from print to online news (see pp. 95–99).

THESIS: CENTRAL CLAIM

The shift from print to online news provides unprecedented opportunities for readers to become more engaged with the news, to hold journalists accountable, and to participate as producers, not simply as consumers.

SUPPORTING CLAIMS

- Print news has traditionally had a one-sided relationship with its readers, delivering information for passive consumption.
- Online news invites readers to participate in a collaborative process—to question and even contribute to the content.
- Links within news stories provide transparency, allowing readers to move easily from the main story to original sources, related articles, or background materials.
- Technology has made it possible for readers to become news producers—posting text, audio, images, and video of news events.
- Citizen journalists can provide valuable information, sometimes more quickly than traditional journalists can.

If you sum up your main lines of argument, as Jacobs did, you will have a rough outline of your essay. In your paper, you will provide evidence for each of your claims.

A4-e Support your claims with specific evidence.

You will need to support your central claim (thesis) and any subordinate claims with evidence: facts, statistics, examples, visuals, expert opinion, and so on. Debatable topics require that you consult sources to establish your *ethos* and to persuade your audience. As you read through or view the sources, you will learn more about the arguments and counterarguments at the centre of your debate.

Using facts and statistics

A fact is something that is known with certainty because it has been objectively verified: Carbon has an atomic weight of 12. Pierre Laporte was assassinated on October 17, 1970. Statistics are collections of numerical facts: Alcohol impairment is a factor in nearly 40 percent of traffic fatalities. About 16 percent of small businesses in Canada are owned by women.

Most arguments are supported at least to some extent by facts and statistics. For example, in the following passage the writer uses statistics to show that US college students' credit card debt is declining.

A recent study revealed that undergraduates are relying less on credit cards and are carrying lower debt than they did five years ago. The study credits the change to wider availability of grant and scholarship money. The average credit card debt per college undergraduate dropped more than 70% from $3,173 in 2008 to $925 in 2013 (Papadimitriou).

Writers often use statistics in selective ways to bolster their own positions. If you suspect that a writer's handling of statistics is not fair, track down the original sources for those statistics or read authors with opposing views, who may give you a fuller understanding of the numbers.

Using examples and illustrations

Examples and illustrations (extended examples, often in story form) rarely prove a point by themselves, but when used in combination with other forms of evidence they flesh out an argument with details and bring it to life. Because examples are often concrete and sometimes vivid, they can reach readers in ways that statistics and abstract ideas cannot.

In a paper arguing that online news provides opportunities for readers that print does not, Sam Jacobs describes how regular citizens using only cell phones and laptops helped save lives during Hurricane Katrina by sending important updates to the rest of the world.

> Citizen reporting made a difference in the wake of Hurricane Katrina in 2005. Armed with cell phones and laptops, regular citizens relayed critical news updates in a rapidly developing crisis, often before traditional journalists were even on the scene.

Using visuals

Visuals can support your argument by providing vivid and detailed evidence and by capturing your readers' attention. Bar or line graphs, for instance, describe and organize complex statistical data; photographs can immediately and evocatively convey abstract ideas; maps can illustrate geography. (See pp. 16–17.)

As you consider using visual evidence, ask yourself these questions:

- Is the visual accurate, credible, and relevant?
- How will the visual appeal to readers? Logically? Ethically? Emotionally?
- How will the visual evidence function? Will it provide background information? Present complex numerical information or an abstract idea? Lend authority? Refute counterarguments?

Citing expert opinion

Although they are no substitute for careful reasoning of your own, the views of an expert can contribute to the force of your argument. For example, to help make the case that print journalism has a one-sided relationship with its readers, Sam Jacobs integrates an expert's key description.

> With the rise of the internet, however, this model has been criticized by journalists such as Dan Gillmor, founder of the Center for Citizen Media, who argues that traditional print journalism treats "news as a lecture," whereas online news is "more of a conversation" (xxiv).

When you rely on expert opinion, make sure that your source is an expert in the field you are writing about. To help readers recognize the expert, provide credentials showing why your source is worth listening to; list the person's position or title alongside his or her name (*Dan Gillmor, founder of the Center for Citizen Media*). When including expert testimony in your paper, you can summarize or paraphrase the expert's opinion or quote the expert's exact words. You will need to document the source, as Jacobs did.

A4-f Anticipate objections; counter opposing arguments.

Readers who already agree with you need no convincing, but skeptical readers may resist your arguments. To be willing to give up a position that seems reasonable, readers need to see that another position is even more reasonable. In addition to presenting your own case, therefore, you should consider the opposing arguments and attempt to counter them.

It might seem at first that drawing attention to an opposing point of view or contradictory evidence would weaken your argument. But by anticipating and countering objections, you show yourself as a reasonable and well-informed writer who has a thorough understanding of the issue.

There is no best place in an essay to deal with opposing views. Often it is useful to summarize the opposing position early in your essay. After stating your thesis but before developing your own arguments, you might have a paragraph that addresses the most important counterargument. Or you can anticipate objections paragraph by paragraph as you develop your case. Wherever you decide to present opposing arguments, you will enhance your credibility if you explain the views of others accurately and fairly.

A4-g Build common ground.

As you counter opposing arguments, try to seek out one or two assumptions you might share with readers who do not initially agree with your views. If you can show that you share their concerns, your readers will be more likely to accept that your argument is valid. For example, to persuade parents that school uniforms will have a positive effect on academic achievement, a school board would want to create common ground with parents to emphasize the shared values around learning. Having established these values in common, the board might persuade parents that school uniforms will reduce distractions, save money, and focus students' attention on learning rather than on clothes.

People believe that intelligence and decency support their side of an argument. To be persuaded, they must see these qualities in your argument.

Anticipating and countering opposing arguments

To anticipate a possible objection to your argument, consider the following questions.

- Could a reasonable person draw a different conclusion from your facts or examples?
- Might a reader question any of your assumptions or offer an alternative explanation?
- Is there any evidence that might weaken your position?

The following questions may help you respond to a potential objection.

- Can you concede the point to the opposition but challenge the point's importance or usefulness?
- Can you explain why readers should consider a new perspective or question a piece of evidence?
- Should you explain how your position responds to contradictory evidence?
- Can you suggest a different interpretation of the evidence?

When you write, use phrasing to signal to readers that you're about to present an objection. Often the signal phrase can go in the lead sentence of a paragraph.

> Critics of this view argue that . . .
> Some readers might point out that . . .
> Researchers challenge these claims by . . .

A4-h Sample student writing: Argument

In the paper that begins on the next page, student writer Sam Jacobs argues that the shift from print to online news benefits readers by providing them with opportunities to produce news and to think more critically as consumers of news. Notice how he appeals to his readers by presenting opposing views fairly before providing his own arguments.

When Jacobs quotes, summarizes, or paraphrases information from a print source or an online source, he cites the source with an in-text citation formatted in MLA style. Citations in the paper refer readers to the list of works cited at the end of the paper. (For more details about citing sources, see MLA-2.)

A guide to writing an argument essay appears on pages 100–01.

Jacobs 1

Sam Jacobs

Professor Alperini

English 101

11 October 2016

From Lecture to Conversation: Redefining What's "Fit to Print"

"All the news that's fit to print," the motto of *The New York Times* since 1896, plays with the word *fit*, asserting that a news story must be newsworthy and must not exceed the limits of the printed page. The increase in online news consumption, however, challenges both meanings of the word *fit*, allowing producers and consumers alike to rethink who decides which topics are worth covering and how extensive that coverage should be. Any cultural shift usually means that something is lost, but in this case there are clear gains. The shift from print to online news provides unprecedented opportunities for readers to become more engaged with the news, to hold journalists accountable, and to participate as producers, not simply as consumers.

Guided by journalism's code of ethics—accuracy, objectivity, and fairness—print news reporters have gathered and delivered stories according to what editors decide is fit for their readers. Except for op-ed pages and letters to the editor, print news has traditionally had a one-sided relationship with its readers. The print news media's reputation for objective reporting has been held up as "a stop sign" for readers, sending a clear message that no further inquiry is necessary (Weinberger). With the rise of the internet, however, this model has been criticized by journalists such as Dan Gillmor, founder of the Center for Citizen Media, who argues that traditional print journalism treats "news as a lecture," whereas online news is "more of a conversation" (xxiv). Print news arrives on the doorstep every morning as a fully formed lecture, a product created without participation from its readership. By contrast, online news invites readers to participate in a collaborative process—to question and even help produce the content.

One of the most important advantages online news offers over print news is the presence of built-in hyperlinks, which carry readers from one electronic document to another. If readers are curious about the definition of a term, the roots of a story, or other perspectives on a topic, links provide a path. Links help readers become more critical consumers of information by engaging them in a totally new way. For instance, the link

In his opening sentences, Jacobs provides background for his thesis.

Thesis states the main point.

Jacobs does not need a citation for common knowledge.

Source is cited in MLA style.

Transition moves from Jacobs's main argument to specific examples.

Marginal annotations indicate MLA-style formatting and effective writing.

Jacobs 2

embedded in the story "Credit-Shy: Younger Generation Is More Likely to Stick to a Cash-Only Policy" (Sapin) allows readers to find out more about the financial trends of young adults and provides statistics that confirm the article's accuracy (see fig. 1). Other links in the article widen the conversation. These kinds of links give readers the opportunity to conduct their own evaluation of the evidence and verify the journalist's claims.

Jacobs clarifies key terms (*transparency* and *accountability*).

Links provide a kind of transparency impossible in print because they allow readers to see through online news to the "sources, disagreements, and the personal assumptions and values" that may have influenced a news story (Weinberger). The International Center for Media and the Public Agenda underscores the importance of news organizations letting "consumers in on the often tightly held little secrets of journalism." To do so, they suggest, will lead to accountability, and "accountability leads to credibility" ("Openness"). These tools alone don't guarantee that news producers will be responsible and trustworthy, but they encourage an open and transparent environment that benefits news consumers.

Jacobs develops the thesis.

Not only has technology allowed readers to become more critical news consumers, but it also has helped some to become news producers. The web gives ordinary people the power to report on the day's events. Anyone with an internet connection can publish on blogs and websites, engage in online discussion forums, and contribute video and audio recordings. Citizen journalists with laptops, cell phones, and digital camcorders have become news producers alongside large news organizations.

Opposing views are presented fairly.

Not everyone embraces the spread of unregulated news reporting online. Critics point out that citizen journalists are not necessarily trained to be fair or ethical, for example, nor are they subject to editorial oversight. Acknowledging that citizen reporting is more immediate and experimental, critics also question its accuracy and accountability: "While it has its place . . . it really isn't journalism at all, and it opens up information flow to the strong probability of fraud and abuse. . . . Information without journalistic standards is called gossip," writes David Hazinski in *The Atlanta Journal-Constitution* (23A). In his book *Losing the News*, media specialist Alex S. Jones argues that what passes for news today is in fact "pseudo news" and is "far less reliable" than traditional print news (27). Even a supporter like Gillmor is willing

Jacobs 3

to agree that citizen journalists are "nonexperts," but he argues that they are "using technology to make a profound contribution, and a real difference" (140).

> Jacobs counters opposing arguments.

Citizen reporting made a difference in the wake of Hurricane Katrina in 2005. Armed with cell phones and laptops, regular citizens relayed critical news updates in a rapidly developing crisis, often before traditional journalists were even on the scene. In 2006, the enormous contributions of citizen journalists were recognized when the New Orleans *Times-Picayune* received the Pulitzer Prize in public service for its online coverage—largely citizen-generated—of Hurricane Katrina. In recognizing the paper's

> A vivid example helps Jacobs make his point.

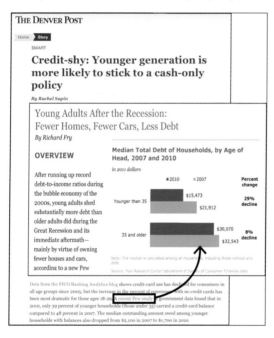

Fig. 1. Links embedded in online news articles allow readers to move from the main story to original sources, related articles, or background materials. The link in this online article (Sapin) points to a statistical report by the Pew Research Center, the original source of the author's data on young adults' spending practices.

Jacobs uses specific evidence for support.

"meritorious public service," the Pulitzer Prize board credited the newspaper's blog for "heroic, multi-faceted coverage of [the storm] and its aftermath" ("2006"). Writing for the *Online Journalism Review*, Mark Glaser emphasizes the role that blog updates played in saving storm victims' lives. Further, he calls *The Times-Picayune*'s partnership with citizen journalists a "watershed for online journalism."

Conclusion echoes the thesis without dully repeating it.

The internet has enabled consumers to participate in a new way in reading, questioning, interpreting, and reporting the news. Decisions about appropriate content and coverage are no longer exclusively in the hands of news editors. Ordinary citizens now have a meaningful voice in the conversation—a hand in deciding what's "fit to print." Some skeptics worry about the apparent free-for-all and loss of tradition. But the expanding definition of news provides opportunities for consumers to be more engaged with events in their communities, their nations, and the world.

Works Cited

Gillmor, Dan. *We the Media: Grassroots Journalism by the People, for the People*. O'Reilly Media, 2006.

Glaser, Mark. "NOLA.com Blogs and Forums Help Save Lives after Katrina." *OJR: The Online Journalism Review*, Knight Digital Media Center, 13 Sept. 2005, www.ojr.org/050913glaser/.

Hazinski, David. "Unfettered 'Citizen Journalism' Too Risky." *The Atlanta Journal-Constitution*, 13 Dec. 2007, p. 23A. *General OneFile*. go.galegroup.com/ps/.

Jones, Alex S. *Losing the News: The Future of the News That Feeds Democracy*. Oxford UP, 2009.

"Openness and Accountability: A Study of Transparency in Global Media Outlets." *ICMPA: International Center for Media and the Public Agenda*, 2006, www.icmpa.umd.edu/pages/studies/transparency/main.html/.

Sapin, Rachel. "Credit-Shy: Younger Generation Is More Likely to Stick to a Cash-Only Policy." *The Denver Post*, 26 Aug. 2013, www.denverpost.com/ci_23929523/credit-shy-younger-generation-stick-cash-only-policy/.

"The 2006 Pulitzer Prize Winners: Public Service." *The Pulitzer Prizes*. Columbia U, www.pulitzer.org/prize-winners-by-year/2006/. Accessed 2 Oct. 2016.

Weinberger, David. "Transparency Is the New Objectivity." *Joho the Blog*, 19 July 2009, www.hyperorg.com/blogger/2009/07/19/transparency-is-the-new-objectivity/.

Works cited page uses MLA style.

List is alphabetized by authors' last names (or by title when a work has no author).

Access date is used for a web source that has no update date.

How to write an argument essay

Composing an **argument** gives you the opportunity to propose a reasonable solution to a debatable issue. You present your position, evidence to support your position, and your response to other views on the issue. A sample argument essay begins on page 95.

Key features

- **A thesis, stated as a clear position on a debatable issue,** frames an argument essay. The issue is debatable because reasonable people disagree about it.

- **An examination of the issue's context** indicates why the issue is important, why readers should care about it, or how your position fits into the debates surrounding the topic.

- **Sufficient, representative, and relevant evidence** supports the argument's claims. Evidence needs to be specific and persuasive; quoted, summarized, or paraphrased fairly and accurately; and cited correctly.

- **Opposing positions are summarized and countered.** By anticipating and countering objections to your position, you establish common ground with readers and show yourself as a reasonable and well-informed writer.

Thinking ahead: Presenting or publishing

You may have some flexibility in how you present or publish your argument. If you submit your argument as an audio or video essay, make sure you understand the genre's conventions and think through how your voice or a combination of sounds and images can help you establish your *ethos*. If you are taking a position on a local issue, consider publishing your argument in the form of a newspaper op-ed or letter to the editor. The benefit? A real-world audience.

Writing your argument

 Explore

Generate ideas by brainstorming responses to questions such as the following.

- What is the debate around your issue? What sources will help you learn more about your issue?

- What position will you take? Why does your position need to be argued?
- What evidence supports your position? What evidence makes you question your position?
- What types of appeals — *ethos, logos, pathos* — might you use to persuade readers? How will you build common ground with your readers?

② Draft

Try to figure out the best way to structure your argument. A typical outline might include the following steps: Capture readers' attention; state your position; give background information; outline your major claims with specific evidence; recognize and respond to opposing points of view; and end by reinforcing your point and why it matters.

As you draft, think about the best order for your claims. You could organize by strength, building to your strongest argument (instead of starting with your strongest), or by concerns your audience might have.

③ Revise

Ask your reviewers for specific feedback. Here are some questions to guide their comments.

- Is the thesis clear? Is the issue debatable?
- Is the evidence persuasive? Is more needed?
- Is your argument organized logically?
- Are there any flaws in your reasoning or assumptions that weaken the argument?
- Have you presented yourself as a knowledgeable, trustworthy writer?
- Does the conclusion pull together your entire argument? How might the conclusion be more effective?

A5 Speaking confidently

- How to deliver a speech or presentation 104

Speaking and writing draw on many of the same skills. Effective speakers, like effective writers, identify their purpose, audience, and context. They project themselves as informed and reasonable, establish common ground with listeners, and use specific, memorable language and persuasive techniques to capture their audience's attention.

In many college or university classes, you'll be assigned to give an oral presentation. The more comfortable you become speaking in different settings, the easier it will be when you give a formal presentation. You can practise your speaking skills as well by contributing to class discussions, responding to the comments of fellow students, and playing an active role in team-based learning.

A5-a Identify your purpose, audience, and context.

As you plan your presentation, strategize a bit: Identify your purpose (reason) for speaking, your audience (listeners), and the context (situation) in which you will speak.

PURPOSE	Begin by asking, "Why am I speaking? What is my goal?" Your goal might be to inform, to persuade, to evaluate, to recommend, or to call to action.
AUDIENCE	Effective speakers identify the needs and expectations of their audience and shape their material to meet those needs and expectations. Assess what your audience may already know and believe, what objections you might need to anticipate, and how you might engage your listeners.
CONTEXT	Ask yourself, "What is the situation for my speech? Is it an assignment for a course? The presentation of a group project? A community meeting? And how much time do I have to speak?" The answers to these questions will help you shape your presentation for your particular speaking situation.

A5-b Prepare a presentation.

Knowing your subject

You need to know your subject well in order to talk about it confidently. Although you should not pack too much material into a short speech, you need to speak knowledgeably to engage your audience. In preparing your speech, do some research to know what evidence — statistics, visuals, expert testimony — will support your points. The more you know about your subject, the more comfortable you'll be in speaking about it.

Developing a clear structure

A good presentation is easy to follow because it has a clear beginning, middle, and end. In your introduction, preview the purpose and structure of your presentation and the question or problem you are addressing so that your audience can anticipate where you are going. Start with an opening hook: a surprising fact, a brief but vivid story, or an engaging question. For an informative speech, organize the body in a way that helps your audience remember key points of information. For a persuasive speech, organize so that you build enthusiasm for your position. And conclude your presentation by giving listeners a sense of completion. Restate the key points, and borrow phrasing or an image from your opening to make the speech come full circle.

Using signposts and repetition

As you speak, use signposts to remind the audience of your purpose and key points. Signposts guide listeners ("The shift to online news has three important benefits for consumers.") and help them to understand the transition from one point to the next ("The second benefit is . . ."). By repeating phrases, you emphasize the importance of key points and help listeners remember them. For more on transitions and repetition, see C5-d.

Writing for the ear, not the eye

Use an engaging, lively style so that the audience will enjoy listening to you. Be sure to use straightforward language that's easy on the ear, not too complicated or too abstract. Occasionally remind listeners of your main point, and keep your sentences short and direct so that listeners can easily follow your presentation. In the following example, the writer adapts a single essay sentence for a speech by breaking it into smaller chunks, engaging the audience with a question, and using plainer language.

SENTENCE FROM AN ARGUMENT ESSAY

In 2006, the enormous contributions of citizen journalists were recognized when the New Orleans *Times-Picayune* received the Pulitzer Prize in public service for its online coverage — largely citizen-generated — of Hurricane Katrina.

ESSAY MATERIAL ADAPTED FOR A SPEECH

The New Orleans *Times-Picayune* newspaper won the 2006 Pulitzer Prize in public service. Why? For its online news about Hurricane Katrina — news generated by ordinary people.

Integrating sources with signal phrases

If you are using sources, do so responsibly. As you speak, be sure to acknowledge your sources with signal phrases ("According to *New York Times* columnist David Brooks . . ."). If you have slides, you can include signal phrases or

Deliver a speech or presentation

1 **Plan and practise.** Think about key details ahead of time. Know the room in which you'll speak and its technology capabilities. Dress both for comfort and for confidence. Most important, practise often and out loud. Practice is critical for both individual and team presentations.

2 **Establish a relationship with your audience.** If you give your audience your full attention, they will return it. Before delivering your speech, make steady eye contact with your listeners, introduce yourself, and help the audience connect with you.

3 **Start strong and end strong.** Beginnings and endings gain and hold an audience's attention. Choose your opening strategy: Will you pose a question and ask for a show of hands? Will you tell a brief personal story? For a strong conclusion, look directly at your audience as you review your key points. Finish by thanking your audience and inviting questions.

4 **Keep slides or other visuals simple.** Slides can help your audience see your presentation's structure, and visual elements, such as images, diagrams, or charts, can engage your listeners. Don't crowd slides with text or data. Make sure the connection between your purpose and any visuals you use is clear.

5 **Use notes.** Confident speakers rely on brief notes to remind them of main points and to capture the exact wording of quotations or the details of research findings.

citations on the slides. For more on integrating and citing sources, see MLA-3 and MLA-4, APA-3 and APA-4, or CMS-3 and CMS-4, depending on the required style.

Using visuals and multimedia purposefully

Well-chosen visuals, video clips, or audio clips can enhance your presentation and add variety. For example, a photograph can highlight an environmental problem, a line graph can quickly show a trend over time, and a brief video clip can capture listeners' attention.

Visuals and multimedia convey information powerfully, but you need to consider how they support your purpose and how your audience will respond. Too many visuals can be distracting, especially when they are difficult to read or don't convey a clear message, so be sure each visual serves a specific purpose. Multimedia can overwhelm a presentation and leave you without sufficient time to achieve your goals.

A5-c Remix an essay for a presentation.

You may be asked to revise an essay into a spoken presentation. Compare the first paragraph of Sam Jacobs's essay (p. 95) with the opening lines for his presentation below. Notice the important adjustments he made in preparing a speaking script from his argument essay.

Good afternoon, everyone. I'm Sam Jacobs.

> Friendly opening establishes a relationship with the audience.

Jacobs starts with his key question and engages the audience immediately.

Today I want to explore this question: How do consumers benefit from reading news online? But first let me have a quick show of hands: How many of you read news online? If you answered yes, you are part of the 71% of young Americans, ages 18 to 29, who read their news online, according to the Pew Research Center. We've grown up in a digital generation, consuming news on every possible mobile device, especially our cell phones. Most of us don't miss the newspaper arriving on the doorstep every morning. And because we expect to read news online, we take it for granted. But if we take it for granted, we might miss the benefits of participating as producers of news, not simply as consumers. The three benefits I want to explore are . . .

> Establishes common ground with the audience.

Jacobs uses a source responsibly and integrates it well.

> Jacobs repeats words and phrases for emphasis and uses signposts to make it easier for his listeners to follow his ideas.

A6 Writing in the disciplines

- Evidence typically used in various disciplines **108**

Postsecondary courses expose you to the thinking of scholars in many disciplines, such as those within the humanities (literature, music, art), the social sciences (psychology, anthropology, sociology), and the sciences (biology, physics, chemistry). No matter what you study, you will be asked to write for a variety of audiences in a variety of formats and to practise the methods used by the discipline's scholars and practitioners. In a criminal justice course, for example, you may be asked to write a policy memo or a legal brief; in a nursing course, you may be asked to write a treatment plan. To write in these courses is to think like a criminologist or a nurse and to engage in the debates of the discipline.

A6-a Find commonalities across disciplines.

Good writing in any field needs to communicate the writer's purpose to an audience and to explore an engaging question about a subject. Effective writers make an argument and support their claims with evidence. Writers in most fields show readers the thesis they're developing (or, in the sciences, the hypothesis they're testing) and counter the objections of other writers. All disciplines require writers to document where they found their evidence and from whom they borrowed ideas.

A6-b Recognize the questions writers in a discipline ask.

Disciplines are characterized by the kinds of questions their scholars attempt to answer. For example, social scientists, who analyze human behaviour, might ask about the factors that cause people to act in certain ways. Historians, who seek an understanding of the past, often ask questions about the causes and effects of events and about the connections between current and past events.

Whenever you write for a college or university course, try to determine the kinds of questions scholars in the field might ask about a topic. You can find clues in assigned readings, lecture topics, discussion groups, and the paper assignment itself.

LaunchPad macmillan learning **MODELS FOR A6**
2 Writing Practice activities, 10 Sample student papers

A6-c Understand the kinds of evidence writers in a discipline use.

Regardless of the discipline in which you're writing, you must support any claims you make with evidence — facts, statistics, examples, and expert opinion.

The kinds of evidence used in different disciplines commonly overlap. Students of geography, media studies, and political science, for example, might use census data to explore different topics. The evidence that one discipline values, however, might not be sufficient to support an interpretation or a conclusion in another field. You might use anecdotes or interviews in an anthropology paper, for example, but such evidence would be irrelevant in a biology lab report. The chart on page 108 lists the kinds of evidence accepted in various disciplines.

A6-d Become familiar with a discipline's language conventions.

Every discipline has a specialized vocabulary. As you read the articles and books in a field, you'll notice certain words and phrases that come up repeatedly. Sociologists, for example, use terms such as *independent variables* and *dyads* to describe social phenomena; computer scientists might refer to *algorithm design* and *loop invariants* to describe programming methods. Practitioners in health fields use terms like *treatment plan* and *systemic assessment* to describe patient care. Use discipline-specific terms only when you are certain that you and your readers understand their meaning.

A6-e Use a discipline's preferred citation style.

In any discipline, you must give credit to those whose ideas or words you have borrowed. Avoid plagiarism by citing sources honestly and accurately.

While all disciplines emphasize careful documentation, each follows a particular system of citation that its members have agreed on. Writers in the humanities usually use the system established by the Modern Language Association (MLA). Scholars in some social sciences, such as psychology and anthropology, follow the style guidelines of the American Psychological Association (APA). Scholars in history and some humanities typically follow *The Chicago Manual of Style*. For guidance on using the MLA, APA, or CMS (*Chicago*) format, see the appropriate tabbed sections in this book.

Evidence typically used in various disciplines

Humanities: literature, art, film, music, philosophy

- Passages of text or lines of a poem
- Details from an image or a work of art
- Passages of a musical composition
- Critical essays that analyze original works

Humanities: history

- Primary sources such as photographs, letters, maps, and government documents
- Scholarly books and articles that interpret evidence

Social sciences: psychology, sociology, political science, anthropology

- Data from original experiments
- Results of field research such as interviews or surveys
- Statistics from government agencies
- Scholarly books and articles that interpret data from original experiments and from other researchers' studies
- Primary sources such as maps and government documents
- Primary sources such as artifacts

Sciences: biology, chemistry, physics

- Data from original experiments
- Scholarly articles that report findings from experiments
- Models, diagrams, or animations

S

Sentence Style

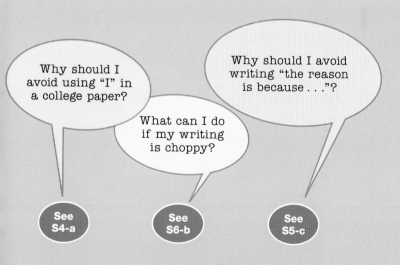

Why should I avoid using "I" in a college paper?

See S4-a

What can I do if my writing is choppy?

See S6-b

Why should I avoid writing "the reason is because . . ."?

See S5-c

S Sentence Style

S1 Parallelism

If two or more ideas are parallel, they are easier to grasp when expressed in parallel grammatical form. Single words should be balanced with single words, phrases with phrases, clauses with clauses.

A kiss can be a comma, a question mark, or an exclamation point.

— Mistinguett

This novel is not to be tossed lightly aside, but to be hurled with great force.

— Dorothy Parker

Politics is about compromise; business is about doing.

— Paul Martin

Writers often use parallelism to create emphasis. (See p. 135.)

S1-a Balance parallel ideas in a series.

Readers expect items in a series to appear in parallel grammatical form. When one or more of the items violate readers' expectations, a sentence will be needlessly awkward.

▶ **Children who study music also learn confidence, discipline,** creativity.
   and ~~they are creative.~~
      ^

   The revision presents all the items in the series as nouns: *confidence, discipline,* and *creativity.*

▶ **Impressionist painters believed in focusing on ordinary**

   subjects, capturing the effects of light on those subjects,
         using
   and ~~to use~~ **short brushstrokes.**
      ^

   The revision uses *-ing* forms for all the items in the series: *focusing, capturing,* and *using.*

   In headings and lists, aim for as much parallelism as the content allows.

Headings

Headings on the same level of organization should be written in parallel form — as single words, phrases, or clauses.

PHRASES AS HEADINGS

Safeguarding Earth's atmosphere

Charting the path to sustainable energy

Conserving global forests

INDEPENDENT CLAUSES AS HEADINGS

Ask the patient to describe current symptoms.

Take a detailed medical history.

Record the patient's vital signs.

Lists

Lists are usually introduced with an independent clause followed by a colon. They are most readable when they are presented in parallel grammatical form. Like headings, lists might consist of words, phrases, or clauses. The following list consists of parallel noun phrases.

Renewable energy technologies include the following: hydroelectric power, solar power, wind energy, and geothermal energy.

S1-b Balance parallel ideas presented as pairs.

When pairing ideas, underscore their connection by expressing them in similar grammatical form. Paired ideas are usually connected in one of these ways:

- with a coordinating conjunction such as *and, but,* or *or*
- with a correlative conjunction such as *either . . . or* or *not only . . . but also*
- with a word introducing a comparison, usually *than* or *as*

Parallel ideas linked with coordinating conjunctions

Coordinating conjunctions (*and, but, or, nor, for, so, yet*) link ideas of equal importance. When those ideas are closely parallel in content, they should be expressed in parallel grammatical form.

▶ Emily Dickinson's poetry features the use of dashes and

the capitalization of
~~capitalizing~~ common words.
^

The revision balances the nouns *use* and *capitalization*.

▶ Many cities are reducing property taxes for homeowners and ~~extend~~ ^*extending*^

tax credits to renters.

> The revision balances the verb *reducing* with the verb *extending*.

Parallel ideas linked with correlative conjunctions

Correlative conjunctions come in pairs: *either . . . or, neither . . . nor, not only . . . but also, both . . . and, whether . . . or.* Make sure that the grammatical structure following the second half of the pair is the same as that following the first half.

▶ George Klein was not only a productive inventor but also ~~was~~

a gifted educator.

> The words *a productive inventor* follow *not only,* so *a gifted educator* should follow *but also.*

▶ The clerk told me either to change my flight or ^*to*^ take the train.

> *To change my flight,* which follows *either,* should be balanced with *to take the train,* which follows *or.*

Comparisons linked with than or as

In comparisons linked with *than* or *as,* the elements being compared should be expressed in parallel grammatical structure.

▶ For some situations, it is better to talk in person than ^*to text.*^ ~~texting.~~

> *To talk* is balanced with *to text.*

Comparisons should also be logical and complete. (See S2-c.)

S1-c Repeat function words to clarify parallels.

Function words such as prepositions (*by, to*) and subordinating conjunctions (*that, because*) signal the grammatical nature of the word groups to follow. Although you can sometimes omit them, be sure to include them whenever they signal parallel structures that readers might otherwise miss.

▶ **Our study revealed that left-handed students were more likely to**

that

have trouble with classroom desks and rearranging desks for

^

exam periods was useful.

A second subordinating conjunction helps readers sort out the two parallel ideas: *that* left-handed students have trouble with classroom desks and *that* rearranging desks was useful.

S2   Needed words

Sometimes writers leave out words intentionally, and the meaning of the sentence is not affected. But leaving out words can occasionally cause confusion for readers or make the sentence ungrammatical. Readers need to see at a glance how the parts of a sentence are connected.

S2-a Add words needed to complete compound structures.

In compound structures, words are often left out for economy: *Tom is a man who means what he says and [who] says what he means.* Such omissions are acceptable as long as the omitted words are common to both parts of the compound structure.

If a sentence defies grammar or idiom because an omitted word is not common to both parts of the compound structure, the simplest solution is to put the word back in.

▶ **Advertisers target customers whom they identify through research**

who

or have purchased their product in the past.

^

The word *who* must be included because *whom . . . have purchased* is not grammatically correct.

accepted

▶ **Mayor Davis never has and never will accept a bribe.**

^

Has . . . accept is not grammatically correct.

in

▶ **Many South Pacific islanders still believe and live by ancient laws.**

^

Believe . . . by is not idiomatic in English. (For a list of common idioms, see W5-d.)

> **Multilingual** Languages sometimes differ in the need for certain words. In particular, be alert for missing articles, verbs, subjects, or expletives. See M2, M3-a, and M3-b.

S2-b Add the word *that* if there is any danger of misreading without it.

If there is no danger of misreading, the word *that* may be omitted when it introduces a subordinate clause (see p. 322). *The value of a principle is the number of things [that] it will explain.* When a sentence might be misread without *that*, however, it is necessary to include the word.

▶ In his famous obedience experiments, psychologist Stanley Milgram
discovered _{that} ordinary people were willing to inflict physical pain on
strangers.

> Milgram didn't discover ordinary people; he discovered that ordinary people were willing to inflict pain on strangers. The word *that* tells readers to expect a clause, not just *ordinary people*, as the direct object of *discovered*.

S2-c Add words needed to make comparisons logical and complete.

Comparisons should be made between items that are alike. To compare unlike items is illogical and distracting.

▶ The forests of North America are much more extensive than _{those of} Europe.

> Forests must be compared with forests, not with all of Europe.

▶ Beyoncé's music videos are better choreographed than any other _{singer's.} ~~singer.~~

> Beyoncé's music videos cannot logically be compared with a singer. The revision uses the possessive form *singer's*, with the word *videos* being implied.

Sometimes the word *other* must be inserted to make a comparison logical.

▶ Jupiter is larger than any ^{other} planet in our solar system.

Jupiter is a planet in our solar system, and it cannot be larger than itself.

Sometimes the word *as* must be inserted to make a comparison grammatically complete.

▶ The city of Lowell is as old, ^{as} if not older than, the neighbouring

city of Lawrence.

The construction *as old* is not complete without a second *as: as old as . . . the neighbouring city of Lawrence.*

Comparisons should be complete enough to ensure clarity. The reader should understand what is being compared.

| INCOMPLETE | Brand X is less salty. |
| COMPLETE | Brand X is less salty than Brand Y. |

Finally, comparisons should leave no ambiguity for readers. If a sentence lends itself to more than one interpretation, revise the sentence to state clearly which interpretation you intend.

AMBIGUOUS	Ken helped me more than my roommate.
CLEAR	Ken helped me more than *he helped* my roommate.
CLEAR	Ken helped me more than my roommate *did*.

S2-d Add the articles *a*, *an*, and *the* where necessary for grammatical completeness.

It is not always necessary to repeat articles with paired items: *We bought a laptop and printer.* However, if one of the items requires *a* and the other requires *an*, both articles must be included.

▶ We bought a laptop and ^{an} e-reader.

> **Multilingual** Choosing and using articles can be challenging for multilingual writers. See M2.

S3 Problems with modifiers

Modifiers, whether they are single words, phrases, or clauses, should point clearly to the words they modify. As a rule, related words should be kept together.

S3-a Put limiting modifiers in front of the words they modify.

Limiting modifiers such as *only*, *even*, *almost*, *nearly*, and *just* should appear in front of a verb only if they modify the verb: *At first, I couldn't even touch my toes, much less grasp them.* If they limit the meaning of some other word in the sentence, they should be placed in front of that word.

▶ The literature reveals that students ~~only~~ learn new vocabulary
            only
  words when they are encouraged to read.
    ^

  Only limits the meaning of the *when* clause.

▶ If you ~~just~~ interview seniors, your understanding of student opinion
        just
  will be incomplete.
        ^

  The adverb *just* limits the meaning of *seniors*, not *interview*.

When the limiting modifier *not* is misplaced, the sentence usually suggests a meaning the writer did not intend.

▶ In Newfoundland and Labrador, all men are ~~not~~ fishermen.
                   not
                             ^

  The original sentence says that no men in Newfoundland and Labrador are fishermen. The revision makes the writer's real meaning clear: Some (but not all) men in Newfoundland and Labrador are fishermen.

LaunchPad macmillan learning **ACTIVITIES FOR S3**
10 Exercises, 1 LearningCurve activity

S3-b Place phrases and clauses so that readers can see at a glance what they modify.

Although phrases and clauses can appear at some distance from the words they modify, make sure your meaning is clear. When phrases or clauses are oddly placed, absurd misreadings can result.

> MISPLACED   The soccer player returned to the clinic where he had undergone emergency surgery in 2012 in a limousine sent by Adidas.
>
> REVISED   Travelling in a limousine sent by Adidas, the soccer player returned to the clinic where he had undergone emergency surgery in 2012.

The revision corrects the false impression that the soccer player underwent emergency surgery in a limousine.

> ▶ ~~There~~ are many pictures of comedians who have performed
>   *On the walls* ^
>   at Gavin's. ~~on the walls.~~
>   ^

The comedians weren't performing on the walls; the pictures were on the walls.

Occasionally the placement of a modifier leads to an ambiguity — a squinting modifier. In such a case, two revisions will be possible, depending on the writer's intended meaning.

> AMBIGUOUS   The exchange students we met for coffee occasionally questioned us about our latest slang.
>
> CLEAR   The exchange students we occasionally met for coffee questioned us about our latest slang.
>
> CLEAR   The exchange students we met for coffee questioned us occasionally about our latest slang.

In the original version, it was not clear whether the meeting or the questioning happened occasionally. Both revisions eliminate the ambiguity.

S3-c Move awkwardly placed modifiers.

As a rule, a sentence should flow from subject to verb to object, without lengthy detours along the way. When a long adverbial word group separates a subject from its verb, a verb from its object, or a helping verb from its main verb, the result is often awkward.

▶ ~~Hong Kong,~~ After more than 150 years of British rule, was transferred back to Chinese control in 1997. Hong Kong

> There is no reason to separate the subject, *Hong Kong*, from the verb, *was transferred*, with a long phrase.

Multilingual English does not allow an adverb to appear between a verb and its object. See M3-f.

- Yolanda lifted ~~easily~~ the twenty-five-kilogram weight. easily

---

S3-d Avoid split infinitives when they are awkward.

An infinitive consists of *to* plus the base form of a verb: *to think, to breathe, to dance*. When a modifier appears between *to* and the verb, an infinitive is said to be "split": *to carefully balance, to completely understand*.

When a long word or a phrase appears between the parts of the infinitive, the result is usually awkward.

▶ ~~The~~ If possible, the patient should try to ~~if possible~~ avoid going up and down stairs.

Attempts to avoid split infinitives can result in equally awkward sentences. When alternative phrasing sounds unnatural, most experts allow — and even encourage — splitting the infinitive.

AWKWARD	We decided actually to enforce the law.
BETTER	We decided to actually enforce the law.

At times, neither the split infinitive nor its alternative sounds particularly awkward. In formal writing, it is usually better not to split the infinitive.

▶ Nursing students learn to ~~accurately~~ record a patient's vital signs/ accurately.

S3-e Repair dangling modifiers.

A dangling modifier fails to refer logically to any word in the sentence. Dangling modifiers are easy to repair, but they can be hard to recognize, especially in your own writing.

Recognizing dangling modifiers

Dangling modifiers are usually word groups (such as verbal phrases) that suggest but do not name an actor. When a sentence opens with such a modifier, readers expect the subject of the next clause to name the actor. If it doesn't, the modifier dangles.

▶ While reading the magazine, ^I was the dog pushed open the door.

The speaker of the sentence (not the dog) was reading the magazine.

▶ After logging into the site, ~~users'~~ users can easily view their account balances. ^ ~~can be easily viewed.~~ ^

Users (not their account balances) log into the site.

The sentences below illustrate four common kinds of dangling modifiers.

DANGLING	*Deciding to join the navy*, the recruiter enthusiastically pumped Joe's hand. [Participial phrase]
DANGLING	*Upon entering the doctor's office*, a skeleton caught my attention. [Preposition followed by a gerund phrase]
DANGLING	*To satisfy her mother*, the piano had to be practised every day. [Infinitive phrase]
DANGLING	*Though not eligible for the clinical trial*, the doctor prescribed the drug for Ethan on compassionate grounds. [Elliptical clause with an understood subject and verb]

These dangling modifiers falsely suggest that the recruiter decided to join the navy, that the skeleton entered the doctor's office, that the piano intended to satisfy the mother, and that the doctor was not eligible for the clinical trial.

Although most readers will understand the writer's intended meaning in such sentences, the unintended humour can be distracting.

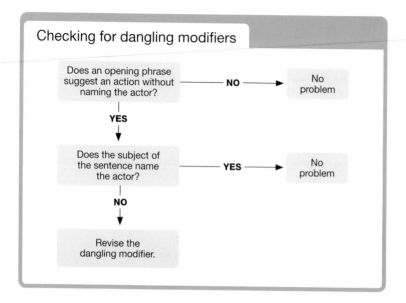

Checking for dangling modifiers

Repairing dangling modifiers

To repair a dangling modifier, you can revise the sentence in one of two ways:

- Name the actor in the subject of the sentence.
- Name the actor in the modifier.

Depending on your sentence, one of these revision strategies may be more appropriate than the other.

ACTOR NAMED IN SUBJECT

▶ Upon entering the doctor's office, a skeleton. I noticed ^ caught my attention. ^

▶ To satisfy her mother, the piano Jing-mei had to practise had to be practised every day. ^

ACTOR NAMED IN MODIFIER

▶ Deciding When Joe decided to join the navy, the recruiter enthusiastically ^ his pumped Joe's hand. ^

▶ Though not eligible for the clinical trial, the doctor Ethan was ^ him prescribed the drug for Ethan on compassionate grounds. ^

NOTE: You cannot repair a dangling modifier just by moving it. Consider, for example, the following sentence about a skeleton. If you put the modifier at the end of the sentence (*A skeleton caught my attention upon entering the doctor's office*), you are still suggesting — absurdly — that the skeleton entered the office. The only way to avoid the problem is to put the word *I* in the sentence, either as the subject or in the modifier.

> Upon entering the doctor's office, a skeleton. ~~caught my attention.~~
>   *I noticed*

> ~~Upon entering~~ the doctor's office, a skeleton caught my attention.
> *As I entered*

S4 Shifts

This section can help you avoid unnecessary shifts that might distract or confuse your readers: shifts in point of view, in verb tense, in mood or voice, or from indirect to direct questions or quotations.

S4-a Make the point of view consistent in person and number.

The point of view of a piece of writing is the perspective from which it is written: first person (*I* or *we*), second person (*you*), or third person (*he, she, it, one, they,* or any noun).

The *I* (or *we*) point of view, which emphasizes the writer, is a good choice for informal letters and writing based on personal experience. The *you* point of view, which emphasizes the reader, works well for giving advice or explaining how to do something. The third-person point of view, which emphasizes the subject, is appropriate in formal academic and professional writing.

Writers who have trouble settling on an appropriate point of view sometimes shift confusingly from one to another. The solution is to choose a suitable perspective and stay with it.

> Our class practised rescuing a victim trapped in a wrecked car.
> We learned to dismantle the car with the essential tools. ~~You~~ *We*
> were graded on ~~your~~ *our* speed and ~~your~~ *our* skill in freeing the victim.

The writer should have stayed with the *we* point of view. *You* is inappropriate because the writer is not addressing readers directly. *You* should not be used in a vague sense meaning "anyone." (See p. 196.)

LaunchPad ACTIVITIES FOR S4
macmillan learning
11 Exercises, 1 LearningCurve activity

> You need
> ~~One needs~~ a password and a credit card number to access the
> ^
> database. You will be billed at an hourly rate.

You is an appropriate choice because the writer is giving advice directly to readers.

S4-b Maintain consistent verb tenses.

Consistent verb tenses clearly establish the time of the actions being described. When a passage begins in one tense and then shifts without warning and for no reason to another, readers are distracted and confused.

> soared
> Our candidate lost in the debate. Just as we gave up hope, she ~~soars~~
> ^
> ahead in the polls.

The writer thought that the present tense (*soars*) would convey excitement. But having begun in the past tense (*lost, gave up*), the writer should follow through in the past tense.

Writers often encounter difficulty with verb tenses when writing about literature. Because fictional events occur outside the time frames of real life, the past tense and the present tense may seem equally appropriate. The literary convention, however, is to describe fictional events consistently in the present tense.

> The scarlet letter is a punishment sternly placed on Hester's breast
> is
> by the community, and yet it ~~was~~ a fanciful and imaginative product
> ^
> of Hester's own needlework.

S4-c Make verbs consistent in mood and voice.

Unnecessary shifts in the mood of a verb can be distracting and confusing to readers. There are three moods in English: the *indicative*, used for facts, opinions, and questions; the *imperative*, used for orders or advice; and the *subjunctive*, used in certain contexts to express wishes or conditions contrary to fact (see G2-g).

Writer's Choice
Choosing a point of view

Using the *I* point of view is not grammatically wrong for postsecondary writing. As you review your options, think about your **purpose** and **audience**, as well as the **genre** (type of writing) expected. When in doubt, ask your instructor.

When you want to focus on your experience, choose the first-person point of view.

FIRST PERSON

Although initially intimidated, I found that my mentor's observations during my student teaching created opportunities for important discussions about learning.

The firsthand experience and personal tone in this sentence help the writer connect with the reader. The first-person point of view is often used in narrative and reflective writing.

When you want to focus on the reader, choose the second-person point of view.

SECOND PERSON

Although initially you may be intimidated, you may find that your mentor's observations during your student teaching create opportunities for important discussions about learning.

The tone here is instructive and establishes the writer as a guide for the reader. Use the second-person point of view when you are giving instructions or advice.

When you want to focus on the topic, choose the third-person point of view.

THIRD PERSON

Although initially they may be intimidated, many student teachers find that their mentor's observations during their student teaching create opportunities for important discussions about learning.

This sentence focuses on the topic, not on the writer or the reader. Use the third-person point of view when you are arguing a point or presenting information.

Once you make a choice, stick with it. Shifting points of view within a piece of writing confuses your reader.

The following passage shifts confusingly from the indicative to the imperative mood.

> The counsellor advised us to spread out our core requirements over
> two or three semesters. ~~Also,~~ pay attention to prerequisites for
> *She also suggested that we*
> elective courses.

The writer began by reporting the counsellor's advice in the indicative mood (*counsellor advised*) and switched to the imperative mood (*pay attention*); the revision puts both sentences in the indicative.

A verb may be in either the active voice (with the subject doing the action) or the passive voice (with the subject receiving the action). (See W3-a.) If a writer shifts without warning from one to the other, readers may be left wondering why.

> Each student completes a self-assessment/, ~~The self-assessment is~~
> *gives it*
> ~~then given~~ to the teacher, and a copy ~~is exchanged~~ with a classmate.
> *exchanges*

Because the passage began in the active voice (*student completes*) and then switched to the passive (*self-assessment is given, copy is exchanged*), readers are left wondering who gives the self-assessment to the teacher and the classmate. The active voice, which is clearer and more direct, leaves no ambiguity.

S4-d Avoid sudden shifts from indirect to direct questions or quotations.

An indirect question reports a question without asking it: *We asked whether we could visit Miriam.* A direct question asks directly: *Can we visit Miriam?* Sudden shifts from indirect to direct questions are awkward. In addition, sentences containing such shifts are impossible to punctuate because indirect questions must end with a period and direct questions must end with a question mark. (See p. 284.)

> LGBT business owners wonder whether their businesses are unfairly
> targeted and ~~can they~~ reverse the trend~~?~~.
> *whether they can*

The revision poses both questions indirectly. The writer could also ask both questions directly: *Are LGBT-owned businesses being unfairly targeted? Can these business owners reverse the trend?*

An indirect quotation reports someone's words without quoting word-for-word: *Senator Kessel said that she wants to see evidence.* A direct quotation presents the exact words of a speaker or writer, set off with quotation marks: *Senator Kessel said, "I want to see evidence."* Unannounced shifts from indirect to direct quotations are distracting and confusing, especially when the writer fails to insert quotation marks, as in the following example.

▶ **The patient said she had been experiencing heart palpitations and**
asked me to
~~please~~ **run as many tests as possible to find out the problem.**
^

The revision reports the patient's words indirectly. The writer also could quote the words directly: *The patient said, "I have been experiencing heart palpitations. Please run as many tests as possible to find out the problem."*

S5 Mixed constructions

A mixed construction contains sentence parts that do not sensibly fit together. The mismatch may be a matter of grammar or of logic.

S5-a Untangle the grammatical structure.

Once you begin a sentence, your choices are limited by the range of grammatical patterns in English. (See B2 and B3.) You cannot begin with one grammatical plan and switch without warning to another. Often you must rethink the purpose of the sentence and revise.

> **MIXED**   For most drivers who have a blood alcohol content of .05 percent double their risk of causing an accident.

The writer begins the sentence with a long prepositional phrase and makes it the subject of the verb *double*. But a prepositional phrase can serve only as a modifier; it cannot be the subject of a sentence.

> **REVISED**   For most drivers who have a blood alcohol content of .05 percent, the risk of causing an accident is doubled.

> **REVISED**   Most drivers who have a blood alcohol content of .05 percent double their risk of causing an accident.

In the first revision, the writer begins with the prepositional phrase and finishes the sentence with a proper subject and verb (*risk . . . is doubled*). In the second revision, the writer stays with the original verb (*double*) and begins the sentence another way, making *drivers* the subject of *double*.

▶ ~~When the country elects~~ a prime minister is the most important

    Electing   ^

responsibility in a democracy.

The adverb clause *When the country elects a prime minister* cannot serve as the subject of the verb *is*. The revision replaces the adverb clause with a gerund phrase, a word group that can function as a subject. (See B3-e and B3-b.)

▶ Although Canada is a wealthy nation, ~~but~~ about 18 percent of

our children live in poverty.

The coordinating conjunction *but* cannot link a subordinate clause (*Although Canada . . .*) with an independent clause (*about 18 percent of our children live in poverty*).

Multilingual English does not allow repeated subjects, objects, nouns, and adverbs in certain situations. See M3-c and M3-d.

● My father ~~he~~ moved to Peru before he met my mother.

S5-b Straighten out the logical connections.

The subject and the predicate (the verb and its modifiers) should make sense together; when they don't, the error is known as *faulty predication.*

▶ The court decided that ~~Tiffany's welfare~~ would not be safe living

    Tiffany ^

with her abusive parents.

Tiffany, not her welfare, would not be safe.

An appositive is a noun that renames a nearby noun. When an appositive and the noun it renames are not logically equivalent, the error is known as *faulty apposition.* (See B3-c.)

▶ ~~The tax accountant,~~ a lucrative profession, requires intelligence,

    Tax accounting, ^

patience, and attention to mathematical detail.

The tax accountant is a person, not a profession.

S5-c Avoid *is when*, *is where*, and *reason . . . is because* constructions.

In formal English, many readers object to *is when*, *is where*, and *reason . . . is because* constructions on either grammatical or logical grounds. Grammatically, the verb *is* (as well as *are*, *was*, and *were*) should be followed by a noun or an adjective, not by an adverb clause beginning with *when*, *where*, or *because*. (See B2-b and B3-e.) Logically, the words *when*, *where*, and *because* suggest relations of time, place, and cause — relations that do not always make sense with *is*, *are*, *was*, or *were*.

> a disorder suffered by people who
> Anorexia nervosa is ~~where people~~ think they are overweight and
> often diet to the point of starvation.

Where refers to places. Anorexia nervosa is a disorder, not a place.

> The ~~reason the~~ experiment failed ~~is~~ because conditions in the lab
> were not sterile.

The writer might have changed *because* to *that* (*The reason the experiment failed is that conditions in the lab were not sterile*), but the preceding revision is more concise.

S6 Sentence emphasis

Within each sentence, emphasize your point by expressing it in the subject and verb of an independent clause, the words that receive the most attention from readers (see S6-a to S6-e).

Within longer stretches of prose, you can draw attention to ideas deserving special emphasis by using a variety of techniques, often involving an unusual twist or some element of surprise (see S6-f).

S6-a Coordinate equal ideas; subordinate minor ideas.

When combining two or more ideas in one sentence, you have two choices: coordination or subordination. Choose coordination to indicate that the ideas are equal or nearly equal in importance. Choose subordination to indicate that one idea is less important than another.

LaunchPad
macmillan learning

ACTIVITIES FOR S6
11 Exercises, 1 LearningCurve activity

Coordination

Coordination draws attention equally to two or more ideas. To coordinate single words or phrases, join them with a coordinating conjunction or with a correlative conjunction: *bananas and strawberries; not only a lackluster plot but also inferior acting* (see B1-g).

To coordinate independent clauses — word groups that express a complete thought and that can stand alone as a sentence — join them with a comma and a coordinating conjunction or with a semicolon:

, and	, but	, or	, nor
, for	, so	, yet	;

The semicolon is often accompanied by a conjunctive adverb such as *moreover, furthermore, therefore,* or *however* or by a transitional phrase such as *for example, in other words,* or *as a matter of fact.* (For a longer list, see p. 130.)

Subordination

To give unequal emphasis to two or more ideas, express the major idea in an independent clause and place any minor ideas in subordinate clauses or phrases. (For specific subordination strategies, see the chart on p. 131.)

Let your intended meaning determine which idea you emphasize. Thinking about your purpose and your audience often helps you decide which ideas deserve emphasis.

S6-b Combine choppy sentences.

Short sentences demand attention, so you should use them primarily for emphasis. Too many short sentences, one after the other, make for a choppy style.

If an idea is not important enough to deserve its own sentence, try combining it with a sentence close by. Put any minor ideas in subordinate structures such as phrases or subordinate clauses. (See B3.)

▶ The Parks Department keeps the use of insecticides to a
                because the
minimum/ ~~The~~ city is concerned about the environment.
         ^

The writer wanted to emphasize that the Parks Department minimizes its use of chemicals, so she put the reason in a subordinate clause beginning with *because*.

▶ The Great Lakes St. Lawrence Seaway, ~~is~~ a 3,700-kilometre waterway
                              ^
that opened in 1959/, ~~It~~ is a major source of transportation for goods
                ^
in North America.

A minor idea is now tucked into an appositive phrase (*a 3,700-kilometre waterway that opened in 1959*).

Although subordination is ordinarily the most effective technique for combining short, choppy sentences, coordination is appropriate when the ideas are equal in importance.

▶ On January 1, lawmakers raised the minimum wage/~~Lawmakers~~ *and*

opened doors for thousands of poor families.

Combining two short sentences by joining their predicates (*raised . . . opened*) is an effective coordination technique.

Using coordination to combine sentences of equal importance

1. Consider using a comma and a coordinating conjunction between the sentences. (See P1-a.)

   | , and | , but | , or | , nor |
   | , for | , so | , yet | |

   ▶ In Orthodox Jewish funeral ceremonies, the shroud is
   a simple linen vestment/, ~~The~~ coffin is plain wood. *and the*

2. Consider using a semicolon with a conjunctive adverb or a transitional phrase. (See p. 272.)

also	however	next
as a result	in addition	now
besides	in fact	of course
consequently	in other words	otherwise
finally	in the first place	still
for example	meanwhile	then
for instance	moreover	therefore
furthermore	nevertheless	thus

   ▶ Alicia scored well on the LSAT/; ~~She also~~ had excellent grades *in addition, she*

   and a record of community service.

3. Consider using a semicolon alone. (See P3-a.)

   ▶ In youth we learn/; ~~In~~ age we understand. *in*

Using subordination to combine sentences of unequal importance

1. Consider putting the less important idea in a subordinate clause beginning with one of the following words. (See B3-e.)

after	before	that	which
although	even though	unless	while
as	if	until	who
as if	since	when	whom
because	so that	where	whose

▶ *When*
John Turner asked Bill Lee to run his campaign./, Lee accepted.

▶ My sister owes much of her recovery to a yoga program/ ~~She~~ *that she*
began ~~the program~~ three years ago.

2. Consider putting the less important idea in an appositive phrase. (See B3-c.)

▶ Karate, ~~is~~ a discipline based on the philosophy of nonviolence/,
~~It~~ teaches the art of self-defence.

3. Consider putting the less important idea in a participial phrase. (See B3-b.)

▶ ~~Canadian writer George Woodcock was~~ *o*ffered full tuition
Canadian author George Woodcock
to university by his grandfather/, ~~He~~ turned it down because of the
condition that he study to be a priest.

Multilingual Unlike some other languages, English does not repeat objects or adverbs in adjective clauses. See M3-d.

● The apartment that we rented ~~it~~ needed repairs.

The pronoun *it* cannot repeat the relative pronoun *that*.

Writer's Choice
Positioning major and minor ideas

There are many ways to organize the ideas in a sentence. If your **purpose** is to convey one particular idea to your readers, put that major idea in the main part of the sentence, and place minor ideas in a subordinate word group to de-emphasize them. Consider these two ideas about social networking sites.

> Social networking websites offer ways for people to connect in the virtual world.

> Social networking sites do not replace face-to-face interaction.

To stress the ways that people can *connect* in the virtual world, the writer should subordinate (or de-emphasize) the idea about the limitations.

> ┌─────────────── MINOR IDEA ────────────────┐┌─MAJOR IDEA─┐
> Although they do not replace face-to-face interaction, social networking
> ──┘
> websites offer ways for people to connect in the virtual world.

> *The writer might be arguing that joining sites such as LinkedIn is the best way to broaden the range of job opportunities for college graduates.*

To focus on the *limitations* of the virtual world, the writer should subordinate the idea about the ways people connect on these websites.

> ┌─────────────────── MINOR IDEA ───────────────────┐
> Although social networking websites offer ways for people to connect in
> ─────────────┐┌──────────── MAJOR IDEA ───────────┐
> the virtual world, they do not replace face-to-face interaction.

> *The writer might be arguing that personal contact is still the best way to build professional relationships.*

When you have both major and minor ideas in a sentence, put your main idea in the independent clause and tuck minor ideas into subordinate word groups.

S6-c Avoid ineffective or excessive coordination.

Coordinate structures are appropriate only when you intend to draw readers' attention equally to two or more ideas: *Professor Liu praises loudly, and she criticizes softly.* If one idea is more important than another — or if a coordinating conjunction does not clearly signal the relationship between the ideas — you should subordinate the less important idea.

INEFFECTIVE COORDINATION	Closets were taxed as rooms, and most colonists stored their clothes in chests or clothespresses.
IMPROVED WITH SUBORDINATION	Because closets were taxed as rooms, most colonists stored their clothes in chests or clothespresses.

The revision subordinates the less important idea (*closets were taxed as rooms*) by putting it in a subordinate clause. Notice that the subordinating conjunction *Because* signals the relation between the ideas more clearly than the coordinating conjunction *and*.

Because it is so easy to string ideas together with *and*, writers often rely too heavily on coordination in their rough drafts. The cure for excessive coordination is simple: Look for opportunities to tuck minor ideas into subordinate clauses or phrases.

> After four hours,
> ▶ ~~Four hours went by, and~~ a rescue truck finally arrived, but by
>   ^
> that time we had been evacuated in a helicopter.

Three independent clauses were excessive. The least important idea has become a prepositional phrase.

S6-d Do not subordinate major ideas.

If a sentence buries its major idea in a subordinate construction, readers may not give the idea enough attention. Make sure to express your major idea in an independent clause and to subordinate any minor ideas.

>   defeated Louis St-Laurent,
> ▶ John Diefenbaker, who was the unexpected winner of the 1957
>   ^
> federal election/. ~~defeated Louis St-Laurent.~~
>   ^

The writer wanted to focus on Diefenbaker's unexpected victory, but the original sentence buried this information in an adjective clause. The revision puts the more important idea in an independent clause and tucks the less important idea into an adjective clause (*who defeated Louis St-Laurent*).

> As
> ▶ I̶ was driving home from my new job, heading down Ranchitos
>   ^
>   Road, ~~when~~ my car suddenly overheated.

The writer wanted to emphasize that the car overheated, not the fact of driving home. The revision expresses the major idea in an independent clause and places the less important idea in an adverb clause (*As I was driving home from my new job*).

S6-e Do not subordinate excessively.

In attempting to avoid short, choppy sentences, writers sometimes go to the opposite extreme, putting more subordinate ideas into a sentence than its structure can bear. If a sentence collapses of its own weight, occasionally it can be restructured. More often, however, such sentences must be divided.

> ▶ Some professional athletes argue that they should not be looked on
>   These athletes
>   as role models. ~~and that they~~ believe that modelling behaviour is a
>   ^^
>   parent's responsibility.

By splitting the original sentence in two, the writer makes it easier for the reader to focus on the main claim, that modeling behaviour is a parent's job.

S6-f Experiment with techniques for gaining emphasis.

By experimenting with certain techniques, usually involving some element of surprise, you can draw attention to ideas that deserve special emphasis. Use such techniques sparingly, however, or they will lose their punch. The writer who tries to emphasize everything ends up emphasizing nothing.

Using sentence endings for emphasis

You can highlight an idea simply by withholding it until the end of a sentence. The technique works something like a punch line. In the following example, the sentence's meaning is not revealed until its very last word.

> The only completely consistent people are the dead.   — Aldous Huxley

An inverted sentence reverses the normal subject-verb order, placing the subject at the end, where it receives unusual emphasis. (See also S7-c.)

> In golden pots are hidden the most deadly poisons.   — Thomas Draxe

Using parallel structure for emphasis

Parallel grammatical structure draws special attention to paired ideas or to items in a series. (See S1.) When parallel ideas are paired, the emphasis falls on words that underscore comparisons or contrasts, especially when they occur at the end of a phrase or clause.

> *Americans* are *benevolently ignorant* about Canada, while *Canadians* are *malevolently well informed* about the United States. — J. Bartlet Brebner

In a parallel series, the emphasis falls at the end, so it is generally best to end with the most dramatic or climactic item in the series.

> My uncle often talks about growing up in Sudan — playing soccer, eating goat stew, and dodging bullets. — Alec Hamza, student

S7 Sentence variety

When a rough draft is filled with too many sentences that begin the same way or have the same structure, try injecting some variety — as long as you can do so without sacrificing clarity or ease of reading.

S7-a Vary your sentence openings.

Most sentences in English begin with the subject, move to the verb, and continue to the object, with modifiers tucked in along the way or put at the end. For the most part, such sentences are fine. Put too many of them in a row, however, and they become monotonous.

Adverbial modifiers are easily movable when they modify verbs; they can often be inserted ahead of the subject. Such modifiers might be single words, phrases, or clauses.

> ▶ Eventually a ~~A~~ few drops of sap ~~eventually~~ began to trickle into the aluminum bucket.

Like most adverbs, *eventually* does not need to appear close to the verb it modifies (*began*).

> ▶ Just as the sun was coming up, a ~~A~~ pair of black ducks flew over the pond. ~~just as the sun was coming up.~~

The adverb clause, which modifies the verb *flew*, is as clear at the beginning of the sentence as it is at the end.

LaunchPad macmillan learning **ACTIVITIES FOR S7**
3 Exercises

Writer's Choice
Strengthening with variety

If you look at a whole paragraph in your draft, you may have difficulty seeing the individual sentences. If a particular passage sounds repetitive, try listing the sentences one after the other so that you can review them.

> I have always loved trains.
>
> As a young boy, I watched the trains from a hillside overlooking the rail yard.
>
> I remember the individual cars rolling down the hill.
>
> I remember how they would couple with other cars.
>
> Sometimes I would hear a loud boom, which always surprised me.

When seen in this format, the sentences look monotonous and sound dull — *I did this, I remember that*. . . . To engage the **audience** and to bring readers into the experience, narrative writing needs variety and detail.

To reduce the repetition, try varying the sentence structure.

REVISED SENTENCES	I have always loved trains, even as a young boy.
	From a hillside overlooking the rail yard, I would watch individual cars roll down the track to couple with other cars.
	The *BOOM!* — the sound of two cars joining — always surprised me.
REVISED PARAGRAPH	I have always loved trains, even as a young boy. From a hillside overlooking the rail yard, I would watch individual cars roll down the track to couple with other cars. The *BOOM!* — the sound of two cars joining — always surprised me.

In the revision, the sentences don't all begin in the same way, and the writer has provided details of sight and sound so that readers can experience the memory.

When you revise for variety, keep your audience in mind. Choose details specific enough to engage the reader, and make choices that add some variety to your sentence structure.

Adjectives and participial phrases can frequently be moved to the beginning of a sentence without loss of clarity.

> *Dejected and down,*
> ▶ Edward/~~dejected and down,~~ nearly gave up his job search.
>   ^

TIP: When beginning a sentence with an adjective or a participial phrase, make sure that the subject of the sentence names the person or thing described in the introductory phrase. If it doesn't, the phrase will dangle. (See S3-e.)

S7-b Use a variety of sentence structures.

A writer should not rely too heavily on simple sentences and compound sentences, for the effect tends to be both monotonous and choppy. (See S6-b and S6-c.) Too many complex or compound-complex sentences, however, can be equally monotonous. If your style tends to one extreme or the other, try to achieve a better mix of sentence types.

The major sentence types are illustrated in the following sentences, all taken from Flannery O'Connor's "The King of the Birds," an essay describing the author's pet peafowl.

SIMPLE	Frequently the cock combines the lifting of his tail with the raising of his voice.
COMPOUND	Any chicken's dusting hole is out of place in a flower bed, but the peafowl's hole, being the size of a small crater, is more so.
COMPLEX	The peacock does most of his serious strutting in the spring and summer when he has a full tail to do it with.
COMPOUND-COMPLEX	The cock's plumage requires two years to attain its pattern, and for the rest of his life, this chicken will act as though he designed it himself.

For a fuller discussion of sentence types, see B4-a.

S7-c Try inverting sentences occasionally.

A sentence is inverted if it does not follow the normal subject-verb-object pattern. Many inversions sound artificial and should be avoided except in the most formal contexts. But if an inversion sounds natural, it can provide a welcome touch of variety.

> *Set at the top two corners of the stage were huge*
> ▶ ~~Huge~~ lavender hearts outlined in bright white lights. ~~were set at the~~
>   ^   ^
> ~~top two corners of the stage.~~

In the revision, the subject, *hearts*, appears after the verb, *were set*. Notice that the two parts of the verb are also inverted — and separated from each other (*Set . . . were*) — without any awkwardness or loss of meaning.

Inverted sentences are used for emphasis as well as for variety (see S6-f).

S7-d Consider adding an occasional question.

An occasional question can provide a change of pace, especially at the beginning of a paragraph, where it engages the reader's interest.

> Virginia Woolf, in her book *A Room of One's Own*, wrote that in order for a woman to write fiction she must have two things, certainly: a room of her own (with key and lock) and enough money to support herself.
> *What then are we to make of Phillis Wheatley, a slave, who owned not even herself?* This sickly, frail black girl who required a servant of her own at times — her health was so precarious — and who, had she been white, would have been easily considered the intellectual superior of all the women and most of the men in the society of her day. [Italics added.]   — Alice Walker

W

Word Choice

What can I do if my writing is too wordy?

See W2

Is it ever OK to use passive voice?

See W3-a

English idioms are difficult. Can I get better at using them?

See W5-d

W Word Choice

W1 Glossary of usage

This glossary includes words commonly confused (such as *accept* and *except*), words commonly misused (such as *anxious*), and words and phrases that are nonstandard (such as *would of*). It also lists colloquialisms and jargon. Colloquialisms are casual expressions that may be appropriate in informal speech but are inappropriate in formal writing. Jargon is needlessly technical or pretentious language that is inappropriate in most academic contexts. If an item is not listed here, consult the index or a dictionary. For irregular verbs (such as *sing, sang, sung*), see G2-a. For idiomatic use of prepositions, see W5-d.

a, an Use *an* before a vowel sound, *a* before a consonant sound: *an apple, a peach.* Problems sometimes arise with words beginning with *h* or *u*. If the *h* is silent, the word begins with a vowel sound, so use *an*: *an hour, an honourable deed.* If the *h* is pronounced, the word begins with a consonant sound, so use *a*: *a hospital, a hotel.* Words such as *university* and *union* begin with a consonant sound (a *y* sound), so use *a*: *a union.* Words such as *uncle* and *umbrella* begin with a vowel sound, so use *an*: *an underground well.* When an abbreviation or an acronym begins with a vowel sound, use *an*: *an EKG, an MRI, an AIDS prevention program.*

accept, except *Accept* is a verb meaning "to receive." *Except* is usually a preposition meaning "excluding." *I will accept all the packages except that one. Except* is also a verb meaning "to exclude." *Please except that item from the list.*

adapt, adopt *Adapt* means "to adjust or become accustomed"; it is usually followed by *to. Adopt* means "to take as one's own." *Our family adopted a Vietnamese child, who quickly adapted to his new life.*

advice, advise *Advice* is a noun, *advise* a verb. *We advise you to follow John's advice.*

affect, effect *Affect* is usually a verb meaning "to influence." *Effect* is usually a noun meaning "result." *The drug did not affect the disease, and it had adverse side effects. Effect* can also be a verb meaning "to bring about." *Only the prime minister can effect such a dramatic change.*

agree to, agree with *Agree to* means "to give consent to." *Agree with* means "to be in accord with" or "to come to an understanding with." *He agrees with me about the need for change, but he won't agree to my plan.*

ain't *Ain't* is nonstandard. Use *am not, are not* (*aren't*), or *is not* (*isn't*). *I am not* (not *ain't*) *going home for spring break.*

all ready, already *All ready* means "completely prepared." *Already* means "previously." *Susan was all ready for the concert, but her friends had already left.*

all right *All right*, written as two words, is correct. *Alright* is nonstandard.

all together, altogether *All together* means "everyone or everything in one place." *Altogether* means "entirely." *We were not altogether certain that we could bring the family all together for the reunion.*

allude   To *allude* to something is to make an indirect reference to it. Do not use *allude* to mean "to refer directly." *In his lecture, the professor referred* (not *alluded*) *to several pre-Socratic philosophers.*

allusion, illusion   An *allusion* is an indirect reference. An *illusion* is a misconception or false impression. *Did you catch my allusion to Shakespeare? Mirrors give the room an illusion of depth.*

a lot   *A lot* is two words. Do not write *alot*. *Sam lost a lot of weight.* See also *lots, lots of.*

among, between   See *between, among.*

amoral, immoral   *Amoral* means "neither moral nor immoral"; it also means "not caring about moral judgments." *Immoral* means "morally wrong." *Until recently, most business courses were taught from an amoral perspective. Murder is immoral.*

amount, number   Use *amount* with quantities that cannot be counted; use *number* with those that can. *This recipe calls for a large amount of sugar. We have a large number of toads in our garden.*

an   See *a, an.*

and/or   Avoid the awkward construction *and/or* except in technical or legal documents.

angry at, angry with   Use *angry with*, not *angry at*, when referring to a person. *The coach was angry with the referee.*

ante-, anti-   The prefix *ante-* means "earlier" or "in front of"; the prefix *anti-* means "against" or "opposed to." *The people running the antismoking campaign put up signs in the antechamber. Anti-* should be used with a hyphen when it is followed by a capital letter or a word beginning with *i.*

anxious   *Anxious* means "worried" or "apprehensive." In formal writing, avoid using *anxious* to mean "eager." *We are eager* (not *anxious*) *to see your new house.*

anybody, anyone   *Anybody* and *anyone* are singular. (See G1-e and G3-a.)

anyone, any one   *Anyone*, an indefinite pronoun, means "any person at all." *Any one*, the pronoun *one* preceded by the adjective *any*, refers to a particular person or thing in a group. *Anyone from the winning team may choose any one of the prizes on display.*

anyways, anywheres   *Anyways* and *anywheres* are nonstandard. Use *anyway* and *anywhere.*

as   Do not use *as* to mean "because" if there is any chance of ambiguity. *We cancelled the picnic because* (not *as*) *it began raining. As* here could mean either "because" or "when."

as, like   See *like, as.*

as to   *As to* is jargon for *about*. *He inquired about* (not *as to*) *the job.*

awhile, a while   *Awhile* is an adverb; it can modify a verb, but it cannot be the object of a preposition such as *for*. The two-word form *a while* is a noun preceded by an article and therefore can be the object of a preposition. *Stay awhile. Stay for a while.*

bad, badly *Bad* is an adjective, *badly* an adverb. *They felt bad about ruining the surprise. Her arm hurt badly after she slid into second base.* (See G4-a, G4-b, and G4-c.)

beside, besides *Beside* is a preposition meaning "at the side of" or "next to." *Annie sleeps with a flashlight beside her bed. Besides* is a preposition meaning "except" or "in addition to." *No one besides Terrie can have that ice cream. Besides* is also an adverb meaning "in addition." *I'm not hungry; besides, I don't like ice cream.*

between, among Ordinarily, use *among* with three or more entities, *between* with two. *The money was divided among several contestants. The money was divided between the animal charity and the church.*

bring, take Use *bring* when an object is being transported toward you, *take* when it is being moved away. *Please bring me a glass of water. Please take these forms to Mr. Scott.*

can, may The distinction between *can* and *may* is fading, but some writers still observe it in formal communication. *Can* is traditionally reserved for ability, *may* for permission. *Can you speak French? May I help you?*

capital, capitol *Capital* refers to a city, *capitol* to a building in the United States where lawmakers meet. *Capital* also refers to wealth or resources. *The residents of the state capital protested plans to close the streets surrounding the capitol.*

censor, censure *Censor* means "to remove or suppress material considered objectionable." *Censure* means "to criticize severely." *The administration's policy of censoring books has been censured by the media.*

cite, site *Cite* means "to quote as an authority or example." *Site* is usually a noun meaning "a particular place." *He cited the zoning law in his argument against the proposed site of the gas station.* Locations on the internet are usually referred to as *sites. The library's website now includes a chat feature.*

climactic, climatic *Climactic* is derived from *climax*, the point of greatest intensity in a series or progression of events. *Climatic* is derived from *climate* and refers to meteorological conditions. *The climactic period in the dinosaurs' reign was reached just before severe climatic conditions brought on an ice age.*

compare to, compare with *Compare to* means "to represent as similar." *She compared him to a wild stallion. Compare with* means "to examine similarities and differences." *The study compared the language ability of apes with that of dolphins.*

complement, compliment *Complement* is a verb meaning "to go with or complete" or a noun meaning "something that completes." As a verb, *compliment* means "to flatter"; as a noun, it means "flattering remark." *Her skill at rushing the net complements his skill at volleying. Martha's flower arrangements receive many compliments.*

conscience, conscious *Conscience* is a noun meaning "moral principles." *Conscious* is an adjective meaning "aware or alert." *Let your conscience be your guide. Were you conscious of his love for you?*

could care less *Could care less* is nonstandard. Write *couldn't care less* instead. *He couldn't* (not *could*) *care less about his psychology final.*

could of *Could of* is nonstandard for *could have. We could have* (not *could of*) *taken the train.*

council, counsel   A *council* is a deliberative body, and a *councillor* is a member of such a body. *Counsel* usually means "advice" and can also mean "lawyer"; a *counsellor* is one who gives advice or guidance. *The councillors met to draft the council's position paper. The pastor offered wise counsel to the troubled teenager.*

criteria   *Criteria* is the plural of *criterion*, which means "a standard or rule or test on which a judgment or decision can be based." *The only criterion for the scholarship is ability.*

data   *Data* is a plural noun technically meaning "facts or propositions." Except in scientific writing, *data* is increasingly being accepted as a singular noun. *The new data suggest* (or *suggests*) *that our theory is correct.*

different from, different than   Ordinarily, write *different from*. *Your sense of style is different from Jim's.* However, in informal writing *different than* is acceptable to avoid an awkward construction. *Please let me know if your plans are different than* (to avoid *from what*) *they were six weeks ago.*

disinterested, uninterested   *Disinterested* means "impartial, objective"; *uninterested* means "not interested." *We sought the advice of a disinterested counsellor to help us solve our problem. Mark was uninterested in anyone's opinion but his own.*

each   *Each* is singular. (See G1-e and G3-a.)

effect   See *affect, effect*.

e.g.   In formal writing, replace the Latin abbreviation *e.g.* with its English equivalent: *for example* or *for instance*.

either   *Either* is singular. (See G1-e and G3-a.) For *either . . . or* constructions, see G1-d and G3-a.

elicit, illicit   *Elicit* is a verb meaning "to bring out" or "to evoke." *Illicit* is an adjective meaning "unlawful." *The reporter was unable to elicit any information from the police about illicit drug traffic.*

emigrate from, immigrate to   *Emigrate* means "to leave one country or region to settle in another." *In 1903, my great-grandfather emigrated from Russia to escape the religious pogroms. Immigrate* means "to enter another country and reside there." *More than 26,000 Syrians immigrated to Canada in 2016.*

eminent, imminent   *Eminent* means "outstanding" or "distinguished." *We met an eminent professor of Greek history. Imminent* means "about to happen." *The snowstorm is imminent.*

etc.   Avoid ending a list with *etc.* It is more emphatic to end with an example, and in most contexts readers will understand that the list is not exhaustive. When you don't wish to end with an example, *and so on* is more graceful than *etc.* Also, since *et cetera* means "and so forth," the phrase *and etc.* is redundant.

everybody, everyone   *Everybody* and *everyone* are singular. (See G1-e and G3-a.)

everyone, every one   *Everyone* is an indefinite pronoun. *Every one*, the pronoun *one* preceded by the adjective *every*, means "each individual or thing in a particular group." *Every one* is usually followed by *of. Everyone wanted to go. Every one of the missing books was found.*

except   See *accept, except.*

explicit, implicit   *Explicit* means "expressed directly" or "clearly defined"; *implicit* means "implied, unstated." *I gave him explicit instructions not to go swimming. My mother's silence indicated her implicit approval.*

farther, further   *Farther* usually describes distances. *Further* usually suggests quantity or degree. *Saskatoon is farther from Kenora than I thought. I would be grateful for further suggestions.*

fewer, less   Use *fewer* for items that can be counted; use *less* for items that cannot be counted. *Fewer people are living in the city. Less rain in the forecast caused the farming community to panic.*

firstly   *Firstly* sounds pretentious, and it leads to the ungainly series *firstly, secondly, thirdly,* and so on. Write *first, second, third* instead.

further   See *farther, further.*

good, well   *Good* is an adjective, *well* an adverb. (See G4-a, G4-b, and G4-c.) *He hasn't felt good about his game since he sprained his wrist last season. She performed well on the uneven parallel bars.*

hanged, hung   *Hanged* is the past-tense and past-participle form of the verb *hang* meaning "to execute." *The prisoner was hanged at dawn. Hung* is the past-tense and past-participle form of the verb *hang* meaning "to fasten or suspend." *The expensive paintings were carefully hung in the gallery.*

hardly   Avoid expressions such as *can't hardly* and *not hardly,* which are considered double negatives. *I can* (not *can't*) *hardly describe my surprise at getting the job.* (See G4-e.)

has got, have got   *Got* is unnecessary and awkward in such constructions. It should be dropped. *We have* (not *have got*) *three days to prepare for the opening.*

hopefully   *Hopefully* means "in a hopeful manner." *We looked hopefully to the future.* Some usage experts object to the use of *hopefully* as a sentence adverb on grounds of clarity. To be safe, avoid using *hopefully* in sentences such as the following: *Hopefully, your son will recover soon.* Instead, indicate who is doing the hoping: *I hope that your son will recover soon.*

however   It is acceptable to start a sentence with the conjunctive adverb *however,* but be careful to place the word in your sentence according to your intended meaning and emphasis. All of the following sentences are correct. *Pam decided, however, to attend the lecture. However, Pam decided to attend the lecture.* (She had been considering other activities.) *Pam, however, decided to attend the lecture.* (Unlike someone else, Pam chose to attend the lecture.) (See P1-f.)

hung   See *hanged, hung.*

i.e.   In formal writing, use *in other words* or *that is* rather than the Latin abbreviation *i.e.* to introduce a clarifying statement. *Exposure to borax usually causes only mild skin irritation; in other words* (not *i.e.*), *it's not usually toxic.*

if, whether   Use *if* to express a condition and *whether* to express alternatives. *If you go on a trip, whether to Idaho or Italy, remember to bring identification.*

illusion   See *allusion, illusion.*

immigrate   See *emigrate from, immigrate to.*

imminent   See *eminent, imminent.*

immoral   See *amoral, immoral.*

imply, infer   *Imply* means "to suggest or state indirectly"; *infer* means "to draw a conclusion." *John implied that he knew all about computers, but the interviewer inferred that John was inexperienced.*

in, into   *In* indicates location or condition; *into* indicates movement or a change in condition. *They found the lost letters in a box after moving into the house.* Some idioms include *in* or *into* (*give in to peer pressure; buy into an idea*); you may have to learn these one at a time.

irregardless   *Irregardless* is nonstandard. Use *regardless.*

is when, is where   These mixed constructions are often incorrectly used in definitions. *A runoff election is a second election held to break a tie* (not *is when a second election is held to break a tie*). (See S5-c.)

its, it's   *Its* is a possessive pronoun; *it's* is a contraction of *it is.* (See P4-b and P4-d.) *It's always fun to watch a dog chase its tail.*

kind of, sort of   Avoid using *kind of* or *sort of* to mean "somewhat." *The movie was somewhat* (not *sort of*) *boring.* Do not put *a* after either phrase. *That kind of* (not *kind of a*) *salesclerk annoys me.*

lay, lie   See *lie, lay.*

licence, license   *Licence* is a noun; *license* is a verb. *I'm finally licensed to drive a motorcycle; I received my licence last week.*

lead, led   *Lead* is a metallic element; it is a noun. *Led* is the past tense of the verb *lead. He led me to the treasure.*

less   See *fewer, less.*

liable   *Liable* means "obligated" or "responsible." Do not use it to mean "likely." *You're likely* (not *liable*) *to trip if you don't tie your shoelaces.*

lie, lay   *Lie* is an intransitive verb meaning "to recline or rest on a surface." Its forms are *lie, lay, lain. Lay* is a transitive verb meaning "to put or place." Its forms are *lay, laid, laid.* (See G2-b.)

like, as   *Like* is a preposition, not a subordinating conjunction. It can be followed only by a noun or a noun phrase. *As* is a subordinating conjunction that introduces a subordinate clause. In casual speech, you may say *She looks like she hasn't slept* or *You don't know her like I do.* But in formal writing, use *as. She looks as if she hasn't slept. You don't know her as I do.* (See also B1-f and B1-g.)

loose, lose   *Loose* is an adjective meaning "not securely fastened." *Lose* is a verb meaning "to misplace" or "to not win." *Did you lose all your loose change?*

lots, lots of   *Lots* and *lots of* are informal substitutes for *many, much,* or *a lot.* Avoid using them in formal writing.

mankind Avoid *mankind* whenever possible. It offends many readers because it excludes women. Use *humanity, humans, the human race,* or *humankind* instead. (See W4-f.)

may See *can, may.*

maybe, may be *Maybe* is an adverb meaning "possibly." *Maybe the sun will shine tomorrow.* *May be* is a verb phrase. *Tomorrow may be brighter.*

may of, might of *May of* and *might of* are nonstandard for *may have* and *might have.* *We might have* (not *might of*) *had too many cookies.*

media, medium *Media* is the plural of *medium. Of all the media that cover the Olympics, television is the medium that best captures the spectacle of the events.*

must of See *may of, might of. Must of* is nonstandard for *must have.*

myself Do not use *myself* in place of *I* or *me. He gave the flowers to Melinda and me* (not *myself*). (*Myself* is a reflexive or intensive pronoun. See B1-b.)

neither *Neither* is singular. (See G1-e and G3-a.) For *neither . . . nor* constructions, see G1-d and G3-a.

none *None* may be singular or plural. (See G1-e.)

nowheres *Nowheres* is nonstandard. Use *nowhere* instead.

number See *amount, number.*

of Use the verb *have,* not the preposition *of,* after the verbs *could, should, would, may, might,* and *must. They must have* (not *must of*) *left early.*

off of *Off* is sufficient. Omit *of. The ball rolled off* (not *off of*) *the table.*

passed, past *Passed* is the past tense of the verb *pass. Ann passed me another slice of cake. Past* usually means "belonging to a former time" or "beyond a time or place." *Our past president spoke until past midnight. The hotel is just past the next intersection.*

percent, per cent, percentage *Percent* (also spelled *per cent*) is always used with a specific number. *Percentage* is used with a descriptive term such as *large* or *small,* not with a specific number. *The candidate won 80 percent of the vote. A large percentage of registered voters turned out for the election.*

phenomena *Phenomena* is the plural of *phenomenon,* which means "an observable occurrence or fact." *Strange phenomena occur at all hours of the night in that house, but last night's phenomenon was the strangest of all.*

plus *Plus* should not be used to join independent clauses. *This raincoat is dirty; moreover* (not *plus*), *it has a hole in it.*

practice, practise *Practice* is a noun; *practise* is a verb. *You should practise the flute at home every day, even if you have band practice at school.*

precede, proceed *Precede* means "to come before." *Proceed* means "to go forward." *As we proceeded up the mountain path, we noticed fresh tracks in the mud, evidence that a group of hikers had preceded us.*

principal, principle *Principal* is a noun meaning "the head of a school or an organization" or "a sum of money." It is also an adjective meaning "most important." *Principle* is a noun meaning "a basic truth or law." *The principal expelled her for three principal reasons. We believe in the principle of equal justice for all.*

proceed, precede   See *precede, proceed.*

quote, quotation   *Quote* is a verb; *quotation* is a noun. Avoid using *quote* as a shortened form of *quotation*. *Quotations* (not *Quotes*) *from his recent book are appearing in various social media channels.*

raise, rise   *Raise* is a transitive verb meaning "to move or cause to move upward." It takes a direct object. *I raised the shades. Rise* is an intransitive verb meaning "to go up." *Heat rises.*

real, really   *Real* is an adjective; *really* is an adverb. *Real* is sometimes used informally as an adverb, but avoid this use in formal writing. *She was really* (not *real*) *angry.* (See G4-a and G4-b.)

reason . . . is because   Use *that* instead of *because*. *The reason she's cranky is that* (not *because*) *she didn't sleep last night.* (See S5-c.)

reason why   The expression *reason why* is redundant. *The reason* (not *The reason why*) *Jones lost the election is clear.*

respectfully, respectively   *Respectfully* means "showing or marked by respect." *Respectively* means "each in the order given." *He respectfully submitted his opinion to the judge. John, Tom, and Larry were a butcher, a baker, and a lawyer, respectively.*

sensual, sensuous   *Sensual* means "gratifying the physical senses," especially those associated with sexual pleasure. *Sensuous* means "pleasing to the senses," especially those involved in the experience of art, music, and nature. *The sensuous music and balmy air led the dancers to more sensual movements.*

set, sit   *Set* is a transitive verb meaning "to put" or "to place." Its past tense is *set. Sit* is an intransitive verb meaning "to be seated." Its past tense is *sat. She set the dough in a warm corner of the kitchen. The cat sat in the doorway.*

should of   *Should of* is nonstandard for *should have*. *They should have* (not *should of*) *been home an hour ago.*

since   Do not use *since* to mean "because" if there is any chance of ambiguity. *Because* (not *Since*) *we won the game, we have been celebrating with pizza and dessert. Since* here could mean "because" or "from the time that."

sit   See *set, sit.*

site   See *cite, site.*

somebody, someone   *Somebody* and *someone* are singular. (See G1-e and G3-a.)

something   *Something* is singular. (See G1-e.)

sometime, some time, sometimes   *Sometime* is an adverb meaning "at an indefinite time." *Some time* is the adjective *some* modifying the noun *time* and means "a period of time." *Sometimes* is an adverb meaning "at times, now and then." *I'll see you sometime soon. I haven't lived there for some time. Sometimes I see him at work.*

suppose to   Write *supposed to.*

sure and   Write *sure to. We were all taught to be sure to* (not *sure and*) *look both ways before crossing a street.*

take See *bring, take.*

than, then *Than* is a conjunction used in comparisons; *then* is an adverb denoting time. *That serving is more than I can eat. Tom laughed, and then we recognized him.*

that See *who, which, that.*

that, which Many writers reserve *that* for restrictive clauses, *which* for nonrestrictive clauses. *Restaurants that allow pets are few in number. Restaurants, which generally don't allow pets, must follow strict health codes.* (See P1-e.)

then, than See *than, then.*

there, their, they're *There* is an adverb specifying place; it is also an expletive (placeholder). Adverb: *Sylvia is sitting there patiently.* Expletive: *There are two plums left. Their* is a possessive pronoun. *Fred and Jane finally washed their car. They're* is a contraction of *they are. They're later than usual today.*

to, too, two *To* is a preposition; *too* is an adverb; *two* is a number. *Too many of your shots slice to the left, but the last two were just right.*

toward, towards *Toward* and *towards* are generally interchangeable, although *toward* is preferred in Canadian English.

try and *Try and* is nonstandard for *try to. The teacher asked us all to try to* (not *try and*) *write an original haiku.*

unique Avoid expressions such as *most unique, more straight, less perfect, very round.* Either something is unique or it isn't. It is illogical to suggest degrees of uniqueness. (See G4-d.)

usage The noun *usage* should not be substituted for *use* when the meaning is "employment of." *The use* (not *usage*) *of insulated shades has cut fuel costs dramatically.*

use to Write *used to.*

utilize *Utilize* means "to make use of." It often sounds pretentious; in most cases, *use* is sufficient. *I used* (not *utilized*) *the 3-D printer.*

wait for, wait on *Wait for* means "to be in readiness for" or "to await." *Wait on* means "to serve." *We're waiting for* (not *waiting on*) *Ruth to take us to the museum.*

ways *Ways* is colloquial when used to mean "distance." *The city is a long way* (not *ways*) *from here.*

weather, whether The noun *weather* refers to the state of the atmosphere. *Whether* is a conjunction referring to a choice between alternatives. *We wondered whether the weather would clear.*

well, good See *good, well.*

which See *that, which* and *who, which, that.*

while Avoid using *while* to mean "although" or "whereas" if there is any chance of ambiguity. *Although* (not *While*) *Gloria lost money in the slot machine, Tom won it at roulette.* Here *While* could mean either "although" or "at the same time that."

who, which, that Do not use *which* to refer to persons. Use *who* instead. *That,* though generally used to refer to things, may be used to refer to a group or class of people. *The player who* (not *that* or *which*) *made the basket at the buzzer was named MVP. The team that scores the most points in this game will win the tournament.*

who, whom *Who* is used for subjects and subject complements; *whom* is used for objects. *Who are the candidates for this year's scholarship? The candidates, whom I met with yesterday, are impressive.* (See G3-d.)

who's, whose *Who's* is a contraction of *who is*; *whose* is a possessive pronoun. *Who's ready for more popcorn? Whose coat is this?* (See P4-b and P4-d.)

would of *Would of* is nonstandard for *would have. She would have* (not *would of*) *had a chance to play if she had arrived on time.*

you In formal writing, avoid *you* in an indefinite sense meaning "anyone." (See G3-b.) *Any spectator* (not *You*) *could tell by the way John caught the ball that his throw would be too late.*

your, you're *Your* is a possessive pronoun; *you're* is a contraction of *you are. Is that your new bike? You're in the finals.* (See P4-b and B1-b.)

W2 Wordy sentences

Long sentences are not necessarily wordy, nor are short sentences always concise. A sentence is wordy if it can be tightened without loss of meaning.

W2-a Eliminate redundancies.

Writers often repeat themselves unnecessarily, thinking that expressions such as *cooperate together* or *basic essentials* add emphasis to their writing. In reality, such redundancies do just the opposite. There is no need to say the same thing twice.

> works
> ▶ Daniel ~~is now employed~~ at a private rehabilitation centre ~~working~~
>   ^
>   as a registered physical therapist.

Though modifiers ordinarily add meaning to the words they modify, occasionally they are redundant.

> ▶ *The Pursuit of Happyness* tells the story of a single father determined
>   ~~in his mind~~ to pull his family out of homelessness.

The word *determined* contains the idea that his resolution formed in his mind.

 LaunchPad macmillan learning **ACTIVITIES FOR W2**
7 Exercises

W2-b Avoid unnecessary repetition of words.

Though words may be repeated deliberately, for effect, repetitions will seem awkward if they are clearly unnecessary. When a more concise version is possible, choose it.

▶ His third speech, delivered in Vancouver, was ~~an~~ outstanding. ~~speech.~~

▶ The best teachers help each student ~~become a better student~~ *grow* both

academically and emotionally.

W2-c Cut empty or inflated phrases.

An empty phrase can be cut with little or no loss of meaning. Common examples are introductory word groups that weaken the writer's authority by apologizing or hedging: *in my opinion, I think that, it seems that,* and so on.

▶ ~~In my opinion,~~ *O*ur current immigration policy is misguided.

   Readers understand without being told that they are hearing the writer's opinion.

Inflated phrases can be reduced to a word or two without loss of meaning.

▶ We are unable to provide funding ~~at this point in time.~~ *now.*

INFLATED	CONCISE
along the lines of	like
as a matter of fact	in fact
at the present time	now, currently
at this point in time	now, currently
because of the fact that	because
by means of	by
due to the fact that	because
for the purpose of	for
have the ability to	be able to, can
in order to	to
in spite of the fact that	although, though
in the event that	if
in the final analysis	finally

W2-d Simplify the structure.

If the structure of a sentence is needlessly indirect, try simplifying it. Look for opportunities to strengthen the verb.

▶ The analyst claimed that because of market conditions she could

not ~~make an~~ estimate ~~of~~ the company's future profits.

The verb *estimate* is more vigorous and concise than *make an estimate of*.

The colourless verbs *is*, *are*, *was*, and *were* frequently generate excess words.

               studied
▶ Investigators ~~were involved in studying~~ the effect of classical music

on unborn babies.

The revision is more direct and concise. The action (*studying*), originally appearing in a subordinate structure, has become a strong verb, *studied*.

The expletive constructions *there is* and *there are* (or *there was* and *there were*) can also lead to wordy sentences. The same is true of expletive constructions beginning with *it*.

       A
▶ ~~There is~~ another module ~~that~~ tells the story of Charles Darwin and

introduces the theory of evolution.

Finally, verbs in the passive voice may be needlessly indirect. When the active voice expresses your meaning as effectively, use it. (See W3-a.)

W2-e Reduce clauses to phrases, phrases to single words.

Word groups functioning as modifiers can often be made more compact. Look for any opportunities to reduce clauses to phrases or phrases to single words.

▶ We took a side trip to Gravenhurst, ~~which was~~ the home of

Dr. Norman Bethune.

     this   problematic
▶ In ~~the~~ essay, ~~that follows,~~ I argue against Kohn's claim that the grading

system discourages thinking, ~~which is a problematic claim.~~

W3 Active verbs

As a rule, choose an active verb and pair it with a subject that names the person or thing doing the action. Active verbs express meaning more emphatically and vigorously than their weaker counterparts — verbs in the passive voice and forms of the verb *be.*

PASSIVE	The pumps *were destroyed* by a surge of power.
***BE* VERB**	A surge of power *was* responsible for the destruction of the pumps.
ACTIVE	A surge of power *destroyed* the pumps.

Verbs in the passive voice lack strength because their subjects receive the action instead of doing it. Forms of the verb *be* (*be, am, is, are, was, were, being, been*) lack vigour because they convey no action.

Although passive verbs and the forms of *be* have legitimate uses, choose an active verb whenever possible.

Even among active verbs, some are more vigorous and colourful than others. Carefully selected verbs can energize a piece of writing.

>   swept   hooked
> ▶ **The goalie crouched low, ~~reached~~ out his stick, and ~~sent~~ the rebound**
>   ^   ^
> **away from the mouth of the net.**

> **Academic English**   Although you may be tempted to avoid the passive voice completely, keep in mind that some writing situations call for it, including some scientific writing. For advice about forming the passive voice, see M1-b.

W3-a Choose the active voice or the passive voice depending on your writing situation.

In the active voice, the subject does the action; in the passive voice, the subject receives the action. Although both voices are grammatically correct, the active voice is usually more effective because it is clearer and more direct.

ACTIVE	Hernando *caught* the fly ball.
PASSIVE	The fly ball *was caught* by Hernando.

 LaunchPad **ACTIVITIES FOR W3**
macmillan learning   6 Exercises, 1 LearningCurve activity

Passive sentences often identify the actor in a *by* phrase, as in the preceding example. Sometimes, however, that phrase is omitted, and who or what is responsible for the action becomes unclear: *The fly ball was caught.*

Most of the time, you will want to emphasize the actor, so you should use the active voice. To replace a passive verb with an active one, make the actor the subject of the sentence.

> The settlers stripped the land of timber before realizing
> ▶ ~~The land was stripped of timber before the settlers realized~~ the
> ^
> consequences of their actions.

The revision emphasizes the actors (*settlers*) by naming them in the subject.

In much scientific writing, the passive voice properly emphasizes the experiment or process being described, not the researcher. Check with your instructor for the preference in your discipline.

W3-b Replace *be* verbs that result in dull or wordy sentences.

Not every *be* verb needs replacing. The forms of *be* (*be, am, is, are, was, were, being, been*) work well when you want to link a subject to a noun that clearly renames it or to an adjective that describes it: *Orchard House was the home of Louisa May Alcott. The harvest will be bountiful after the summer rains.*

Be verbs also are essential as helping verbs before present participles (*is flying, are disappearing*) to express ongoing action: *Derrick was fighting the fire when his wife went into labour.* (See G2-f.)

If using a *be* verb makes a sentence needlessly dull and wordy, however, consider replacing it. Often a phrase following the verb contains a noun or an adjective (such as *violation* or *resistant*) that suggests a more vigorous, active verb (*violate, resist*).

> violate
> ▶ Burying nuclear waste in Antarctica would ~~be in violation of~~ an
> ^
> international treaty.

Violate is less wordy and more vigorous than *be in violation of.*

> resisted
> ▶ When Rosa Parks ~~was resistant to~~ giving up her seat on the bus,
> ^
> she became a civil rights hero.

Resisted is stronger than *was resistant to.*

Writer's Choice
Using the active or the passive voice

You will usually choose whether to write in the active voice or the passive voice. While your instructors often expect you to use the active voice, some situations and fields of study will require you to write in the passive voice. This choice will be influenced primarily by your **purpose** but also by your **audience's expectations** and the **genre** in which you are writing (see C1-a).

To emphasize the actor and not the receiver of the action, choose the active voice.

ACTIVE   <u>Provincial officials forced</u> nearly 28,000 Calgarians to leave their homes after the flood.

> *This sentence focuses on the government's displacing the people. Emphasizing the province's action may be better for the writer whose purpose is to make an argument about that action.*

To focus attention on the receiver of the action, choose the passive voice.

PASSIVE   Nearly <u>28,000 Calgarians were forced</u> to leave their homes after the flood.

> *This sentence focuses on the people displaced by the flood. Emphasizing the number of homeless Calgarians may be better for the writer whose purpose is to discuss how the flood affected residents.*

What idea are you emphasizing in your sentence? Considering your purpose and audience, what would be more effective — focusing on the actor or on the person or thing being acted on? It's your choice.

W3-c As a rule, choose a subject that names the person or thing doing the action.

In weak, unemphatic prose, both the actor and the action may be buried in sentence elements other than the subject and the verb. In the following weak sentence, for example, both the actor and the action appear in prepositional phrases, word groups that do not receive much attention from readers.

WEAK	The institution of Bennett's New Deal had the effect of reversing some of the economic inequalities of the Great Depression.
EMPHATIC	Bennett's New Deal reversed some of the economic inequalities of the Great Depression.

Consider the subjects and verbs of the two versions — *institution had* versus *New Deal reversed*. The latter expresses the writer's point more emphatically.

> ~~The use of~~ pure oxygen can ~~cause healing in~~ wounds that are
>
> otherwise untreatable.

In the original sentence, the subject and verb — *use can cause* — express the point blandly. *Oxygen can heal* makes the point more emphatically and directly.

W4 Appropriate language

Language is appropriate when it suits your subject, engages your audience, and blends naturally with your own voice.

To some extent, the conventions of the genre in which you are writing will determine your choice of language. When in doubt about the conventions of a particular genre — lab reports, informal essays, business memos, and so on — consult your instructor or look at models written by experts in the field.

W4-a Avoid jargon, except in specialized writing situations.

Jargon is special language used among members of a trade, profession, or group. Use jargon only when readers will be familiar with it and when plain English will not do as well.

JARGON	We outsourced the work to an outfit in New Brunswick because we didn't have the bandwidth to tackle it in-house.
REVISED	We hired a company in New Brunswick because we had too few employees to do the work.

Broadly defined, jargon includes puffed-up language designed more to impress readers than to inform them. The following are examples from business, government, higher education, and the military, with plain English alternatives in parentheses.

ameliorate (improve)   optimal (best, most favourable)
commence (begin)   parameters (boundaries, limits)
components (parts)   peruse (read, look over)
endeavour (try)   prior to (before)
facilitate (help)   utilize (use)
indicator (sign)   viable (workable)

Sentences with jargon are hard to read and are often wordy.

▶ The CEO should ~~dialogue~~ with investors about ~~partnering~~ with
     talk   working
  clients to buy land in ~~economically deprived zones.~~
    poor neighbourhoods.

W4-b Avoid pretentious language, most euphemisms, and "doublespeak."

Hoping to sound profound or poetic, some writers embroider their thoughts with large words and flowery phrases. Such pretentious language is so ornate and wordy that it obscures the writer's meaning.

▶ Taylor's ~~employment of multihued means of expression draws~~
    use of colourful language reveals that she has a
  ~~back the curtains and lets slip the~~ nostalgic ~~vantage point from~~
                     view of
  ~~which she observes~~ American society.

The writer of the original sentence had turned to a thesaurus in an attempt to sound authoritative. When such a writer gains enough confidence to speak in his or her own voice, pretentious language disappears.

Euphemisms — nice-sounding words or phrases substituted for words thought to sound harsh — are sometimes appropriate. Many cultures, for example, accept euphemisms when speaking or writing about excretion (*I have to go to the bathroom*), sexual intercourse (*They did not sleep together*), and the like. We may also use euphemisms out of concern for someone's

Writer's Choice
Using discipline-specific terms

In general, try to minimize jargon and instead use plain language in your writing. Some disciplines, however, have specific terminology that is not only standard but also expected. When you use a discipline's terms effectively, you show yourself to be a member of that community and increase your authority with your **audience**.

For example, the following terms have specialized meanings in chemistry and economics and are understood by readers in those disciplines.

absolute	deadweight loss	hybridization
consumer surplus	degenerate	utility

UNNECESSARY USE OF A SPECIALIZED TERM

Although Canada's love affair with the automobile has not diminished, more Canadians have embraced automotive *hybridization* as their concern for the environment has grown.

In this example, hybridization *is not discipline-specific. The writer has used the word to sound impressive.*

NECESSARY USE OF A SPECIALIZED TERM

As shown, sp^2 *hybridization* leaves one nonhybridized *p* orbital.

Here, hybridization *has a specific meaning for chemists.*

When writing for a specific disciplinary audience, familiarize yourself with the language and terminology of the discipline through course readings and other materials. Use discipline-specific terms only when you know that you and your readers understand their meaning. Doing so will help you make effective word choices.

feelings. Telling parents, for example, that their daughter is "unmotivated" is more sensitive than saying she's lazy. Tact or politeness, then, can justify an occasional euphemism.

Most euphemisms, however, are needlessly evasive or even deceitful. Like pretentious language, they obscure the intended meaning.

EUPHEMISM	PLAIN ENGLISH
adult entertainment	pornography
preowned automobile	used car
economically deprived	poor
negative savings	debts
strategic withdrawal	retreat, defeat
chemical dependency	drug addiction
downsize	lay off, fire
correctional facility	prison, jail

The term *doublespeak* applies to any deliberately evasive or deceptive language, including euphemisms. Doublespeak is especially common in politics and business. A military retreat is described as *tactical redeployment*; *enhanced interrogation* is a euphemism for "torture"; and *downsizing* really means "firing employees."

W4-c Avoid obsolete and invented words.

Although dictionaries list obsolete words such as *recomfort* and *reechy*, these words are not appropriate for current use. Invented words or expressions (called *neologisms*) are too recently created to be part of Standard English. Many fade out of use without becoming standard. *YOLO* and *MOOC* are neologisms that may not last. *Prequel* and *email* are no longer neologisms; they have become Standard English. Avoid using invented words in formal writing unless they are given in the dictionary as standard or unless no other word expresses your meaning.

W4-d In most contexts, avoid slang, regional expressions, and nonstandard English.

Slang is an informal and sometimes private vocabulary that expresses the solidarity of a group such as teenagers, rap musicians, or sports fans; it is subject to more rapid change than Standard English. For example, the slang teenagers use to express approval changes every few years; *cool, groovy, neat, awesome, sick,* and *dope* have replaced one another within the last three decades. Sometimes slang becomes so widespread that it is accepted as standard vocabulary. *Jazz,* for example, started out as slang but is now a standard term for a style of music.

Although slang has a certain vitality, it is a code that not everyone understands, and it is very informal. Therefore, it is inappropriate in most written work.

▶ When the server crashed unexpectedly, three hours of unsaved

  data. ~~went down the tubes.~~

  we lost

▶ The government's "filth" guidelines for food will ~~gross you out.~~

  disgust you.

Regional expressions are common to a group in a geographic area. *He's from away* (for *He wasn't born here*) is an expression in Prince Edward Island, for example. Regional expressions have the same limitations as slang and are therefore inappropriate in most writing.

▶ John was four blocks from the house before he remembered to ~~cut~~

  the headlights. ~~on.~~

  turn on

▶ With the law enforcement budget severely cut, the city's gangs will
  ~~have a field day.~~

  take advantage.

Standard English is the language used in all academic, business, and professional fields. Nonstandard English is spoken by people with a common regional or social heritage. Although nonstandard English may be appropriate when spoken within a close group, it is out of place in most formal and informal writing.

▶ The premier said he ~~don't~~ know whether he will approve the budget

  doesn't

  without the clean air provision.

If you speak a nonstandard dialect, try to identify the ways in which your dialect differs from Standard English. You will find help in other sections of this book for the following features of nonstandard English, which commonly cause problems in writing.

Misusing verb forms such as *began* and *begun* (G2-a)

Leaving *-s* endings off verbs (G2-c)

Leaving *-ed* endings off verbs (G2-d)

Leaving out necessary verbs (G2-e)

Using double negatives (G4-e)

W4-e Choose an appropriate level of formality.

In deciding on a level of formality, consider both your subject and your audience. Does the subject demand a dignified treatment, or is a relaxed tone more suitable? Will readers be put off if you assume too close a relationship with them, or might you alienate them by seeming too distant?

For most postsecondary and professional writing, some degree of formality is appropriate. In a job application letter, for example, it is a mistake to sound too breezy and informal.

TOO INFORMAL	I'd like to get that sales job you've got on the website
MORE FORMAL	I would like to apply for the position of sales manager posted on LinkedIn.

Informal writing is appropriate for private letters, personal email and text messages, and business correspondence between close associates. Like spoken conversation, informal writing allows contractions (*don't, I'll*) and colloquial words (*kids, kinda*). Vocabulary and sentence structure are rarely complex.

In choosing a level of formality, above all be consistent. When a writer's voice shifts from one level of formality to another, readers receive mixed messages.

> Jorge's pitching lesson ~~commenced~~ with his famous curveball, [*began*]
> ~~implemented~~ by tucking the little finger behind the ball. Next [*thrown*]
> he ~~elucidated~~ the mysteries of the sucker pitch, a slow ball coming [*revealed*]
> behind a fast windup.

Words such as *commenced* and *elucidated* are inappropriate for the subject matter, and they clash with informal terms such as *sucker pitch* and *fast windup*.

W4-f Avoid sexist language.

Sexist language is language that stereotypes or demeans women or men. Using nonsexist language is a matter of courtesy — of respect for and sensitivity to the feelings of others.

Recognizing sexist language

Some sexist language is easy to recognize because it reflects genuine contempt for women: referring to a woman as a "chick," for example, or calling a lawyer a "lady lawyer."

Other forms of sexist language are less blatant. The following practices, while they may not result from conscious sexism, reflect stereotypical thinking: referring to members of one profession as exclusively male or exclusively female (teachers as women or engineers as men, for instance) or using different conventions when naming or identifying women and men.

STEREOTYPICAL LANGUAGE

After a nursing student graduates, *she* must face a difficult licensing examination. [Not all nursing students are women.]

Running for city council are Boris Stotsky, a lawyer, and *Mrs.* Cynthia Jones, a professor of English and *mother of three.* [The title *Mrs.* and the phrase *mother of three* are irrelevant.]

All executives' *wives* are invited to the welcome dinner. [Not all executives are married to women.]

Still other forms of sexist language result from outdated traditions. The pronouns *he, him,* and *his,* for instance, were traditionally used to refer generically to persons of either sex. Nowadays, to avoid sexist usage, some writers substitute the female pronouns (*she, her, hers*) alternately with the male pronouns.

GENERIC PRONOUNS

A journalist is motivated by *his* deadline.

A good interior designer treats *her* clients' ideas respectfully.

But both forms are sexist — for excluding one sex entirely and for making assumptions about the members of particular professions.

Similarly, terms including *man* and *men* were once used to refer generically to persons of either sex. Current usage demands gender-neutral terms for references to both men and women.

INAPPROPRIATE	APPROPRIATE
chairman	chairperson, moderator, chair, head
clergyman	priest, minister, rabbi, imam
congressman	member of Congress, representative, legislator
fireman	firefighter
foreman	supervisor
mailman	mail carrier, postal worker, letter carrier
to man	to operate, to staff
mankind	people, humans
manpower	personnel, staff
policeman	police officer
salesman	salesperson, sales associate, salesclerk
weatherman	forecaster, meteorologist

Revising sexist language

When revising sexist language, you may be tempted to substitute *he or she* and *his or her*. This strategy is wordy and can become awkward when repeated throughout an essay. Also, some readers may think *he or she* or *his or her* excludes transgender individuals. A better revision strategy is to write in the plural; yet another strategy is to recast the sentence so that the problem does not arise.

SEXIST

A journalist is motivated by *his* deadline.

A good interior designer treats *her* clients' ideas respectfully.

BETTER: USING THE PLURAL

Journalists are motivated by *their* deadlines.

Good interior designers treat *their* clients' ideas respectfully.

BETTER: REVISING THE SENTENCE

A journalist is motivated by *a* deadline.

A good interior designer treats clients' ideas respectfully.

For more examples of these revision strategies, see G3-a.

W4-g Revise language that may offend groups of people.

Your writing should be respectful and free of stereotypical, biased, or other offensive language. Be especially careful when describing or labelling people. Labels can become dated, and it is important to recognize when their continued use is not acceptable. When naming groups of people, choose labels that the groups currently use to describe themselves. For example, *Negro* is not an acceptable label for Black Canadians; instead of *Eskimo*, use *Inuit*; for other Indigenous peoples, name the specific group when possible.

► Nunavut takes its name from the ~~Eskimo~~ word meaning "our land."
  Inuit

► Many ~~Oriental~~ immigrants have recently settled in our town.
  Asian

Negative stereotypes (such as "drives like a teenager" or "sour as a spinster") are of course offensive. But you should avoid stereotyping a person or a group even if you believe your generalization to be positive.

> It was no surprise that Greer, ~~a Chinese Canadian,~~ was selected for
>
>   *an excellent math and science student,*
>
> the honours chemistry program in her second year.

W5   Exact language

Two reference works will help you find words to express your meaning exactly: a good dictionary, such as *The Canadian Oxford Dictionary*, and a collection of synonyms and antonyms, such as *Roget's International Thesaurus*.

TIP: Do not turn to a thesaurus in search of impressive words. Look instead for words that exactly express your meaning.

W5-a   Select words with appropriate connotations.

In addition to their strict dictionary meanings (or *denotations*), words have *connotations*, emotional colourings that affect how readers respond to them. The word *steel* denotes "commercial iron that contains carbon," but it also calls up images associated with steel. These associations give the word its connotations — cold, hard, smooth, unbending.

If the connotation of a word does not seem appropriate for your purpose, your audience, or your subject matter, you should change the word. When a more appropriate synonym does not come quickly to mind, consult a dictionary or a thesaurus.

> When Canadian soldiers returned home after World War II, many
>
>   *left*
>
> women ~~abandoned~~ their jobs in favour of marriage.

The word *abandoned* is too negative for the context.

>   *sweat*
>
> As I covered the boats with marsh grass, the ~~perspiration~~ I had
>
> worked up evaporated in the wind, and the cold morning air
>
> seemed even colder.

The term *perspiration* is too dainty for the context, which suggests vigorous exercise.

W5-b Prefer specific, concrete nouns.

Unlike general nouns, which refer to broad classes of things, specific nouns point to particular items. *Film*, for example, names a general class, *fantasy film* names a narrower class, and *Alice through the Looking Glass* is more specific still. Other examples: *team, football team, Montreal Alouettes; music, symphony, Beethoven's Ninth.*

Unlike abstract nouns, which refer to qualities and ideas (*justice, beauty, realism, dignity*), concrete nouns point to immediate, often sensory experiences and to physical objects (*steeple, asphalt, lilac, stone, garlic*).

Specific, concrete nouns express meaning more vividly than general or abstract ones. Although general and abstract language is sometimes necessary to convey your meaning, use specific, concrete words whenever possible.

> The senator spoke about the challenges of the future:
> pollution, dwindling resources, and terrorism.
> ~~the environment and world peace.~~
>   ^

Nouns such as *thing, area, aspect, factor,* and *individual* are especially dull and imprecise.

> motherhood, and memory.
> Toni Morrison's *Beloved* is about slavery, ~~among other things.~~
>   ^

W5-c Do not misuse words.

If a word is not in your active vocabulary, you may find yourself misusing it, sometimes with embarrassing consequences. When in doubt, check the dictionary.

> climbing
> The fans were ~~migrating~~ up the bleachers in search of seats.
>   ^

> permeated
> The internet has so ~~diffused~~ our culture that it touches all segments
>   ^
> of society.

Also be alert for misused word forms — using a noun such as *absence* or *significance,* for example, when your meaning requires the adjective *absent* or *significant.*

> persistent
> Most dieters are not ~~persistence~~ enough to make a permanent change
>   ^
> in their eating habits.

W5-d Use standard idioms.

Idioms are speech forms that follow no easily specified rules. The English say "Bernice went *to hospital*," an idiom strange to some Canadian ears, which are accustomed to hearing *the* in front of *hospital*. Native speakers of a language seldom have problems with idioms, but prepositions (such as *with, to, at,* and *of*) sometimes cause trouble, especially when they follow certain verbs and adjectives. When in doubt, consult a dictionary.

UNIDIOMATIC	IDIOMATIC
abide with (a decision)	abide by (a decision)
according with	according to
agree to (an idea)	agree with (an idea)
angry at (a person)	angry with (a person)
capable to	capable of
comply to	comply with
different than (a person or thing)	different from (a person or thing)
intend on doing	intend to do
off of	off
plan on doing	plan to do
preferable than	preferable to
prior than	prior to
sure and	sure to
think on	think of, about
try and	try to
type of a	type of

> **Multilingual** Because idioms follow no particular rules, you must learn them individually. You may find it helpful to keep a list of idioms that you frequently encounter in conversation and in reading.

W5-e Do not rely heavily on clichés.

The pioneer who first announced that he had "slept like a log" no doubt amused his companions with a fresh, unlikely comparison. Today, however, that comparison is a cliché, a saying that can no longer add emphasis or surprise.

To see just how dully predictable clichés are, put your hand over the right-hand column and then finish the phrases on the left.

beat around	the bush
busy as a	bee, beaver
cool as a	cucumber
crystal	clear
dead as a	doornail
light as a	feather
like a bull	in a china shop
out of the frying pan and	into the fire
playing with	fire
selling like	hotcakes
starting out at the bottom	of the ladder
water under the	bridge
avoid clichés like the	plague

The solution for clichés is simple: Just delete them or rewrite them.

▶ When I received a full scholarship from my second-choice
               felt pressured to settle for second best.
  school, I ~~found myself between a rock and a hard place.~~
        ^

Sometimes you can write around a cliché by adding an element of surprise. One student revised a cliché about butterflies in her stomach like this:

> If all of the action in my stomach is caused by butterflies, there must be a horde of them, with horseshoes on.

The image of butterflies wearing horseshoes is fresh and unlikely, not predictable like the original cliché.

W5-f Use figures of speech with care.

A figure of speech is an expression that uses words imaginatively (rather than literally) to make abstract ideas concrete. Most often, figures of speech compare two seemingly unlike things to reveal surprising similarities.

In a *simile*, the writer makes the comparison explicitly, usually by introducing it with *like* or *as*: *By the time cotton had to be picked, Grandfather's neck was as red as the clay he plowed.* In a *metaphor*, the *like* or *as* is omitted, and the comparison is implied. For example, in William Shakespeare's *As You Like It*, a young man compares life to a play: *All the world's a stage, and all the men and women merely players.*

Although figures of speech are useful devices, writers sometimes use them without thinking through the images they evoke. The result is sometimes a *mixed metaphor,* the combination of two or more images that don't make sense together.

▶ **Our manager decided to put all controversial issues** ~~in a holding pattern~~ **on a back burner until after the annual meeting.**

Here the writer is mixing airplanes and stoves. Simply deleting one of the images corrects the problem.

G

Grammatical Sentences

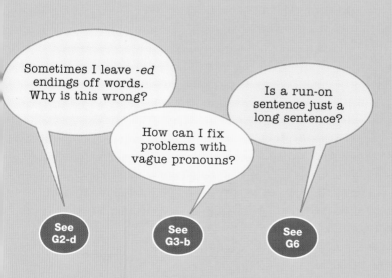

Sometimes I leave -*ed* endings off words. Why is this wrong?

See G2-d

How can I fix problems with vague pronouns?

See G3-b

Is a run-on sentence just a long sentence?

See G6

G — Grammatical Sentences

G1 Subject-verb agreement

In the present tense, verbs agree with their subjects in number (singular or plural) and in person (first, second, third): *I sing, you sing, she sings, we sing, they sing.* Even if your ear recognizes the standard subject-verb combinations in G1-a, you may encounter tricky situations such as those described in G1-b to G1-k.

G1-a Learn to recognize standard subject-verb combinations.

This section describes the basic guidelines for making present-tense verbs agree with their subjects. The present-tense ending *-s* (or *-es*) is used on a verb if its subject is third-person singular (*he, she, it,* and singular nouns); otherwise the verb takes no ending. Consider, for example, the present-tense forms of the verbs *love* and *try,* given at the beginning of the chart on page 172.

The verb *be* varies from this pattern; it has special forms in *both* the present and the past tense (see the end of the chart).

If you aren't sure of the standard forms, use the charts on pages 172 and 173 as you proofread your work. See also G2-c on *-s* endings of regular and irregular verbs.

G1-b Make the verb agree with its subject, not with a word that comes between.

Word groups often come between the subject and the verb. Such word groups, usually modifying the subject, may contain a noun that at first appears to be the subject. By mentally stripping away such modifiers, you can isolate the noun that is in fact the subject.

The *samples* on the tray in the lab *need* testing.

▶ High levels of air pollution causes damage to the respiratory tract.

The subject is *levels,* not *pollution.* Strip away the phrase *of air pollution* to hear the correct verb: *levels cause.*

▶ The slaughter of pandas for their pelts has̲ caused the panda population to decline drastically.

The subject is *slaughter,* not *pandas* or *pelts.*

LaunchPad **ACTIVITIES FOR G1**
macmillan learning   7 Exercises, 1 LearningCurve activity

Subject-verb agreement at a glance

Present-tense forms of *love* and *try* (typical verbs)

	Singular		**Plural**	
FIRST PERSON	I	love	we	love
SECOND PERSON	you	love	you	love
THIRD PERSON	he/she/it*	loves	they**	love

	Singular		**Plural**	
FIRST PERSON	I	try	we	try
SECOND PERSON	you	try	you	try
THIRD PERSON	he/she/it*	tries	they**	try

Present-tense forms of *have*

	Singular		**Plural**	
FIRST PERSON	I	have	we	have
SECOND PERSON	you	have	you	have
THIRD PERSON	he/she/it*	has	they**	have

Present-tense forms of *do* (including negative forms)

	Singular		**Plural**	
FIRST PERSON	I	do/don't	we	do/don't
SECOND PERSON	you	do/don't	you	do/don't
THIRD PERSON	he/she/it*	does/doesn't	they**	do/don't

Present-tense and past-tense forms of *be*

	Singular		**Plural**	
FIRST PERSON	I	am/was	we	are/were
SECOND PERSON	you	are/were	you	are/were
THIRD PERSON	he/she/it*	is/was	they**	are/were

*And singular nouns (*child, Roger*)
**And plural nouns (*children, the Mannings*)

NOTE: Phrases beginning with the prepositions *as well as, in addition to, accompanied by, together with,* and *along with* do not make a singular subject plural. *The premier as well as his press secretary was on the plane.* To emphasize that two people were on the plane, the writer could use *and* instead: *The premier and his press secretary were on the plane.*

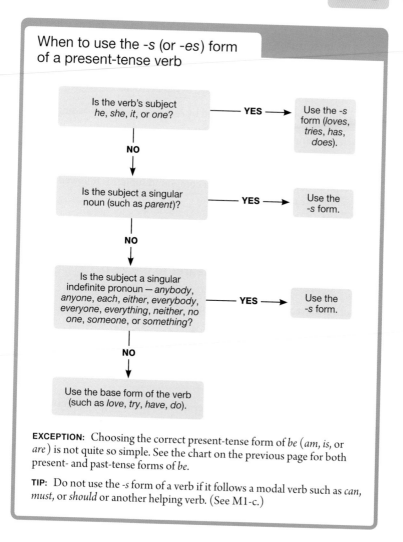

When to use the *-s* (or *-es*) form of a present-tense verb

Is the verb's subject *he, she, it,* or *one*? —— **YES** → Use the *-s* form (*loves, tries, has, does*).

NO ↓

Is the subject a singular noun (such as *parent*)? —— **YES** → Use the *-s* form.

NO ↓

Is the subject a singular indefinite pronoun — *anybody, anyone, each, either, everybody, everyone, everything, neither, no one, someone,* or *something*? —— **YES** → Use the *-s* form.

NO ↓

Use the base form of the verb (such as *love, try, have, do*).

EXCEPTION: Choosing the correct present-tense form of *be* (*am, is,* or *are*) is not quite so simple. See the chart on the previous page for both present- and past-tense forms of *be*.

TIP: Do not use the *-s* form of a verb if it follows a modal verb such as *can, must,* or *should* or another helping verb. (See M1-c.)

G1-c Treat most subjects joined with *and* as plural.

A subject with two or more parts is said to be compound. If the parts are connected with *and*, the subject is nearly always plural.

Leon and Jan often *jog* together.

▶ The Supreme Court's willingness to hear the case and its
affirmation of the original decision ~~has~~ set a new precedent.
      have

EXCEPTIONS: When the parts of the subject form a single unit or when they refer to the same person or thing, treat the subject as singular.

Fish and chips was a last-minute addition to the menu.

Sue's friend and adviser was surprised by her decision.

When a compound subject is preceded by *each* or *every*, treat it as singular.

Each tree, shrub, and vine needs to be sprayed.

Every car, truck, and van is required to pass inspection.

This exception does not apply when a compound subject is followed by *each*: *Alan and Marcia each have different ideas.*

G1-d With subjects joined with *or* or *nor* (or with *either . . . or* or *neither . . . nor*), make the verb agree with the part of the subject nearer to the verb.

A driver's *licence* or credit *card is* required.

A driver's *licence* or two credit *cards are* required.

▶ If an infant or a child ~~have~~ **has** a high fever, call a doctor.

▶ Neither the chief financial officer nor the marketing managers ~~was~~ **were** able to convince the client to reconsider.

The verb must be matched with the part of the subject closer to it: *child has* in the first sentence, *managers were* in the second.

NOTE: If one part of the subject is singular and the other is plural, put the plural one last to avoid awkwardness.

G1-e Treat most indefinite pronouns as singular.

Indefinite pronouns are pronouns that do not refer to specific persons or things. The following commonly used indefinite pronouns are singular.

anybody	each	everyone	nobody	somebody
anyone	either	everything	no one	someone
anything	everybody	neither	nothing	something

Many of these words appear to have plural meanings, and they are often treated as such in casual speech. In formal written English, however, they are nearly always treated as singular. (See G3-a.)

> *Everyone* on the team *supports* the coach.

▶ Each of the essays ~~have~~ been graded.
   has

▶ Nobody who participated in the clinical trials ~~were~~ given a placebo.
   was

The subjects of these sentences are *Each* and *Nobody*. These indefinite pronouns are third-person singular, so the verbs must be *has* and *was*.

A few indefinite pronouns (*all, any, none, some*) may be singular or plural depending on the noun or pronoun they refer to.

SINGULAR   *Some* of our *luggage was* lost.

None of his *advice makes* sense.

PLURAL   *Some* of the *rocks are* slippery.

None of the *eggs were* broken.

NOTE: When the meaning of *none* is emphatically "not one," *none* may be treated as singular: *None* [meaning "Not one"] *of the eggs was broken.* Using *not one* is sometimes clearer: *Not one of the eggs was broken.*

G1-f Treat collective nouns as singular unless the meaning is clearly plural.

Collective nouns such as *jury, committee, audience, crowd, troop, family,* and *couple* name a class or a group. In Canadian English, collective nouns are nearly always treated as singular: They emphasize the group as a unit. Occasionally, when there is some reason to draw attention to the individual members of the group, a collective noun may be treated as plural. (See also p. 193.)

SINGULAR   The *class respects* the teacher.

PLURAL   The *class are* debating among themselves.

To underscore the notion of individuality in the second sentence, many writers would add a clearly plural noun.

PLURAL   The class *members are* debating among themselves.

> *meets*
> **The board of trustees ~~meet~~ in Dartmouth twice a year.**

The board as a whole meets; there is no reason to draw attention to its individual members.

> *were*
> **A young couple ~~was~~ arguing about politics while holding hands.**

The meaning is clearly plural. Only separate individuals can argue and hold hands.

NOTE: The phrase *the number* is treated as singular, *a number* as plural.

SINGULAR   *The number* of school-age children *is* declining.

PLURAL   *A number* of children *are* attending the wedding.

NOTE: In general, when fractions or units of measurement are used with a singular noun, treat them as singular; when they are used with a plural noun, treat them as plural.

SINGULAR   *Three-fourths* of the salad *has* been eaten.

SINGULAR   Fifty *centimetres* of wallboard *was* covered with mud.

PLURAL   *One-fourth* of the drivers *were* texting.

PLURAL   Two *kilograms* of blueberries *were* used to make the jam.

G1-g Make the verb agree with its subject even when the subject follows the verb.

Verbs ordinarily follow subjects. When this order is reversed, it is easy to become confused. Sentences beginning with *there is* or *there are* (or *there was* or *there were*) are inverted; the subject follows the verb.

There *are* surprisingly few *honeybees* left in southern China.

were

▶ There ~~was~~ a social worker and a journalist at the meeting.
^

The subject, *worker and journalist*, is plural, so the verb must be *were*.

Occasionally you may decide to invert a sentence for variety or effect. When you do so, check to make sure that your subject and verb agree.

are

▶ Of particular concern ~~is~~ penicillin and tetracycline, antibiotics
^

used to make animals more resistant to disease.

The subject, *penicillin and tetracycline*, is plural, so the verb must be *are*.

G1-h Make the verb agree with its subject, not with a subject complement.

One basic sentence pattern in English consists of a subject, a linking verb, and a subject complement: *Jack is a lawyer*. Because the subject complement (*lawyer*) names or describes the subject (*Jack*), it is sometimes mistaken for the subject. (See B2-b on subject complements.)

These *exercises are* a way to test your ability to perform under pressure.

are

▶ A tent and a sleeping bag ~~is~~ the required equipment.
^

Tent and bag is the subject, not *equipment*.

is

▶ A major force in today's economy ~~are~~ children — as consumers,
^

decision makers, and trend spotters.

Force is the subject, not *children*. If the corrected version seems too awkward, make *children* the subject: *Children are a major force in today's economy — as consumers, decision makers, and trend spotters.*

G1-i Who, which, and *that* take verbs that agree with their antecedents.

Like most pronouns, the relative pronouns *who, which,* and *that* have antecedents, nouns or pronouns to which they refer. Relative pronouns used as subjects of subordinate clauses take verbs that agree with their antecedents.

ANT   PN   V

Take a *course that prepares* you for classroom management.

One of the

Constructions such as *one of the students who* (or *one of the things that*) cause problems for writers. Do not assume that the antecedent must be *one*. Instead, consider the logic of the sentence.

▶ Our ability to use language is one of the things that sets̸ us apart

from animals.

The antecedent of *that* is *things*, not *one*. Several things set us apart from animals.

Only one of the

When the word *only* comes before *one*, you are safe in assuming that *one* is the antecedent of the relative pronoun.

▶ Veronica was the only one of the first-year French students who

was
~~were~~ fluent enough to apply for the exchange program.
^
The antecedent of *who* is *one*, not *students*. Only one student was fluent enough.

G1-j Words such as *athletics, economics, mathematics, physics, politics, statistics, measles,* and *news* are usually singular, despite their plural form.

is
▶ Politics ~~are~~ among my mother's favourite pastimes.
^

EXCEPTIONS: Occasionally some of these words, especially *mathematics, economics, politics,* and *statistics,* have plural meanings: *Office politics often sway decisions about hiring and promotion. The economics of the building plan are prohibitive.*

G1-k Titles of works, company names, words mentioned as words, and gerund phrases are singular.

describes
▶ *Lost Cities* ~~describe~~ the discoveries of fifty ancient civilizations.
^

specializes
▶ *Delmonico Brothers* ~~specialize~~ in organic produce and
^

additive-free meats.

is
▶ *Controlled substances* ~~are~~ a euphemism for illegal drugs.
^

A gerund phrase consists of an *-ing* verb form followed by any objects, complements, or modifiers (see B3-b). Treat gerund phrases as singular.

▶ **Encountering long hold times ~~make~~ makes customers impatient with telephone tech support.**

G2 Verb forms, tenses, and moods

In speech, some people use verb forms and tenses that match a home dialect or variety of English. In writing, use Standard English verb forms unless you are quoting nonstandard speech or using alternative forms for literary effect. (See W4-d.)

Except for the verb *be*, all verbs in English have five forms. The following list shows the five forms and provides a sample sentence in which each might appear.

BASE FORM	Usually I (*walk, ride*).
PAST TENSE	Yesterday I (*walked, rode*).
PAST PARTICIPLE	I have (*walked, ridden*) many times before.
PRESENT PARTICIPLE	I am (*walking, riding*) right now.
-S FORM	He/she/it (*walks, rides*) regularly.

The verb *be* has eight forms instead of the usual five: *be, am, is, are, was, were, being, been.*

G2-a Choose Standard English forms of irregular verbs.

For all regular verbs, the past-tense and past-participle forms are the same (ending in *-ed* or *-d*), so there is no danger of confusion. This is not true, however, for irregular verbs, such as the following.

BASE FORM	PAST TENSE	PAST PARTICIPLE
go	went	gone
break	broke	broken
fly	flew	flown

LaunchPad macmillan learning **ACTIVITIES FOR G2**
11 Exercises, 1 LearningCurve activity

> **Multilingual** If English is not your native language, see also M1 for more help with verbs.

The past-tense form always occurs alone, without a helping verb. It expresses action that occurred entirely in the past: *I rode to work yesterday. I walked to work last Tuesday.* The past participle is used with a helping verb. It forms the perfect tenses with *has, have,* or *had*; it forms the passive voice with *be, am, is, are, was, were, being,* or *been.* (See B1-c for a list of helping verbs and G2-f for a survey of tenses.)

PAST TENSE   Last July, we *went* to Seoul.

HELPING VERB + PAST PARTICIPLE   We *have gone* to Seoul twice.

The list of common irregular verbs beginning below will help you distinguish between the past tense and the past participle. Choose the past-participle form if the verb in your sentence requires a helping verb; choose the past-tense form if the verb does not require a helping verb. (See verb tenses in G2-f.)

>   saw
> Yesterday we ~~seen~~ a documentary about Isabel Allende.
>
> The past-tense *saw* is required because there is no helping verb.

>   stolen
> The truck was apparently ~~stole~~ while the driver ate lunch.

>   fallen
> By Friday, the stock market had ~~fell~~ two hundred points.
>
> Because of the helping verbs *was* and *had,* the past-participle forms are required: *was stolen, had fallen.*

Common irregular verbs

BASE FORM	PAST TENSE	PAST PARTICIPLE
arise	arose	arisen
awake	awoke, awaked	awaked, awoke, awoken
be	was, were	been
beat	beat	beaten, beat
become	became	become
begin	began	begun
bend	bent	bent
bite	bit	bitten, bit
blow	blew	blown
break	broke	broken

BASE FORM	PAST TENSE	PAST PARTICIPLE
bring	brought	brought
build	built	built
burst	burst	burst
buy	bought	bought
catch	caught	caught
choose	chose	chosen
cling	clung	clung
come	came	come
cost	cost	cost
deal	dealt	dealt
dig	dug	dug
dive	dived, dove	dived
do	did	done
draw	drew	drawn
dream	dreamed, dreamt	dreamed, dreamt
drink	drank	drunk
drive	drove	driven
eat	ate	eaten
fall	fell	fallen
fight	fought	fought
find	found	found
fly	flew	flown
forget	forgot	forgotten, forgot
freeze	froze	frozen
get	got	gotten, got
give	gave	given
go	went	gone
grow	grew	grown
hang (execute)	hanged	hanged
hang (suspend)	hung	hung
have	had	had
hear	heard	heard
hide	hid	hidden
hurt	hurt	hurt
keep	kept	kept
know	knew	known
lay (put)	laid	laid
lead	led	led
lend	lent	lent
let (allow)	let	let
lie (recline)	lay	lain
lose	lost	lost
make	made	made
prove	proved	proved, proven
read	read	read
ride	rode	ridden
ring	rang	rung
rise (get up)	rose	risen

BASE FORM	PAST TENSE	PAST PARTICIPLE
run	ran	run
say	said	said
see	saw	seen
send	sent	sent
set (place)	set	set
shake	shook	shaken
shoot	shot	shot
shrink	shrank	shrunk
sing	sang	sung
sink	sank	sunk
sit (be seated)	sat	sat
slay	slew	slain
sleep	slept	slept
speak	spoke	spoken
spin	spun	spun
spring	sprang	sprung
stand	stood	stood
steal	stole	stolen
sting	stung	stung
strike	struck	struck, stricken
swear	swore	sworn
swim	swam	swum
swing	swung	swung
take	took	taken
teach	taught	taught
throw	threw	thrown
wake	woke, waked	waked, woken
wear	wore	worn
win	won	won
wring	wrung	wrung
write	wrote	written

G2-b Distinguish among the forms of *lie* and *lay*.

Writers and speakers frequently confuse the various forms of *lie* (meaning "to recline or rest on a surface") and *lay* (meaning "to put or place something"). *Lie* is an intransitive verb; it does not take a direct object: *The tax forms lie on the table.* The verb *lay* is transitive; it takes a direct object: *Please lay the tax forms on the table.* (See B2-b.)

In addition to confusing the meaning of *lie* and *lay*, writers and speakers are often unfamiliar with the Standard English forms of these verbs.

BASE FORM	PAST TENSE	PAST PARTICIPLE	PRESENT PARTICIPLE
lie ("recline")	lay	lain	lying
lay ("put")	laid	laid	laying

lay
▶ Sue was so exhausted that she ~~laid~~ down for a nap.
 ^

The past-tense form of *lie* ("to recline") is *lay*.

lain
▶ The patient had ~~laid~~ in an uncomfortable position all night.
 ^

The past-participle form of *lie* ("to recline") is *lain*. If the correct English seems too stilted, recast the sentence: *The patient had been lying in an uncomfortable position all night.*

laid
▶ The customer gently ~~lay~~ the iPad on the help desk counter.
 ^

The past-tense form of *lay* ("to place") is *laid*.

lying
▶ Letters dating from 1915 were ~~laying~~ in a corner of the chest.
 ^

The present participle of *lie* ("to rest on a surface") is *lying*.

G2-c Use -s (or -es) endings on present-tense verbs that have third-person singular subjects.

All singular nouns (*child, tree*) and the pronouns *he, she,* and *it* are third-person singular; indefinite pronouns such as *everyone* and *neither* are also third-person singular. When the subject of a sentence is third-person singular, its verb takes an -s or -es ending in the present tense. (See also G1.)

	SINGULAR		PLURAL	
FIRST PERSON	I	know	we	know
SECOND PERSON	you	know	you	know
THIRD PERSON	he/she/it	knows	they	know
	child	knows	parents	know
	everyone	knows		

drives
▶ My neighbour ~~drive~~ to the Thousand Islands every weekend.
 ^

turns   dissolves   eats
▶ Sulphur dioxide ~~turn~~ leaves yellow, ~~dissolve~~ marble, and ~~eat~~
 ^   ^   ^
away iron and steel.

The subjects *neighbour* and *sulphur dioxide* are third-person singular, so the verbs must end in -s.

TIP: Do not add the *-s* ending to the verb if the subject is not third-person singular. The writers of the following sentences, knowing they sometimes dropped *-s* endings from verbs, overcorrected by adding the endings where they don't belong.

▶ I prepare~~s~~ system specifications for every installation.

> The pronoun *I* is first-person singular, so its verb does not require the *-s*.

▶ The wood floors require~~s~~ continual sweeping.

> The *-s* ending is used only on present-tense verbs with third-person *singular* subjects.

G2-d Do not omit *-ed* endings on verbs.

Speakers who do not fully pronounce *-ed* endings sometimes omit them unintentionally in writing. Failure to pronounce *-ed* endings is common in many dialects and in informal speech even in Standard English. In the following frequently used words and phrases, for example, the *-ed* ending is not always fully pronounced.

advised	prejudiced
asked	pronounced
concerned	stereotyped
developed	supposed to
fixed	used to

When a verb is regular, both the past tense and the past participle are formed by adding *-ed* (or *-d*) to the base form of the verb.

Past tense

Use the ending *-ed* or *-d* to express the past tense of regular verbs. The past tense is used when the action occurred entirely in the past.

▶ In 1998, journalist Barbara Ehrenreich ~~decide~~ decided to try to live on minimum wage.

▶ Last summer, my counsellor ~~advise~~ advised me to ask my graphic arts instructor for a recommendation.

Past participles

Past participles are used in three ways: (1) following *have, has,* or *had* to form one of the perfect tenses; (2) following *be, am, is, are, was, were, being,* or *been* to form the passive voice; and (3) as adjectives modifying nouns or pronouns. The perfect tenses are listed on page 187, and the passive voice is discussed in W3-a. For a discussion of participles as adjectives, see B3-b.

▶ Robin has ~~ask~~ the Office of Student Affairs for more housing staff
       asked

for next year.

    Has asked is present perfect tense (*have* or *has* followed by a past participle).

▶ Though it is not a new phenomenon, domestic violence is now
   publicized
~~publicize~~ more than ever.

    Is publicized is a verb in the passive voice (a form of *be* followed by a past participle).

G2-e Do not omit needed verbs.

Although Standard English allows some linking verbs and helping verbs to be contracted in informal contexts, it does not allow them to be omitted.

    Linking verbs, used to link subjects to subject complements, are frequently a form of *be: be, am, is, are, was, were, being, been.* (See B2-b.) Some of these forms may be contracted (*I'm, she's, we're, you're, they're*), but they should not be omitted altogether.

▶ When we quiet in the evening, we can hear the crickets.
     are

▶ Mordecai Richler a Jewish Canadian author whose stories have
      was
been made into films.

Helping verbs, used with main verbs, include forms of *be, do,* and *have* and the modal verbs *can, will, shall, could, would, should, may, might,* and *must.* (See B1-c.) Some helping verbs may be contracted (*he's leaving, we'll celebrate, they've been told*), but they should not be omitted altogether.

▶ We been in Red Deer since last Thursday.
  have

> **Multilingual**   Some languages do not require a linking verb between a subject and its complement. English, however, requires a verb in every sentence. See M3-a.
>
> *am*
> - Every night, I read to my daughter. When I ∧ too busy, my
>
>   husband reads to her.

G2-f Choose the appropriate verb tense.

Tenses indicate the time of an action in relation to the time of the speaking or writing about that action.

The most common problem with tenses — shifting confusingly from one tense to another — is discussed in section S4. Other problems with tenses are detailed in this section, after the following survey of tenses.

Survey of tenses

Tenses are classified as present, past, and future, with simple, perfect, and progressive forms for each.

SIMPLE TENSES   The simple tenses indicate relatively simple time relations. The *simple present* tense is used primarily for actions occurring at the same time they are being discussed or for actions occurring regularly. The *simple past* tense is used for actions completed in the past. The *simple future* tense is used for actions that will occur in the future. In the following table, the simple tenses are given for the regular verb *walk*, the irregular verb *ride*, and the highly irregular verb *be*.

SIMPLE PRESENT

SINGULAR		PLURAL	
I	walk, ride, am	we	walk, ride, are
you	walk, ride, are	you	walk, ride, are
he/she/it	walks, rides, is	they	walk, ride, are

SIMPLE PAST

SINGULAR		PLURAL	
I	walked, rode, was	we	walked, rode, were
you	walked, rode, were	you	walked, rode, were
he/she/it	walked, rode, was	they	walked, rode, were

SIMPLE FUTURE

I, you, he/she/it, we, they	will walk, ride, be

PERFECT TENSES   More complex time relations are indicated by the perfect tenses. A verb in one of the perfect tenses (a form of *have* plus the past participle) expresses an action that was or will be completed at the time of another action.

PRESENT PERFECT

| I, you, we, they | have walked, ridden, been |
| he/she/it | has walked, ridden, been |

PAST PERFECT

| I, you, he/she/it, we, they | had walked, ridden, been |

FUTURE PERFECT

| I, you, he/she/it, we, they | will have walked, ridden, been |

PROGRESSIVE FORMS   The simple and perfect tenses have progressive forms that describe actions in progress. A progressive verb consists of a form of *be* followed by a present participle. The progressive forms are not normally used with certain verbs, such as *believe, know, hear,* and *seem*.

PRESENT PROGRESSIVE

I	am walking, riding, being
he/she/it	is walking, riding, being
you, we, they	are walking, riding, being

PAST PROGRESSIVE

| I, he/she/it | was walking, riding, being |
| you, we, they | were walking, riding, being |

FUTURE PROGRESSIVE

| I, you, he/she/it, we, they | will be walking, riding, being |

PRESENT PERFECT PROGRESSIVE

| I, you, we, they | have been walking, riding, being |
| he/she/it | has been walking, riding, being |

PAST PERFECT PROGRESSIVE

| I, you, he/she/it, we, they | had been walking, riding, being |

FUTURE PERFECT PROGRESSIVE

| I, you, he/she/it, we, they | will have been walking, riding, being |

Multilingual   See M1-a for more specific examples of verb tenses that can be challenging for multilingual writers.

Special uses of the present tense

Use the present tense when expressing general truths, when writing about literature, and when quoting, summarizing, or paraphrasing an author's views.

General truths or scientific principles should appear in the present tense unless such principles have been disproved.

> ▸ Galileo taught that the earth ~~revolved~~ ^{revolves} around the sun.

Because Galileo's teaching has not been discredited, the verb should be in the present tense. The following sentence, however, is acceptable: *Ptolemy taught that the sun revolved around the earth.*

When writing about a work of literature, you may be tempted to use the past tense. The convention in the humanities, however, is to describe fictional events in the present tense.

> ▸ In Masuji Ibuse's *Black Rain,* a child ~~reached~~ ^{reaches} for a pomegranate
> in his mother's garden, and a moment later he ~~was~~ ^{is} dead, killed
> by the blast of the atomic bomb.

When you are quoting, summarizing, or paraphrasing the author of a nonliterary work, use present-tense verbs such as *writes, reports, asserts,* and so on to introduce the source. This convention is usually followed even when the author is dead (unless a date or the context specifies the time of writing).

> ▸ Dr. Jerome Groopman ~~argued~~ ^{argues} that doctors are "susceptible to the
> subtle and not so subtle efforts of the pharmaceutical industry to
> sculpt our thinking" (9).

In MLA style, signal phrases are written in the present tense, not the past tense. (See also MLA-3c.)

APA NOTE: When you are documenting a paper with the APA (American Psychological Association) style of in-text citations, use past tense verbs such as *reported* or *demonstrated* or present perfect verbs such as *has reported* or *has demonstrated* to introduce the source. (See APA-3c.)

The past perfect tense

The past perfect tense consists of a past participle preceded by *had* (*had worked, had gone*). This tense is used for an action already completed by the time of another past action or for an action already completed at some specific past time.

> Everyone *had spoken* by the time I arrived.

> I pleaded my case, but Paula *had made up* her mind.

Writers sometimes use the simple past tense when they should use the past perfect.

▶ By the time dinner was served, the guest of honour ~~left~~. *had*

> The past perfect tense is needed because the action of leaving was already completed at a specific past time (when dinner was served).

Some writers tend to overuse the past perfect tense. Do not use the past perfect if two past actions occurred at the same time.

▶ When Ernest Hemingway lived in Cuba, he ~~had written~~ *For Whom the Bell Tolls.* *wrote*

Sequence of tenses with infinitives and participles

An infinitive is the base form of a verb preceded by *to*. (See B3-b.) Use the present infinitive to show action at the same time as or later than the action of the verb in the sentence.

▶ Barb had hoped to ~~have paid~~ the bill by May 1. *pay*

> The action expressed in the infinitive (*to pay*) occurred later than the action of the sentence's verb (*had hoped*).

Use the perfect form of an infinitive (*to have* followed by the past participle) for an action occurring earlier than that of the verb in the sentence.

▶ Dan would like to ~~join~~ the navy, but he could not swim. *have joined*

> The liking occurs in the present; the joining would have occurred in the past.

Like the tense of an infinitive, the tense of a participle is governed by the tense of the sentence's verb. Use the present participle (ending in *-ing*) for an action occurring at the same time as that of the sentence's verb.

> *Hiking* the Great Divide Trail, we spotted many wildflowers.

Use the past participle (such as *given* or *helped*) or the present perfect participle (*having* plus the past participle) for an action occurring before that of the verb.

> *Discovered* off the coast of Nova Scotia, the three-masted barque yielded many treasures.

> *Having worked* her way through university, Lee graduated debt-free.

G2-g Use the subjunctive mood in the few contexts that require it.

There are three moods in English: the *indicative*, used for facts, opinions, and questions; the *imperative*, used for orders or advice; and the *subjunctive*, used in certain contexts to express wishes, requests, or conditions contrary to fact. For many writers, the subjunctive causes the most problems.

Forms of the subjunctive

In the subjunctive mood, present-tense verbs do not change form to indicate the number and person of the subject (see G1). Instead, the subjunctive uses the base form of the verb (*be, drive, employ*) with all subjects. Also, in the subjunctive mood, there is only one past-tense form of *be: were* (never *was*).

It is important that you *be* [not *are*] prepared for the interview.

We asked that she *drive* [not *drives*] more slowly.

If I *were* [not *was*] you, I'd try a new strategy.

Uses of the subjunctive

The subjunctive mood appears only in a few contexts: in contrary-to-fact clauses beginning with *if* or expressing a wish; in *that* clauses following verbs such as *ask, insist, recommend, request,* and *suggest;* and in certain set expressions.

IN CONTRARY-TO-FACT CLAUSES BEGINNING WITH *IF*   When a subordinate clause beginning with *if* expresses a condition contrary to fact, use the subjunctive *were* in place of *was.*

▶ If I ~~was~~ a member of Parliament, I would vote for that bill.
       were

▶ The astronomers would be able to see the moons of Jupiter
  tonight if the weather ~~was~~ clearer.
                        were

The writer is not a member of Parliament, and the weather is not clear.

Do not use the subjunctive mood in *if* clauses expressing conditions that exist or may exist.

If Dana *wins* the contest, she will leave for Barcelona in June.

IN CONTRARY-TO-FACT CLAUSES EXPRESSING A WISH   In formal English, use the subjunctive *were* in clauses expressing a wish or desire.

INFORMAL   I wish that Dr. Vaughn *was* my professor.

FORMAL   I wish that Dr. Vaughn *were* my professor.

IN *THAT* CLAUSES FOLLOWING VERBS SUCH AS *ASK, INSIST, REQUEST,* AND *SUGGEST* Because requests have not yet become reality, they are expressed in the subjunctive mood.

▶ Professor Moore insists that her students ~~are~~ on time.
  be

▶ We recommend that Lambert ~~files~~ form NR73 soon.
  file

IN CERTAIN SET EXPRESSIONS The subjunctive mood, once more widely used, remains in certain set expressions: *be that as it may, as it were, far be it from me,* and so on.

G3 Pronouns

Pronouns are words that substitute for nouns (see B1-b). Pronoun errors are typically related to the four topics discussed in this section:

  a. pronoun-antecedent agreement (singular vs. plural)
  b. pronoun reference (clarity)
  c. pronoun case (personal pronouns such as *I* vs. *me, she* vs. *her*)
  d. pronoun case (*who* vs. *whom*)

For more help with pronouns, consult the glossary of usage (W1).

G3-a Make pronouns and antecedents agree.

Many pronouns have antecedents, nouns or pronouns to which they refer. A pronoun and its antecedent agree when they are both singular or both plural.

SINGULAR   Dr. Ava Berto finished *her* rounds.

PLURAL   The hospital *interns* finished *their* rounds.

Indefinite pronouns

Indefinite pronouns refer to nonspecific persons or things.

anybody	each	everyone	nobody	somebody
anyone	either	everything	no one	someone
anything	everybody	neither	nothing	something

LaunchPad macmillan learning **ACTIVITIES FOR G3**
11 Exercises, 1 LearningCurve activity

> **Multilingual** The pronouns *he, his, she, her, it,* and *its* must agree in gender (masculine, feminine, or neuter) with their antecedents, not with the words they modify.
>
> *Steve* visited *his* [not *her*] sister in Gander.

Traditionally, indefinite pronouns have been treated as singular in formal English. Using a singular pronoun usually results in a sentence that is sexist, and the traditional alternative (*he or she*) is now often considered noninclusive.

SEXIST	*Everyone* performs at *his* own fitness level.
SEXIST	*Everyone* performs at *her* own fitness level.
NONINCLUSIVE	*Everyone* performs at *his or her* own fitness level.

Using *he/his* or *she/her* to refer generically to any person is considered sexist. Using *he or she* or *his or her* is wordy, and it doesn't include people who prefer not to refer to themselves as *he* or *she*. It is therefore becoming increasingly acceptable in many contexts, including formal writing, to use the plural pronoun *they* to refer to an indefinite pronoun: *everyone performs at their own fitness level.* (You may want to check with your instructor for any preferences.)

The following are usually your best options for revision.

1. Make the antecedent plural.
2. Rewrite the sentence so that no problem of agreement exists.
3. Use the plural pronoun *they* to refer to the singular antecedent.

> When ~~someone travels~~ people travel outside Canada for the first time, ~~he needs~~ they need to apply for a passport.

> ~~When someone travels outside Canada for the first time,~~ Anyone who travels outside Canada for the first time he needs to apply for a passport.

> When someone travels outside Canada for the first time, ~~he needs~~ they need to apply for a passport.

If you change a pronoun from singular to plural (or vice versa), check to be sure that the verb agrees with the new pronoun (see G1-e).

See W4-f for more on avoiding sexist language.

NOTE: When using pronouns to refer to people, choose the pronouns that people would use to refer to themselves. Doing so shows respect and communicates your audience awareness. Some transgender and gender-fluid individuals refer to themselves by new pronouns (*ze/hir*, for example), but if you are unfamiliar with such preferences, *they* and *them* are acceptable gender-neutral options.

Generic nouns

A generic noun represents a typical member of a group, such as a typical student, or any member of a group, such as a lawyer. Although generic nouns may seem to have plural meanings, they traditionally have been considered singular. However, you should avoid using *he* to refer to generic nouns, as in *A runner must train if he wants to excel*. As with indefinite pronouns, the singular use of *they* is becoming increasingly acceptable with generic nouns.

When you have trouble with generic nouns, you will usually have the same revision options as mentioned on page 192 for indefinite pronouns.

▸ A ~~medical student~~ must study hard if ~~he wants~~ to succeed.
   Medical students   they want

▸ A medical student must study hard ~~if he wants~~ to succeed.

▸ A medical student must study hard if ~~he wants~~ to succeed.
                         they want

Collective nouns

Collective nouns such as *jury, committee, audience, crowd, class, troop, family, team*, and *couple* name a group. Ordinarily the group functions as a unit, so the noun should be treated as singular; if the members of the group function as individuals, however, the noun should be treated as plural. (See also G1-f.)

AS A UNIT   The *committee* granted *its* permission to build.

AS INDIVIDUALS   The *committee* put *their* signatures on the document.

When treating a collective noun as plural, many writers prefer to add a clearly plural antecedent such as *members* to the sentence: *The members of the committee put their signatures on the document.*

▸ After only an hour of deliberation, the jury returned ~~their~~ verdict.
                                        its

There is no reason to draw attention to the individual members of the jury, so *jury* should be treated as singular.

Compound antecedents

In 1988, *Reagan and Mulroney* held a summit at which *they* signed the Canada–United States Free Trade Agreement.

With compound antecedents joined with *or* or *nor* (or with *either . . . or* or *neither . . . nor*), make the pronoun agree with the nearer antecedent.

Either *Bruce* or *Tom* should receive first prize for *his* poem.

Neither the *mouse* nor the *rats* could find *their* way through the maze.

NOTE: If one of the antecedents is singular and the other plural, as in the second example, put the plural one last to avoid awkwardness.

EXCEPTION: If one antecedent is male and the other female, do not follow the traditional rule. The sentence *Either Bruce or Elizabeth should receive first prize for her short story* makes no sense. The best solution is to recast the sentence: *The prize for best short story should go to either Bruce or Elizabeth.*

G3-b Make pronoun references clear.

In a sentence like *After Andrew intercepted the ball, he kicked it as hard as he could,* the pronouns *he* and *it* substitute for the nouns *Andrew* and *ball*. The word a pronoun refers to is called its *antecedent*.

Ambiguous reference

Ambiguous pronoun reference occurs when a pronoun could refer to two possible antecedents.

► ~~When Gloria set the pitcher~~ on the glass-topped table /. ~~it broke.~~
   The pitcher broke when Gloria set it

► Tom told James, ~~that he had~~ won the lottery.
   "You have"

What broke — the pitcher or the table? Who won the lottery — Tom or James? The revisions eliminate the ambiguity.

Implied reference

A pronoun should refer to a specific antecedent, not to a word that is implied but not present in the sentence.

▶ After braiding Ann's hair, Sue decorated ~~them~~ with ribbons.
the braids ^

The pronoun *them* referred to Ann's braids (implied by the term *braiding*), but the word *braids* did not appear in the sentence.

Modifiers, such as possessives, cannot serve as antecedents. A modifier may strongly imply the noun that a pronoun might logically refer to, but it is not itself that noun.

▶ In ~~Jamaica Kincaid's~~ "Girl," ~~she~~ portrays a mother-daughter
Jamaica Kincaid ^

relationship laced with tension.

Using the possessive form of an author's name to introduce a source leads to a problem later in this sentence: The pronoun *she* cannot refer logically to a possessive modifier (*Jamaica Kincaid's*). The revision substitutes the noun *Jamaica Kincaid* for the pronoun *she*, thereby eliminating the problem.

Broad reference of this, that, which, and it

For clarity, the pronouns *this, that, which,* and *it* should ordinarily refer to specific antecedents rather than to whole ideas or sentences. When a pronoun's reference is needlessly broad, either replace the pronoun with a noun or supply an antecedent to which the pronoun clearly refers.

▶ By pooling their money, members of an investment club gain
The larger sum
purchasing power. ~~This~~ allows for more diversification, which lowers
^
the risks.

The writer substituted the noun *sum* for the pronoun *this*, which referred broadly to the idea expressed in the preceding sentence.

▶ Romeo and Juliet were both too young to have acquired much
a fact
wisdom, ~~and~~ that accounts for their rash actions.
^

The writer added an antecedent (*fact*) that the pronoun *that* clearly refers to.

Indefinite use of they, it, *and* you

Do not use the pronoun *they* to refer indefinitely to persons who have not been specifically mentioned. *They* should always refer to a specific antecedent.

> the school board
> ► In June, ~~they~~ voted to charge a fee for students to participate in
>   ^
> sports and music programs.

The word *it* should not be used indefinitely in constructions such as *It is said on television . . .* or *In the book, it says that. . . .*

> The
> ► ~~In the~~ article ~~it~~ states that male moths can smell female moths from
>   ^
> several kilometres away.

The pronoun *you* is appropriate only when the writer is addressing the reader directly: *Once you have kneaded the dough, let it rise in a warm place.* Except in informal contexts, however, *you* should not be used to mean "anyone in general." Use a noun instead.

> a guest
> ► Ms. Pickersgill's *Guide to Etiquette* stipulates that ~~you~~ should
>   ^
> not arrive at a party too early or leave too late.

G3-c Distinguish between pronouns such as *I* and *me*.

The personal pronouns in the following chart change *case form* according to their grammatical function in a sentence. Pronouns functioning as subjects or subject complements appear in the *subjective* case; those functioning as objects appear in the *objective* case; and those showing ownership appear in the *possessive* case.

	SUBJECTIVE CASE	OBJECTIVE CASE	POSSESSIVE CASE
SINGULAR	I	me	my
	you	you	your
	he/she/it	him/her/it	his/her/its
PLURAL	we	us	our
	you	you	your
	they	them	their

Pronouns in the subjective and objective cases are frequently confused. Most of the rules in this section specify when to use one or the other of these cases (*I* or *me*, *he* or *him*, and so on). See page 199 for a special use of pronouns and nouns in the possessive case.

Subjective case (*I, you, he, she, it, we, they*)

When a pronoun is used as a subject complement (a word following a linking verb), your ear may mislead you, since the incorrect form is frequently heard in casual speech. (See "subject complement," B2-b.)

▶ During the trial, David Milgaard repeatedly denied that the
       he.
killer was ~~him.~~
       ^

If *killer was he* seems too stilted, rewrite the sentence: *During the trial, David Milgaard repeatedly denied that he was the killer.*

Objective case (*me, you, him, her, it, us, them*)

When a personal pronoun is used as a direct object, an indirect object, or the object of a preposition, it must be in the objective case.

DIRECT OBJECT	Bruce found Tony and brought *him* home.
INDIRECT OBJECT	Alice gave *me* a surprise party.
OBJECT OF A PREPOSITION	Jessica wondered if the call was for *her*.

Compound word groups

When a subject or an object appears as part of a compound structure, you may occasionally become confused. To test for the correct pronoun, mentally strip away all of the compound word group except the pronoun in question.

▶ Janice was indignant when she realized that the salesclerk was
               her.
insulting her mother and ~~she.~~
              ^

Her mother and her is the direct object of the verb *was insulting*. Strip away the words *her mother and* to hear the correct pronoun: *was insulting her* (not *was insulting she*).

When a pronoun functions as a subject or a subject complement, it must be in the subjective case.

SUBJECT	Sylvia and *he* shared the award.
SUBJECT COMPLEMENT	Greg announced that the winners were Sylvia and *he*.

                                          me
▶ The most traumatic experience for her father and ~~I~~ occurred
                                       ^
long after her operation.

Her father and me is the object of the preposition *for*. Strip away the words *her father and* to test for the correct pronoun: *for me* (not *for I*).

When in doubt about the correct pronoun, some writers try to avoid making the choice by using a reflexive pronoun such as *myself*. Using a reflexive pronoun in such situations is nonstandard.

> ► Nidra gave my cousin and ~~myself~~ *me* some good tips on travelling in
>
>   New Delhi.

My cousin and me is the indirect object of the verb *gave*. For correct uses of *myself*, see the glossary of usage (W1).

Appositives

Appositives are noun phrases that rename nouns or pronouns. A pronoun used as an appositive has the same function (usually subject or object) as the word(s) it renames.

> ► The managers, Dr. Bell and ~~me,~~ *I,* could not agree on a plan.

The appositive *Dr. Bell and I* renames the subject, *managers*. Test: *I could not agree* (not *me could not agree*).

> ► The reporter found only two witnesses, the bicyclist and ~~I.~~ *me.*

The appositive *the bicyclist and me* renames the direct object, *witnesses*. Test: *found me* (not *found I*).

Comparisons with than *or* as

When a comparison begins with *than* or *as*, your choice of a pronoun will depend on your intended meaning. To test for the correct pronoun, mentally complete the sentence: *My roommate likes football more than I* [*do*].

> ► In our report on nationalized health care in the United States,
>
>   we argued that Canadians are better off than ~~us.~~ *we.*

We is the subject of the verb *are*, which is understood: *Canadians are better off than we* [*are*]. If the correct English seems too formal, you can always add the verb.

> ► We respected no other candidate as much as ~~she.~~ *her.*

This sentence means that we respected no other candidate as much as *we respected her*. *Her* is the direct object of the understood verb *respected*.

We *or* us *before a noun*

When deciding whether *we* or *us* should precede a noun, choose the pronoun that would be appropriate if the noun were omitted.

▶ <u>~~Us~~</u> tenants would rather fight than move.

(We)

▶ Management is shortchanging ~~we~~ tenants.

(us)

No one would say *Us would rather fight than move* or *Management is shortchanging we.*

Subjects and objects of infinitives

An infinitive is the word *to* followed by the base form of a verb. (See B3-b.) Subjects of infinitives are an exception to the rule that subjects must be in the subjective case. Whenever an infinitive has a subject, it must be in the objective case. Objects of infinitives also are in the objective case.

▶ Sue asked John and ~~I~~ to drive the mayor and ~~she~~ to the airport.

(me) *(her)*

John and me is the subject of the infinitive *to drive*; *mayor and her* is the direct object of the infinitive.

Possessive case to modify a gerund

A pronoun that modifies a gerund or a gerund phrase should be in the possessive case (*my, our, your, his, her, its, their*). A gerund is a verb form ending in *-ing* that functions as a noun. Gerunds frequently appear in phrases; when they do, the whole gerund phrase functions as a noun. (See B3-b.)

▶ The chances of ~~you~~ being hit by lightning are slim.

(your)

Your modifies the gerund phrase *being hit by lightning.*

Nouns as well as pronouns may modify gerunds. To form the possessive case of a noun, use an apostrophe and an *-s* (*victim's*) or just an apostrophe (*victims'*). (See P4-a.)

▶ The old order in France paid a high price for the ~~aristocracy~~

(aristocracy's)

exploiting the lower classes.

The possessive noun *aristocracy's* modifies the gerund phrase *exploiting the lower classes.*

G3-d Distinguish between *who* and *whom*.

The choice between *who* and *whom* (or *whoever* and *whomever*) occurs primarily in subordinate clauses and in questions. *Who* and *whoever*, subjective-case pronouns, are used for subjects and subject complements. *Whom* and *whomever*, objective-case pronouns, are used for objects. (See pp. 200–02.)

An exception to this general rule occurs when the pronoun functions as the subject of an infinitive (see p. 201).

Consult the chart on page 202 for a summary of the trouble spots with *who* and *whom*.

In subordinate clauses

When *who* and *whom* (or *whoever* and *whomever*) introduce subordinate clauses, their case is determined by their function *within the clause they introduce*.

In the following two examples, the pronouns *who* and *whoever* function as the subjects of the clauses they introduce.

> who
> ▶ First prize goes to the runner ~~whom~~ earns the most points.
>   ^
>
> The subordinate clause is *who earns the most points*. The verb of the clause is *earns*, and its subject is *who*.

> ▶ Maya Angelou's *I Know Why the Caged Bird Sings* should be read
>   whoever
>   by ~~whomever~~ is interested in the effects of racism on children.
>   ^
>   The writer selected the pronoun *whomever*, thinking that it was the object of the preposition *by*. However, the object of the preposition is the entire subordinate clause *whoever is interested in the effects of racial prejudice on children*. The verb of the clause is *is*, and the subject of the verb is *whoever*.

When functioning as an object in a subordinate clause, *whom* (or *whomever*) also appears out of order, before the subject and verb. To choose the correct pronoun, you can mentally restructure the clause.

> whom
> ▶ You will work with our senior traders, ~~who~~ you will meet later.
>   ^
>
> The subordinate clause is *whom you will meet later*. The subject of the clause is *you*, and the verb is *will meet*. *Whom* is the direct object of the verb. The correct choice becomes clear if you mentally restructure the clause: *you will meet whom*.

When functioning as the object of a preposition in a subordinate clause, *whom* is often separated from its preposition.

>   *whom*
> ▸ The tutor ~~who~~ I was assigned to was very supportive.

Whom is the object of the preposition *to*. In this sentence, the writer might choose to drop *whom*: *The tutor I was assigned to was very supportive.*

NOTE: Inserted expressions such as *they know, I think,* and *she says* should be ignored in determining whether to use *who* or *whom*.

>   *who*
> ▸ The speech pathologist worked with a stroke patient ~~whom~~ she
>
> knew was suffering from aphasia.

Who is the subject of *was suffering*, not the object of *knew*.

In questions

When *who* and *whom* (or *whoever* and *whomever*) are used to open questions, their case is determined by their function within the question.

>   *Who*
> ▸ ~~Whom~~ was responsible for creating that computer virus?

Who is the subject of the verb *was*.

When *whom* functions as the object of a verb or the object of a preposition in a question, it appears out of normal order. To choose the correct pronoun, mentally restructure the question.

>   *Whom*
> ▸ ~~Who~~ did the New Democratic Party nominate in 1961?

Whom is the direct object of the verb *did nominate*. This becomes clear if you restructure the question: *The New Democratic Party did nominate whom in 1961?*

For subjects or objects of infinitives

An infinitive is the word *to* followed by the base form of a verb. (See B3-b.) Subjects of infinitives are an exception to the rule that subjects must be in the subjective case. The subject of an infinitive must be in the objective case. Objects of infinitives also are in the objective case.

>   *whom*
> ▸ When it comes to money, I know ~~who~~ to believe.

The infinitive phrase *whom to believe* is the direct object of the verb *know*, and *whom* is the subject of the infinitive *to believe*.

Checking for problems with *who* and *whom*

In subordinate clauses

Isolate the subordinate clause. Then read its subject, verb, and any objects, restructuring the clause if necessary. Some writers find it helpful to substitute *he* for *who* and *him* for *whom*.

> Samuels hoped to become the business partner of (whoever/whomever) found the treasure.
>
> > **TEST:** . . . *whoever* found the treasure. [. . . *he* found the treasure.]
>
> Ada always seemed to be bestowing a favour on (whoever/whomever) she worked for.
>
> > **TEST:** . . . she worked for *whomever*. [. . . she worked for *him*.]

In questions

Read the subject, verb, and any objects, rearranging the sentence structure if necessary.

> (Who/Whom) conferred with Roosevelt and Stalin at Yalta in 1945?
>
> > **TEST:** *Who* conferred . . . ?
>
> (Who/Whom) did the committee nominate?
>
> > **TEST:** The committee did nominate *whom*?

G4 Adjectives and adverbs

Adjectives modify nouns or pronouns. They usually come before the word they modify; occasionally they function as complements following the word they modify. Adverbs modify verbs, adjectives, or other adverbs. (See B1-d and B1-e.)

Many adverbs are formed by adding *-ly* to adjectives (*normal, normally; smooth, smoothly*). But don't assume that all words ending in *-ly* are adverbs or that all adverbs end in *-ly*. Some adjectives end in *-ly* (*lovely, friendly*), and some adverbs don't (*always, here, there*). When in doubt, consult a dictionary.

Multilingual Placement of adjectives and adverbs can be a tricky matter for multilingual writers. See M3-f and M4-b.

G4-a Use adjectives to modify nouns.

Adjectives ordinarily precede the nouns they modify (*tall building*). But they can also function as subject complements or object complements, following the nouns they modify.

Subject complements

A subject complement follows a linking verb and completes the meaning of the subject. (See B2-b.) When an adjective functions as a subject complement, it describes the subject.

Justice is blind.

Problems can arise with verbs such as *smell, taste, look,* and *feel,* which sometimes, but not always, function as linking verbs. If the word following one of these verbs describes the subject, use an adjective; if the word following the verb modifies the verb, use an adverb.

ADJECTIVE	The detective looked *cautious.*
ADVERB	The detective looked *cautiously* for fingerprints.

The adjective *cautious* describes the detective; the adverb *cautiously* modifies the verb *looked.*

Linking verbs suggest states of being, not actions. Notice, for example, the different meanings of *looked* in the preceding examples. To look cautious suggests the state of being cautious; to look cautiously is to perform an action in a cautious way.

▶ The lilacs in our yard smell especially ~~sweetly~~ *sweet* this year.

The verb *smell* suggests a state of being, not an action. Therefore, it should be followed by an adjective, not an adverb.

▶ The drawings looked ~~well~~ *good* after the architect made changes.

The verb *looked* is a linking verb suggesting a state of being, not an action. The adjective *good* is appropriate following the linking verb to describe *drawings.* (See also G4-c.)

> **Multilingual** In English, adjectives are not pluralized to agree with the words they modify: *The red* [not *reds*] *roses were a surprise.*

Object complements

An object complement follows a direct object and completes its meaning. (See B2-b.) When an adjective functions as an object complement, it describes the direct object.

Sorrow makes *us wise.*

Object complements occur with verbs such as *call, consider, create, find, keep,* and *make.* When a modifier follows the direct object of one of these verbs, use an adjective to describe the direct object; use an adverb to modify the verb.

ADJECTIVE	The referee called the plays *perfect.*
ADVERB	The referee called the plays *perfectly.*

The first sentence means that the referee considered the plays to be perfect; the second means that the referee did an excellent job of calling the plays.

G4-b Use adverbs to modify verbs, adjectives, and other adverbs.

When adverbs modify verbs (or verbals), they nearly always answer the question When? Where? How? Why? Under what conditions? How often? or To what degree? When adverbs modify adjectives or other adverbs, they usually qualify or intensify the meaning of the word they modify. (See B1-e.)

Adjectives are often used incorrectly in place of adverbs in casual or non-standard speech.

▶ The travel arrangement worked out ~~perfect~~ for everyone.
        perfectly

▶ The manager must see that the office runs ~~smooth~~ and ~~efficient.~~
        smoothly   *efficiently.*

The adverb *perfectly* modifies the verb *worked out*; the adverbs *smoothly* and *efficiently* modify the verb *runs.*

▶ The chance of recovering lost property looks ~~real~~ slim.
        really

Only adverbs can modify adjectives or other adverbs. *Really* intensifies the meaning of the adjective *slim.*

G4-c Distinguish between *good* and *well*, *bad* and *badly*.

Good is an adjective (*good performance*). *Well* is an adverb when it modifies a verb (*speak well*). The use of the adjective *good* in place of the adverb *well* to modify a verb is nonstandard and especially common in casual speech.

▶ We were glad that Sanya had done ~~good~~ ^{well} on the CPA exam.

The adverb *well* modifies the verb *had done*.

Confusion can arise because *well* is an adjective when it modifies a noun or pronoun and means "healthy" or "satisfactory" (*The babies were well and warm*).

▶ Adrienne did not feel ~~good,~~ ^{well,} but she performed anyway.

As an adjective following the linking verb *did feel*, *well* describes Adrienne's health.

Bad is always an adjective and should be used to describe a noun; *badly* is always an adverb and should be used to modify a verb. The adverb *badly* is often used inappropriately to describe a noun, especially following a linking verb.

▶ The sisters felt ~~badly~~ ^{bad} when they realized they had left their brother out of the planning.

The adjective *bad* is used after the linking verb *felt* to describe the noun *sisters*.

G4-d Use comparatives and superlatives with care.

Most adjectives and adverbs have three forms: the positive, the comparative, and the superlative.

POSITIVE	COMPARATIVE	SUPERLATIVE
fast	faster	fastest
friendly	friendlier	friendliest
carefully	more carefully	most carefully
bad	worse	worst
good	better	best

Comparative versus superlative

Use the comparative to compare two things, the superlative to compare three or more.

▶ Which of these two protein shakes is ~~best?~~ better?

▶ Though Shaw and Jackson are impressive, Zhao is the ~~more~~ most qualified of the three candidates running for mayor.

Forming comparatives and superlatives

To form comparatives and superlatives of most one- and two-syllable adjectives, use the endings -er and -est: *smooth, smoother, smoothest; easy, easier, easiest.* With longer adjectives, use *more* and *most* (or *less* and *least* for downward comparisons): *exciting, more exciting, most exciting; helpful, less helpful, least helpful.*

Some one-syllable adverbs take the endings -er and -est (*fast, faster, fastest*), but longer adverbs and all of those ending in -*ly* form the comparative and superlative with *more* and *most* (or *less* and *least*).

The comparative and superlative forms of some adjectives and adverbs are irregular: *good, better, best; well, better, best; bad, worse, worst; badly, worse, worst.*

▶ The Kirov is the ~~talentedest~~ most talented ballet company we have seen.

▶ According to our projections, sales at local businesses will be
~~worser~~ worse than those at the chain stores this winter.

Double comparatives or superlatives

Do not use double comparatives or superlatives. When you have added -er or -est to an adjective or adverb, do not also use *more* or *most* (or *less* or *least*).

▶ Of all her family, Julia is the ~~most~~ happiest about the move.

▶ All the polls indicated that Trudeau was more ~~likelier~~ likely to win than Harper.

Absolute concepts

Avoid expressions such as *more straight, less perfect, very round,* and *most unique.* Either something is unique or it isn't. It is illogical to suggest that absolute concepts come in degrees.

>   unusual
> ▶ That is the most ~~unique~~ wedding gown I have ever seen.
>   ^

>   valuable
> ▶ The painting is more ~~priceless~~ because it is signed.
>   ^

G4-e Avoid double negatives.

Standard English allows two negatives only if a positive meaning is intended: *The orchestra was not unhappy with its performance* (meaning that the orchestra was happy). Using a double negative to emphasize a negative meaning is nonstandard.

Negative modifiers such as *never, no,* and *not* should not be paired with other negative modifiers or with negative words such as *neither, none, no one, nobody,* and *nothing.*

>   anything
> ▶ The city is not doing ~~nothing~~ to see that the trash is collected
>   ^
>
>   during the strike.

The double negative *not . . . nothing* is nonstandard.

The modifiers *hardly, barely,* and *scarcely* are considered negatives in Standard English, so they should not be used with negatives such as *not, no one,* or *never.*

>   can
> ▶ Maxine is so weak that she ~~can't~~ hardly climb stairs.
>   ^

G5 Sentence fragments

A sentence fragment is a word group that pretends to be a sentence. Sentence fragments are easy to recognize when they appear out of context, like these:

When the cat leaped onto the table.

Running for the bus.

When fragments appear next to related sentences, however, they are harder to spot.

> We had just sat down to dinner. When the cat leaped onto the table.

> I tripped and twisted my ankle. Running for the bus.

Recognizing sentence fragments

To be a sentence, a word group must consist of at least one full independent clause. An independent clause includes a subject and a verb, and it either stands alone or could stand alone.

To test whether a word group is a complete sentence or a fragment, use the flowchart on page 209. By using the flowchart, you can see exactly why *When the cat leaped onto the table* is a fragment: It has a subject (*cat*) and a verb (*leaped*), but it begins with a subordinating word (*When*). *Running for the bus* is a fragment because it lacks a subject and a verb (*Running* is a verbal, not a verb). (See also B3-b and B3-e.)

Repairing sentence fragments

You can repair most fragments in one of two ways:

- Pull the fragment into a nearby sentence.
- Rewrite the fragment as a complete sentence.

▶ We had just sat down to dinner/~~When~~ the cat leaped onto the
                                      when
  table.

▶ *Running for the bus,*
   I tripped and twisted my ankle. ~~Running for the bus.~~

Multilingual Unlike some other languages, English requires a subject and a verb in every sentence (except in commands, where the subject *you* is understood but not present: *Sit down*). See M3-a and M3-b.

- *It is*
  ~~Is~~ often hot and humid during the summer.

- *are*
  Students usually very busy at the end of the semester.

Test for fragments

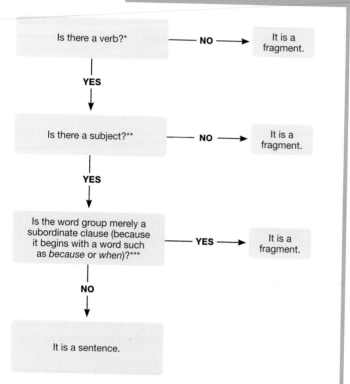

*Do not mistake verbals for verbs. A verbal is a verb form (such as *walking* or *to act*) that does not function as the verb of a clause. (See B3-b.)

**The subject of a sentence may be *you*, understood but not present in the sentence. (See B2-a.)

***A sentence may open with a subordinate clause, but the sentence must also include an independent clause. (See G5-a and B4-a.)

If you find any fragments, try one of these methods of revision (see G5-a to G5-c):

1. Attach the fragment to a nearby sentence.

2. Rewrite the fragment as a complete sentence.

G5-a Attach fragmented subordinate clauses or turn them into sentences.

A subordinate clause is patterned like a sentence, with both a subject and a verb, but it begins with a word that marks it as subordinate. The following words commonly introduce subordinate clauses.

after	since	where
although	so that	whether
as	than	which
as if	that	while
because	though	who
before	unless	whom
even though	until	whose
how	when	why
if		

Subordinate clauses function within sentences as adjectives, as adverbs, or as nouns. They cannot stand alone. (See B3-e.)

Most fragmented clauses beg to be pulled into a sentence nearby.

▶ Canadians have come to fear the Zika virus/~~Because~~ it is ^{because}

transmitted by the common mosquito.

Because introduces a subordinate clause, so it cannot stand alone. (For punctuation of subordinate clauses appearing at the end of a sentence, see P2-f.)

▶ Although psychiatrist Peter Kramer expresses concerns about

Prozac/, ~~Many~~ other doctors believe that the benefits of ^{many}

antidepressants outweigh the risks.

Although introduces a subordinate clause, so it cannot stand alone. (For punctuation of subordinate clauses at the beginning of a sentence, see P1-b.)

If a fragmented clause cannot be attached to a nearby sentence or if you feel that attaching it would be awkward, try turning the clause into a sentence. The simplest way to do this is to delete the opening word or words that mark it as subordinate.

▶ Uncontrolled development is taking a toll on the environment.

~~So that across~~ the globe, fragile ecosystems are collapsing. ^{Across}

G5-b Attach fragmented phrases or turn them into sentences.

Like subordinate clauses, phrases function within sentences as adjectives, as adverbs, or as nouns. They cannot stand alone. Fragmented phrases are often prepositional or verbal phrases; sometimes they are appositives, words or word groups that rename nouns or pronouns. (See B3-a, B3-b, and B3-c.)

Often a fragmented phrase may simply be pulled into a nearby sentence.

▶ The archaeologists worked slowly/, ~~Examining~~ *examining* and labelling every pottery shard they uncovered.

The word group beginning with *Examining* is a verbal phrase.

▶ The patient displayed symptoms of ALS/, ~~A~~ *a* neurodegenerative disease.

A neurodegenerative disease is an appositive renaming the noun *ALS*. (For punctuation of appositives, see P1-e.)

If a fragmented phrase cannot be pulled into a nearby sentence effectively, turn the phrase into a sentence. You may need to add a subject, a verb, or both.

▶ Jamie explained how to access our new database. ~~Also~~ *She also taught us* how to submit expense reports and request vendor payments.

The revision turns the fragmented phrase into a sentence by adding a subject and a verb.

G5-c Attach other fragmented word groups or turn them into sentences.

Other word groups that are commonly fragmented include parts of compound predicates, lists, and examples introduced by *for example, in addition,* or similar expressions.

Parts of compound predicates

A predicate consists of a verb and its objects, complements, and modifiers (see B2-b). A compound predicate includes two or more predicates joined with a coordinating conjunction such as *and, but,* or *or.* Because the parts of a compound predicate have the same subject, they should appear in the same sentence.

▶ The woodpecker finch of the Galápagos Islands carefully selects

a twig of a certain size and shape/ ~~And~~ then uses this tool to pry
    ^{and}   ^

out grubs from trees.

The subject is *finch*, and the compound predicate is *selects . . . and . . . uses.* (For punctuation of compound predicates, see P2-a.)

Lists

To correct a fragmented list, often you can attach it to a nearby sentence with a colon or a dash. (See P3-d and P6-b.)

▶ The smallest bones in the human body are in the middle ear/ :

~~The~~ incus, the malleus, and the stapes.
^{the}
^

Sometimes terms such as *especially, namely, like,* and *such as* introduce fragmented lists. Such fragments can usually be attached to the preceding sentence.

▶ In the twentieth century, Canada produced some of its best writers/ ,
                                                                      ^
~~Such~~ as Robertson Davies, Michael Ondaatje, Alice Munro, and
^{such}

June Callwood.

Examples introduced by for example, in addition, *or similar* expressions

Other expressions that introduce examples or explanations can lead to unintentional fragments. Although you may begin a sentence with some of the following words or phrases, make sure that what follows has a subject and a verb.

also	for example	mainly
and	for instance	or
but	in addition	that is

Often the easiest solution is to turn the fragment into a sentence.

▶ In his memoir, Primo Levi describes the horrors of living in a

concentration camp. For example, ~~working~~ without food and
                                 ^{he worked}   ^

~~suffering~~ emotional abuse.
^{suffered}
^
The writer corrected this fragment by adding a subject — *he* — and substituting verbs for the verbals *working* and *suffering.*

G5-d Exception: A fragment may be used for effect.

Writers occasionally use sentence fragments for special purposes.

FOR EMPHASIS	Following the dramatic Americanization of their children, even my parents grew more publicly confident. *Especially my mother.* — Richard Rodriguez
TO ANSWER A QUESTION	Are these new drug tests 100 percent reliable? *Not in the opinion of most experts.*
TRANSITIONS	*And now the opposing arguments.*
EXCLAMATIONS	*Not again!*
IN ADVERTISING	*Fewer carbs. Improved taste.*

Although fragments are sometimes appropriate, writers and readers do not always agree on when they are appropriate. That's why you will find it safer to write in complete sentences.

G6 Run-on sentences

Run-on sentences are independent clauses that have not been joined correctly. An independent clause is a word group that can stand alone as a sentence. (See B4-a.) When two independent clauses appear in one sentence, they must be joined in one of these ways:

- with a comma and a coordinating conjunction (*and, but, or, nor, for, so, yet*)
- with a semicolon (or occasionally with a colon or a dash)

Recognizing run-on sentences

There are two types of run-on sentences. When a writer puts no mark of punctuation and no coordinating conjunction between independent clauses, the result is called a *fused sentence.*

FUSED   ┌────── INDEPENDENT CLAUSE ──────┐ ┌──────
Air pollution poses risks to all humans it can be

─ INDEPENDENT CLAUSE ─┐
deadly for asthma sufferers.

LaunchPad **ACTIVITIES FOR G6**
macmillan learning
9 Exercises, 1 LearningCurve activity

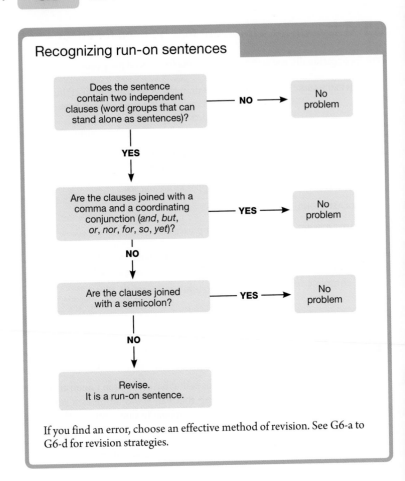

Recognizing run-on sentences

Does the sentence contain two independent clauses (word groups that can stand alone as sentences)? — **NO** → No problem

YES ↓

Are the clauses joined with a comma and a coordinating conjunction (*and, but, or, nor, for, so, yet*)? — **YES** → No problem

NO ↓

Are the clauses joined with a semicolon? — **YES** → No problem

NO ↓

Revise. It is a run-on sentence.

If you find an error, choose an effective method of revision. See G6-a to G6-d for revision strategies.

A far more common type of run-on sentence is the *comma splice* — two or more independent clauses joined with a comma but without a coordinating conjunction. In some comma splices, the comma appears alone.

> **COMMA SPLICE** Air pollution poses risks to all humans, it can be deadly for asthma sufferers.

In other comma splices, the comma is accompanied by a joining word that is *not* a coordinating conjunction. There are only seven coordinating conjunctions in English: *and, but, or, nor, for, so,* and *yet*.

> **COMMA SPLICE** Air pollution poses risks to all humans, however, it can be deadly for asthma sufferers.

However is a transitional expression, not a coordinating conjunction, and cannot be used with only a comma to join two independent clauses (see G6-b).

Writer's Choice
Clustering ideas in meaningful ways

When you draft, you may rush to write down your ideas before you forget them. Writers at all levels of experience do this. When you're generating ideas, you may not worry too much about grammar and punctuation, so you may end up with some run-on sentences. In later drafts you will need to revise so that your **audience** understands your meaning.

RUN-ON SENTENCE	Students can succeed in college or university by attending classes and keeping up with homework, visiting instructors during office hours can also be important, participating in campus events and clubs can help students succeed, too.

Several ideas compete for attention in this draft sentence:

- Students can succeed in college or university.
- Attending classes is important.
- Doing homework is important.
- Visiting instructors during office hours is important.
- Participating in campus events can help students succeed.
- Participating in campus clubs can help students succeed.

As a writer, ask yourself: How can I cluster the ideas in a way that best communicates my meaning?

POSSIBLE REVISION	Students can succeed in college or university by attending classes and keeping up with homework, by visiting instructors during office hours, and by participating in campus events and clubs.
POSSIBLE REVISION	In addition to attending class and keeping up with homework, students can succeed in college by visiting instructors during office hours. Participating in campus events and clubs is another way to foster success.

In each revision, the ideas are clustered, making the passage easier to read. The first revision places equal emphasis on all the different actions students can take to succeed in college. The second revision focuses on the importance of communicating with instructors.

Identifying, separating, and grouping ideas — all with your **purpose** and **audience** in mind — can help you revise run-on sentences.

Revising run-on sentences

To revise a run-on sentence, you have four choices.

1. Use a comma and a coordinating conjunction (*and, but, or, nor, for, so, yet*).

    ▶ Air pollution poses risks to all humans, _{but} it can be deadly for

    people with asthma.

2. Use a semicolon (or, if appropriate, a colon or a dash). A semicolon may be used alone; it can also be accompanied by a transitional expression.

    ▶ Air pollution poses risks to all humans/; it can be deadly for

    people with asthma.

    ▶ Air pollution poses risks to all humans/; _{however,} it can be deadly for

    people with asthma.

3. Make the clauses into separate sentences.

    ▶ Air pollution poses risks to all humans/. _{It} ~~it~~ can be deadly for

    people with asthma.

4. Restructure the sentence; try subordinating a clause.

    ▶ _{Although air} ~~Air~~ pollution poses risks to all humans, it can be deadly for

    people with asthma.

One of these revision techniques usually works better than the others for a particular sentence. The fourth technique, the one requiring the most extensive revision, is often the most effective.

G6-a Consider separating the clauses with a comma and a coordinating conjunction.

There are seven coordinating conjunctions in English: *and, but, or, nor, for, so,* and *yet.* When a coordinating conjunction joins independent clauses, it is usually preceded by a comma. (See P1-a.)

▶ Some lesson plans include exercises, _{but} completing them should not

be the focus of all class periods.

▶ Many law enforcement officials admit that the polygraph is

unreliable, ~~however,~~ *yet* they still use it as an assessment tool.

However is a transitional expression, not a coordinating conjunction, so it cannot be used with only a comma to join independent clauses. (See also G6-b.)

G6-b Consider separating the clauses with a semicolon, a colon, or a dash.

When the independent clauses are closely related and their relation is clear without a coordinating conjunction, a semicolon is an acceptable method of revision. (See P3-a.)

▶ Tragedy depicts the individual confronted with the fact of

death/; comedy depicts the adaptability of human nature.

A semicolon is required between independent clauses that have been linked with a transitional expression such as *however, therefore, moreover, in fact,* or *for example.* (For a longer list, see p. 272.)

▶ In his film adaptation, the director changed key details of the

plot/; in fact, he added whole scenes that do not appear in the

story.

A colon or a dash may be more appropriate if the first independent clause introduces the second or if the second clause summarizes or explains the first. (See P3-d and P6-b.) In formal writing, the colon is usually preferred to the dash.

▶ Nuclear waste is hazardous; ~~this~~ *This* is an indisputable fact.

▶ The female black widow spider is often a widow of her own

making/she has been known to eat her partner after mating.

A colon is an appropriate method of revision if the first independent clause introduces a quoted sentence.

▶ Saul Bellow, winner of the Nobel Prize for Literature, had this to say

about characters/: "We all know what it is to be tired of 'characters.'

Human types have become false and boring."

G6-c Consider making the clauses into separate sentences.

> We
> ▶ Why should we spend money on space exploration/? ~~we~~ have
>   ^
>
> enough underfunded programs here on Earth.

A question and a statement should be separate sentences.

> ▶ Some studies have suggested that sexual relationships set
>   According
> bonobos apart from common chimpanzees/. ~~according~~ to
>   ^
> some scientists, these differences have been exaggerated.

Using a comma alone to join two independent clauses creates a comma splice.

NOTE: When two quoted independent clauses are divided by explanatory words, make each clause its own sentence.

> ▶ "It's always smart to learn from your mistakes," my supervisor
>   "It's
> declared/. ~~"it's~~ even smarter to learn from the mistakes of others."
>   ^

G6-d Consider restructuring the sentence, perhaps by subordinating one of the clauses.

If one of the independent clauses is less important than the other, turn the less important clause into a subordinate clause or phrase. (For more about subordination, see S6, especially the chart on p. 131.)

> ▶ One of the most famous advertising slogans is Wheaties cereal's
>   which
> "Breakfast of Champions," ~~it~~ associated the cereal with famous
>   ^
> athletes.

> ▶ Alfred Fitzpatrick , was a reverend and a pioneer in education, ~~he~~
>   ^
> founded Frontier College in 1899.

Minor ideas in these sentences are now expressed in subordinate clauses or phrases.

M

Multilingual Writers and ESL Topics

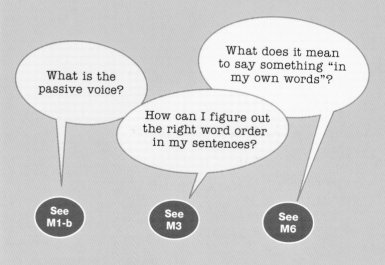

What is the passive voice?

See M1-b

What does it mean to say something "in my own words"?

See M6

How can I figure out the right word order in my sentences?

See M3

Multilingual Writers and ESL Topics

This section of *A Canadian Writer's Reference* is primarily for multilingual writers. You may find this section helpful if you learned English as a second language (ESL) or if you speak a language other than English with your friends and family.

M1 Verbs

Both native and nonnative speakers of English encounter challenges with verbs. Section M1 focuses on specific challenges that multilingual writers sometimes face. You can find more help with verbs in other sections in the book:

making subjects and verbs agree (G1)

using irregular verb forms (G2-a, G2-b)

using correct verb endings (G2-c, G2-d)

choosing the correct verb tense (G2-f)

avoiding inappropriate uses of the passive voice (W3-a)

M1-a Use the appropriate verb form and tense.

This section offers a brief review of English verb forms and tenses. For additional help, see G2-f and B1-c.

Basic verb forms

Every main verb in English has five forms, which are used to create all of the verb tenses in Standard English. The following chart shows these forms for the regular verb *help* and the irregular verbs *give* and *be*. See G2-a for a list of common irregular verbs.

Basic verb forms

	Regular verb *help*	Irregular verb *give*	Irregular verb *be**
BASE FORM	help	give	be
PAST TENSE	helped	gave	was, were
PAST PARTICIPLE	helped	given	been
PRESENT PARTICIPLE	helping	giving	being
-S FORM	helps	gives	is

Be also has the forms *am* and *are*, which are used in the present tense.

Verb tenses commonly used in the active voice

For descriptions and examples of all verb tenses, see G2-f. For verb tenses commonly used in the passive voice, see the chart on page 225.

Simple tenses

For general facts, states of being, habitual actions

Simple present	**Base form or -s form**
● general facts	University students often *study* late at night.
● states of being	Water *becomes* steam at 100 degrees Celsius.
● habitual, repetitive actions	We *donate* to a different charity each year.
● scheduled future events	The train *arrives* tomorrow at 6:30 p.m.

NOTE: For other uses of the present tense, see page 188.

Simple past	**Base form + -ed or -d or irregular form**
● actions completed at a specific time in the past	The storm *destroyed* their property. She *drove* to Montreal three years ago.
● facts or states of being in the past	When I *was* young, I usually *walked* to school with my sister.

Simple future	***will* + base form**
● future actions, promises, or predictions	I *will exercise* tomorrow. The snowfall *will begin* around midnight.

Simple progressive forms

For continuing actions

Present progressive	***am, is, are* + present participle**
● actions in progress at the present time, not continuing indefinitely	The students *are taking* an exam in Room 105. The valet *is parking* the car.
● future actions (with *leave, go, come, move*, etc.)	I *am leaving* tomorrow morning.

Past progressive	***was, were* + present participle**
● actions in progress at a specific time in the past	They *were swimming* when the storm struck.
● *was going to, were going to* for past plans that did not happen	We *were going to* drive to Banff for March Break, but the car broke down.

Verb tenses commonly used in the active voice, *continued*

NOTE: Some verbs are not normally used in the progressive: *appear, believe, belong, contain, have, hear, know, like, need, see, seem, taste, understand,* and *want.*

> want
> ► I ~~am wanting~~ to see August Wilson's *Radio Golf.*
>   ∧

Perfect tenses

For actions that happened before another present or past time

Present perfect   *has, have* + past participle

- repetitive or constant actions that began in the past and continue to the present

  I *have loved* cats since I was a child.
  Amy *has worked* in Kenya for ten years.

- actions that happened at an unknown or unspecific time in the past

  Ola *has visited* Aleppo three times.

Past perfect   *had* + past participle

- actions that began or occurred before another time in the past

  She *had* just *crossed* the street when the runaway car crashed into the building.

NOTE: For more on the past perfect, see G2-f. For uses of the past perfect in conditional sentences, see M1-e.

Perfect progressive forms

For continuous past actions before another present or past time

Present perfect progressive   *has, have* + *been* + present participle

- continuous actions that began in the past and continue to the present

  Yolanda *has been trying* to get a job in Toronto for five years.

Past perfect progressive   *had* + *been* + present participle

- actions that began and continued in the past until another past action

  By the time I moved to British Columbia, I *had been supporting* myself for five years.

Verb tenses

Section G2-f describes all the verb tenses in English, showing the forms of a regular verb (*walk*), an irregular verb (*ride*), and the verb *be* in each tense. The chart on pages 222–23 provides more details about the tenses commonly used in the active voice in writing; the chart on page 225 gives details about tenses commonly used in the passive voice.

M1-b To write a verb in the passive voice, use a form of *be* with the past participle.

When a sentence is written in the passive voice, the subject receives the action instead of doing it. (See W3-a.)

> The solution *was measured* by the lab assistant.

> The picnic *has been rescheduled* twice because of rain.

To form the passive voice, use a form of *be*—*am, is, are, was, were, being, be,* or *been*—followed by the past participle of the main verb: *was chosen, are remembered.* (Sometimes a form of *be* follows another helping verb: *will be considered, could have been broken.*)

>   written
> ▶ *Dreaming in Cuban* was ~~writing~~ by Cristina García.
>   ^

In the passive voice, the past participle *written*, not the present participle *writing*, must follow *was* (the past tense of *be*).

>   tested.
> ▶ The child is being ~~test.~~
>   ^

The past participle *tested*, not the base form *test*, must be used with *is being* to form the passive voice.

For details on forming the passive voice in various tenses, consult the chart on page 225. (The active voice is generally stronger and more direct than the passive. The passive voice does have appropriate uses; see W3-a.)

> ▶ The accident ~~was~~ happened suddenly.

Verb tenses commonly used in the passive voice

For details about commonly used verb tenses in the active voice, see the chart on pages 222–23.

Simple tenses (passive voice)

Simple present

- general facts
- habitual, repetitive actions

am, is, are + past participle
Breakfast *is served* daily.
The receipts *are counted* every night.

Simple past

- completed past actions

was, were + past participle
He *was punished* for being late.

Simple future

- future actions, promises, or predictions

will be + past participle
The decision *will be made* by the committee next week.

Simple progressive forms (passive voice)

Present progressive

- actions in progress at the present time
- future actions (with *leave, go, come, move,* etc.)

am, is, are + *being* + past participle
The new stadium *is being built* with private money.
Jo *is being moved* to a new class next month.

Past progressive

- actions in progress at a specific time in the past

was, were + *being* + past participle
We thought we *were being followed*.

Perfect tenses (passive voice)

Present perfect

- actions that began in the past and continue to the present
- actions that happened at an unknown or unspecific time in the past

has, have + *been* + past participle
The flight *has been delayed* because of storms over the Prairies.

Wars *have been fought* throughout history.

Past perfect

- actions that began or occurred before another time in the past

had + *been* + past participle
He *had been given* all the hints he needed to complete the puzzle.

NOTE: Future progressive, future perfect, and perfect progressive forms are not used in the passive voice.

M1-c Use the base form of the verb after a modal.

The modal verbs are *can, could, may, might, must, shall, should, will,* and *would.* (*Ought to* is also considered a modal verb.) The modals are used with the base form of a verb to show ability, certainty, necessity, permission, obligation, or possibility.

Modals and the verbs that follow them do not change form to indicate tense. For a summary of modals and their meanings, see the chart below. (See also G2-e.)

▶ The art museum will ~~launches~~ ^launch^ its fundraising campaign next month.

The modal *will* must be followed by the base form *launch,* not the present-tense form *launches.*

▶ The translator could ~~spoke~~ ^speak^ many languages, so the ambassador hired her for the European tour.

The modal *could* must be followed by the base form *speak,* not the past-tense form *spoke.*

TIP: Do not use *to* before a main verb that follows a modal.

▶ Gina can ~~to~~ drive us home if we miss the last train.

For the use of modals in conditional sentences, see M1-e.

Modals and their meanings

can
- general ability (present)

  Ants *can survive* anywhere, even in space. Jorge *can run* a marathon faster than his brother.
- informal requests or permission

  Can you *tell* me where the light is? Sandy *can borrow* my calculator.

could
- general ability (past)

  Lea *could read* when she was only three years old.
- polite, informal requests or permission

  Could you *give* me that pen?

Modals and their meanings, *continued*

may

- formal requests or permission
- possibility

May I *see* the report? Students *may park* only in the yellow zone.

I *may try* to finish my homework tonight, or I *may wake up* early and *finish* it tomorrow.

might

- possibility

Funding for the language lab *might double* by 2021.

NOTE: *Might* usually expresses a stronger possibility than *may*.

must

- necessity (present or future)
- strong probability
- near certainty (present or past)

To be effective, welfare-to-work programs *must provide* access to job training.

Amy *must be* nervous. [She is probably nervous.]

I *must have left* my wallet at home. [I almost certainly left my wallet at home.]

should

- suggestions or advice
- obligations or duties
- expectations

People *should drink* plenty of water every day.

The government *should protect* citizens' rights.

The books *should arrive* soon. [We expect the books to arrive soon.]

will

- certainty
- requests
- promises and offers

If you don't leave now, you *will be* late for your rehearsal.

Will you *help* me study for my psychology exam?

Jonah *will arrange* the carpool.

would

- polite requests
- habitual or repeated actions (in the past)

Would you *help* me carry these books? I *would like* some tea. [*Would like* is more polite than *want*.]

Whenever Elena needed help with sewing, she *would call* her aunt.

M1-d To make negative verb forms, add *not* in the appropriate place.

If the verb is the simple present or past tense of *be* (*am, is, are, was, were*), add *not* after the verb.

George is *not* a member of the club.

For simple present-tense verbs other than *be*, use *do* or *does* plus *not* before the base form of the verb. (For the correct forms of *do* and *does,* see the chart in G1-a.)

> does
> ▶ Mariko not want more dessert.

> ▶ Mariko does not wants more dessert.

For simple past-tense verbs other than *be*, use *did* plus *not* before the base form of the verb.

> plant
> ▶ They did not planted corn this year.

In a verb phrase consisting of one or more helping verbs and a present or past participle (*is watching, were living, has played, could have been driven*), use the word *not* after the first helping verb.

> not
> ▶ Inna should have not gone dancing last night.

> not
> ▶ Bonnie is no singing this weekend.

NOTE: English allows only one negative in an independent clause to express a negative idea; using more than one is an error known as a *double negative* (see G4-e).

> any
> ▶ We could not find no books about the history of our school.

M1-e In a conditional sentence, choose verb tenses according to the type of condition expressed in the sentence.

Conditional sentences contain two clauses: a subordinate clause (usually starting with *if, when,* or *unless*) and an independent clause. The subordinate clause (sometimes called the *if* or *unless* clause) states the condition or cause;

the independent clause states the result or effect. In each example in this section, the subordinate clause (*if* clause) is marked SUB, and the independent clause is marked IND. (See B3-e, on subordinate clauses.)

Factual

Factual conditional sentences express relationships based on facts. If the relationship is a scientific truth, use the present tense in both clauses.

> ┌──────────── SUB ────────────┐ ┌─IND─┐
> If water *cools* to 0 degrees Celsius, it *freezes.*

If the sentence describes a condition that is (or was) habitually true, use the same tense in both clauses.

> ┌──────────── SUB ────────────┐ ┌──────────── IND ────────────┐
> When Sue *jogs* along the canal, her dog *runs* ahead of her.

> ┌──────────── SUB ────────────┐ ┌──IND──┐
> Whenever the coach *asked* for help, I *volunteered.*

Predictive

Predictive conditional sentences are used to predict the future or to express future plans or possibilities. To form a predictive sentence, use a present-tense verb in the subordinate clause; in the independent clause, use the modal *will, can, may, should,* or *might* plus the base form of the verb.

> ┌──────── SUB ────────┐ ┌──────── IND ────────┐
> If you *practise* regularly, your tennis game *should improve.*

> ┌──────────── IND ────────────┐ ┌──── SUB ────┐
> We *will lose* our remaining wetlands unless we *act* now.

TIP: In all types of conditional sentences (factual, predictive, and speculative), *if* or *unless* clauses do not use the modal verb *will.*

>   passes
> ▶ If Liv ~~will pass~~ her history test, she will graduate this year.
>   ^

Speculative

Speculative conditional sentences express unlikely, contrary-to-fact, or impossible conditions. English uses the past or past perfect tense in the *if* clause, even for conditions in the present or the future.

UNLIKELY POSSIBILITIES   If the condition is possible but unlikely in the present or the future, use the past tense in the subordinate clause; in the independent clause, use *would*, *could*, or *might* plus the base form of the verb.

┌──────SUB──────┐ ┌──────IND──────┐
If I *won* the lottery, I *would travel* to Egypt.

The writer does not expect to win the lottery. Because this is a possible but unlikely present or future situation, the past tense is used in the subordinate clause.

CONDITIONS CONTRARY TO FACT   In conditions that are currently unreal or contrary to fact, use the past-tense verb *were* (not *was*) in the *if* clause for all subjects. (See also G2-g, on the subjunctive mood.)

▶ If I ~~was~~ *were* prime minister, I would make student loan debt a priority.

The writer is not prime minister, so *were* is correct in the *if* clause.

EVENTS THAT DID NOT HAPPEN   In a conditional sentence that speculates about an event that did not happen or was impossible in the past, use the past perfect tense in the *if* clause; in the independent clause, use *would have*, *could have*, or *might have* with the past participle. (See also past perfect tense, p. 223.)

┌──────SUB──────┐ ┌──────IND──────┐
If I *had saved* more money, I *would have visited* Laos last year.

The writer did not save more money and did not travel to Laos. This sentence shows a possibility that did not happen.

M1-f Become familiar with verbs that may be followed by gerunds or infinitives.

A gerund is a verb form that ends in *-ing* and is used as a noun: *sleeping, dreaming*. An infinitive is the word *to* plus the base form of the verb: *to sleep, to dream*. The word *to* is an infinitive marker, not a preposition, in this use. (See B3-b.)

A few verbs may be followed by either a gerund or an infinitive; others may be followed by a gerund but not by an infinitive; still others may be followed by an infinitive but not by a gerund.

Verb + gerund or infinitive (no change in meaning)

The following commonly used verbs may be followed by a gerund or an infinitive, with little or no difference in meaning:

begin	hate	love
continue	like	start

I love *skiing*. I love *to ski*.

Verb + gerund or infinitive (change in meaning)

With a few verbs, the choice of a gerund or an infinitive changes the meaning dramatically:

forget	stop
remember	try

She stopped *speaking* to Lucia. [She no longer spoke to Lucia.]

She stopped *to speak* to Lucia. [She paused so that she could speak to Lucia.]

Verb + gerund

These verbs may be followed by a gerund but not by an infinitive:

admit	discuss	imagine	put off	risk
appreciate	enjoy	miss	quit	suggest
avoid	escape	postpone	recall	tolerate
deny	finish	practise	resist	

Bill enjoys *playing* [not *to play*] the piano.

Jamie quit *smoking*.

Verb + infinitive

These verbs may be followed by an infinitive but not by a gerund:

agree	decide	manage	plan	wait
ask	expect	mean	pretend	want
beg	help	need	promise	wish
claim	hope	offer	refuse	would like

Jill has offered *to water* [not *watering*] the plants while we are away.

Joe finally managed *to find* a parking space.

A few of these verbs may be followed either by an infinitive directly or by a noun or pronoun plus an infinitive:

ask	help	promise	would like
expect	need	want	

We asked *to speak* to the congregation.

We asked *Rabbi Abrams to speak* to our congregation.

Verb + noun or pronoun + infinitive

With certain verbs in the active voice, a noun or pronoun must come between the verb and the infinitive that follows it. The noun or pronoun usually names a person who is affected by the action of the verb.

advise	instruct
allow	order
cause	persuade
command	remind
convince	require
encourage	tell
have ("own")	warn

$$\overset{\text{V}}{\text{The class}} \underset{}{\text{encouraged}} \overset{\text{N}}{\text{Luis}} \overset{\lceil\text{INF}\rceil}{\text{to tell}} \text{ the story of his escape.}$$

The counsellor *advised Haley to take* four courses instead of five.

Verb + noun or pronoun + unmarked infinitive

An unmarked infinitive is an infinitive without *to*. A few verbs (often called *causative verbs*) may be followed by a noun or pronoun and an unmarked infinitive.

have ("cause")
help
let ("allow")
make ("force")

▶ **Rose had the attendant ~~to~~ wash the windshield.**

▶ **Frank made me ~~to~~ carry his book for him.**

Help can be followed by a noun or pronoun and either an unmarked or a marked infinitive.

Emma *helped Brian wash* the dishes.

Emma *helped Brian to wash* the dishes.

NOTE: The infinitive is used in some typical constructions with *too* and *enough*.

TOO + ADJECTIVE + INFINITIVE
The gift is *too large to wrap.*

ENOUGH + NOUN + INFINITIVE
Our emergency pack has *enough bottled water to last* a week.

ADJECTIVE + *ENOUGH* + INFINITIVE
Some of the hikers felt *strong enough to climb* another thousand feet.

M2 Articles

Articles (*a, an, the*) are part of a category of words known as *noun markers* or *determiners*.

M2-a Be familiar with articles and other noun markers.

Standard English uses noun markers to help identify the nouns that follow. In addition to articles (*a, an,* and *the*), noun markers include the following, which are covered in other sections of this book:

- possessive nouns, such as *Elena's* (P4-a)
- possessive pronoun/adjectives: *my, your, his, her, its, our, their* (B1-b)
- demonstrative pronoun/adjectives: *this, that, these, those* (B1-b)
- quantifiers: *all, any, each, either, every, few, many, more, most, much, neither, several, some,* and so on (M2-d)
- numbers: *one, twenty-three,* and so on

Using articles and other noun markers

Articles and other noun markers always appear before nouns; sometimes other modifiers, such as adjectives and adverbs, come between a noun marker and a noun.

>   ART N
> Felix is reading a book about mythology.

>   ART ADJ   N
> We took an exciting trip to Yukon last summer.

> NOUN
> MARKER ADV   ADJ   N
> That very delicious meal was expensive.

In most cases, do not use an article with another noun marker.

▶ ~~The~~ Natalie's older brother lives in Alberta.

Expressions like *a few, the most,* and *all the* are exceptions: *a few potatoes, all the rain.* See also M2-d.

Types of articles and types of nouns

To choose an appropriate article for a noun, first determine whether the noun is *common* or *proper, count* or *noncount, singular* or *plural,* and *specific* or *general.* The chart on pages 236–37 describes the types of nouns.

Articles are classified as *indefinite* and *definite.* The indefinite articles, *a* and *an,* are used with general nouns. The definite article, *the,* is used with specific nouns. (The last section of the chart on p. 237 explains general and specific nouns.)

A and *an* both mean "one" or "one among many." Use *a* before a consonant sound: *a banana, a vacation, a happy child, a united family.* Use *an* before a vowel sound: *an eggplant, an uncle, an honourable person.* (See also *a, an* in W1.)

The shows that a noun is specific; use *the* with one or more than one specific thing: *the newspaper, the soldiers.*

M2-b Use *the* with most specific common nouns.

The definite article, *the,* is used with most nouns—both count and noncount—that the reader can identify specifically. Usually the identity will be clear to the reader for one of the following reasons. (See also the chart on p. 238.)

1. The noun has been previously mentioned.

                                       the

▶ A truck cut in front of our van. When truck skidded a few seconds

   later, we almost crashed into it.

     The article *A* is used before *truck* when the noun is first mentioned. When the noun is mentioned again, it needs the article *the* because readers can now identify which truck skidded—the one that cut in front of the van.

2. A phrase or clause following the noun restricts its identity.

▶ Bryce warned me that $\overset{the}{\underset{\wedge}{GPS}}$ in his car was not working.

The phrase *in his car* identifies the specific GPS.

NOTE: Descriptive adjectives do not necessarily make a noun specific. A specific noun is one that readers can identify within a group of nouns of the same type.

▶ If I win the lottery, I will buy $\overset{a}{\underset{\wedge}{\text{the}}}$ brand-new bright red sports car.

The reader cannot identify which specific brand-new bright red sports car the writer will buy. Even though *car* has many adjectives in front of it, it is a general noun in this sentence.

3. A superlative adjective such as *best* or *most intelligent* makes the noun's identity specific. (See also G4-d.)

▶ Our petite daughter dated $\overset{the}{\underset{\wedge}{\text{tallest}}}$ boy in her class.

The superlative *tallest* makes the noun *boy* specific. Although there might be several tall boys, only one boy can be the tallest.

4. The noun describes a unique person, place, or thing.

▶ During an eclipse, one should not look directly at $\overset{the}{\underset{\wedge}{\text{sun}}}$.

There is only one sun in our solar system, so its identity is clear.

5. The context or situation makes the noun's identity clear.

▶ Please don't slam $\overset{the}{\underset{\wedge}{\text{door}}}$ when you leave.

Both the speaker and the listener know which door is meant.

6. The noun is singular and refers to a scientific class or category of items (most often animals, musical instruments, and inventions).

▶ $\overset{The\ tin}{\underset{\wedge}{\text{Tin}}}$ whistle is common in traditional Irish music.

The writer is referring to the tin whistle as a class of musical instruments.

Types of nouns

Common or proper

Common nouns	Examples	
• name general persons, places, things, or ideas	religion	beauty
	knowledge	student
• begin with lowercase	rain	country

Proper nouns	Examples	
• name specific persons, places, things, or ideas	Hinduism	Prime Minister Pearson
	Philip	CN Tower
	Yellowknife	Supreme Court
• begin with capital letter	Vietnam	Renaissance

Count or noncount (common nouns only)

Count nouns	Examples
• name persons, places, things, or ideas that can be counted	girl, girls
	city, cities
	goose, geese
• have plural forms	philosophy, philosophies

Noncount nouns	Examples	
• name things or abstract ideas that cannot be counted	water	patience
	silver	knowledge
	furniture	air
• cannot be made plural		

NOTE: See the chart on page 239 for lists of commonly used noncount nouns.

Singular or plural (both common and proper)

Singular nouns (count and noncount)	Examples	
• represent one person, place, thing, or idea	backpack	rain
	country	beauty
	woman	Nile River
	achievement	Salt Spring Island

Plural nouns (count only)	Examples	
• represent more than one person, place, thing, or idea	backpacks	Ural Mountains
	countries	Falkland Islands
	women	achievements
• must be count nouns		

Types of nouns, *continued*

Specific (definite) or general (indefinite) (count and noncount)

Specific nouns

- name persons, places, things, or ideas that can be identified within a group of the same type

Examples

The students in Professor Martin's *class* should study.

The airplane carrying *the senator* was late.

The furniture in *the truck* was damaged.

General nouns

- name categories of persons, places, things, or ideas (often plural)

Examples

Students should study.

Books bridge *gaps* between *cultures*.

The airplane has made commuting between *cities* easy.

M2-c Use *a* (or *an*) with common singular count nouns that refer to "one" or "any."

If a count noun refers to one unspecific item (not a whole category), use the indefinite article, *a* or *an*. *A* and *an* usually mean "one among many" but can also mean "any one." (See also the chart on p. 238.)

▶ My English professor asked me to bring ^a^ dictionary to class.

> The noun *dictionary* refers to "one unspecific dictionary" or "any dictionary."

▶ We want to rent ^an^ apartment close to the lake.

> The noun *apartment* refers to "any apartment close to the lake," not a specific apartment.

Choosing articles for common nouns

Use *the*

- if the reader has enough information to identify the noun specifically

COUNT: Please turn on *the lights*. We're going to *the zoo* tomorrow.

NONCOUNT: *The food* throughout Italy is excellent.

Use *a* or *an*

- if the noun refers to one item *and* if the item is singular but not specific

COUNT: Bring *a pencil* to class. Charles wrote *an essay* about his first job.

NOTE: Do not use *a* or *an* with plural or noncount nouns.

Use a quantifier (*enough, many, some,* etc.)

- if the noun represents an unspecified amount of something
- if the amount is more than one but not all items in a category

COUNT (PLURAL): Amir showed us *some photos* of India. *Many turtles* return to the same nesting site each year.

NONCOUNT: We didn't get *enough rain* this summer.

NOTE: Sometimes no article conveys an unspecified amount: *Amir showed us photos of India.*

Use no article

- if the noun represents all items in a category
- if the noun represents a category in general

COUNT (PLURAL): *Students* can attend the show for free.

NONCOUNT: *Coal* is a natural resource.

NOTE: *The* is occasionally used when a singular count noun refers to all items in a class or a specific category: *The North Atlantic right whale is endangered in Canada.*

Commonly used noncount nouns

Food and drink

beef, bread, butter, candy, cereal, cheese, cream, meat, milk, pasta, rice, salt, sugar, water, wine

Nonfood substances

air, cement, coal, dirt, gasoline, gold, paper, petroleum, plastic, rain, silver, snow, soap, steel, wood, wool

Abstract nouns

advice, anger, beauty, confidence, courage, employment, fun, happiness, health, honesty, information, intelligence, knowledge, love, poverty, satisfaction, wealth

Other

biology (and other areas of study), clothing, equipment, furniture, homework, jewellery, luggage, machinery, mail, money, news, poetry, pollution, research, scenery, traffic, transportation, violence, weather, work

NOTE: A few noncount nouns (such as *love*) can also be used as count nouns: *He had two loves: music and archery.*

M2-d Use a quantifier such as *some* or *more*, not *a* or *an*, with a noncount noun to express an approximate amount.

Do not use *a* or *an* with noncount nouns. Also do not use numbers or words such as *several* or *many*; they must be used with plural nouns, and noncount nouns do not have plural forms. (See the chart above for lists of commonly used noncount nouns.)

▶ Dr. Snyder gave us ~~an~~ information about Cuso International.

▶ Do you have ~~many~~ money with you?

You can use quantifiers such as *enough, less,* and *some* to suggest approximate amounts or nonspecific quantities of noncount nouns: *a little salt, any homework, enough wood, less information, much pollution.*

M2-e Do not use articles with nouns that refer to all of something or to something in general.

When a noncount noun refers to all of its type or to a concept in general, it is not marked with an article.

> Kindness
> ▶ ~~The kindness~~ is a virtue.
>   ∧
>
> The noun represents kindness in general; it does not represent a specific type of kindness, such as *the kindness he showed me after my mother's death*.

> ▶ In some places, ~~the~~ rice is preferred to all other grains.
>
> The noun *rice* represents rice in general. To refer to a specific type or serving of rice, the definite article is appropriate: *The rice my husband served last night is the best I've ever tasted.*

In most cases, when you use a count noun to represent a general category, make the noun plural. Do not use unmarked singular count nouns to represent whole categories.

> Fountains are
> ▶ ~~Fountain is~~ an expensive element of landscape design.
>   ∧
>
> *Fountains* is a count noun that represents fountains in general.

EXCEPTION: In some cases, *the* can be used with singular count nouns to represent a class or specific category: *The Chinese alligator is smaller than the American alligator.* See also number 6 in M2-b.

M2-f Do not use articles with most singular proper nouns. Use *the* with most plural proper nouns.

Since singular proper nouns are already specific, they typically do not need an article: *Prime Minister Trudeau, Jamaica, Lake Huron, Mount Etna.*

There are, however, many exceptions. In most cases, if the proper noun consists of a common noun with modifiers (adjectives or an *of* phrase), use *the* with the proper noun.

> the
> ▶ We visited Great Wall of China last year.
>   ∧

> the
> ▶ Rob wants to be a translator for Canadian Security Intelligence Service.
>   ∧

The is used with most plural proper nouns: *the McGregors, the Bahamas, the Finger Lakes, the Northwest Territories.*

Using *the* with geographic nouns

When to omit *the*

streets, squares, parks	Ivy Street, Union Square, Glacier National Park
cities, provinces and most territories, counties	Halifax, Saskatchewan, Bee County
most countries, continents	Italy, China, South America, Africa
bays, single lakes	Hudson Bay, Lake Geneva
single mountains, islands	Mount Everest, Crete

When to use *the*

country names with *of* phrase	the United States (of America), the People's Republic of China
large regions, deserts	the East Coast, the Sahara
peninsulas	the Bruce Peninsula, the Avalon Peninsula
oceans, seas, gulfs	the Pacific Ocean, the Dead Sea, the Persian Gulf
canals and rivers	the Panama Canal, the Amazon
mountain ranges	the Rocky Mountains, the Alps
groups of islands	the Thousand Islands

Geographic names create problems because there are so many exceptions to the rules. When in doubt, consult the chart above, check a dictionary, or ask a native speaker.

M3 Sentence structure

Although their structure can vary widely, sentences in English generally flow from subject to verb to object or complement: *Bears eat fish.* This section focuses on the major challenges that multilingual students face when writing sentences in English. For more details on the parts of speech and the elements of sentences, consult sections B1–B4.

M3-a Use a linking verb between a subject and its complement.

Some languages, such as Russian and Turkish, do not use linking verbs (*is*, *are*, *was*, *were*) between subjects and complements (nouns or adjectives that rename or describe the subject). Every English sentence, however, must include a verb. For more on linking verbs, see G2-e.

> ▶ Jim ^is^ intelligent.

> ▶ Many streets in San Francisco ^are^ very steep.

M3-b Include a subject in every sentence.

Some languages, such as Spanish and Japanese, do not require a subject in every sentence. Every English sentence, however, needs a subject.

> ▶ Your aunt is very energetic. ~~Seems~~ ^She seems^ young for her age.

Commands are an exception: The subject *you* is understood but not present in the sentence.

> [You] Give me the book.

The word *it* is used as the subject of a sentence describing the weather or temperature, stating the time, indicating distance, or suggesting an environmental fact.

> ▶ ~~Is~~ ^It is^ raining in the valley and snowing in the mountains.

> ▶ ~~Is~~ ^It is^ 9:15 a.m.

In most English sentences, the subject appears before the verb. Some sentences, however, are inverted: The subject comes after the verb. In these sentences, a placeholder called an *expletive* (*there* or *it*) often comes before the verb.

> EXP　V　┌──S──┐
> There are many people here today.

> ┌──S──┐　V
> (Many people are here today.)

There is
▶ ~~Is~~ an apple pie in the refrigerator.
 ^

 there are
▶ As you know, ~~~~many religious sects in India.
 ^

Notice that the verb agrees with the subject that follows it: *apple pie is, sects are.* (See G1-g.)

Sometimes an inverted sentence has an infinitive (*to work*) or a noun clause (*that she is intelligent*) as the subject. In such sentences, the placeholder *it* is needed before the verb. (See also B3-b and B3-e.)

EXP V ┌─ S ─┐
 It is important to study daily.

 ┌─ S ─┐ V
 (To study daily is important.)

 it
▶ Because the road is flooded, is necessary to change our route.
 ^

TIP: The words *here* and *there* can be used as placeholders, but they cannot be used as subjects. When they mean "in this place" (*here*) or "in that place" (*there*), they are adverbs, which are never subjects.

 It there.
▶ I just returned from Japan. ~~There~~ is very beautiful~~/~~
 ^ ^

 This school that school
▶ ~~Here~~ offers a master's degree in physical therapy; ~~there~~ has
 ^ ^

 only a bachelor's program.

M3-c Do not use both a noun and a pronoun to perform the same grammatical function in a sentence.

English does not allow a subject to be repeated in its own clause.

▶ The doctor ~~she~~ advised me to cut down on salt.

The pronoun *she* cannot repeat the subject, *doctor.*

Do not add a pronoun even when a word group comes between the subject and the verb.

▶ **The watch that I lost on vacation ~~it~~ was in my backpack.**

The pronoun *it* cannot repeat the subject, *watch.*

Some languages allow "topic fronting," placing a word or phrase (a "topic") at the beginning of a sentence and following it with an independent clause that explains something about the topic. This form is not allowed in English because the sentence seems to start with one subject but then introduces a new subject in an independent clause.

INCORRECT   ⌐TOPIC¬ ⌐—— IND CLAUSE——¬
                The seeds I planted them last fall.

The sentence can be corrected by bringing the topic (*seeds*) into the independent clause.

                      the seeds
▶ ~~The seeds~~ I planted ~~them~~ last fall.
                 ^

M3-d Do not repeat a subject, an object, or an adverb in an adjective clause.

Adjective clauses begin with relative pronouns (*who, whom, whose, which, that*) or relative adverbs (*when, where*). Relative pronouns usually serve as subjects or objects in the clauses they introduce; another word in the clause cannot serve the same function. Relative adverbs should not be repeated by other adverbs later in the clause.

               ⌐—— ADJ CLAUSE ——¬
The cat ran under the car that was parked on the street.

▶ **The cat ran under the car that ~~it~~ was parked on the street.**

The relative pronoun *that* is the subject of the adjective clause, so the pronoun *it* cannot be added as a subject.

▶ **Myrna enjoyed the investment seminars that she attended ~~them~~**

last week.

The relative pronoun *that* is the object of the verb *attended.* The pronoun *them* cannot also serve as an object.

Sometimes the relative pronoun is understood but not present in the sentence. In such cases, do not add another word with the same function as the omitted pronoun.

▶ Myrna enjoyed the investment seminars she attended ~~them~~ last week.

The relative pronoun *that* is understood after *seminars* even though it is not present in the sentence.

If the clause begins with a relative adverb, do not use another adverb with the same meaning later in the clause.

▶ The office where I work ~~there~~ is one hour from the city.

The adverb *there* cannot repeat the relative adverb *where*.

M3-e Avoid mixed constructions beginning with *although* or *because*.

A word group that begins with *although* cannot be linked to a word group that begins with *but* or *however*. The result is an error called a *mixed construction* (see also S5-a). Similarly, a word group that begins with *because* cannot be linked to a word group that begins with *so* or *therefore*.

If you want to keep *although* or *because*, drop the other linking word.

▶ Although Linda Holeman is best known for her novels for adults,

~~but~~ she has written several books for teens.

▶ Because German and Dutch are related languages, ~~therefore~~

tourists from Berlin can usually read a few signs in Amsterdam.

If you want to keep the other linking word, omit *although* or *because*.

▶ ~~Although~~ Linda Holeman is best known for her novels for adults,

but she has written several books for teens.

▶ ~~Because~~ German and Dutch are related languages/; therefore,

tourists from Berlin can usually read a few signs in Amsterdam.

For advice about using commas and semicolons with linking words, see P1-a and P3-a.

M3-f Do not place an adverb between a verb and its direct object.

Adverbs modifying verbs can appear in various positions: at the beginning or end of a sentence, before or after a verb, or between a helping verb and its main verb.

> *Slowly*, we drove along the rain-slick road.

> Mia handled the teapot *very carefully*.

> Martin *always* wins our tennis matches.

> Christina is *rarely* late for our lunch dates.

> My daughter has *often* spoken of you.

> The election results were being *closely* followed by analysts.

However, an adverb cannot appear between a verb and its direct object.

> ▶ Mother wrapped ~~carefully~~ the gift. ^{carefully}

> The adverb *carefully* cannot appear between the verb, *wrapped*, and its direct object, *the gift*.

M4 Using adjectives

M4-a Distinguish between present participles and past participles used as adjectives.

Both present and past participles may be used as adjectives. The present participle always ends in -*ing*. Past participles usually end in -*ed, -d, -en, -n*, or -*t*. (See G2-a.)

PRESENT PARTICIPLES	confusing, speaking, boring
PAST PARTICIPLES	confused, spoken, bored

Like all other adjectives, participles can come before nouns; they also can follow linking verbs, in which case they describe the subject of the sentence. (See B2-b.)

Use a present participle to describe a person or thing *causing or stimulating an experience.*

The *boring lecture* put us to sleep. [The lecture caused boredom.]

Use a past participle to describe a person or thing *undergoing an experience.*

The *audience* was *bored.* [The audience experienced boredom.]

Participles that describe emotions or mental states often cause the most confusion.

annoying/annoyed	exhausting/exhausted
boring/bored	fascinating/fascinated
confusing/confused	frightening/frightened
depressing/depressed	satisfying/satisfied
exciting/excited	surprising/surprised

Order of cumulative adjectives

FIRST

ARTICLE OR OTHER NOUN MARKER   a, an, the, her, Joe's, two, many, some

EVALUATIVE WORD   attractive, dedicated, delicious, ugly, disgusting

SIZE   large, enormous, small, little

LENGTH OR SHAPE   long, short, round, square

AGE   new, old, young, antique

COLOUR   yellow, blue, crimson

NATIONALITY   French, Peruvian, Vietnamese

RELIGION   Catholic, Protestant, Jewish, Muslim

MATERIAL   silver, walnut, wool, marble

LAST

NOUN/ADJECTIVE   tree (as in *tree* house), kitchen (as in *kitchen* table)

THE NOUN MODIFIED   house, coat, bicycle, bread, woman, coin

My large blue wool **coat** is in the attic.

M4-b Place cumulative adjectives in an appropriate order.

Adjectives usually come before the nouns they modify and may also come after linking verbs. (See B1-d and B2-b.)

> ADJ N   V ADJ
> Janine wore a new necklace. Janine's necklace was new.

Cumulative adjectives are adjectives that build on one another, cannot be joined by the word *and*, and are not separated by commas (P2-d). These adjectives must be listed in a particular order. If you use cumulative adjectives before a noun, see the chart on page 247. The chart is only a guide; don't be surprised if you encounter exceptions.

> stained red plastic
> ▶ My dorm room has only a desk and a ~~plastic red stained~~ chair.

M5 Prepositions and idiomatic expressions

M5-a Become familiar with prepositions that show time and place.

The most frequently used prepositions in English are *at, by, for, from, in, of, on, to,* and *with.* Prepositions can be difficult to master because the differences among them are subtle and idiomatic. The chart on page 249 is limited to three troublesome prepositions that show time and place: *at, on,* and *in.*

Not every possible use is listed in the chart, so don't be surprised when you encounter exceptions and idiomatic uses that you must learn one at a time. For example, in English a person rides *in* a car but *on* a bus, plane, train, or subway.

> at
> ▶ My first class starts ~~on~~ 8:00 a.m.
>   ^

> on
> ▶ The farmers go to market ~~in~~ Wednesday.
>   ^

LaunchPad **ACTIVITIES FOR M5**
macmillan learning
3 Exercises, 1 LearningCurve activity

At, *on*, and *in* to show time and place

Showing time

AT   *at* a specific time: *at* 7:20, *at* dawn, *at* dinner

ON   *on* a specific day or date: *on* Tuesday, *on* June 4

IN   *in* a part of a 24-hour period: *in* the afternoon, *in* the daytime [but *at* night]

in a year or month: *in* 2008, *in* July

in a period of time: finished *in* three hours

Showing place

AT   *at* a meeting place or location: *at* home, *at* the club

at the edge of something: sitting *at* the desk

at the corner of something: turning *at* the intersection

at a target: throwing the snowball *at* Lucy

ON   *on* a surface: placed *on* the table, hanging *on* the wall

on a street: the house *on* Spring Street

on an electronic medium: *on* television, *on* the internet

IN   *in* an enclosed space: *in* the garage, *in* an envelope

in a geographic location: *in* Ottawa, *in* New Brunswick

in a print medium: *in* a book, *in* a magazine

M5-b Use nouns (including *-ing* forms) after prepositions.

In a prepositional phrase, use a noun (not a verb) after the preposition. Sometimes the noun will be a gerund, the *-ing* verb form that functions as a noun (see B3-b).

> Our student government is good at ~~save~~ money.
>   saving^

Distinguish between the preposition *to* and the infinitive marker *to*. If *to* is a preposition, it should be followed by a noun or a gerund.

> We are dedicated to ~~help~~ the poor.
>   helping^

If *to* is an infinitive marker, it should be followed by the base form of the verb.

▶ We want to ~~helping~~ the poor.
   _{help} ^

To test whether *to* is a preposition or an infinitive marker, insert a word that you know is a noun after the word *to*. If the noun makes sense in that position, *to* is a preposition. If the noun does not make sense after *to*, then *to* is an infinitive marker.

Zoe is addicted *to* _____.

They are planning *to* _____.

In the first sentence, a noun (such as *magazines*) makes sense after *to*, so *to* is a preposition and should be followed by a noun or a gerund: Zoe is addicted *to magazines*. Zoe is addicted *to running*.

In the second sentence, a noun (such as *magazines*) does not make sense after *to*, so *to* is an infinitive marker and must be followed by the base form of the verb: They are planning *to build* a new school.

M5-c Become familiar with common adjective + preposition combinations.

Some adjectives appear only with certain prepositions. These expressions are idiomatic and may be different from the combinations used in your native language.

▶ Paula is married ~~with~~ Jon.
   _{to} ^

Check an ESL dictionary for combinations that are not listed in the chart on page 251.

M5-d Become familiar with common verb + preposition combinations.

Many verbs and prepositions appear together in idiomatic phrases. Pay special attention to the combinations that are different from the combinations used in your native language.

▶ Your success depends ~~of~~ your effort.
   _{on} ^

Check an ESL dictionary for combinations that are not listed in the chart on page 251.

Adjective + preposition combinations

accustomed to
addicted to
afraid of
angry with
ashamed of
aware of
committed to
concerned
  about
concerned with

connected to
covered with
dedicated to
devoted to
different from
engaged in
engaged to
excited about
familiar with
full of

guilty of
interested in
involved in
involved with
known as
known for
made of (*or*
  made from)
married to
opposed to

preferable to
proud of
responsible
  for
satisfied with
scared of
similar to
tired of
worried about

Verb + preposition combinations

agree with
apply to
approve of
arrive at
arrive in
ask for
believe in
belong to
care about
care for
compare to

compare with
concentrate on
consist of
count on
decide on
depend on
differ from
disagree with
dream about
dream of
feel like

forget about
happen to
hope for
insist on
listen to
participate in
rely on
reply to
respond to
result in
search for

speak to (*or*
  speak with)
stare at
succeed at
succeed in
take advantage of
take care of
think about
think of
wait for
wait on

M6 Paraphrasing sources effectively

Effective paraphrasing is an important skill for writing in university and college. You will frequently paraphrase information from your textbooks to answer homework and exam questions, and you will especially need this skill when you are writing essays that incorporate information from other writers. However, learning how to paraphrase can be challenging because often the topics and the vocabulary are new and unfamiliar to multilingual writers.

The purpose of paraphrasing is to restate an author's ideas in your own words. Most writers find the following process for paraphrasing useful:

1. Read and understand the text.
2. Put the text aside.
3. Express the information in your own words.
4. Compare your paraphrase to the original text to check that you have used different words and different sentence structures but have kept the author's meaning.

This process provides an effective way to paraphrase; it requires that the writer have a large vocabulary and well-developed sentence-writing abilities. Sometimes it's hard to find the right words to paraphrase a sentence or to know whether a paraphrase has the same meaning as the original source.

The following sections provide rules of thumb that can help you develop skill with paraphrasing.

M6-a Avoid replacing a source's words with synonyms.

Learning to paraphrase will help you communicate the ideas of authors effectively and avoid plagiarism — using another person's ideas or words without giving credit to that person. However, even if you tell your reader that information comes from another author, you can still commit plagiarism if you change only the words but do not make the *presentation* of the information your own.

Some writers misinterpret the instructions to "use your own words"; they simply replace words in the source with synonyms, words that have similar meanings. Such word-by-word paraphrases frequently result in awkward sentence structures and inaccuracy. Meaning in English often comes from phrases and sentences rather than from individual words. Also, synonyms have similar meanings, but they rarely have *identical* meanings. Sometimes a synonym requires a different sentence structure than the original word does.

The following examples illustrate some of the problems that can arise with word-by-word paraphrasing.

Here is a short passage from Rebecca Webber's article "Make Your Own Luck."

ORIGINAL SOURCE

People who spot and seize opportunity are different. They are more open to life's forking paths, so they see possibilities others miss. And if things don't work out the way they'd hoped, they brush off disappointment and launch themselves headlong toward the next fortunate circumstance. As a result, they're happier and more likely to achieve their goals.

— Rebecca Webber, "Make Your Own Luck," p. 64

The following is a word-by-word paraphrase of the sentences highlighted in yellow.

UNACCEPTABLE PARAPHRASE: MEANING CHANGED

Persons who see and grab chances are diverse. They are further exposed to life's dividing trails, and they view prospects others ignore.

The first problem with this paraphrase is that the student who wrote it used the same sentence structure as in the original passage. Because she did not use her own sentence structure, this paraphrase is plagiarized. Second, the words that the student substituted are not exact synonyms, so the paraphrase has lost some of the meaning of the original passage.

- The word *grab* is an informal synonym of the word *seize* and may not be acceptable in a formal paper.
- *Diverse* and *different* have similar, but not identical, meanings. The word *different* in the original passage implies that people who are open to opportunities are different from people who are not open to opportunities. Using *diverse* in this context implies that people who welcome opportunity are different from one another. Using *diverse* distorts the meaning of the sentence.
- Using *exposed* instead of *open* changes the meaning in a significant way. *Exposed* implies that something negative has happened to these people, while *open* is a positive character trait.

As you paraphrase, keep in mind that simply substituting synonyms into the original passage does not guarantee an accurate paraphrase.

The following paraphrase of the sentence highlighted in blue demonstrates another potential problem with word-by-word paraphrases. Using synonyms often requires changing the surrounding sentence structure because in English the same word can be more than one part of speech (see p. 305).

For example, *work* can be either a noun or a verb; in the following paraphrase, the student has substituted the noun *effort* for the verb *work*, but it is not an appropriate substitution.

> **UNACCEPTABLE PARAPHRASE: AWKWARD RESULT**
>
> And if everything don't effort out the manner they'd wanted, they rebuff disappointment and throw themselves impulsive toward the next lucky situation.

- When the student changed *things* to *everything*, she also needed to change the verb from the plural form (*don't*) to the singular form (*doesn't*).
- Using *effort* in place of *work* is inappropriate. *Effort* is a synonym for the noun *work* but not a synonym for the verb *work*. The part of speech of a word is an important consideration when choosing a synonym.
- When the student substituted *manner* for *way*, she should have used a different structure: *in the manner*.
- Although *headlong* has a similar meaning to *impulsive*, in the original passage *headlong* is an adverb modifying the verb *launch*; *impulsive* is an adjective. An adjective cannot replace an adverb in a sentence.

M6-b Determine the meaning of the original source.

Rather than trying to paraphrase word-for-word within each sentence, a better approach is to look at an entire passage and try to understand its meaning as well as how the information is organized before you try to present it in your own words. Look at the meaning of each phrase or clause rather than just the meaning of each word.

> **ORIGINAL SOURCE**
>
> People who spot and seize opportunity are different. They are more open to life's forking paths, so they see possibilities others miss. And if things don't work out the way they'd hoped, they brush off disappointment and launch themselves headlong toward the next fortunate circumstance. As a result, they're happier and more likely to achieve their goals.

The topic sentence of a paragraph is important. The topic sentence here (the first sentence in the paragraph) tells you about a particular group of people; from the title of the article, you can tell that Webber is talking about people who create their own luck. Lucky people, according to the author, have different characteristics from people who are not lucky. The rest of the paragraph then describes how lucky people are different.

Here is the original passage as the student writer annotated it. She worked through the original passage, repeatedly asking herself, "What is the author's point here?"

ORIGINAL SOURCE WITH STUDENT ANNOTATIONS

↙ Lucky people?
People who spot and seize opportunity are different. They are

↙ More willing to take risks?
more open to life's forking paths, so they see possibilities others

miss. And if things don't work out the way they'd hoped, they

↙ Don't get discouraged/upset   Keep looking? ↘
brush off disappointment and launch themselves headlong

toward the next fortunate circumstance. As a result, they're

↙ More positive personalities overall
happier and more likely to achieve their goals.

M6-c Present the author's meaning in your own words.

If you analyze a paragraph in its entirety rather than look at each word individually, you should be able to organize your information differently from the way the original author did and write a better paraphrase. As you analyze a source, you may still need to figure out the meaning of certain words, but do not focus on word-for-word substitutions. Here is one student's paraphrase of Rebecca Webber's work using her annotations of the text (see M6-b).

ACCEPTABLE PARAPHRASE

Individuals notice and respond to life's chances in different ways. Some people notice opportunities that other people might not notice, they are more willing to take risks, and they do not get discouraged if their decisions do not work out. Because they do not get discouraged easily, they are able to stay positive and content and to continue to search enthusiastically for the next opportunity (Webber 64).

This paraphrase presents the student's understanding of the author's meaning — without using words or sentence structure from the original. Notice that the paraphrase includes a citation. The idea is still Webber's idea, so a citation is needed, but the student uses her own words to communicate the information from Webber's article.

P

Punctuation and Mechanics

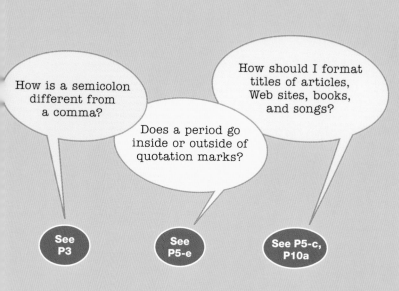

How is a semicolon different from a comma?

See P3

Does a period go inside or outside of quotation marks?

See P5-e

How should I format titles of articles, Web sites, books, and songs?

See P5-c, P10a

P Punctuation and Mechanics

P1 The comma

The comma was invented to help readers. Without it, sentence parts can collide into one another unexpectedly, causing misreadings.

| CONFUSING | If you cook Elmer will do the dishes. |
| CONFUSING | While we were eating a rattlesnake approached our campsite. |

Add commas in the logical places (after *cook* and *eating*), and suddenly all is clear. No longer is Elmer being cooked and the rattlesnake being eaten.

Various rules have evolved to prevent such misreadings and to speed readers along through complex grammatical structures. Those rules are detailed in this section. (Section P2 explains when not to use commas.)

P1-a Use a comma before a coordinating conjunction joining independent clauses.

When a coordinating conjunction connects two or more independent clauses — word groups that could stand alone as separate sentences — a comma must come before the conjunction. There are seven coordinating conjunctions in English: *and, but, or, nor, for, so,* and *yet.*

A comma tells readers that one independent clause has come to a close and that another is about to begin.

▶ The department sponsored a seminar on postsecondary survival skills,
  ^
  and it also hosted a barbecue for new students.

EXCEPTION: If the two independent clauses are short and there is no danger of misreading, the comma may be omitted.

The plane took off and we were on our way.

TIP: As a rule, do *not* use a comma with a coordinating conjunction that joins only two words, phrases, or subordinate clauses. (See P2-a. See also P1-c for commas with coordinating conjunctions joining three or more elements.)

▶ A good money manager controls expenses/and invests surplus

  dollars to meet future needs.

The word group following *and* is not an independent clause; it is the second half of a compound predicate (*controls . . . and invests*).

 LaunchPad
macmillan learning

ACTIVITIES FOR P1

11 Exercises, 1 LearningCurve activity

P1-b Use a comma after an introductory clause or phrase.

The most common introductory word groups are clauses and phrases functioning as adverbs. Such word groups usually tell when, where, how, why, or under what conditions the main action of the sentence occurred. (See B3-a, B3-b, and B3-e.)

A comma tells readers that the introductory clause or phrase has come to a close and that the main part of the sentence is about to begin.

> **When Irwin was ready to iron, his cat tripped on the cord.**
> ^
>
> Without the comma, readers may think that Irwin is ironing his cat. The comma signals that *his cat* is the subject of a new clause, not part of the introductory one.

EXCEPTION: The comma may be left out after a short adverb clause or phrase if there is no danger of misreading. *In no time we were at 900 metres.*

Sentences also frequently begin with participial phrases that function as adjectives, describing the noun or pronoun immediately following them. The comma tells readers that they are about to learn the identity of the person or thing described; therefore, the comma is usually required even when the phrase is short. (See B3-b.)

> **Buried under layers of younger rocks, the earth's oldest rocks**
> ^
>
> **contain no fossils.**

NOTE: Other introductory word groups include transitional expressions and absolute phrases (see P1-f).

P1-c Use a comma between all items in a series.

When three or more items are presented in a series, those items should be separated from one another with commas. Items in a series may be single words, phrases, or clauses.

> **Leonard Cohen was inducted into the Canadian Music Hall of Fame,**
>
> **the Canadian Songwriters Hall of Fame, and the American Rock and**
> ^
>
> **Roll Hall of Fame.**

Although some writers view the last comma in a series as optional, most experts advise using the comma because its omission can result in ambiguity or misreading.

▶ **My uncle willed me all of his property, houses, and boats.**
^

Did the uncle will his property *and* houses *and* boats — or simply his property, consisting of houses and boats? If the former meaning is intended, a comma is necessary to prevent ambiguity.

P1-d Use a comma between coordinate adjectives not joined with *and*. Do not use a comma between cumulative adjectives.

When two or more adjectives each modify a noun separately, they are coordinate.

Roberto is a *warm, gentle, affectionate* father.

If the adjectives can be joined with *and*, the adjectives are coordinate, so you should use commas: *warm* and *gentle* and *affectionate* (*warm, gentle, affectionate*). Adjectives that do not modify the noun separately are cumulative.

Three large grey shapes moved slowly toward us.

Beginning with the adjective closest to the noun *shapes*, these modifiers lean on one another, piggyback-style, with each modifying a larger word group. *Grey* modifies *shapes*, *large* modifies *grey shapes*, and *three* modifies *large grey shapes*. Cumulative adjectives cannot be joined with *and* (not *three and large and grey shapes*).

COORDINATE ADJECTIVES

▶ **Should patients with severe, irreversible brain damage be put on life**
^
support systems?

Adjectives are coordinate if they can be connected with *and*: *severe* and *irreversible*.

CUMULATIVE ADJECTIVES

▶ **Ira ordered a rich/chocolate/layer cake.**

Ira didn't order a cake that was rich and chocolate and layer. He ordered a *layer cake* that was *chocolate*, a *chocolate layer cake* that was *rich*.

P1-e Use commas to set off nonrestrictive (nonessential) elements. Do not use commas to set off restrictive (essential) elements.

Certain word groups that modify nouns or pronouns can be restrictive or nonrestrictive — that is, essential or not essential to the meaning of a sentence. These word groups are usually adjective clauses, adjective phrases, or appositives.

Restrictive elements

A restrictive element defines or limits the meaning of the word it modifies; it is therefore essential to the meaning of the sentence and is not set off with commas. If you remove a restrictive modifier from a sentence, the meaning changes significantly, becoming more general than you intended.

> **RESTRICTIVE (NO COMMAS)**
>
> The campers need clothes *that are durable.*
>
> Scientists *who study the earth's structure* are called geologists.

The first sentence does not mean that the campers need clothes in general. The intended meaning is more limited: The campers need durable clothes. The second sentence does not mean that scientists in general are called geologists; only those scientists who specifically study the earth's structure are called geologists. The italicized word groups are essential and are therefore not set off with commas.

Nonrestrictive elements

A nonrestrictive modifier describes a noun or pronoun whose meaning has already been clearly defined or limited. Because the modifier contains nonessential or parenthetical information, it is set off with commas. If you remove a nonrestrictive element from a sentence, the meaning does not change dramatically. Some meaning may be lost, but the defining characteristics of the person or thing described remain the same.

> **NONRESTRICTIVE (WITH COMMAS)**
>
> The campers need sturdy shoes, *which are expensive.*
>
> The scientists, *who represented five different universities,* met to review applications for the prestigious Northern Science Award.

In the first sentence, the campers need sturdy shoes, and the shoes happen to be expensive. In the second sentence, the scientists met to review applications for the award; that they represented five different universities is informative but not critical to the meaning of the sentence. The nonessential information in both sentences is set off with commas.

NOTE: Often it is difficult to tell whether a word group is restrictive or nonrestrictive without seeing it in context and considering the writer's meaning. Both of the following sentences are grammatically correct, but their meanings are slightly different.

> The dessert made with fresh raspberries was delicious.
>
> The dessert, made with fresh raspberries, was delicious.

In the first example, the phrase *made with fresh raspberries* tells which of two or more desserts the writer is referring to. In the example with commas, the phrase merely adds information about one dessert.

Adjective clauses

Adjective clauses are patterned like sentences, containing subjects and verbs, but they function within sentences as modifiers of nouns or pronouns. They always follow the word they modify, usually immediately. Adjective clauses begin with a relative pronoun (*who, whom, whose, which, that*) or with a relative adverb (*where, when*). (See also B3-e.)

Nonrestrictive adjective clauses are set off with commas; restrictive adjective clauses are not.

NONRESTRICTIVE CLAUSE (WITH COMMAS)

▶ Ed's house, which is located on five hectares, was completely
furnished with bats in the rafters and mice in the kitchen.

The adjective clause *which is located on five hectares* does not restrict the meaning of *Ed's house*; the information is nonessential and is therefore set off with commas.

RESTRICTIVE CLAUSE (NO COMMAS)

▶ The trumpeter swans/that are born at the Toronto Zoo/
are released into the wild.

Because the adjective clause *that are born at the Toronto Zoo* identifies one particular type of swan out of many, the information is essential and is therefore not set off with commas.

NOTE: Use *that* only with restrictive (essential) clauses. Many writers prefer to use *which* only with nonrestrictive (nonessential) clauses, but usage varies.

Adjective phrases

Prepositional or verbal phrases functioning as adjectives may be restrictive or nonrestrictive. Nonrestrictive phrases are set off with commas; restrictive phrases are not.

NONRESTRICTIVE PHRASE (WITH COMMAS)

▶ The helicopter, with its million-candlepower spotlight
illuminating the area, circled above.

The *with* phrase is nonessential because its purpose is not to specify which of two or more helicopters is being discussed. The phrase is not required for readers to understand the meaning of the sentence.

RESTRICTIVE PHRASE (NO COMMAS)

▶ One corner of the attic was filled with newspapers/dating from
the early 1900s.

Dating from the early 1900s restricts the meaning of *newspapers*, so the comma
should be omitted.

Appositives

An appositive is a noun or noun phrase that renames a nearby noun. Nonrestrictive appositives are set off with commas; restrictive appositives are not.

NONRESTRICTIVE APPOSITIVE (WITH COMMAS)

▶ Darwin's most important book, *On the Origin of Species,* was the
  ^   ^
result of many years of research.

Most important restricts the meaning to one book, so the appositive *On the Origin of Species* is nonrestrictive and should be set off with commas.

RESTRICTIVE APPOSITIVE (NO COMMAS)

▶ The song/"Viva la Vida/" was blasted out of huge amplifiers at the
concert.

Once they've read *song,* readers still don't know precisely which song the writer means. The appositive following *song* restricts its meaning, so the appositive should not be set off with commas.

P1-f Use commas to set off transitional and parenthetical expressions, absolute phrases, and word groups expressing contrast.

Transitional expressions

Transitional expressions serve as bridges between sentences or parts of sentences. They include conjunctive adverbs such as *however, therefore,* and *moreover* and transitional phrases such as *for example, as a matter of fact,* and *in other words.* (For complete lists of these expressions, see P3-a.)

When a transitional expression appears between independent clauses in a compound sentence, it is preceded by a semicolon and is usually followed by a comma. (See P3-a.)

▶ Minh did not understand our language; moreover, he was
                                                 ^
unfamiliar with our customs.

When a transitional expression appears at the beginning of a sentence or in the middle of an independent clause, it is usually set off with commas.

> ► **Natural foods are not always salt-free; celery, for example, contains**
> ^   ^
> **more sodium than most people think.**

EXCEPTION: If a transitional expression blends smoothly with the rest of the sentence, calling for little or no pause in reading, it does not need to be set off with a comma. Expressions such as *also, at least, certainly, consequently, indeed, of course, moreover, no doubt, perhaps, then,* and *therefore* do not always call for a pause.

Alice's bicycle is broken; *therefore* you will need to borrow Sue's.

Parenthetical expressions

Expressions that are distinctly parenthetical, providing only supplemental information, should be set off with commas. They interrupt the flow of a sentence or appear at the end as afterthoughts.

> ► **Evolution, as far as we know, doesn't work this way.**
> ^   ^

Absolute phrases

An absolute phrase, which modifies the whole sentence, usually consists of a noun followed by a participle or participial phrase. (See B3-d.) Absolute phrases may appear at the beginning or at the end of a sentence and should be set off with commas.

```
┌──────── ABSOLUTE PHRASE ────────┐
│   N   PARTICIPLE                 │
```
The sun appearing for the first time in a week, we were at last able to begin the archaeological dig.

> ► **Elvis Presley made music industry history in the 1950s, his**
> ^
> **records having sold more than ten million copies.**

NOTE: Do not insert a comma between the noun and the participle in an absolute construction.

> ► **The next contestant/being five years old, the host adjusted the**
> **height of the microphone.**

Word groups expressing contrast

Sharp contrasts beginning with words such as *not*, *never*, and *unlike* are set off with commas.

► Unlike Robert, Celia loves using Instagram.
      ^

P1-g Use commas to set off nouns of direct address, the words *yes* and *no*, interrogative tags, and mild interjections.

► Forgive me, Angela, for forgetting your birthday.
      ^   ^

► The film was faithful to the book, wasn't it?
      ^

P1-h Use commas with expressions such as *he said* to set off direct quotations.

► In his book *Shake Hands with the Devil*, Romeo Dallaire

   wrote, "We all helped to create the mess that has murdered and
      ^

   displaced millions and destabilized the whole central African

   region" (5).

See P5 on the use of quotation marks and pages 391–92 on citing literary sources in MLA style.

P1-i Use commas with dates, addresses, titles, and numbers.

Dates

In dates, set off the year with a pair of commas.

► On October 5, 1813, Tecumseh was killed in the Battle of the
      ^   ^
   Thames.

EXCEPTIONS: Commas are not needed if the date is inverted or if only the month and year are given: 15 April 2009; January 2018.

Addresses

The elements of an address or a place name are separated with commas. A postal code, however, is not preceded by a comma.

▶ **Please send the package to Greg Tarvin at 708 Spring Street,**
˄

Hamilton, ON L8N 2P1.
˄

Titles

If a title follows a name, set off the title with a pair of commas.

▶ **Ann Hall, MD, has been appointed to the board of trustees.**
˄   ˄

Numbers

In numbers more than four digits long, use commas or spaces to separate the numbers into groups of three, starting from the right. In numbers four digits long, a comma or space is optional.

3,500 or 3500 or 3 500   100,000 or 100 000   5,000,000 or 5 000 000

EXCEPTIONS: Do not use commas in street numbers, telephone numbers, or years with four or fewer digits.

P2 Unnecessary commas

Many common misuses of the comma result from a misunderstanding of the major comma rules presented in P1.

P2-a Do not use a comma with a coordinating conjunction that joins only two words, phrases, or subordinate clauses.

Though a comma should be used before a coordinating conjunction joining independent clauses (see P1-a) or with a series of three or more elements (see P1-c), these rules should not be extended to other compound word groups.

▶ **Ron discovered a leak/and came back to fix it.**

The coordinating conjunction *and* links two verbs in a compound predicate: *discovered* and *came.*

 LaunchPad ACTIVITIES FOR P2
macmillan learning   5 Exercises

▶ We knew that she had won/but that the election was close.

The coordinating conjunction *but* links two subordinate clauses, each beginning with *that*.

P2-b Do not use a comma to separate a verb from its subject or object.

A sentence should flow from subject to verb to object without unnecessary pauses. Commas may appear between these major sentence elements only when a specific rule calls for them.

▶ Zoos large enough to give the animals freedom to roam/are

becoming more popular.

The comma should not separate the subject, *Zoos*, from the verb, *are becoming*.

P2-c Do not use a comma before the first or after the last item in a series.

Though commas are required between items in a series (P1-c), do not place them either before or after the whole series.

▶ Other causes of asthmatic attacks are/stress, change in temperature,

and cold air.

▶ Even novels that focus on horror, evil, and alienation/often have

themes of spiritual renewal and redemption.

P2-d Do not use a comma between cumulative adjectives, between an adjective and a noun, or between an adverb and an adjective.

Commas are required between coordinate adjectives (those that can be joined with *and*), but they do not belong between cumulative adjectives (those that cannot be joined with *and*). (For a full discussion, see P1-d.)

▶ In the corner of the closet, we found an old/maroon hatbox.

A comma should never be used between an adjective and the noun that follows it.

▶ **It was a senseless, dangerous/mission.**

Nor should a comma be used between an adverb and an adjective that follows it.

▶ **Rehabilitation often helps severely/injured patients.**

P2-e Do not use commas to set off restrictive elements.

Restrictive elements are modifiers or appositives that restrict the meaning of the nouns they follow. Because they are essential to the meaning of the sentence, they are not set off with commas. (For a full discussion of restrictive and nonrestrictive elements, see P1-e.)

▶ **Drivers/who think they own the road/make cycling a dangerous**

sport.

The modifier *who think they own the road* restricts the meaning of *Drivers* and is essential to the meaning of the sentence. Putting commas around the *who* clause falsely suggests that all drivers think they own the road.

▶ **Margaret Mead's book/ *Coming of Age in Samoa*/stirred up**

considerable controversy when it was published in 1928.

Since Mead wrote more than one book, the appositive contains information essential to the meaning of the sentence.

P2-f Do not use a comma to set off a concluding adverb clause that is essential for meaning.

When adverb clauses introduce a sentence, they are nearly always followed by a comma (see P1-b). When they conclude a sentence, however, they are not set off by a comma if their content is essential to the meaning of the earlier part of the sentence. Adverb clauses beginning with *after, as soon as, because, before, if, since, unless, until,* and *when* are usually essential.

▶ **Don't visit Paris at the height of the tourist season/unless you**

have booked hotel reservations.

Without the *unless* clause, the meaning of the sentence might at first seem broader than the writer intended.

P2-g

When a concluding adverb clause is nonessential, it should be preceded by a comma. Clauses beginning with *although, even though, though,* and *whereas* are usually nonessential.

▶ The lecture seemed to last only a short time, although it had

actually gone on for more than an hour.

P2-g Do not use a comma after a phrase that begins an inverted sentence.

Though a comma belongs after most introductory phrases (see P1-b), it does not belong after phrases that begin an inverted sentence. In an inverted sentence, the subject follows the verb, and a phrase that ordinarily would follow the verb is moved to the beginning.

▶ At the bottom of the hill/sat the stubborn mule.

P2-h Avoid other common misuses of the comma.

Do not use a comma in the following situations.

AFTER A COORDINATING CONJUNCTION (*AND, BUT, OR, NOR, FOR, SO, YET*)

▶ Occasionally TV talk shows are performed live, but/more

often they are recorded.

AFTER *SUCH AS* OR *LIKE*

▶ Shade-loving plants such as/begonias, impatiens, and coleus

can add colour to a shady garden.

AFTER *ALTHOUGH*

▶ Although/the air was balmy, the water was cold.

BEFORE A PARENTHESIS

▶ Though Sylvia's CAEL score was low/(only 60), her application

essay was superior.

TO SET OFF AN INDIRECT (REPORTED) QUOTATION

▶ Samuel Goldwyn once said/that a verbal contract isn't worth

the paper it's written on.

WITH A QUESTION MARK OR AN EXCLAMATION POINT

▶ "Why don't you try it?/" she coaxed. "You can't do any worse

than the rest of us."

P3 The semicolon and the colon

The semicolon is used to connect major sentence elements of equal grammatical rank. The colon is used primarily to call attention to the words that follow it.

P3-a Use a semicolon between closely related independent clauses.

Between independent clauses with no coordinating conjunction

When two independent clauses appear in one sentence, they are usually linked with a comma and a coordinating conjunction (*and, but, or, nor, for, so, yet*). If the clauses are closely related and the relation is clear without a conjunction, they may be linked with a semicolon instead.

> In film, a low-angle shot makes the subject look powerful; a high-angle shot does just the opposite.

A semicolon must be used whenever a coordinating conjunction has been omitted between independent clauses. To use merely a comma creates a type of run-on sentence known as a *comma splice*. (See G6.)

▶ In 1534, Jacques Cartier sailed to Canada while trying to find a route

to Asia/; in 1535, he made a second voyage to Canada.

LaunchPad macmillan learning
ACTIVITIES FOR P3
9 Exercises, 1 LearningCurve activity

Between independent clauses linked with a transitional expression

Transitional expressions include conjunctive adverbs and transitional phrases.

CONJUNCTIVE ADVERBS

accordingly	however	now
also	incidentally	otherwise
anyway	indeed	similarly
besides	instead	specifically
certainly	likewise	still
consequently	meanwhile	subsequently
conversely	moreover	then
finally	nevertheless	therefore
furthermore	next	thus
hence	nonetheless	

TRANSITIONAL PHRASES

after all	even so	in fact
as a matter of fact	for example	in other words
as a result	for instance	in the first place
at any rate	in addition	on the contrary
at the same time	in conclusion	on the other hand

When a transitional expression appears between independent clauses, it is preceded by a semicolon and usually followed by a comma.

▶ Many corals grow very gradually/; in fact, the creation of a coral

reef can take centuries.

When a transitional expression appears in the middle or at the end of the second independent clause, the semicolon goes *between the clauses.*

▶ Biologists have observed laughter in primates other than humans/;

chimpanzees, however, sound more like they are panting than

laughing.

Transitional expressions should not be confused with the coordinating conjunctions *and, but, or, nor, for, so,* and *yet,* which are preceded by a comma when they link independent clauses. (See P1-a.)

P3-b Use a semicolon between items in a series containing internal punctuation.

▶ Researchers point to key benefits of positive thinking: It leads to high self-esteem, especially in people who focus on their achievements/; it helps make social interactions, such as those
  ⌃
with co-workers, more enjoyable/; and, most important, it
  ⌃
results in better sleep and overall health.

Without the semicolons, the reader would have to sort out the major groupings, distinguishing between important and less important pauses according to the logic of the sentence. By inserting semicolons at the major breaks, the writer does this work for the reader.

P3-c Avoid common misuses of the semicolon.

Do not use a semicolon in the following situations.

BETWEEN A SUBORDINATE CLAUSE AND THE REST OF THE SENTENCE

▶ Although legislating radio stations to include Canadian content was
controversial/, it has helped many Canadian artists to gain recognition.
  ⌃

BETWEEN AN APPOSITIVE AND THE WORD IT REFERS TO

▶ The scientists were fascinated by the species *Argyroneta aquatica/*,
  ⌃
a spider that lives underwater.

TO INTRODUCE A LIST

▶ Some of my favourite celebrities have their own blogs/: Katy Perry,
  ⌃
Beyoncé, and Zooey Deschanel.

BETWEEN INDEPENDENT CLAUSES JOINED BY *AND, BUT, OR, NOR, FOR, SO,* OR *YET*

▶ Five of the applicants had worked with spreadsheets/, but only
  ⌃
one was familiar with database management.

EXCEPTION: If one or both of the independent clauses contain a comma, you may use a semicolon with a coordinating conjunction between the clauses.

P3-d Use a colon after an independent clause to direct attention to a list, an appositive, a quotation, or a summary or an explanation.

A LIST

The daily exercise routine should include at least the following: ten minutes of stretching, forty abdominal crunches, and a twenty-minute run.

AN APPOSITIVE

My roommate seems to live on two things: sushi and social media.

A QUOTATION

Consider the words of Justin Trudeau: "I fundamentally believe our society works better when women are at the forefront."

A SUMMARY OR AN EXPLANATION

Faith is like love: It cannot be forced.

The novel is clearly autobiographical: The author even gives his own name to the main character.

NOTE: For other ways of introducing quotations, see "Introducing quoted material" on pages 282–83. When an independent clause follows a colon, begin with a capital letter. Some disciplines use a lowercase letter instead. See MLA-5a, APA-5a, and CMS-5a for variations.

P3-e Use a colon according to convention.

SALUTATION IN A LETTER   Dear Editor:

HOURS AND MINUTES   5:30 p.m.

PROPORTIONS   The ratio of women to men was 2:1.

TITLE AND SUBTITLE   *The Glory of Hera: Greek Mythology and the Greek Family*

BIBLIOGRAPHIC ENTRIES   Boston: Bedford/St. Martin's, 2018

CHAPTER AND VERSE IN SACRED TEXT   Luke 2:14, Qur'an 67:3

P3-f Avoid common misuses of the colon.

A colon must be preceded by a full independent clause. Therefore, avoid using it in the following situations.

BETWEEN A VERB AND ITS OBJECT OR COMPLEMENT

▶ Some important vitamins found in vegetables are̸ vitamin A, thiamine, niacin, and vitamin C.

BETWEEN A PREPOSITION AND ITS OBJECT

▶ The heart's two pumps each consist of̸ an upper chamber, or atrium, and a lower chamber, or ventricle.

AFTER *SUCH AS*, *INCLUDING*, OR *FOR EXAMPLE*

▶ U Sports governs university athletic sports, including̸ basketball, soccer, ice hockey, and football.

P4 The apostrophe

P4-a Use an apostrophe to indicate that a noun is possessive.

Possessive nouns usually indicate ownership, as in *Tim's hat* or *the lawyer's desk*. Frequently, however, ownership is only loosely implied: *the tree's roots, a day's work*. If you are not sure whether a noun is possessive, try turning it into an *of* phrase: *the roots of the tree, the work of a day*. (Pronouns also have possessive forms. See p. 276 and P4-d.)

When to add -'s

1. If the noun does not end in -*s*, add -'*s*.

   Luck often propels a rock musician's career.

   The Children's Wish Foundation of Canada is a nonprofit organization that fulfills wishes for children who have life-threatening illnesses.

LaunchPad macmillan learning **ACTIVITIES FOR P4**
6 Exercises, 1 LearningCurve activity

2. If the noun is singular and ends in -*s* or an *s* sound, add -'*s* to show possession.

   Lois's sister spent last year in India.

   Her article presents an overview of Marx's teachings.

NOTE: To avoid potentially awkward pronunciation, some writers use only the apostrophe with a singular noun ending in -*s*: *Sophocles'*.

When to add only an apostrophe

If the noun is plural and ends in -*s*, add only an apostrophe.

   Both diplomats' briefcases were searched by guards.

Joint possession

To show joint possession, use -'*s* or (-*s*') with the last noun only; to show individual possession, make all nouns possessive.

   Have you seen Joyce and Greg's new camper?

   John's and Marie's expectations of marriage couldn't have been more different.

Joyce and Greg jointly own one camper. John and Marie individually have different expectations.

Compound nouns

If a noun is compound, use -'*s* (or -*s*') with the last element.

   My father-in-law's memoir about life in Sri Lanka was just published.

Indefinite pronouns

Indefinite pronouns refer to no specific person or thing: *everyone, someone, no one, something.* (See B1-b.)

   Someone's raincoat has been left behind.

P4-b Use an apostrophe to mark omissions in contractions and numbers.

In a contraction, the apostrophe takes the place of one or more missing letters. *It's* stands for *it is, can't* for *cannot.*

   It's a shame that Frank can't go on the tour.

   The apostrophe is also used to mark the omission of the first two digits of a year or years.

   The reunion for the class of '12 is tonight.

   I am studying the music of the '60s generation.

P4-c Do not use an apostrophe in certain situations.

An apostrophe typically is not used to pluralize numbers, letters, abbreviations, and words mentioned as words. Note the few exceptions and be consistent throughout your paper.

Plural of numbers

Do not use an apostrophe in the plural of any numbers.

> Oksana skated nearly perfect figure 8s.

> The 1920s are known as the Jazz Age.

Plural of letters

Italicize the letter and use roman (regular) font style for the -s ending. (Do not italicize academic grades.)

> Two large *P*s were painted on the door.

> He received two Ds for the first time in his life.

EXCEPTIONS: To avoid misreading, use an apostrophe to form the plural of lowercase letters and the capital letters *A* and *I*.

> Beginning readers often confuse *b*'s and *d*'s.

> Students with straight A's earn high honours.

MLA NOTE: MLA recommends using an apostrophe for the plural of single capital and lowercase letters: *H*'s, *p*'s.

Plural of abbreviations

Do not use an apostrophe to pluralize an abbreviation.

> Harriet has thirty DVDs on her desk.

> Marco earned two PhDs before his thirtieth birthday.

Plural of words mentioned as words

Generally, omit the apostrophe to form the plural of words mentioned as words. If the word is italicized, the -s ending appears in roman (regular) type.

> We've heard enough *maybe*s.

Words mentioned as words may also appear in quotation marks. When you choose this option, use the apostrophe.

> We've heard enough "maybe's."

P4-d Avoid common misuses of the apostrophe.

Do not use an apostrophe with nouns that are not possessive or with the possessive pronouns *its, whose, his, hers, ours, yours,* and *theirs.*

> ▶ Some ~~outpatient's~~ ^{outpatients} have special parking permits.

> ▶ Each area has ~~it's~~ ^{its} own conference room.

> *It's* means "it is." The possessive pronoun *its* contains no apostrophe despite the fact that it is possessive.

> ▶ We attended a reading by Junot Díaz, ~~who's~~ ^{whose} work focuses on the Dominican immigration experience.

> *Who's* means "who is." The possessive pronoun is *whose.*

P5 Quotation marks

Writers use quotation marks primarily to enclose direct quotations of another person's spoken or written words. You will also find these other uses and exceptions:

- for quotations within quotations (single quotation marks: P5-b)
- for titles of short works (P5-c)
- for words used as words (P5-d)
- with other marks of punctuation (P5-e)
- with brackets and ellipsis marks (pp. 286–87, P6-c)
- no quotation marks for indirect quotations, paraphrases, and summaries (p. 279)
- no quotation marks for long quotations (pp. 279–80)

LaunchPad macmillan learning   **ACTIVITIES FOR P5**
5 Exercises, 1 LearningCurve activity

P5-a Use quotation marks to enclose direct quotations.

Direct quotations of a person's words, whether spoken or written, must be in quotation marks.

> "Twitter," according to social media researcher Jameson Brown, "is the best social network for brand to customer engagement."

In dialogue, begin a new paragraph to mark a change in speaker.

> "Mom, his name is Willie, not William. A thousand times I've told you, it's *Willie*."
> "Willie is a derivative of William, Lester. Surely his birth certificate doesn't have Willie on it, and I like calling people by their proper names."
> "Yes, it does, ma'am. My mother named me Willie K. Mason."
> — Gloria Naylor

If a single speaker utters more than one paragraph, introduce each paragraph with a quotation mark, but do not use a closing quotation mark until the end of the speech.

Exception: indirect quotations

Do not use quotation marks around indirect quotations. An indirect quotation reports someone's ideas without using that person's exact words. In academic writing, indirect quotation is called *paraphrase* or *summary*. (See R2-c.)

> Social media researcher Jameson Brown finds Twitter the best social media tool for companies that want to reach their consumers.

Exception: long quotations

Long quotations of prose or poetry are generally set off from the text by indenting. Quotation marks are not used because the indented format tells readers that the quotation is taken word-for-word from the source. The long quotation below is from an essay about Billy the Kid, a notorious outlaw of the American Old West.

> After making an exhaustive study of the historical record, James Horan evaluates Billy the Kid like this:
>
> > The portrait that emerges of [the Kid] from the thousands of pages of affidavits, reports, trial transcripts, his letters, and his testimony is neither the mythical Robin Hood nor the stereotyped adenoidal moron and pathological killer. Rather Billy appears as a disturbed, lonely young man, honest, loyal to his friends, dedicated to his beliefs, and betrayed by our institutions and the corrupt, ambitious, and compromising politicians of his time. (158)

The number in parentheses is a citation handled according to MLA style (see MLA-4a).

MLA, APA, and CMS have specific guidelines for what constitutes a long quotation and how it should be indented (see pp. 376, 446, and 503, respectively).

P5-b Use single quotation marks to enclose a quotation within a quotation.

> Megan Marshall notes that Elizabeth Peabody's school focused on "not merely 'teaching' but 'educating children morally and spiritually as well as intellectually from the first' " (107).

P5-c Use quotation marks around the titles of short works.

Short works include newspaper and magazine articles, poems, short stories, songs, episodes of television and radio programs, and chapters or subdivisions of books.

> Roch Carrier's short story "The Hockey Sweater" is based on a true story from his childhood.

NOTE: Titles of long works such as books, plays, television and radio programs, films, magazines, and so on are put in italics. (See P10-a.)

P5-d Quotation marks may be used to set off words used as words.

Although words used as words are ordinarily italicized (see p. 302), quotation marks are also acceptable. Be consistent throughout your paper.

> The terms "migrant" and "refugee" are frequently confused.

> The terms *migrant* and *refugee* are frequently confused.

P5-e Use punctuation with quotation marks according to convention.

This section describes the conventions Canadian publishers use in placing various marks of punctuation inside or outside quotation marks. It also explains how to punctuate when introducing quoted material. (For the use of quotation marks in MLA, APA, and CMS styles, see MLA-4, APA-4a, and CMS-4, respectively. The examples in this section show MLA style.)

Periods and commas

Place periods and commas inside quotation marks.

> "I'm here as part of my service-learning project," I told the classroom teacher. "I'm hoping to become a reading specialist."

This rule applies to single quotation marks as well as double quotation marks. (See P5-b.) It also applies to all uses of quotation marks: for quoted material, for titles of works, and for words used as words.

EXCEPTION: In the MLA and APA styles of parenthetical in-text citations, the period follows the citation in parentheses.

> David M. Quiring notes that in 1944, poverty in Saskatchewan "had reached legendary proportions, dashing the hopes of the immigrants who had come to this place once thought to be a Garden of Eden" (3).

Colons and semicolons

Put colons and semicolons outside quotation marks.

> Harold wrote, "I regret that I am unable to attend the fundraiser for diabetes research"; his letter, however, came with a substantial contribution.

Question marks and exclamation points

Put question marks and exclamation points inside quotation marks unless they apply to the whole sentence.

> Dr. Abram's first question on the first day of class was "What three goals do you have for the course?"

> Have you heard the old proverb "Do not climb the hill until you reach it"?

In the first sentence, the question mark applies only to the quoted question. In the second sentence, the question mark applies to the whole sentence.

NOTE: In MLA and APA styles for a quotation that ends with a question mark or an exclamation point, the parenthetical citation and a period should follow the entire quotation.

> Rosie Thomas asks, "Is nothing in life ever straight and clear, the way children see it?" (77).

Introducing quoted material

After a word group introducing a quotation, choose a colon, a comma, or no punctuation at all, whichever is appropriate in context.

FORMAL INTRODUCTION If a quotation is formally introduced, a colon is appropriate. A formal introduction is a full independent clause, not just an expression such as *he writes* or *she remarked*.

> Thomas Friedman provides a challenging yet optimistic view of the future: "We need to get back to work on our country and on our planet. The hour is late, the stakes couldn't be higher, the project couldn't be harder, the payoff couldn't be greater" (25).

EXPRESSION SUCH AS *HE WRITES* If a quotation is introduced with an expression such as *he writes* or *she remarked* — or if it is followed by such an expression — a comma is needed.

> "As soon as I get that first big laugh," Howie Mandel explains, "it's like a warm blanket covering me" (141).

> "The written record signed, sealed, and swiftly transmitted was essential to military power and the extension of government," Harold Innis wrote about the connection between successful empires and communication (30).

BLENDED QUOTATION When a quotation is blended into the writer's own sentence, either a comma or no punctuation is appropriate, depending on the way in which the quotation fits into the sentence structure.

> The future champion could, as he put it, "float like a butterfly and sting like a bee."

> Virginia Woolf wrote in 1928 that "a woman must have money and a room of her own if she is to write fiction" (4).

BEGINNING OF SENTENCE If a quotation appears at the beginning of a sentence, use a comma after it unless the quotation ends with a question mark or an exclamation point.

> "The truth is I rarely know where I am going to be from one day to the next," Canadian humourist Rick Mercer claims (xii).

> "What is it?" she asked, bracing herself.

INTERRUPTED QUOTATION If a quoted sentence is interrupted by explanatory words, use commas to set off the explanatory words. If two successive quoted sentences from the same source are interrupted by explanatory words, use a comma before the explanatory words and a period after them.

> "Everyone agrees journalists must tell the truth," Bill Kovach and Tom Rosenstiel write. "Yet people are befuddled about what 'the truth' means" (37).

P5-f Avoid common misuses of quotation marks.

Do not use quotation marks to draw attention to familiar slang, to disown trite expressions, or to justify an attempt at humour.

> ▶ The economist noted that his prediction for a 5 percent decline was only a ⁄ballpark figure.⁄

Do not use quotation marks around the title of your own essay.

P6 Other punctuation marks

P6-a End punctuation

The period

Use a period to end all sentences except direct questions or genuine exclamations. Also use periods in abbreviations according to convention.

TO END SENTENCES Most sentences should end with a period. A sentence that reports a question instead of asking it directly (an indirect question) should end with a period, not a question mark.

> ▶ The professor asked whether talk therapy was more beneficial than antidepressants⁄.
>   ^

If a sentence is not a genuine exclamation, it should end with a period, not an exclamation point. (See also p. 284.)

> ▶ After years of research, Dr. Low finally solved the equation⁄.
>   ^

LaunchPad macmillan learning   **ACTIVITIES FOR P6**
5 Exercises

IN ABBREVIATIONS   A period is conventionally used in abbreviations of titles and Latin words or phrases, including the time designations for morning and afternoon.

Mr.	i.e.	a.m. (or AM)
Ms.	e.g.	p.m. (or PM)
Dr.	etc.	

NOTE: If a sentence ends with a period marking an abbreviation, do not add a second period.

Do not use a period with postal abbreviations for provinces and territories: AB, NU, PE.

Current usage is to omit the period in abbreviations of organization names, academic degrees, and designations for eras.

NATO	NIH
CRA	BS
UNESCO	PhD
CUPE	BC
UBC	BCE

The question mark

A direct question should be followed by a question mark.

What is the horsepower of a 777 engine?

TIP: Do not use a question mark after an indirect question, one that is reported rather than asked directly. Use a period instead.

▶ He asked me who was teaching the math course this year~~?~~.
                                                            ^

The exclamation point

Use an exclamation point after a word group or sentence to express exceptional feeling or to provide special emphasis. The exclamation point is rarely appropriate in academic writing.

When Mischa entered the room, I switched on the lights, and we all yelled, "Surprise!"

TIP: Do not overuse the exclamation point.

▶ In the angler's memory, the fish lives on, increasing in length

and weight with each passing year, until at last it is big enough

to shade a fishing boat~~!~~.
                        ^

This sentence doesn't need to be pumped up with an exclamation point. It is emphatic enough without it.

P6-b The dash, parentheses, and brackets

The dash

When typing, use two hyphens to form a dash (--). Do not put spaces before or after the dash. If your word processing program has what is known as an "em-dash" (—), you may use it instead, with no space before or after it.

Use a dash to set off parenthetical material that deserves emphasis.

> One of music's rising trends — lyrics that promote the use of synthetic drugs — is leading some artists to speak out against their peers.

Use a dash to set off appositives that contain commas. An appositive is a noun or noun phrase that renames a nearby noun. Ordinarily most appositives are set off with commas (P1-e), but when the appositive itself contains commas, a pair of dashes helps readers see the relative importance of all the pauses.

> In my hometown, people's basic needs — food, clothing, and shelter — are less costly than in a big city like Toronto.

A dash can also be used to introduce a list, a restatement, an amplification, or a dramatic shift in tone or thought.

> Along the wall are the bulk liquids — sesame seed oil, honey, safflower oil, and that half-liquid "peanuts only" peanut butter.

> In his last semester, Peter tried to pay more attention to his priorities — applying to graduate school and getting financial aid.

> Everywhere we looked there were little kids — a bag of Skittles in one hand and their mommy or daddy's sleeve in the other.

> Kiere took a few steps back, came running full speed, kicked a mighty kick — and missed the ball.

In the first two examples, the writer could also use a colon. (See P3-d.) The colon is more formal than the dash and not quite as dramatic.

TIP: Unless there is a specific reason for using the dash, avoid it. Unnecessary dashes create a choppy effect.

Parentheses

Use parentheses to enclose supplemental material, minor digressions, and afterthoughts.

> Nurses record patients' vital signs (temperature, pulse, and blood pressure) several times a day.

Use parentheses to enclose letters or numbers labelling items in a series.

Regulations stipulated that only the following equipment could be used on the survival mission: (1) a knife, (2) ten metres of parachute line, (3) a book of matches, (4) two ponchos, (5) an E tool, and (6) a signal flare.

TIP: Rough drafts are likely to contain unnecessary parentheses. As writers head into a sentence, they often think of additional details, using parentheses to work them in as best they can. Such sentences usually can be revised to add the details without parentheses.

> **Researchers have said that three million** ~~(estimates run~~ *from* *to*
>
> ~~as high as~~ **five million)** **Canadians have diabetes.**

Brackets

Use brackets to enclose any words or phrases that you have inserted into an otherwise word-for-word quotation.

Audubon reports that "if there are not enough young to balance deaths, the end of the species [California condor] is inevitable" (4).

The sentence quoted from the *Audubon* article did not contain the words *California condor* (since the context of the full article made clear what species was meant), so the writer needed to add the name in brackets.

The Latin word "sic" in brackets indicates that an error in a quoted sentence appears in the original source.

According to the review, Adele's performance was brilliant, "exceding [sic] the expectations of even her most loyal fans."

Do not overuse "sic," however, since calling attention to others' mistakes can appear snobbish. The preceding quotation, for example, might have been paraphrased instead: *According to the review, even Adele's most loyal fans were surprised by the brilliance of her performance.*

NOTE: For advice on using "sic" in MLA, APA, and CMS styles, see MLA-3b, APA-3b, and CMS-3a, respectively.

P6-c The ellipsis mark

The ellipsis mark consists of three spaced periods. Use an ellipsis mark to indicate that you have deleted words from an otherwise word-for-word quotation.

Shute acknowledges that treatment for autism can be expensive: "Sensory integration therapy . . . can cost up to $200 an hour" (82).

If you delete a full sentence or more in the middle of a quoted passage, use a period before the three ellipsis dots.

> "If we don't properly train, teach, or treat our growing prison population," says Luis Rodríguez, "somebody else will. . . . This may well be the safety issue of the new century" (16).

TIP: Ordinarily, do not use the ellipsis mark at the beginning or at the end of a quotation. Readers will understand that the quoted material is taken from a longer passage. (If you have cut some words from the end of the final quoted sentence, however, MLA requires an ellipsis mark.)

In quoted poetry, use a full line of ellipsis dots to indicate that you have dropped a line or more from the poem, as in this example from "To His Coy Mistress" by Andrew Marvell:

> Had we but world enough, and time,
> This coyness, lady, were no crime.
> . . . .
> But at my back I always hear
> Time's wingèd chariot hurrying near; (1-2, 21-22)

P6-d The slash

Use the slash to separate two or three lines of poetry that have been run into your text. Add a space both before and after the slash.

> In the opening lines of "Jordan," George Herbert pokes gentle fun at popular poems of his time: "Who says that fictions only and false hair / Become a verse? Is there in truth no beauty?" (1-2).

Four or more lines of poetry should be handled as an indented quotation. (See p. 279.)

The slash may occasionally be used to separate paired terms such as *pass/fail* and *producer/director*. Do not use a space before or after the slash. Be sparing in this use of the slash. In particular, avoid the use of *and/or*, *he/she*, and *his/her*. Instead of using *he/she* and *his/her* to solve sexist language problems, you can usually find more graceful alternatives. (See W4-f and G3-a.)

P7 Spelling and hyphenation

You learned to spell from repeated experience with words in both reading and writing. As you proofread, you can probably tell if a word doesn't look quite right. In such cases, the solution is simple: Look up the word in a dictionary.

P7-a Become familiar with the major spelling rules.

i *before* e *except after* c

In general, use *i* before *e* except after *c* and except when it sounds like *ay*, as in *neighbour* and *weigh*.

I BEFORE *E*	relieve, believe, sieve, niece, fierce, piece
E BEFORE *I*	receive, deceive, sleigh, freight, eight
EXCEPTIONS	seize, either, weird, height, foreign, leisure

Suffixes

FINAL SILENT -*e*   Generally, drop a final silent -*e* when adding a suffix that begins with a vowel. Keep the final -*e* if the suffix begins with a consonant.

combine, combination	achieve, achievement
desire, desiring	care, careful
prude, prudish	entire, entirety
remove, removable	gentle, gentleness

Words such as *changeable, judgment, argument,* and *truly* are exceptions.

FINAL -*y*   When adding -*s* or -*d* to words ending in -*y*, ordinarily change -*y* to -*ie* when the -*y* is preceded by a consonant but not when it is preceded by a vowel.

comedy, comedies	monkey, monkeys
dry, dried	play, played

With proper names ending in -*y*, however, do not change the -*y* to -*ie* even if it is preceded by a consonant: *the Doughertys.*

FINAL CONSONANTS   If a final consonant is preceded by a single vowel *and* the consonant ends a one-syllable word or a stressed syllable, double the consonant when adding a suffix beginning with a vowel.

bet, betting	occur, occurrence
commit, committed	

Plurals

-s OR -es   Add *-s* to form the plural of most nouns; add *-es* to singular nouns ending in *-s*, *-sh*, *-ch*, and *-x*.

table, tables	church, churches
paper, papers	dish, dishes

Ordinarily add *-s* to nouns ending in *-o* when the *-o* is preceded by a vowel. Add *-es* when it is preceded by a consonant.

radio, radios	hero, heroes
video, videos	tomato, tomatoes

OTHER PLURALS   To form the plural of a hyphenated compound word, add *-s* to the chief word even if it does not appear at the end.

mother-in-law, mothers-in-law

English words derived from other languages such as Latin, Greek, or French sometimes form the plural as they would in their original language.

medium, media	chateau, chateaux
criterion, criteria	

Multilingual   Spelling varies slightly among English-speaking countries. Variations can be confusing for some multilingual students in Canada. Following is a list of some common words with different Canadian, American, and British spellings. Consult a dictionary for others.

CANADIAN	AMERICAN	BRITISH
cancelled, travelled	canceled, traveled	cancelled, travelled
colour, humour	color, humor	colour, humour
judgment or judgement	judgment	judgement
cheque	check	cheque
realize, apologize	realize, apologize	realise, apologise
defence	defense	defence
anemia, anaesthetic	anemia, anesthetic	anaemia, anaesthetic
theatre, centre	theater, center	theatre, centre
fetus	fetus	foetus
mould, smoulder	mold, smolder	mould, smoulder
civilization	civilization	civilisation
connection, inflection	connection, inflection	connexion, inflexion
licorice or liquorice	licorice	liquorice

P7-b Discriminate between words that sound alike but have different meanings.

Words that sound alike or nearly alike but have different meanings and spellings are called *homophones*. The following sets of words are commonly confused. A careful writer will double-check their every use. (See also the glossary of usage, W1.)

affect (verb: to exert an influence)
effect (verb: to accomplish; noun: result)

its (possessive pronoun: of or belonging to it)
it's (contraction of *it is* or *it has*)

loose (adjective: free, not securely attached)
lose (verb: to fail to keep, to be deprived of)

principal (adjective: most important; noun: head of a school)
principle (noun: a fundamental guideline or truth)

their (possessive pronoun: belonging to them)
they're (contraction of *they are*)
there (adverb: that place or position)

who's (contraction of *who is* or *who has*)
whose (possessive form of *who*)

your (possessive pronoun: belonging to you)
you're (contraction of *you are*)

P7-c Be alert to commonly misspelled words.

absence	arrangement	committee	emphasize
accidentally	ascend	competitive	environment
accommodate	athlete	conceivable	especially
achievement	attendance	conscience	exaggerated
acknowledge	basically	conscientious	exercise
acquaintance	beautiful	conscious	exhaust
acquire	beginning	criticism	existence
address	believe	criticize	extraordinary
all right	benefited	decision	familiar
amateur	bureau	definitely	fascinate
analyze	business	descendant	February
answer	calendar	desperate	foreign
apparently	cemetery	different	forty
appearance	changeable	disastrous	fourth
arctic	column	eighth	friend
argument	commitment	eligible	government
arithmetic	committed	embarrass	grammar

harass	mischievous	presence	siege
height	necessary	prevalent	similar
humorous	noticeable	privilege	sincerely
incidentally	occasion	proceed	sophomore
incredible	occurred	pronunciation	strictly
independence	occurrence	publicly	subtly
indispensable	pamphlet	quiet	succeed
inevitable	parallel	quite	surprise
intelligence	particularly	quizzes	thorough
irrelevant	pastime	receive	tomorrow
irresistible	permanent	recognize	tragedy
knowledge	permissible	referred	transferred
library	perseverance	restaurant	truly
license/licence	phenomenon	rhythm	unnecessarily
lightning	physically	roommate	usually
loneliness	practically	sandwich	vacuum
maintenance	precede	schedule	villain
manoeuvre	preference	seize	weird
marriage	preferred	separate	whether
mathematics	prejudice	sergeant	writing

P7-d Consult the dictionary to determine how to treat a compound word.

The dictionary indicates whether to treat a compound word as hyphenated (*water-repellent*), as one word (*waterproof*), or as two words (*water table*). If the compound word is not in the dictionary, treat it as two words.

▶ The prosecutor chose not to cross-examine any witnesses.

▶ All students are expected to record their data in a small

  note book.

▶ Alice walked through the looking glass into a backward world.

P7-e Hyphenate two or more words used together as an adjective before a noun.

▶ Today's teachers depend on both traditional textbook material

  and web-delivered content.

▶ Richa Gupta is not yet a well-known candidate.
^

Generally, do not use a hyphen when such compounds follow the noun.

▶ After our social media campaign, Richa Gupta will be well/known.

Do not use a hyphen to connect -ly adverbs to the words they modify.

▶ A slowly/moving truck tied up traffic.

P7-f Hyphenate fractions and certain numbers when they are spelled out.

For numbers written as words, use a hyphen in all fractions (*two-thirds*) and in all forms of compound numbers from twenty-one to ninety-nine (*thirty-five, sixty-seventh*).

P7-g Use a hyphen with the prefixes *all-*, *ex-* (meaning "former"), and *self-* and with the suffix *-elect*.

▶ The private foundation is funnelling more money into self-help projects.
^

▶ The Student Council bylaws require the president-elect to attend all
^
council meetings before the transfer of office.

P7-h Use a hyphen in certain words to avoid ambiguity.

Without the hyphen, there would be no way to distinguish between words such as *re-creation* and *recreation*.

Bicycling in the city has always been my favourite form of recreation.

The film was praised for its astonishing re-creation of nineteenth-century London.

Hyphens are sometimes used to separate awkward double or triple letters in compound words (*anti-intellectual*, *cross-stitch*).

P7-i Check for correct word breaks when words must be divided at the end of a line.

In academic writing, it's best to set your computer applications not to hyphenate automatically. This setting will ensure that only words already containing a hyphen (such as *long-distance* or *pre-Roman*) will be hyphenated at the ends of lines.

Email addresses and URLs need special attention when they occur at the end of a line of text or in bibliographic citations. You must make a decision about hyphenation in each case.

Do not insert a hyphen to divide electronic addresses. Instead, break an email address after the @ symbol or before a period. It is common practice to break a URL before most marks of punctuation. (For specific guidelines, see MLA-5, APA-5, and CMS-5.)

P8 Capitalization

In addition to the rules in this section, a good dictionary can tell you when to use capital letters.

P8-a Capitalize proper nouns and words derived from them; do not capitalize common nouns.

Proper nouns are the names of specific persons, places, and things. All other nouns are common nouns. The following types of words are usually capitalized: names of deities, religions, religious followers, sacred books; words of family relationship used as names; particular places; nationalities and their languages, races, bands; educational institutions, departments, particular courses; government departments, organizations, political parties; historical movements, periods, events, documents; and trade names.

PROPER NOUNS	COMMON NOUNS
God (used as a name)	a god
Book of Common Prayer	a sacred book
Uncle Pedro	my uncle
Father (used as a name)	my father
Lake Superior	a picturesque lake
the Peter Wall Institute	a centre for advanced studies
the Maritimes	an eastern province
Commonwealth Stadium	a football stadium
University of Windsor	a university
Geology 101	geology
the New Democratic Party	a political party
the Enlightenment	the eighteenth century
Advil	a painkiller

Months, holidays, and days of the week are treated as proper nouns; the seasons and numbers of the days of the month are not.

Our academic year begins on a Tuesday in early September, right after Labour Day.

Graduation is in late spring, on the second of June.

EXCEPTION: Capitalize Fourth of July (or July Fourth) when referring to the US holiday.

Names of school subjects are capitalized only if they are names of languages. Names of particular courses are capitalized.

This semester Lee is taking math, physics, French, and English.

Professor Obembe offers Modern Canadian Fiction 501 to graduate students.

The terms *web* and *website* have become widely accepted as lowercase. Style guidelines vary: MLA uses *Web* and *Web site*; APA and CMS use *web* and *website*. Other online and computer terminology is considered generic and is not capitalized: *home page* (or *homepage*), *operating system, app,* and so on. Check with your instructor about whether you should follow the guidelines in MLA-5, APA-5, or CMS-5.

NOTE: Do not capitalize common nouns to make them seem important.

P8-b Capitalize titles of persons when used as part of a proper name but usually not when used alone.

Professor Margaret Barnes; Dr. Eun Ju Kim; John Scott Williams Jr.

Crown Attorney Marshall was reprimanded for badgering the witness.

The lieutenant-governor was appointed last year.

Usage varies when the title of an important public figure is used alone: *The governor general* [or *Governor General*] *refused to give the bill Royal Assent.*

P8-c Capitalize titles according to convention.

In both titles and subtitles of works mentioned in the text of a paper, major words such as nouns, pronouns, verbs, adjectives, and adverbs should be capitalized. Minor words such as articles, prepositions, and coordinating conjunctions are not capitalized unless they are the first or last word of a title or subtitle. (In APA style, also capitalize all words of four or more letters. See APA-5.)

Capitalize the second part of a hyphenated term in a title if it is a major word but not if it is a minor word. Capitalize chapter titles and the titles of other major divisions of a work following the same guidelines used for titles of complete works.

> *Seizing the Enigma: The Race to Break the German U-Boat Codes*
> *A River Runs through It*
> "I Want to Hold Your Hand"

To see why some of the titles in the list are italicized and some are put in quotation marks, see P10-a and P5-c.

Titles of works are handled differently in the APA reference list. See "Preparing the list of references" in APA-5.

P8-d Capitalize the first word of a sentence.

The first word of a sentence should be capitalized. When a sentence appears within parentheses, capitalize its first word unless the parentheses appear within another sentence.

> Early detection of breast cancer significantly increases survival rates. (See table 2.)

> Early detection of breast cancer significantly increases survival rates (see table 2).

P8-e Capitalize the first word of a quoted sentence but not a quoted word or phrase.

> Loveless writes, "If failing schools are ever to be turned around, much more must be learned about how schools age as institutions" (25).

> Russell Baker has written that in the United States, sports are "the opiate of the masses" (46).

If a quoted sentence is interrupted by explanatory words, do not capitalize the first word after the interruption. (See also P5-e.)

> "If you want to go out," he said, "tell me now."

When quoting poetry, copy the poet's capitalization exactly. Many poets capitalize the first word of every line of poetry; a few contemporary poets dismiss capitalization altogether.

> it was the week   that
> i felt the city's narrow breezes rush about
> me   — Don L. Lee

P8-f Capitalize the first word after a colon if it begins an independent clause.

If a group of words following a colon could stand on its own as a complete sentence, capitalize the first word.

> Clinical trials called into question the safety profile of the drug:
> A high percentage of participants reported hypertension and kidney
> problems.

Preferences vary among academic disciplines. See MLA-5, APA-5, and CMS-5.
Always use lowercase for a list or an appositive that follows a colon (see P3-d).

> Students were divided into two groups: residents and commuters.

P9 Abbreviations and numbers

P9-a Use standard abbreviations for titles immediately before and after proper names.

**TITLES BEFORE
PROPER NAMES**

Mr. Rafael Zabala
Ms. Nancy Linehan
Dr. Margaret Simmons
Rev. John Stone

**TITLES AFTER
PROPER NAMES**

William Albert Sr.
Thomas Hines Jr.
Robert Simkowski, MD
Mia Chin, LLD

Do not abbreviate a title if it is not used with a proper name: *My history professor* [not *prof.*] *is an expert on race relations in South Africa.*
Avoid redundant titles such as *Dr. Amy Day, MD.* Choose one title or the other: *Dr. Amy Day* or *Amy Day, MD.*

P9-b Use abbreviations only when you are sure your readers will understand them.

Familiar abbreviations for the names of organizations, companies, countries, academic degrees, and common terms, written without periods, are generally acceptable.

DNA	MD
NBA	PhD
FBI	CBC
CEO	DVD

Game show host Alex Trebek graduated from the University of Ottawa with a BA in philosophy.

When using an unfamiliar abbreviation (such as *CASW* for Canadian Association of Social Workers) or a potentially ambiguous abbreviation (such as *CSA*, which can refer to either the Canadian Standards Association or the Canadian Space Agency), write the full name followed by the abbreviation in parentheses at the first mention of the name. Then use just the abbreviation throughout the rest of the paper.

NOTE: An abbreviation that can be pronounced as a word is called an *acronym*: *NATO, MADD, OPEC.*

P9-c Use *BC, AD, a.m., p.m., No.,* and *$* only with specific dates, times, numbers, and amounts.

The abbreviations *CE* ("common era") and *BCE* ("before the common era") both follow a date. Instead of *CE*, you may use the alternative form *AD* ("*anno Domini*"), which precedes a date; instead of *BCE*, you may use the alternative form *BC* ("before Christ"), which follows a date.

40 BCE (or 40 BC)

44 CE (or AD 44)

4:00 a.m. (or AM)

6:00 p.m. (or PM)

No. 12 (or no. 12)

$150

Avoid using *a.m., p.m., No.,* or *$* when not accompanied by a specific numeral: *in the morning* (not *in the a.m.*).

P9-d Units of measurement

The following are typical symbols and abbreviations for units of measurement. Most measurements in Canada are given in metric units (*km, mg*), but imperial or US standard units (*mi, lb*) are often still used. Generally, use symbols for metric units when they appear with numerals; spell out the units when they are used alone or when they are used with spelled-out numbers (see also P9-h).

METRIC UNITS	IMPERIAL OR US STANDARD UNITS
m, cm, mm	yd, ft, in.
km, kph	mi, mph
kg, g, mg	lb, oz

Results were measured in pounds.

Runners in the 5–km race had to contend with pouring rain.

Use no periods after metric symbols and abbreviations for units of measurement, except the abbreviation for "inch" (*in.*), to distinguish it from the preposition *in*.

P9-e Be sparing in your use of Latin abbreviations.

Latin abbreviations are acceptable in notes and bibliographies.

cf. (Latin *confer*, "compare")

e.g. (Latin *exempli gratia*, "for example")

et al. (Latin *et alia*, "and others")

etc. (Latin *et cetera*, "and so forth")

i.e. (Latin *id est*, "that is")

N.B. (Latin *nota bene*, "note well")

In the text of a paper in most academic fields, use the appropriate English phrases.

P9-f Plural of abbreviations

To form the plural of most abbreviations, add -*s*, without an apostrophe: *PhDs, DVDs*. Do not add -*s* to indicate the plural of units of measurement: *mm* (not *mms*), *lb* (not *lbs*), *in.* (not *ins.*).

P9-g Avoid inappropriate abbreviations.

In academic writing, abbreviations for the following are not commonly accepted.

PERSONAL NAMES   Charles (not Chas.)

DAYS OF THE WEEK   Monday (not Mon.)

HOLIDAYS   Christmas (not Xmas)

MONTHS   January, February, March (not Jan., Feb., Mar.)

COURSES OF STUDY   political science (not poli. sci.)

DIVISIONS OF WRITTEN WORKS   chapter, page (not ch., p.)

PROVINCES, TERRITORIES, COUNTRIES   Saskatchewan (not SK or Sask.)

PARTS OF A BUSINESS NAME   Adams Lighting Company (not Adams Lighting Co.); Zeiss and Brothers (not Zeiss and Bros.)

NOTE: Use symbols or abbreviations for units of measurement when they are preceded by numerals (*13 cm*). Do not abbreviate them or use symbols when they are used alone. See P9-d.

EXCEPTION: Abbreviate states, provinces, and territories in complete addresses, and always abbreviate *DC* when used with *Washington*.

P9-h Follow the conventions in your discipline for spelling out or using numerals to express numbers.

In the humanities, which generally follow Modern Language Association (MLA) style, use numerals only for specific numbers larger than one hundred: *353; 1,020*. Spell out numbers one hundred and below and large round numbers: *eleven, thirty-five, fifteen million*. Treat related numbers in a passage consistently: *The survey found that 9 of the 157 students had not taken a course on alcohol use.*

The social sciences and other disciplines that follow American Psychological Association (APA) style use numerals for all but the numbers one through nine. Spell out numbers from one to nine even when they are used with related numerals in a passage: *The survey found that nine of the 157 respondents had not taken a course on alcohol use.* (An exception is the abstract of a paper, where numerals are used for all numbers. See APA-5.)

If a sentence begins with a number, spell out the number or rewrite the sentence.

> One hundred fifty
> ▶ ~~150~~ children in our program need expensive dental treatment.
>   ^

Rewriting the sentence may be less awkward if the number is long: *In our program, 150 children need expensive dental treatment.*

P9-i Use numerals according to convention in dates, addresses, and so on.

DATES   July 4, 1776; 56 BCE; 30 CE

ADDRESSES   77 Latches Lane, 4147 42nd Street SW

PERCENTAGES   55 percent (or 55%)

FRACTIONS, DECIMALS   ⅞, 0.047

SCORES   7 to 3, 21–18

STATISTICS   average age 37, average weight 80 kg

SURVEYS   4 out of 5

EXACT AMOUNTS OF MONEY $105.37, $106,000

DIVISIONS OF BOOKS   volume 3, chapter 4, page 189

DIVISIONS OF PLAYS   act 3, scene 3 (or act III, scene iii)

TIME OF DAY   4:00 p.m., 1:30 a.m.

NOTE: When not using *a.m.* or *p.m.*, write out the time in words (*two o'clock in the afternoon, twelve noon, seven in the morning*).

P10 Italics

This section describes conventional uses for italics. (If your instructor prefers underlining, simply substitute underlining for italics in the examples in this section.)

Some computer and online applications do not allow for italics. To indicate words that should be italicized, you can use underscore marks or asterisks before and after the words.

I am planning to write my senior thesis on _The Book Thief_.

NOTE: Excessive use of italics to emphasize words or ideas, especially in academic writing, is distracting and should be avoided.

 LaunchPad macmillan learning   **ACTIVITIES FOR P10**
3 Exercises

P10-a Italicize the titles of works according to convention.

Titles of the following types of works should be italicized.

TITLES OF BOOKS   *The Color Purple, The Round House*

MAGAZINES   *Time, Maclean's, Canadian Business*

NEWSPAPERS   *The Toronto Sun, Calgary Herald*

PAMPHLETS   *Common Sense, Facts about Marijuana*

LONG POEMS   *The Waste Land, Paradise Lost*

PLAYS   *The Humans, Hamilton*

FILMS   *Casablanca, Argo*

TELEVISION PROGRAMS   *Trailer Park Boys, Orphan Black*

RADIO PROGRAMS   *All Things Considered*

MUSICAL COMPOSITIONS   *Porgy and Bess*

CHOREOGRAPHIC WORKS   *Brief Fling*

WORKS OF VISUAL ART   *The Jack Pine*

VIDEO GAMES   *Everquest, Call of Duty*

DATABASES [MLA]   *JSTOR*

WEBSITES [MLA]   *Salon, Google*

COMPUTER SOFTWARE OR APPS [MLA]   *Photoshop, Instagram*

The titles of other works — including short stories, essays, episodes of radio and television programs, songs, and short poems — are enclosed in quotation marks. (See P5-c.)

NOTE: Do not use italics when referring to the Bible, titles of books in the Bible (Genesis, not *Genesis*), or titles of legal documents (the Charter of Rights and Freedoms, not the *Charter of Rights and Freedoms*).

P10-b Italicize other terms according to convention.

Ships, spacecraft, and aircraft

Queen Mary 2, Endeavour, Wright Flyer

The success of the Soviets' *Sputnik* energized the US space program.

Foreign words

Shakespeare's Falstaff is a comic character known for both his excessive drinking and his general *joie de vivre*.

EXCEPTION: Do not italicize foreign words that have become a standard part of the English language — "laissez-faire," "fait accompli," "modus operandi," and "per diem," for example.

Words mentioned as words, letters mentioned as letters, and numbers mentioned as numbers

Tomás assured us that the chemicals could probably be safely mixed, but his *probably* stuck in our minds.

Some toddlers have trouble pronouncing the letters *f* and *s*.

A big *3* was painted on the stage door.

NOTE: Quotation marks may be used instead of italics to set off words mentioned as words. (See P5-d.)

B

Basic Grammar

Will I be a better writer if I know grammar basics?

See
B1–B4

B Basic Grammar

B1 Parts of speech

Traditional grammar recognizes eight parts of speech: noun, pronoun, verb, adjective, adverb, preposition, conjunction, and interjection. Many words can function as more than one part of speech. For example, depending on its use in a sentence, the word *paint* can be a noun (*The paint is wet*) or a verb (*Please paint the ceiling next*).

B1-a Nouns

A noun is the name of a person, place, thing, or concept.

>   N   N   N
> The *lion* in the *cage* growled at the *zookeeper*.

Nouns sometimes function as adjectives modifying other nouns. Because of their dual roles, nouns used in this manner may be called *noun/adjectives*.

>   N/ADJ   N/ADJ
> The *leather* notebook was tucked in the *student's* backpack.

Nouns are classified in a variety of ways. *Proper* nouns are capitalized, but *common* nouns are not (see P8-a). For clarity, writers choose between *concrete* and *abstract* nouns (see W5-b). The distinction between *count* nouns and *non-count* nouns can be especially helpful to multilingual writers (see M2-a). Most nouns have singular and plural forms; *collective* nouns may be either singular or plural, depending on how they are used (see G1-f and G3-a). *Possessive* nouns require an apostrophe (see P4-a).

B1-b Pronouns

A pronoun is a word used in place of a noun. Usually the pronoun substitutes for a specific noun, known as its *antecedent*.

>   ANT   PN
> When the *battery* wears down, we recharge *it*.

Although most pronouns function as substitutes for nouns, some can function as adjectives modifying nouns. Such pronouns may be called *pronoun/adjectives*.

>   PN/ADJ
> *That* bird was at the same window yesterday morning.

 LaunchPad
macmillan learning

ACTIVITIES FOR B1
9 Exercises, 3 LearningCurve activities

Pronouns are classified in the following ways.

PERSONAL PRONOUNS Personal pronouns refer to specific persons or things. They always function as substitutes for nouns.

Singular: I, me, you, she, her, he, him, it

Plural: we, us, you, they, them

POSSESSIVE PRONOUNS Possessive pronouns indicate ownership.

Singular: my, mine, your, yours, her, hers, his, its

Plural: our, ours, your, yours, their, theirs

Some of these possessive pronouns function as adjectives modifying nouns: *my, your, his, her, its, our, their.*

INTENSIVE AND REFLEXIVE PRONOUNS Intensive pronouns emphasize a noun or another pronoun (The mayor *herself* met us at the door). Reflexive pronouns name a receiver of an action identical with the doer of the action (Paula cut *herself*).

Singular: myself, yourself, himself, herself, itself

Plural: ourselves, yourselves, themselves

RELATIVE PRONOUNS Relative pronouns introduce subordinate clauses functioning as adjectives (The writer *who won the award* refused to accept it). The relative pronoun, in this case *who*, also points back to a noun or pronoun that the clause modifies (*writer*). (See B3-e.)

who, whom, whose, which, that

The pronouns *whichever, whoever, whomever, what,* and *whatever* are sometimes considered relative pronouns, but they introduce noun clauses and do not point back to a noun or pronoun. (See "Noun clauses" in B3-e.)

INTERROGATIVE PRONOUNS Interrogative pronouns introduce questions (*Who* is expected to win the election?).

who, whom, whose, which, what

DEMONSTRATIVE PRONOUNS Demonstrative pronouns identify or point to nouns. Frequently they function as adjectives (*This* chair is my favourite), but they may also function as substitutes for nouns (*This* is my favourite chair).

this, that, these, those

INDEFINITE PRONOUNS Indefinite pronouns refer to nonspecific persons or things. Most are always singular (*everyone, each*); some are always plural (*both, many*); a few may be singular or plural (see G1-e). Most indefinite pronouns function as substitutes for nouns (*Something* is burning), but some can also function as adjectives (*All* campers must check in at the lodge).

all	anything	everyone	nobody	several
another	both	everything	none	some
any	each	few	no one	somebody
anybody	either	many	nothing	someone
anyone	everybody	neither	one	something

RECIPROCAL PRONOUNS Reciprocal pronouns refer to individual parts of a plural antecedent (By turns, the penguins fed *one another*).

each other, one another

NOTE: See also pronoun-antecedent agreement (G3-a), pronoun reference (G3-b), distinguishing between pronouns such as *I* and *me* (G3-c), and distinguishing between *who* and *whom* (G3-d).

B1-c Verbs

The verb of a sentence usually expresses action (*jump, think*) or being (*is, become*). It is composed of a main verb possibly preceded by one or more helping verbs.

MV
The horses *exercise* every day.

HV MV
The task force report *was* not *completed* on schedule.

HV HV MV
No one *has been defended* with more passion than our pastor.

Notice that words, usually adverbs, can intervene between the helping verb and the main verb (was *not* completed). (See B1-e.)

Helping verbs

There are twenty-three helping verbs in English: forms of *have, do,* and *be,* which may also function as main verbs; and nine modals, which function only as helping verbs. *Have, do,* and *be* change form to indicate tense; the nine modals do not.

FORMS OF *HAVE, DO,* AND *BE*
have, has, had
do, does, did
be, am, is, are, was, were, being, been

MODALS
can, could, may, might, must, shall, should, will, would

The verb phrase *ought to* is often classified as a modal as well.

Main verbs

The main verb of a sentence is always the kind of word that would change form if put into these test sentences:

BASE FORM	Usually I (*walk, ride*).
PAST TENSE	Yesterday I (*walked, rode*).
PAST PARTICIPLE	I have (*walked, ridden*) many times before.
PRESENT PARTICIPLE	I am (*walking, riding*) right now.
-S FORM	Usually he/she/it (*walks, rides*).

If a word doesn't change form when slipped into the test sentences, you can be certain that it is not a main verb. For example, the noun *revolution*, though it may seem to suggest an action, can never function as a main verb. Just try to make it behave like one (*Today I revolution . . . , Yesterday I revolutioned . . .*) and you'll see why.

When both the past-tense and the past-participle forms of a verb end in -*ed*, the verb is regular (*walked, walked*). Otherwise, the verb is irregular (*rode, ridden*). (See G2-a.)

The verb *be* is highly irregular, having eight forms instead of the usual five: the base form *be*; the present-tense forms *am, is,* and *are*; the past-tense forms *was* and *were*; the present participle *being*; and the past participle *been*.

Helping verbs combine with main verbs to create tenses. See G2-f.

NOTE: Some verbs are followed by words that look like prepositions but are so closely associated with the verb that they are a part of its meaning. These words are known as particles. Common verb-particle combinations include *bring up, drop off, give in, look up, run into,* and *take off.*

TIP: For more information about using verbs, see these sections of the handbook: active verbs (W3), subject-verb agreement (G1), Standard English verb forms (G2-a to G2-d), verb tense and mood (G2-f and G2-g), and verbs for multilingual writers (M1).

B1-d Adjectives

An adjective is a word used to modify, or describe, a noun or pronoun. An adjective usually answers one of these questions: Which one? What kind of? How many?

ADJ
the *playful* dog [Which dog?]

ADJ
qualified applicants [What kind of applicants?]

ADJ
nine months [How many months?]

Adjectives usually precede the words they modify. They may also follow linking verbs, in which case they describe the subject. (See B2-b.)

ADJ
The decision was *unpopular.*

The definite article *the* and the indefinite articles *a* and *an* are also classified as adjectives.

ART   ART   ART
A defendant should be judged on *the* evidence provided to *the* jury, not on hearsay.

Some possessive, demonstrative, and indefinite pronouns can function as adjectives: *their, its, this, all* (see B1-b). And nouns can function as adjectives when they modify other nouns: *apple pie* (the noun *apple* modifies the noun *pie*; see B1-a).

TIP: You can find more details about using adjectives in G4. If you are a multilingual writer, you may find help with articles and specific uses of adjectives in M2 and M4.

B1-e Adverbs

An adverb is a word used to modify, or qualify, a verb (or verbal), an adjective, or another adverb. It usually answers one of these questions: When? Where? How? Why? Under what conditions? To what degree?

Pull *firmly* on the emergency handle. [Pull how?]

Read the text *first* and *then* complete the exercises. [Read when? Complete when?]

Place the flowers *here.* [Place where?]

Adverbs modifying adjectives or other adverbs usually intensify or limit the intensity of the word they modify.

ADV
Be *extremely* kind, and you will have many friends.

ADV
We proceeded *very* cautiously in the dark house.

The words *not* and *never* are classified as adverbs.

B1-f Prepositions

A preposition is a word placed before a noun or a pronoun to form a phrase that modifies another word in the sentence. The prepositional phrase functions as an adjective or an adverb.

$$\overset{P}{} \quad \overset{P}{} \quad \overset{P}{}$$
The winding road *to* the summit travels *past* craters *from* an extinct volcano.

To the summit functions as an adjective modifying the noun *road*; *past craters* functions as an adverb modifying the verb *travels*; *from an extinct volcano* functions as an adjective modifying the noun *craters*. (For more on prepositional phrases, see B3-a.)

English has a limited number of prepositions. The most common are included in the following list.

about	beyond	next	through
above	but	of	throughout
across	by	off	till
after	concerning	on	to
against	considering	onto	toward
along	despite	opposite	under
among	down	out	underneath
around	during	outside	unlike
as	except	over	until
at	for	past	unto
before	from	plus	up
behind	in	regarding	upon
below	inside	respecting	with
beside	into	round	within
besides	like	since	without
between	near	than	

Some prepositions are more than one word long. *Along with, as well as, in addition to, next to,* and *rather than* are examples.

TIP: Prepositions are used in idioms such as *capable of* and *dig up* (see W5-d). For specific issues for multilingual writers, see M5.

B1-g Conjunctions

Conjunctions join words, phrases, or clauses, and they indicate the relation between the elements joined.

COORDINATING CONJUNCTIONS   A coordinating conjunction is used to connect grammatically equal elements. (See S1-b and S6.) The coordinating conjunctions are *and, but, or, nor, for, so,* and *yet.*

> The sociologist interviewed children *but* not their parents.

> Write clearly, *and* your readers will appreciate your efforts.

In the first sentence, *but* connects two noun phrases; in the second, *and* connects two independent clauses.

CORRELATIVE CONJUNCTIONS   Correlative conjunctions come in pairs; they connect grammatically equal elements.

> either . . . or
>
> neither . . . nor
>
> not only . . . but also
>
> whether . . . or
>
> both . . . and

> *Either* the painting was brilliant *or* it was a forgery.

SUBORDINATING CONJUNCTIONS   A subordinating conjunction introduces a subordinate clause and indicates the relation of the clause to the rest of the sentence. (See B3-e.) The most common subordinating conjunctions are *after, although, as, as if, because, before, if, in order that, once, since, so that, than, that, though, unless, until, when, where, whether,* and *while.* (For a complete list, see p. 322.)

> *When* the fundraiser ends, we expect to have raised more than half a million dollars.

CONJUNCTIVE ADVERBS   Conjunctive adverbs connect independent clauses and indicate the relation between the clauses. They can be used with a semicolon to join two independent clauses in one sentence, or they can be used alone with an independent clause. The most common conjunctive adverbs are *finally, furthermore, however, moreover, nevertheless, similarly, then, therefore,* and *thus.* (For a complete list, see p. 272.)

> The photographer failed to take a light reading; *therefore,* all the pictures were underexposed.

> During the day, the kitten sleeps peacefully. *However,* when night falls, the kitten is wide awake and ready to play.

Conjunctive adverbs can appear at the beginning or in the middle of a clause.

> When night falls, *however*, the kitten is wide awake and ready to play.

TIP: The ability to distinguish between conjunctive adverbs and coordinating conjunctions will help you avoid run-on sentences and make punctuation decisions (see G6, P1-a, and P1-f). The ability to recognize subordinating conjunctions will help you avoid sentence fragments (see G5).

B1-h Interjections

An interjection is a word used to express surprise or emotion (*Oh! Hey! Wow!*).

B2 Sentence patterns

The vast majority of English sentences conform to one of these five patterns:

> subject/verb/subject complement
> subject/verb/direct object
> subject/verb/indirect object/direct object
> subject/verb/direct object/object complement
> subject/verb

Adverbial modifiers (single words, phrases, or clauses) may be added to any of these patterns, and they may appear nearly anywhere — at the beginning, in the middle, or at the end.

> *Predicate* is the grammatical term given to the verb plus its objects, complements, and adverbial modifiers.

B2-a Subjects

The subject of a sentence names whom or what the sentence is about. The simple subject is always a noun or pronoun; the complete subject consists of the simple subject and any words or word groups modifying the simple subject.

The complete subject

To find the complete subject, ask Who? or What?, insert the verb, and finish the question. The answer is the complete subject.

⌐——— COMPLETE SUBJECT ———⌐
The devastating effects of famine can last for many years.

Who or what can last for many years? *The devastating effects of famine.*

⌐———————— COMPLETE SUBJECT ————————⌐
Adventure novels that contain multiple subplots are often made into successful movies.

Who or what are often made into movies? *Adventure novels that contain multiple subplots.*

COMPLETE
⌐—— SUBJECT——⌐
In our program, student teachers work full-time for ten months.

Who or what works full-time for ten months? *Student teachers.* Notice that *In our program, student teachers* is not a sensible answer to the question. (It is not wise to assume that the subject must always appear first in a sentence.)

The simple subject

To find the simple subject, strip away all modifiers in the complete subject. This includes single-word modifiers such as *the* and *devastating*, phrases such as *of famine*, and subordinate clauses such as *that contain multiple subplots.*

⌐ SS ⌐
The devastating *effects* of famine can last for many years.

⌐ SS ⌐
Adventure *novels* that contain multiple subplots are often made into successful movies.

A sentence may have a compound subject containing two or more simple subjects joined with a coordinating conjunction such as *and, but,* or *or.*

⌐—— SS ——⌐   ⌐SS⌐
Great *commitment* and a little *luck* make a successful actor.

Understood subjects

In imperative sentences, which give advice or issue commands, the subject is understood but not actually present in the sentence. The subject of an imperative sentence is understood to be *you.*

[*You*] Put your hands on the steering wheel.

Subject after the verb

Although the subject ordinarily comes before the verb (*The planes took off*), occasionally it does not. When a sentence begins with *There is* or *There are* (or *There was* or *There were*), the subject follows the verb. In such inverted constructions, the word *There* is an expletive, an empty word serving merely to get the sentence started.

┌ SS ┐
There are *eight planes waiting to take off.*

Occasionally a writer will invert a sentence for effect.

┌SS┐
Joyful is *the child whose school closes for snow.*

Joyful is an adjective, so it cannot be the subject. Turn this sentence around and its structure becomes obvious.

The *child* whose school closes for snow is joyful.

In questions, the subject frequently appears between the helping verb and the main verb.

HV ┌── SS ──┐ MV
Do *Kenyan marathoners* train year-round?

TIP: The ability to recognize the subject of a sentence will help you edit for fragments (G5), subject-verb agreement (G1), pronouns such as *I* and *me* (G3-c), missing subjects (M3-b), and repeated subjects (M3-c).

B2-b Verbs, objects, and complements

Section B1-c explains how to find the verb of a sentence. A sentence's verb is classified as linking, transitive, or intransitive, depending on the kinds of objects or complements the verb can (or cannot) take.

Linking verbs and subject complements

Linking verbs connect the subject to a subject complement, a word or word group that completes the meaning of the subject by renaming or describing it.

If the subject complement renames the subject, it is a noun or noun equivalent (sometimes called a *predicate noun*).

┌──────── S ────────┐┌ V ┐┌ SC ┐
An email message requesting personal information may be a scam.

If the subject complement describes the subject, it is an adjective or adjective equivalent (sometimes called a *predicate adjective*).

```
        ┌──────── S ────────┐ V   SC
        Last month's temperatures were mild.
```

Whenever they appear as main verbs (rather than helping verbs), the forms of *be* — *be, am, is, are, was, were, being, been* — usually function as linking verbs. In the preceding examples, for instance, the main verbs are *be* and *were*.

Verbs such as *appear, become, feel, grow, look, make, seem, smell, sound,* and *taste* are linking when they are followed by a word or word group that renames or describes the subject.

```
              ┌─ S ─┐┌─ V ─┐   SC
        As it thickens, the sauce will look unappealing.
```

Transitive verbs and direct objects

A transitive verb takes a direct object, a word or word group that names a receiver of the action.

```
        ┌──── S ────┐  V   ┌──── DO ────┐
        The hungry cat clawed the bag of dry food.
```

The simple direct object is always a noun or pronoun, in this case *bag*. To find it, simply strip away all modifiers.

Transitive verbs usually appear in the active voice, with the subject doing the action and a direct object receiving the action. Active-voice sentences can be transformed into passive, with the subject receiving the action.

Transitive verbs, indirect objects, and direct objects

The direct object of a transitive verb is sometimes preceded by an indirect object, a noun or pronoun telling to whom or for whom the action of the sentence is done.

```
        S   V   IO ┌─ DO ─┐      S ┌─ V ─┐ IO ┌ DO ┐
        You give her some yarn, and she will knit you a scarf.
```

The simple indirect object is always a noun or pronoun. To test for an indirect object, insert the word *to* or *for* before the word or word group in question. If the sentence makes sense, the word or word group is an indirect object.

You give [to] *her* some yarn, and she will knit [for] *you* a scarf.

Transitive verbs, direct objects, and object complements

The direct object of a transitive verb is sometimes followed by an object complement, a word or word group that renames or describes the object.

```
    S           V       DO    ┌──── OC ────┐
People often consider chivalry a thing of the past.
```

```
 ┌─ S ─┐  V    DO   ┌──── OC ────┐
The kiln makes clay firm and strong.
```

When the object complement renames the direct object, it is a noun or pronoun (such as *thing*). When it describes the direct object, it is an adjective (such as *firm* and *strong*).

Intransitive verbs

Intransitive verbs take no objects or complements.

```
 ┌──── S ────┐  V
The audience laughed.
```

```
 ┌── S ──┐   V
The driver accelerated in the straightaway.
```

Nothing receives the actions of laughing and accelerating in these sentences, so the verbs are intransitive. Notice that such verbs may or may not be followed by adverbial modifiers. In the second sentence, *in the straightaway* is an adverbial prepositional phrase modifying *accelerated*. See B3-a.

NOTE: The dictionary will tell you whether a verb is transitive or intransitive. Some verbs can be both transitive and intransitive.

> **TRANSITIVE**   Sandra *flew* her small plane over the canyon.
>
> **INTRANSITIVE**   A flock of migrating geese *flew* overhead.

In the first example, *flew* has a direct object that receives the action: *her small plane*. In the second example, the verb is followed by an adverb (*overhead*), not by a direct object.

B3 Subordinate word groups

Subordinate word groups include phrases and clauses. Phrases are subordinate because they lack a subject and a verb; they are classified as prepositional, verbal, appositive, and absolute (see B3-a to B3-d). Subordinate clauses have a subject and a verb, but they begin with a word (such as *although, that,* or *when*) that marks them as subordinate (see B3-e).

B3-a Prepositional phrases

A prepositional phrase begins with a preposition such as *at, by, for, from, in, of, on, to,* or *with* (see B1-f) and usually ends with a noun or noun equivalent: *on the table, for him, by sleeping late.* The noun or noun equivalent is known as the *object of the preposition.*

Prepositional phrases function as adjectives or as adverbs. As an adjective, a prepositional phrase nearly always appears immediately following the noun or pronoun it modifies.

The hut had *walls of mud.*

Adjective phrases usually answer one or both of the questions Which one? and What kind of? If we ask Which walls? or What kind of walls? we get a sensible answer: *walls of mud.*

Adverbial prepositional phrases usually modify the verb, but they can also modify adjectives or other adverbs. When a prepositional phrase modifies the verb, it can appear nearly anywhere in a sentence.

James *walked* his dog *on a leash.*

Sabrina *will in time adjust* to life in Ecuador.

During a mudslide, the terrain *can change* drastically.

If a prepositional phrase is movable, you can be certain that it is adverbial.

In the cave, the explorers found well-preserved prehistoric drawings.

The explorers found well-preserved prehistoric drawings *in the cave.*

Adverbial word groups usually answer one of these questions: When? Where? How? Why? Under what conditions? To what degree?

James walked his dog *how? On a leash.*

Sabrina will adjust to life in Ecuador *when? In time.*

The terrain can change drastically *under what conditions? During a mudslide.*

In questions and subordinate clauses, a preposition may appear after its object.

What are you afraid *of*?

We avoided the bike trail *that* John had warned us *about*.

B3-b Verbal phrases

A verbal is a verb form that does not function as the verb of a clause. Verbals include infinitives (the word *to* plus the base form of the verb), present participles (the *-ing* form of the verb), and past participles (the verb form usually ending in *-d*, *-ed*, *-n*, *-en*, or *-t*). (See G2-a and B1-c.)

INFINITIVE	PRESENT PARTICIPLE	PAST PARTICIPLE
to dream	dreaming	dreamed or dreamt
to choose	choosing	chosen
to build	building	built

Instead of functioning as the verb of a clause, a verbal functions as an adjective, a noun, or an adverb.

ADJECTIVE	*Broken* promises cannot be fixed.
NOUN	Constant *complaining* becomes wearisome.
ADVERB	Can you wait *to celebrate*?

Verbals with objects, complements, or modifiers form verbal phrases.

In my family, *singing loudly* is more appreciated than *singing well*.

Like verbals, verbal phrases function as adjectives, nouns, or adverbs. Verbal phrases are ordinarily classified as participial, gerund, and infinitive.

Participial phrases

Participial phrases always function as adjectives. Their verbals are either present participles (such as *dreaming, asking*) or past participles (such as *stolen, reached*).
    Participial phrases frequently appear immediately following the noun or pronoun they modify.

Jamal saw his *cousin waving from across the street.*

Participial phrases are often movable. They can precede the word they modify.

Being a weight-bearing joint, the *knee* is among the most frequently injured.

They may also appear at some distance from the word they modify.

Last night we saw a *play* that affected us deeply, *written with profound insight into the lives of immigrants.*

Gerund phrases

Gerund phrases are built around present participles (verb forms that end in -*ing*), and they always function as nouns: usually as subjects, subject complements, direct objects, or objects of a preposition.

S
Rationalizing a fear can eliminate it.

SC
The key to good sauce is browning the mushrooms.

DO
Lizards usually enjoy sunning themselves.

The Heart and Stroke Foundation of Canada has documented the benefits of diet
OBJ OF PREP
and exercise in reducing the risk of heart attack.

Infinitive phrases

Infinitive phrases, usually constructed around *to* plus the base form of the verb (*to call, to drink*), can function as nouns, as adjectives, or as adverbs. When functioning as a noun, an infinitive phrase may appear in almost any noun slot in a sentence, usually as a subject, subject complement, or direct object.

S
To give her speech without fainting was her goal.

Infinitive phrases functioning as adjectives usually appear immediately following the noun or pronoun they modify.

You have the *right to vote.*

The infinitive phrase modifies the noun *right*. Which right? The *right to vote*.
Adverbial infinitive phrases usually qualify the meaning of the verb, telling when, where, how, why, under what conditions, or to what degree an action occurred.

Volunteers *rolled up* their pants *to wade through the flood waters.*

NOTE: In some constructions, the infinitive is unmarked; that is, the *to* does not appear. (See M1-f.)

> Graphs and charts can help researchers [*to*] *present complex data.*

B3-c Appositive phrases

Appositive phrases describe nouns or pronouns. Instead of modifying nouns or pronouns, however, appositive phrases rename them. In form they are nouns or noun equivalents. In the following example, the appositive *conversationalists at heart* renames the noun *Bloggers*.

> Bloggers, *conversationalists at heart*, are the online equivalent of radio talk show hosts.

B3-d Absolute phrases

An absolute phrase modifies a whole clause or sentence, not just one word. It consists of a noun or noun equivalent usually followed by a participial phrase.

> *Her words reverberating in the hushed arena*, the premier urged the crowd to support her former opponent.

B3-e Subordinate clauses

Subordinate clauses are patterned like sentences, having subjects and verbs and sometimes objects or complements. But they function within sentences as adjectives, adverbs, or nouns. They cannot stand alone as complete sentences.

A subordinate clause usually begins with a subordinating conjunction or a relative pronoun. The chart on page 322 classifies these words according to the kinds of clauses (adjective, adverb, or noun) they introduce.

Adjective clauses

Adjective clauses modify nouns or pronouns, usually answering the question Which one? or What kind of? Most adjective clauses begin with a relative pronoun (*who, whom, whose, which,* or *that*). In addition to introducing the clause, the relative pronoun points back to the noun that the clause modifies.

> The coach chose *players who would benefit from intense drills.*

> A *book that goes unread* is a writer's worst nightmare.

Writer's Choice
Building credibility with appositives

Appositives rename a noun or pronoun. Writers often use them to help an **audience** better understand a person or thing or to give that person or thing fuller context. Consider the following pair of sentences.

> Helene Aumais surprised everyone by winning the Crescent City 10k road race.

> Helene Aumais, a woman who had never run more than a kilometre before last month, surprised everyone by winning the Crescent City 10k road race.

In the second example, the writer uses an appositive to give more information about Helene Aumais, the subject of the sentence, and to suggest to readers why the win was so surprising.

As a college or university research writer, you will often use appositives to build your own credibility as you cite sources within your own text. To come across as a knowledgeable researcher who draws on relevant and reliable sources of information, you can give the credentials for your source in an appositive phrase.

CITATION WITH NO CREDENTIALS	According to John Dunlosky, regular use of practice tests "can substantially boost student learning" (14).
CITATION WITH CREDENTIALS	According to John Dunlosky, a researcher and professor of psychology at Kent State University in the United States, regular use of practice tests "can substantially boost student learning" (14).
	The first sentence, while not incorrect, may prompt your readers to question who John Dunlosky is and, further, why anyone should care. The second sentence adds language that suggests Dunlosky's authority on the subject and that positions you as a credible researcher.

As a research writer, you use sources to help you fulfill your purpose — to inform or to persuade — and to help you meet the needs of your audience. Choosing to use appositives to introduce sources builds your credibility as a researcher.

Words that introduce subordinate clauses

Words introducing adjective clauses

RELATIVE PRONOUNS: that, which, who, whom, whose

RELATIVE ADVERBS: when, where, why

Words introducing adverb clauses

SUBORDINATING CONJUNCTIONS: after, although, as, as if, because, before, even though, if, in order that, once, since, so that, than, that, though, unless, until, when, where, whether, while

Words introducing noun clauses

RELATIVE PRONOUNS: which, who, whom, whose

OTHER PRONOUNS: what, whatever, whichever, whoever, whomever

OTHER SUBORDINATING WORDS: how, if, that, when, whenever, where, wherever, whether, why

Relative pronouns are sometimes "understood."

The things [*that*] *we cherish most* are the things [*that*] *we might lose.*

Occasionally an adjective clause is introduced by a relative adverb, usually *when, where,* or *why.*

The aging actor returned to the *stage where he had made his debut as Hamlet half a century earlier.*

The parts of an adjective clause are often arranged as in sentences (subject/verb/object or complement).

Sometimes it is our closest friends who disappoint us.

Frequently, however, the object or complement appears first, out of the normal order of subject/verb/object.

They can be the very friends whom we disappoint.

TIP: For punctuation of adjective clauses, see P1-e and P2-e. For advice about avoiding repeated words in adjective clauses, see M3-d.

Adverb clauses

Adverb clauses modify verbs, adjectives, or other adverbs, usually answering one of these questions: When? Where? Why? How? Under what conditions? To what degree? They always begin with a subordinating conjunction (such as *after, although, because, that, though, unless,* or *when*). (For a complete list, see the chart on p. 322.)

When the sun went down, the hikers *prepared* their camp.

Kate *would have made* the team *if she hadn't broken her ankle.*

Noun clauses

A noun clause functions just like a single-word noun, usually as a subject, a subject complement, a direct object, or an object of a preposition. It usually begins with one of the following words: *how, if, that, what, whatever, when, where, whether, which, who, whoever, whom, whomever, whose, why.* (For a complete list, see the chart on p. 322.)

           — S —
Whoever leaves the house last must double-lock the door.

               — DO —
Copernicus argued that the sun is the centre of the universe.

     The subordinating word introducing the clause may or may not play a significant role in the clause. In the preceding examples, *Whoever* is the subject of its clause, but *that* does not perform a function in its clause.

     As with adjective clauses, the parts of a noun clause may appear in normal order (subject/verb/object or complement) or out of their normal order.

          S   V   — DO —
Loyalty is what keeps a friendship strong.

          DO   S V
Quebec is where we live.

B4 Sentence types

Sentences are classified in two ways: according to their structure (simple, compound, complex, or compound-complex) and according to their purpose (declarative, imperative, interrogative, or exclamatory).

B4-a Sentence structures

Depending on the number and the types of clauses they contain, sentences are classified as simple, compound, complex, or compound-complex.

Clauses come in two varieties: independent and subordinate. An independent clause contains a subject and a predicate, and it either stands alone or could stand alone as a sentence. A subordinate clause also contains a subject and a predicate, but it functions within a sentence as an adjective, an adverb, or a noun; it cannot stand alone. (See B3-e.)

Simple sentences

A simple sentence is one independent clause with no subordinate clauses.

———————— INDEPENDENT CLAUSE ————————
Without a passport, Eva could not visit her aunt in Peru.

A simple sentence may contain compound elements—a compound subject, verb, or object, for example—but it does not contain more than one full sentence pattern. The following sentence is simple because its two verbs (*comes in* and *goes out*) share a subject (*Spring*).

———————— INDEPENDENT CLAUSE ————————
Spring comes in like a lion and goes out like a lamb.

Compound sentences

A compound sentence is composed of two or more independent clauses with no subordinate clauses. The independent clauses are usually joined with a comma and a coordinating conjunction (*and, but, or, nor, for, so, yet*) or with a semicolon. (See P1-a and P3-a.)

INDEPENDENT   INDEPENDENT
——CLAUSE——   ———— CLAUSE ————
The car broke down, but a rescue van arrived within minutes.

                   INDEPENDENT
—— INDEPENDENT CLAUSE ——   ———— CLAUSE ————
A shark was spotted near shore; people left immediately.

LaunchPad **ACTIVITIES FOR B4**
macmillan learning   2 Exercises

Complex sentences

A complex sentence is composed of one independent clause with one or more subordinate clauses. (See B3-e.)

	SUBORDINATE
ADJECTIVE	┌── CLAUSE ──┐ The pitcher who won the game is a rookie.

	SUBORDINATE
ADVERB	┌── CLAUSE ──┐ If you leave late, take a cab home.

	SUBORDINATE
NOUN	┌──── CLAUSE ────┐ What matters most to us is a quick commute.

Compound-complex sentences

A compound-complex sentence contains at least two independent clauses and at least one subordinate clause. The following sentence contains two independent clauses, each of which contains a subordinate clause.

┌────── INDEPENDENT CLAUSE ──────┐   ┌─ INDEPENDENT CLAUSE ─
                ┌── SUB CL ──┐   ┌─ SUB CL ─
Tell the nurse practitioner how you feel, and she will decide whether you

┌──────────────┐
can go home.

B4-b Sentence purposes

Writers use declarative sentences to make statements, imperative sentences to issue requests or commands, interrogative sentences to ask questions, and exclamatory sentences to make exclamations.

DECLARATIVE	The echo sounded in our ears.
IMPERATIVE	Love your neighbour.
INTERROGATIVE	Did the better team win tonight?
EXCLAMATORY	We're here to save you!

R

Researching

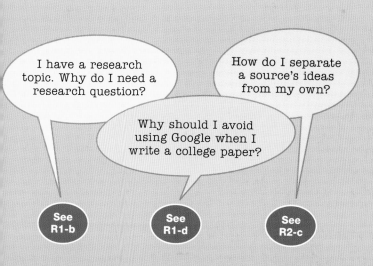

I have a research topic. Why do I need a research question?

See R1-b

How do I separate a source's ideas from my own?

See R2-c

Why should I avoid using Google when I write a college paper?

See R1-d

R Researching

A postsecondary research assignment asks you to pose questions worth exploring, read widely in search of possible answers, interpret what you read, draw reasoned conclusions, and support those conclusions with evidence. In short, it asks you to enter a research conversation by being *in* conversation with other writers and thinkers who have explored and studied your topic. As you listen to and learn from the voices already in the conversation, you'll find entry points where you can add your own insights and ideas.

R1 Thinking like a researcher; gathering sources

- How to enter a research conversation 332
- Testing a research question 333
- How to go beyond a Google search 336

Keep an open mind throughout the research process, and enjoy the detective work of finding answers to questions that matter to you. Take time to find out what has been written about your topic and what's missing from the research conversation. You can stay organized by planning the search with a solid research question in mind and maintaining accurate records of the sources you consult.

R1-a Manage the project.

When you start on a research project, you need to understand the assignment, choose a direction, and ask questions about your topic. The following tips will help you manage the beginning phase of research.

Managing time

When you receive your assignment, set a realistic schedule of deadlines. Think about how much time you might need for each step of your project. One student created a calendar to map out her tasks for a paper assigned on October 3 and due October 31 (see p. 330), keeping in mind that some tasks might overlap or need to be repeated.

Sample calendar for a research assignment

2	3	4	5	6	7	8
	Receive and analyze the assignment.	Pose questions you might explore. →	Talk with a reference librarian; plan a search strategy. →	Start research log.	Settle on a topic; narrow the focus.	Revise research questions. Locate sources. →
9	**10**	**11**	**12**	**13**	**14**	**15**
Read, take notes, and compile a working bibliography. →				Draft a working thesis and an outline.	Draft the paper. →	
16	**17**	**18**	**19**	**20**	**21**	**22**
→ Draft the paper. →			Visit the writing centre for feedback.	Do additional research if needed. →		
23	**24**	**25**	**26**	**27**	**28**	**29**
Ask peers for feedback. Revise the paper; if necessary, revise the thesis. →				Prepare a list of works cited. →		Proofread the final draft. →
30	**31**					
Proofread the final draft. →	Submit the final draft.					

Getting the big picture

As you consider a possible research topic, set aside some time to learn what people are saying about it by reading sources on the web or in library databases. Ask yourself questions such as these:

- What aspects of the topic are generating the most debate?
- Why and how are people disagreeing?
- Which arguments and approaches seem worth exploring?

Once you have an aerial view of the topic and are familiar with some of the existing research, you can zoom in closer to examine subtopics and debates that look interesting.

Keeping a research log

Research is a process. As your topic evolves, you may find yourself asking new questions that require you to create a new search strategy, find additional sources, or revise your initial assumptions. A research log — a hard-copy notebook or a set of digital files — helps you maintain orderly records of the sources you read and your ideas about those sources. Keeping an accurate source trail and working bibliography, and separating your own insights and ideas from those of your sources, will help you become an efficient and responsible researcher.

R1-b Pose questions worth exploring.

Every research project starts with questions. Working within the guidelines of your assignment, come up with a few preliminary questions that seem worth researching — questions that you are interested in exploring, that you feel would engage your audience, and about which there is substantial debate. You might try using the journalist's questions — What? Who? Why? When? Where? and How? — to help you answer a research question. Here, for example, are a few students' preliminary questions.

- Why are boys diagnosed with attention deficit disorder more often than girls are?

- How can nutritional food labels be redesigned so that they inform rather than confuse consumers?

- Under what circumstances should juvenile offenders be tried as adults?

As you think about possible questions, choose those that are focused (not too broad), challenging (not just factual), and grounded (not too speculative) as possible entry points in a research conversation.

Choosing a focused question

If your initial question is too broad, given the length of the paper you plan to write, look for ways to restrict your focus. Here, for example, is how two students narrowed their initial questions.

TOO BROAD	NARROWER
What causes depression?	How has the widespread use of antidepressant drugs affected teenage suicide rates?
What are the benefits of stricter auto emissions standards?	How will stricter auto emissions standards create new auto industry jobs and make Canadian carmakers more competitive in the world market?

Enter a research conversation

A postsecondary research project asks you to be in conversation with writers and researchers who have studied your topic — responding to their ideas and arguments and contributing your own insights to move the conversation forward. As you ask preliminary research questions, you may wonder where and how to step into a research conversation.

1 **Identify the experts and ideas in the conversation.** Ask: Who are the major writers and most influential people researching your topic? What are their credentials? What positions have they taken? How and why do the experts disagree?

2 **Identify any gaps in the conversation.** What is missing from the conversation? Where are the gaps in the existing research? What questions haven't been asked yet? What positions need to be challenged?

3 **Try using an orienting statement** to help you find a point of entry:

- *On one side of the debate is position X, on the other side is Y, but there is a middle position, Z.*

- *The conventional view about the problem needs to be challenged because . . .*

- *Key details in this debate that have been overlooked are . . .*

- *Researchers have drawn conclusion X from the evidence, but one could also draw conclusion Y.*

Testing a research question

As you draft research questions, explore your topic from multiple perspectives. You may find that your research leads you in unexpected directions and challenges your assumptions. As your ideas evolve, keep testing your research question.

- Does the question allow you to enter into a research conversation that you care about?
- Is the question flexible enough to allow for many possible answers?
- Is the question focused, challenging, and grounded?
- Can you show your audience why the question needs to be asked and why the answer matters?

Choosing a challenging question

Your research paper will be more interesting to both you and your audience if you base it on an intellectually challenging line of inquiry. Avoid factual questions that fail to provoke thought or engage readers in a debate; such questions lead to reports or lists of facts, not to researched arguments.

TOO FACTUAL	CHALLENGING
Is autism on the rise?	Why is autism so difficult to treat?
Where is wind energy being used?	What makes wind farms economically viable?

You will need to address a factual question in the course of answering a more challenging one. For example, if you were writing about promising treatments for autism, you would no doubt answer the question "What is autism?" at some point in your paper and even analyze competing definitions of autism to help support your arguments about the challenges of treating the condition. A factual question, though, is too limited to be the focus for the whole paper.

Choosing a grounded question

Make sure that your research question is grounded, not too speculative. Although speculative questions — such as those that address morality or beliefs — are worth asking in a research paper, they are unsuitable central questions. For most college or university courses, the central argument of a research paper should be grounded in facts and should not be based entirely on beliefs.

TOO SPECULATIVE	GROUNDED
Is it wrong to share pornographic personal photos by cell phone?	What role should the Canadian government play in regulating mobile content?
Do medical scientists have the right to experiment on animals?	How have technical breakthroughs made medical experiments on animals increasingly unnecessary?

R1-c Map out a search strategy.

Before you search for sources, think about what kinds of sources will be appropriate for your project. Considering the kinds of sources you need will help you develop a research strategy — a systematic plan for locating sources. To create an effective search strategy for your research question, consult a reference librarian and study your library's website for an overview of available resources.

No single search strategy works for every topic. For some topics, it may be useful to search for information in newspapers, government publications, and websites. For others, the best sources might be found in scholarly journals and books, research reports from think tanks, and specialized reference works. Still other topics might be enhanced by field research — interviews, surveys, or observation.

With the help of a librarian, each of the students whose research essays appear in this handbook constructed a search strategy appropriate for his or her research question.

SOPHIE HARBA (See her full research paper in MLA-5b.) Sophie Harba's topic, the role of government in legislating food choices, is the subject of lively debates in scholarly articles and in publications aimed at the general public. To find information on her topic, Harba decided to

- search the web to locate current news, government publications, and information from organizations that focus on issues surrounding government regulation of food
- check a library database for current peer-reviewed research articles
- use the library catalogue to search for a recently published book that was cited in a blog and on several well-respected websites

APRIL WANG (See her full paper in APA-5b.) April Wang's topic, the role of technology in the shift from teacher-delivered to student-centred learning, is the subject of educational studies as well as articles and books aimed at both educators and the general public. To find information on her topic, Wang decided to

- search Google Scholar and *CQ Researcher* to learn what aspects of her research question are generating the most debate
- listen to a TED talk to deepen her understanding about educational technology
- search specialized databases related to education and technology for recent scholarly articles and reports
- track down a scholarly article that several of her sources cited as an influential study

NED BISHOP (See pages from his paper in CMS-5b.) Ned Bishop's topic, Nathan Bedford Forrest's role in the Fort Pillow massacre during the American Civil War, has been investigated and debated by professional historians. Given the nature of his historical topic, Bishop decided to

- locate books through the library's online catalogue
- locate scholarly articles by searching a database specializing in history sources
- locate newspaper articles from 1864 by searching a historical newspaper database
- use the web to track down additional primary documents mentioned in his sources

Using sources responsibly: Use your research log to record information for every source you read or view. If you gather complete publication information from the start of your project, you'll easily find it when you need to document your sources.

R1-d Search efficiently; master a few shortcuts to finding good sources.

Most students use a combination of library databases and the web in their research. You can save yourself a lot of time by becoming an efficient searcher.

Using the library

The website hosted by your college or university library links to databases and other references containing articles, studies, and reports from scholarly journals and other sources written by the key researchers debating your topic. Use your library's resources, designed for academic researchers, to find the most authoritative sources for your project.

Go beyond a Google search

You might start with Google to gain an overview of your topic, but relying on the popular search engine to choose your sources isn't a research strategy. Good research involves going beyond the information available from a quick Google search. To locate reliable, authoritative sources, be strategic about *how* and *where* to search.

1 **Familiarize yourself with the research conversation.** Identify the current debate about the topic you have chosen and the most influential writers and experts in the debate. Where is the research conversation happening? In scholarly sources? Government agencies? The popular media?

2 **Generate keywords to focus your search.** Use specific words and combinations to search. Add words such as *debate*, *disagreements*, *proponents*, or *opponents* to track down the various positions in the research conversation. Use a journalist's questions— Who? When? Where? What? Why?—to refine a search.

3 **Search discipline-specific databases available through your school library** to locate carefully chosen scholarly (peer-reviewed) content that doesn't appear in search results on the open web. Use databases such as JSTOR and Academic Search Premier, designed for academic researchers, to locate sources in the most influential publications.

4 **If your topic has been in the news, try *CQ Researcher*,** available through many college and university libraries. Its brief articles provide pro/con arguments on current controversies in criminal justice, law, environment, technology, health, and education, although it focuses mostly on the United States.

5 **Explore the Pew Research Center** (pewresearch.org) original research and nonpartisan discussions of findings and trends in a wide range of academic fields.

6 **Explore Canadian content** in the Canadian Business & Current Affairs Database (CBCA), the largest source of scholarly articles about Canada. This database, available through many college and university libraries, contains over seven hundred full-text periodicals in fields ranging from politics to the medical sciences.

Many libraries offer one-on-one help from research librarians, who can tell you what resources are available and who can suggest ways to refine your keywords or narrow your search.

Savvy searchers cut down on the clutter of a broad search by adding additional search terms, limiting a search to recent publications, or clicking on a database option to look at only one type of source, such as peer-reviewed articles. When looking for books, use your library's online catalogue.

Using the web

When conducting searches, use terms that are as specific as possible. The keywords you use will determine the quality of the results you see. You can refine your search by date or by domain; for example, *autism site:.gc.ca* will search for information about autism on federal government (.gc.ca) websites. Use clues in what you find (such as organizations or government agencies that seem particularly informative) to refine your search.

As you examine sites, look for "about" links to learn about a site's author or sponsoring agency. Examine URLs for clues. Those that contain .k12 may be intended for young audiences; URLs ending in .gc.ca and those beginning with canada.ca lead to official information from Canadian federal government entities. If you aren't sure where a page originated, erase everything in the URL after the first slash in your address bar; the result should be the root page of the site, which may offer useful information about the site's purpose and audience (see p. 338). Avoid sites that provide information but no explanation of who the authors are or why the site was created. For more on evaluating websites, see R3-c.

Using bibliographies and citations

Scholarly books and articles list the works the author has cited, usually at the end. These lists are useful shortcuts to additional reliable sources on your topic. For example, most of the scholarly articles that student writer Sophie Harba consulted contained citations to related research studies and helped her identify the most influential authors contributing to her research conversation. Through these citations, she quickly located other sources and a network of relevant research related to her topic. Even popular sources such as news articles and TED talks may refer to additional relevant sources that may be worth tracking down.

R1-e Conduct field research, if appropriate.

Your own field research can enhance or be the focus of a writing project. For a composition class, for example, you might want to interview a local politician about a current issue, such as the initiation of a city bike-share program. For a sociology class, you might decide to conduct a survey about campus trends in community service.

Check URLs for clues about sponsorship

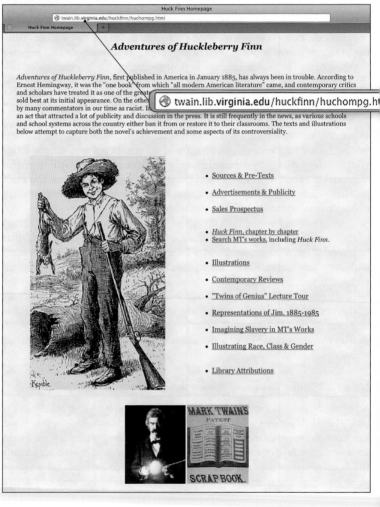

This source, from an internal page of a website, provides no indication of an author or a sponsor. Shortening the URL to **http://twain.lib.virginia.edu/** leads to a main page that lists a US university literature professor as the author and the University of Virginia Library as the sponsor.

Tips for smart searching

For currency

If you need current information, news outlets such as the *Globe and Mail* and the BBC, think tanks, and government agencies may provide appropriate sources for your research. When using Google, limit a search to the most recent year, month, week, or day.

For authority

Keep an eye out for experts being cited in sources you examine. Following the trail of citations may lead you to sources by those experts — or the organizations they represent — that may be even more helpful. You can limit a Google search by type of website and type of source. Add *site:. gc.ca* to focus on federal government sources or *filetype:pdf* to zero in on reports and research papers as PDF files.

For scholarship

Use a library database to look for reports of original scholarly research written by the people who conducted it. Read the abstract of a long article or the article's introductory paragraphs and conclusion to see if the source is worth further investigation.

For context

Books provide context that articles cannot. You may find a single chapter or even a few pages that are just what you need to gain a deeper perspective.

For firsthand authenticity

In some fields, primary sources may be required. In historical research, for example, a primary source is one that originated in the historical period under discussion or is a firsthand account from a witness. In the sciences, a primary source (sometimes called a *primary article*) is a published report of research written by the scientist who conducted it. For more information, see page 352.

RESEARCH TIP: Colleges and universities often require researchers to submit projects to an institutional review board (IRB) if the research involves human subjects outside a classroom setting. Before administering a survey or conducting other fieldwork, check with your instructor to see whether IRB approval is required.

Interviewing

Interviews can often shed new light on a topic. Look for an expert who has firsthand knowledge of the subject, or seek out someone whose personal experience and expertise provide a valuable perspective.

When asking for an interview, be clear about who you are, what the purpose of the interview is, and how you would prefer to conduct it: by email, over the phone, or in person. Ask questions that lead to facts, anecdotes, and opinions that will add a meaningful dimension to your paper.

Using sources responsibly: When quoting your source (the interviewee), be accurate and fair. Do not change the meaning of your interviewee's words or take them out of context. To ensure accuracy, you might ask permission to record the interview or conduct it by email.

Surveying opinion

For some topics, you may find it useful to survey opinions through written questionnaires, phone or email polls, or questions posted on a social media site. Many people resist long questionnaires, so for a good response rate, limit your questions with your purpose in mind.

Surveys with yes/no questions or multiple-choice options can be completed quickly, and the results are easy to tally. You may also want to ask a few open-ended questions to elicit more individual responses, some of which may be worth quoting in your paper.

Other field methods

Your firsthand visits to and observations of significant places, people, or events can enhance a paper in a variety of disciplines. If you aren't able to visit an organization, a company, or a historic site, you may find useful information on an official website or a phone number or an email address to use to contact a representative.

R1-f Write a research proposal.

One effective way to manage your research project and focus your thinking is to write a research proposal. A proposal gives you an opportunity to look back — to remind you why you chose your topic — and to look forward — to predict any difficulties or obstacles that might arise during your project. In a research proposal, you identify the question you plan to explore, the sources you plan to use, and the feasibility of the project, given the time and resources available. As you take stock of your project, you also have the opportunity to seek feedback about your research question and search strategy.

The following questions will help you organize your proposal.

- **Research question.** What question will you be exploring? Why does this question need to be asked? What do you hope to learn from the project?

- **Research conversation.** What have you learned so far about the debate or the specific research conversation you will enter? What entry point have you found to offer your own insights and ideas?

- **Search strategy.** Explain your search strategy: What kinds of sources will you use to explore your question? What sources will be most useful, and why? How will you locate a variety of sources (primary/secondary, textual/visual)?

- **Research challenges.** What challenges, if any, do you anticipate (locating sufficient sources, managing the project, finding a position to take)? What resources are available to help you meet these challenges?

R2 Managing information; taking notes responsibly

- Information to collect for a working bibliography 343
- How to avoid plagiarizing from the web 347

An effective researcher is a good record keeper. Whether you decide to keep records on paper or on a computer or mobile device, you will need methods for managing information: maintaining a working bibliography (see R2-a) and taking notes without plagiarizing your sources (see R2-c). (For more on avoiding plagiarism, see MLA-2 for MLA style, APA-2 for APA style, and CMS-2 for CMS style.)

R2-a Maintain a working bibliography.

Keep a record of any sources you read or view. This record, called a *working bibliography*, will help you keep track of publication information for the sources you might use so that you can refer to them as you write. You can also start to compile the list of sources that will appear at the end of your paper. The format of this list depends on the documentation style you are using (for MLA style, see MLA-4; for APA style, see APA-4; for CMS style, see CMS-4).

LaunchPad **ACTIVITIES FOR R2**
macmillan learning
    1 Writing Practice activity

See R3-e for advice on using your working bibliography as the basis for an annotated bibliography.

Most researchers save bibliographic information from the library's catalogue and databases and the web. The information you need to collect is given in the chart on page 343. If you download a visual, gather the same information as for a print source.

For web sources, some bibliographic information may not be available, but spend time looking for it before assuming that it doesn't exist. When information isn't available on the home page, you may have to drill into the site, following links to interior pages. (See also pp. 339 and 354 for more details about finding bibliographic information in online sources.)

Using sources responsibly: Be careful when using the copy-and-paste function with an online source; don't lose track of which words come from the source. To avoid plagiarism, put quotation marks around any language you copy from a source.

R2-b Keep track of source materials.

Save a copy of each potential source as you conduct your research. Many database services will allow you to email, text, save, or print citations or full texts, and you can easily download, copy, or take screen shots of information from the web.

Working with photocopies, printouts, and electronic files — as opposed to relying on memory or hastily written notes — lets you annotate the source as you read. You can highlight key passages, perhaps even colour-coding them to reflect topics in your outline. You also reduce the chances of unintentional plagiarism since you will be able to compare your use of a source with the actual source, not just with your notes.

R2-c As you take notes, avoid unintentional plagiarism.

Plagiarism, using someone's words or ideas without giving credit, is often accidental. After spending so much time thinking through your topic and reading sources, it's sometimes easy to forget where a helpful idea came from or to remember that the idea wasn't yours to begin with. When you take notes and jot down ideas, be careful to put quotation marks around any borrowed words or phrases. Even if you half-copy an author's sentences — either by mixing the author's phrases with your own without using quotation marks or by plugging your synonyms into an author's sentence structure — you are committing plagiarism, a serious academic offence. (For examples of this kind of plagiarism, sometimes referred to as *patchwriting*, see MLA-2, APA-2, and CMS-2.)

Information to collect for a working bibliography

For an entire book

- All authors; any editors or translators
- Title and subtitle
- Edition (if not the first)
- Publication information: city, publisher, and date
- Medium: print, web, DVD, and so on
- Date you accessed the source (for an online source)

For an article

- All authors of the article
- Title and subtitle of the article
- Title of the journal, magazine, or newspaper
- Date, volume, issue, and page numbers
- Medium: print, web, DVD, and so on
- Date you accessed the source (for an online source)

For an article retrieved from a database (in addition to preceding information)

- Name of the database
- Accession number or other number assigned by the database
- Digital object identifier (DOI), if there is one
- URL of the database home page or of the journal's home page, if there is no DOI
- Date you accessed the source

For a web source (including visual, audio, and multimedia sources)

- All authors, editors, or composers of the source
- Editor or compiler of the web source, if there is one
- Title and subtitle of the source
- Title of the longer work, if the source is contained in a longer work
- Title of the website
- Print publication information for the source, if available
- Online page or paragraph numbers, if the source provides them
- Date of online publication (or latest update)
- Sponsor or publisher of the site
- Date you accessed the source
- URL or permalink of the page on which the source appears

NOTE: For more details, see MLA-4b, APA-4b, or CMS-4c.

To take notes responsibly, make sure you understand the ideas in the source. What is the meaning of certain words? What is the argument? What is the evidence? Then, resist the temptation to look at the source as you take notes — except when you are quoting. Keep the source close by so that you can check for accuracy, but don't try to put ideas in your own words with the source's sentences in front of you. When you need to quote a source, make sure you copy the words exactly and put quotation marks around them.

Summarizing, paraphrasing, and quoting exact language are three ways to take notes on a source. Make sure that your notes also include information about where the words and ideas come from so that you can easily integrate and document the source in your paper. And indicate in your notes if you have summarized, paraphrased, or quoted an author's words to avoid unintentionally plagiarizing a source.

Summarizing without plagiarizing

A summary condenses information and captures main ideas, perhaps reducing a chapter to a short paragraph or a paragraph to a single sentence. A summary should be written in your own words; if you use phrases from the source, put them in quotation marks.

Here is a passage about marine pollution from a US National Oceanic and Atmospheric Administration (NOAA) website. Following the passage are the student's annotations — notes and questions that help him figure out the meaning — and then his summary of the passage. (The bibliographic information is recorded in MLA style.)

ORIGINAL SOURCE

A question that is often posed to the NOAA Marine Debris Program (MDP) is "How much debris is actually out there?" The MDP has recognized the need for this answer as well as the growing interest and value of citizen science. To that end, the MDP is developing and testing two types of monitoring and assessment protocols: 1) rigorous scientific survey and 2) volunteer at-sea visual survey. These types of monitoring programs are necessary in order to compare marine debris, composition, abundance, distribution, movement, and impact data on national and global scales.

— NOAA Marine Debris Program. "Efforts and Activities Related to the 'Garbage Patches.'" *Marine Debris*, 2012, pm22100.net/docs/pdf/enercoop/pollutions/noaa-plastiques.pdf.

ORIGINAL SOURCE WITH STUDENT ANNOTATIONS

             ⌐ by whom?⌐   ocean ⌐   ⌐ trash
A question that is often posed to the NOAA Marine Debris

Program (MDP) is "How much debris is actually out there?" The

MDP has recognized the need for this answer as well as the
                 aha
growing interest and value of citizen science. To that end, the MDP

is developing and testing two types of monitoring and assessment
         ways of gathering information
protocols: 1) rigorous scientific survey and 2) volunteer at-sea visual

survey. These types of monitoring programs are necessary in order
        kinds of materials ⌐   ⌐ how much?
to compare marine debris, composition, abundance, distribution,
          ⌐ why it matters
movement, and impact data on national and global scales.

SUMMARY

Source: NOAA Marine Debris Program. "Efforts and Activities Related to the
    'Garbage Patches.'" *Marine Debris*. 2012, pm22100.net/docs/pdf/enercoop/
    pollutions/noaa-plastiques.pdf.

Having to field citizens' questions about the size of debris fields in Earth's oceans,
the Marine Debris Program, an arm of the US National Oceanic and Atmospheric
Administration, is currently implementing methods to monitor and draw
conclusions about our oceans' patches of pollution (NOAA Marine Debris Program).

Academic English When you are summarizing or paraphrasing
ideas from a source, keep these guidelines in mind: (1) Avoid replacing a
source's words with synonyms. (2) Determine the meaning of the source.
(3) Present your understanding of the author's meaning.

Paraphrasing without plagiarizing

Like a summary, a paraphrase is written in your own words; but whereas a summary reports significant information in fewer words than the source, a paraphrase restates the information in roughly the same number of words. A successful paraphrase also uses sentence structure that's different from the original. If you retain occasional choice phrases from the source, use quotation marks so that later you will know which phrases are not your own. If you paraphrase a source, you must still cite the source.

As you read the following paraphrase of the original source (see p. 344), notice that the language is significantly different from that in the original.

PARAPHRASE

Source: NOAA Marine Debris Program. "Efforts and Activities Related to the 'Garbage Patches.'" *Marine Debris*, 2012, pm22100.net/docs/pdf/enercoop/ pollutions/noaa-plastiques.pdf.

Citizens concerned and curious about the amount, makeup, and locations of debris patches in our oceans have been pressing NOAA's Marine Debris Program for answers. In response, the organization is preparing to implement plans and standards for expert study and nonexpert observation, both of which will yield results that will be helpful in determining the significance of the pollution problem (NOAA Marine Debris Program).

For additional practical advice on how to paraphrase, see section M6.

Using quotation marks to avoid plagiarizing

A quotation consists of the exact words from a source. In your notes, put all quoted material in quotation marks; do not assume that you will remember later which words, phrases, and passages you have quoted and which are your own. When you quote, be sure to copy the words of your source exactly, including punctuation and capitalization.

QUOTATION

Source: NOAA Marine Debris Program. "Efforts and Activities Related to the 'Garbage Patches.'" *Marine Debris*, 2012, pm22100.net/docs/pdf/enercoop/ pollutions/noaa-plastiques.pdf.

The NOAA Marine Debris Program has noted that, as our oceans become increasingly polluted, surveillance is "necessary in order to compare marine debris, composition, abundance, distribution, movement, and impact data on national and global scales."

Note that because the source is from a website without page numbers, the in-text citation includes only the author name and not a page number.

Avoid plagiarizing from the web

1 **Understand what plagiarism is.** When you use another author's intellectual property (language, visuals, or ideas) in your own writing without giving proper credit, you commit a kind of academic theft called *plagiarism*.

2 **Treat online sources the same way you treat print sources.** Language, data, or images that you find on the web must be cited, even if the material is in the public domain (which includes older works no longer protected by copyright law), is publicly accessible on free sites or social media, or is on a government website.

3 **Keep track of words and ideas borrowed from sources.** When you copy and paste passages from online sources, put quotation marks around any text that you have copied. Develop a system for distinguishing your words and ideas from anything you've summarized, paraphrased, or quoted.

4 **Create a complete bibliographic entry for each source to keep track of publication information.** From the start of your research project, maintain accurate records for all online sources you read or view.

For details on avoiding plagiarism while working with sources, see MLA-2 (MLA), APA-2 (APA), and CMS-2 (CMS).

R3 Evaluating sources

You can often locate far more potential sources for your topic than you will have time to read. Your challenge will be to determine what kinds of sources you need and what you need these sources to do and to select a reasonable number of trustworthy sources. This kind of decision making is referred to as *evaluating sources*. When you evaluate a source, you make a judgment about how useful the source is to your project.

Evaluating sources isn't something you do in one sitting, and often it doesn't follow a formula (*find sources > evaluate sources > write the paper*). After you do some planning, searching, and reading, for example, you may reflect on the information you have and conclude that you need to rethink your research question — and so you return to assessing the kinds of sources you need. Or you may be midway through drafting your paper when you begin to question a particular source's credibility, at which point you return to searching and reading.

Viewing evaluation as a process

When you use sources in your writing, make a habit of evaluating, or judging the value of, those sources at each stage of your project. The following questions may help.

Evaluate as you PLAN

What kinds of sources do I need?

What do I need these sources to help me do: Define? Persuade? Inform?

Evaluate as you SEARCH

How can I find the most reliable sources?

Which sources will help me build my credibility as a researcher?

Evaluate as you READ

What positions do these sources take in the debate on my topic? What are their biases?

How do these sources inform my own understanding of the topic and the position I will take?

Evaluate as you WRITE

How do the sources I've chosen help me make my point?

How do my own ideas fit into the conversation on my research topic?

LaunchPad **ACTIVITIES FOR R3**
macmillan learning
3 Writing Practice activities, 2 Sample student papers, 4 Video tutorials

R3-a Think about how sources might contribute to your writing.

How you plan to use sources will affect how you evaluate them. Sources can have a range of functions in a paper. You can use them to

- provide background information or context for your topic
- explain terms or concepts that your readers might not understand
- provide evidence for your argument
- lend authority to your argument
- identify a gap or contradiction in the conversation
- offer counterarguments and alternative interpretations to your argument

As you plan your writing, you will need to think through the kinds of sources that will help you answer your research question and support your thesis.

For examples of how student writers use sources for a variety of purposes, see MLA-1c and APA-1c.

R3-b Select sources worth your time and attention.

As you search for sources in databases, the library catalogue, and search engines, you're likely to find many more results than you can read or use. This section explains how to scan through the results for the most promising sources and how to preview those sources to see whether they meet your needs.

Scanning search results

As you scan through a list of search results, look for clues indicating whether a source might be useful for your purposes or not worth pursuing. You will need to use somewhat different strategies when scanning search results from a database, a library catalogue, and a web search engine.

DATABASES Most databases list at least the following information, which can help you decide if a source is relevant, current, and scholarly (see the chart on p. 351).

The title and brief description (How relevant?)

A date (How current?)

The name of periodical (How scholarly?)

The length (How extensive in coverage?)

Many databases allow you to sort your list of results by relevance or date; sorting may help you scan the information more efficiently.

CATALOGUES A library's catalogue usually lists basic information about books, periodicals, DVDs, and other material — enough to give you a first impression. As in database search results, the title and date of publication of books and other sources listed in the catalogue will often be your first clues as to whether a source is worth consulting. If details such as the subject matter, currency, and authority of a potential source seem appropriate, it's probably worth taking a look at the source itself.

WEB SEARCH ENGINES Reliable and unreliable sources live side by side online. As you scan through search results, look for the following clues about the probable relevance, currency, and reliability of a website.

> The title, keywords, and lead-in text (How relevant?)
>
> A date (How current?)
>
> An indication of the site's sponsor or purpose (How reliable?)
>
> The URL, especially the URL ending: for example, .com, .edu, .gc.ca, or .org (How relevant? How reliable?)

Previewing sources

Once you have decided that a source looks promising, preview it quickly to see whether it lives up to its promise.

PREVIEWING AN ARTICLE

- Consider the publication in which the article is printed. Is it a scholarly journal (see the chart on p. 351)? A popular magazine? A newspaper with a national reputation?

- For a magazine or journal article, look for an abstract or a statement of purpose at the beginning; also look for a summary at the end.

- For a newspaper article, focus on the headline and the opening paragraphs for relevance.

- Scan any headings and look at any visuals — charts, graphs, diagrams, or illustrations — that might indicate the article's focus and scope.

PREVIEWING A WEBSITE

- Check to see if the sponsor is a reputable organization, a government agency, or a university. Is the group likely to look at only one side of a debatable issue?

- If you have landed on an internal page of a site and no author or sponsor is evident, try viewing the home page, either by clicking on a link or by shortening the URL (see the tip on p. 338).

- Try to determine the purpose of the website. Is the site trying to sell a product? Promote an idea? Inform the public? Is the purpose consistent with your research?

- If the site includes statistical data (tables, graphs, charts), can you tell how and by whom the statistics were compiled? Is research cited?

- Find out when the site was created or last updated. Is it current enough for your purposes?

Determining whether a source is scholarly

For many postsecondary assignments, you will be asked to use scholarly sources. These are written by experts for a knowledgeable audience and usually go into more depth than books and articles written for a general audience. (Scholarly sources are sometimes called *refereed* or *peer-reviewed* because the work is evaluated by experts in the field before publication.) To determine whether a source is scholarly, look for the following:

- Formal language and presentation
- Authors who are academics or scientists
- Footnotes or a bibliography documenting the works cited by the author in the source
- Original research and interpretation, rather than a summary of other people's work
- Quotations from and analysis of primary sources (in humanities disciplines such as literature, history, and philosophy)
- A description of research methods or a review of related research (in the sciences and social sciences)

NOTE: In some databases, searches can be limited to refereed or peer-reviewed journals.

PREVIEWING A BOOK

- Glance through the table of contents, keeping your research question in mind. Even if the entire book is not relevant, parts of it may be useful.
- Scan the preface in search of a statement of the author's purposes.
- Use the index to look up a few words related to your topic.
- If a chapter looks useful, read its opening and closing paragraphs and skim any headings.

Selecting appropriate versions of digital sources

An online source may appear as an abstract, an excerpt, or a full-text work. It is important to distinguish among these versions of sources and to use a complete version of a source, preferably one with page numbers, for your research.

Abstracts and excerpts are shortened versions of complete works. An abstract — a summary of a work's contents — might appear in a database record for a source and can give you clues about the usefulness of the source for your research. An excerpt is the first few sentences or paragraphs of a newspaper or magazine article and sometimes appears in a list of results from an online search. Reading a complete article is the best way to understand an author's argument before referring to it in your own writing. Also, working with a file that includes page numbers, such as a PDF, will be helpful when you cite the source.

R3-c Read with an open mind and a critical eye.

As you begin reading the sources you have chosen, keep an open mind. Do not let your personal beliefs prevent you from listening to new ideas and opposing viewpoints. Be curious about the wide range of positions in the research conversation you are entering. Your research question should guide you as you read your sources.

Distinguishing between primary and secondary sources

As you begin assessing evidence in a source, determine whether you are reading a primary or a secondary source. Primary sources include original documents such as letters, diaries, films, legislative bills, laboratory studies, field research reports, and eyewitness accounts. Secondary sources are commentaries on primary sources — another writer's opinions about or interpretation of a primary source.

Although a primary source is not necessarily more reliable than a secondary source, it has the advantage of being a firsthand account. You can better evaluate what a secondary source says if you have first read any primary sources it discusses.

Reading like a researcher

To read like a researcher is to read with an open, curious mind, to find out not only what has been written about a topic but also what is missing from the research conversation.

- **Read carefully.** Read to understand and summarize the main ideas of a source and an author's point of view. Ask questions: What does the source say? What is the author's central claim or thesis? What evidence does the author use to support the thesis?

- **Read skeptically.** Read to examine an author's assumptions, evidence, and conclusions and to pose counterarguments. Ask questions: Are any of the author's arguments or conclusions problematic? Is the author's evidence persuasive and sufficient?

- **Read evaluatively.** Read to judge the usefulness of a source for your research project. You may disagree with an author's argument or use of evidence, but refuting the author's ideas will help you clarify your position. Ask questions: Is the author an expert on the topic? Will the source provide background information, lend authority, explain a concept, or offer counterevidence for your claims?

- **Read responsibly.** Take time to read the entire source and to understand its author's arguments, assumptions, and conclusions. Avoid taking quotations from the first few pages of a source before you understand whether the ideas are representative of the work as a whole.

Evaluating all sources

Checking for signs of bias

- Does the author or publisher endorse political or religious views that could affect objectivity?
- Is the author or publisher associated with a special-interest group, such as PETA or the National Firearms Association of Canada, that might emphasize one side of an issue?
- Are alternative views presented and addressed? How fairly does the author treat opposing views? (See A3-c.)
- Does the author's language show signs of bias?

Assessing an argument

- What is the author's central claim or thesis?
- How does the author support this claim — with relevant and sufficient evidence or with just a few anecdotes or emotional examples?
- Are statistics consistent with those you encounter in other sources? Does the author explain where the statistics come from?
- Are any of the author's assumptions questionable?
- Does the author consider opposing arguments and refute them persuasively? (See A4-f.)
- Does the author use flawed logic? (See A3-a.)

Being alert for signs of bias

Bias is a way of thinking, a tendency to be partial, that prevents people and publications from viewing a topic objectively. Both in print and online, some sources are more objective than others. If you are exploring the rights of organizations like WikiLeaks to distribute sensitive government documents over the internet, for example, you may not find objective, unbiased information in a Global Affairs Canada report. If you are researching timber harvesting practices, you are likely to encounter bias in publications sponsored by environmental groups. As a researcher, you will need to consider any suspected bias as you assess each source. If you are uncertain about a source's special interests, seek the help of a reference librarian.

Like publishers, some authors are more objective than others. If you have reason to believe that a writer is particularly biased, you will want to assess his or her arguments with special care. For a list of questions worth asking, see the chart above.

Assessing the author's argument

In nearly all subjects worth writing about, there is some element of argument, so expect to encounter debates and disagreements among authors. In fact, areas of disagreement give you entry points in a research conversation.

Evaluating sources you find on the web

Authorship

- Does the website or document have an author? You may need to dig to find the author's name. For example, you may need to navigate to the home page or find an "about this site" link.
- Is the author knowledgeable and credible? When the author's credentials aren't listed on the specific interior page, look for links to the site's home page.

Sponsorship

- Who sponsors the site? The sponsor of a site is often named and described on the home page.
- What does the URL tell you? The domain name extension often signals the type of group hosting the site: commercial (.com), educational (.edu), nonprofit (.org), governmental (.gc.ca), military (.mil), or network (.net). URLs may also indicate a country of origin: .uk (United Kingdom) or .jp (Japan), for instance. Some Canadian federal government websites use the root URL canada.ca.

Purpose and audience

- Why was the site created: To argue a position? To sell a product? To inform readers?
- Who is the site's intended audience?

Currency

- How current is the site? Check for the date of publication or the date of the latest update, often located at the bottom of the home page or at the beginning or end of an internal page.
- How current are the site's links? If many of the links no longer work, the site may be too dated for your purposes.

Evaluating a website: Checking reliability

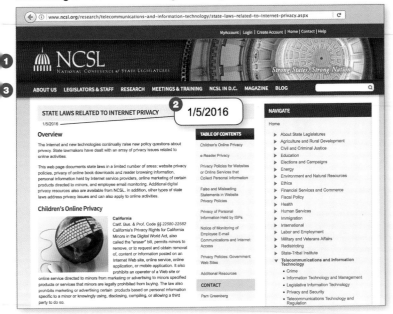

1 This page on internet monitoring and workplace privacy appears on a website sponsored by the US National Conference of State Legislatures. The NCSL is a bipartisan group that functions as a clearinghouse of ideas and research of interest to state lawmakers. It is also a lobby for state issues before the US government. The URL ending .org marks this sponsor as a nonprofit organization.

2 A clear date of publication shows currency.

3 An "About Us" page confirms that this is a credible organization whose credentials can be verified.

Evaluating a website: Checking purpose

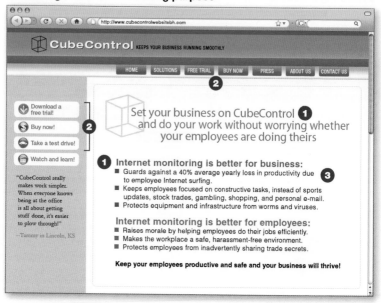

1   The site is sponsored by a company that specializes in employee-monitoring software.

2   Repeated links for trial downloads and purchase suggest the site's intended audience: consumers seeking to purchase software (probably not researchers seeking detailed information about employees' use of the internet in the workplace).

3   The site appears to provide information and even shows statistics from studies, but ultimately the purpose of the site is to sell a product.

R3-d Assess web sources with special care.

Before using a web source in your paper, make sure you know who created the material and for what purpose. Sources with reliable information can stand up to scrutiny. For a checklist on evaluating web sources, see the chart on page 354.

RESEARCH TIP: Many instructors do not consider wikis, such as *Wikipedia*, to be appropriate sources for college or university research. The information found on wikis is often general, and the authors are enthusiasts but not experts. Most wiki entries include a reference section, however, that can point you to valuable, credible sources.

Assessing multimodal sources with your research question in mind

The best sources for your topic may be videos such as public service ads, interviews delivered as podcasts or blog posts, or infographics that present information as a combination of data and visuals. Though not scholarly sources, such sources may be appropriate given your topic, your purpose, and your audience. When student writer Sophie Harba entered a debate about the rise of chronic diseases from harmful diets, she used a graph from the US Department of Agriculture to demonstrate the dangers of the typical American diet. (Her essay begins on p. 427.) The graph added needed evidence to help answer her research question: Should the government enact laws to regulate eating choices? The guidelines in the chart on page 353 will be helpful as you evaluate multimodal sources.

R3-e Construct an annotated bibliography.

Writing an annotated bibliography allows you to summarize, evaluate, and record publication information for your sources before drafting your research paper. You summarize each source to understand its main ideas; you evaluate (judge) each source for accuracy and relevance and to assess how the source contributes to your research project; and you record bibliographic information to keep track of publication details for each source.

Constructing an annotated bibliography focuses your attention on the most promising sources you've located, providing you with an opportunity to reflect on *how* and *why* these sources will help you answer your research question. Clarifying your sources' ideas will help you separate them from your own ideas and from each other, and it will also help you move toward a draft in which you synthesize sources and present your own thesis. (See MLA-3d and APA-3d for more on synthesis.)

SAMPLE ANNOTATED BIBLIOGRAPHY ENTRY (MLA STYLE)

Resnik, David. "Trans Fat Bans and Human Freedom." *American Journal of Bioethics*, vol. 10, no. 3, Mar. 2010, pp. 27-32.

Summarize the source in the present tense.

Annotations should be three to seven sentences long.

In this scholarly article, bioethicist David Resnik argues that bans on unhealthy foods set a dangerous precedent to threaten our personal freedom. He claims that researchers don't have enough evidence to know whether banning trans fats will save lives or money; all we know is that such bans restrict dietary choices. Resnik explains why most Americans oppose food restrictions, noting our multiethnic heritage and regional traditions, as well as our desire for the freedom to choose our own food, even food with long-term health risks. The author acknowledges that few people would probably miss eating trans fats if they were banned entirely, but he fears that such bans would be a slippery slope and could lead to further restrictions on products such as red meat and sugary sodas, which are also known to have harmful effects. Resnik, a bioethicist, offers a well-reasoned argument, but he goes too far by insisting that all proposed food restrictions will do more harm than good. This article contributes important perspectives on why many Americans see government legislation as unreasonable and provides counterarguments to other sources that claim it would be unreasonable not to enact legislation to advance public health.

Evaluate the source for bias and relevance.

Evaluate the source for its contribution to the research project.

How to write an annotated bibliography

An **annotated bibliography** gives you an opportunity to summarize, evaluate, and record publication information for your sources before drafting your research paper. You summarize each source to understand its main ideas; you evaluate each source for accuracy, quality, and relevance. Finally, you reflect, asking yourself how the source will contribute to your research project. A sample annotated bibliography entry appears on page 358.

Key features

- **A list of sources arranged in alphabetical order by author** includes complete bibliographic information for each source.

- **A brief entry for each source** is typically one hundred to two hundred words and is written in paragraph form.

- **A summary** of each source states the work's main ideas and key points briefly and accurately. The summary is written in the third person and the present tense. Summarizing helps you test your understanding of a source and restate its meaning responsibly.

- **An evaluation** of the source's role and usefulness in your project includes an assessment of the source's strengths and limitations, the author's qualifications and expertise, and the function of the source in your project. Evaluating a source helps you analyze how the source fits into your project and separate the source's ideas from your own.

Thinking ahead: Presenting or publishing

You may be asked to submit your annotated bibliography electronically. If this is the case, be sure that any entries for web sources include functioning links to the sources so that your reader can easily access them, if necessary.

Writing your annotated bibliography

1 Explore

For each source, begin by brainstorming responses to questions such as the following.

- What is the purpose of the source? Who is the author's intended audience?

- What is the author's thesis? What evidence supports the thesis?
- What qualifications and expertise does the author bring? Does the author have any biases or make any questionable assumptions?
- Why do you think this source is useful for your project?
- How does this source relate to the other sources in your bibliography?

2 Draft

- Arrange the sources in alphabetical order by author (or by title for works with no author).
- Provide consistent bibliographic information for each source. For the exact bibliographic format, see MLA-4b, APA-4b, or CMS-4c.
- Start your summary by identifying the thesis and purpose of the source as well as the credentials of the source's author.
- Keep your research question in mind. How does this source contribute to your project? How does it help you take your place in the conversation?

3 Revise

Ask reviewers for specific feedback. Here are some questions to guide their comments.

- Is each source summarized clearly? Have you identified the author's main idea?
- For each source, have you made a clear judgment about how and why the source is useful for your project?
- Have you used quotation marks around exact words from a source?

MLA

MLA Papers

Why do I have to cite a source even if I put the idea in my own words?

See MLA-2d

What rules do I have to follow to set up my paper?

See MLA-5b

How can I work sources into my writing more smoothly?

See MLA-3

MLA MLA Papers

Directory to MLA in-text citation models

Directory to MLA works cited models

Directory to MLA works cited models, *continued*

MLA Papers

In English and other humanities courses, you may be asked to document your sources with the Modern Language Association (MLA) system of citations described in MLA-4. When writing an MLA paper that is based on sources, you face three main challenges: (1) supporting a thesis, (2) citing your sources accurately and avoiding plagiarism, and (3) integrating source material effectively.

Examples in this tabbed section are drawn from one student's research. Sophie Harba's research essay, in which she argues that US state governments have the responsibility to advance health policies and to regulate healthy eating choices, appears on pages 427–32.

MLA-1 Supporting a thesis

Most research assignments ask you to form a thesis, or main idea, and to support that thesis with well-organized evidence.

MLA-1a Form a working thesis.

Once you have read a variety of sources, considered your subject from different perspectives, and chosen an entry point in the research conversation (see R1-b), you are ready to form a working thesis: a one-sentence (or occasionally a two-sentence) statement of your central idea (see also C1-c). The thesis expresses your informed, reasoned answer to your research question.

Here, for example, are student writer Sophie Harba's research question and working thesis.

RESEARCH QUESTION

Should state governments enact laws to regulate healthy eating choices?

WORKING THESIS

State governments have the responsibility to regulate healthy eating choices because of the rise of chronic diseases.

LaunchPad **ACTIVITIES FOR MLA-1**
macmillan learning
2 Exercises, 1 Writing prompt

Testing your thesis

Keep the following guidelines in mind to develop an effective thesis statement.

- A thesis should be your answer to a question and should take a position that needs to be argued and supported. It should not be a fact or a description.
- A thesis should match the scope of the research project. If your thesis is too broad, explore a subtopic of your original topic. If your thesis is too narrow, ask a research question that has more than one answer.
- A thesis should be focused. Avoid vague words such as *interesting* or *good*. Use concrete language and make sure your thesis lets readers know your position.
- A thesis should stand up to the "So what?" test. Ask yourself why readers should be interested in your essay and care about your thesis.

After you have written a rough draft and perhaps done more reading, you may decide to revise your thesis, as Harba did, to give it a sharper and more specific focus.

REVISED THESIS

In the name of public health and safety, state governments have the responsibility to shape health policies and to regulate healthy eating choices, especially since doing so offers a potentially large social benefit for a relatively small cost.

The thesis usually appears at the end of the introductory paragraph. To read Harba's thesis in the context of her introduction, see page 427.

MLA-1b Organize ideas with a rough outline.

The body of your paper will consist of evidence in support of your thesis. It will be useful to sketch an informal plan that helps you begin to organize your ideas. Sophie Harba, for example, used this simple plan to outline the structure of her argument.

- Debates about the government's role in regulating food have a long history in the United States.
- Some experts argue that we should focus on the dangers of unhealthy eating habits and on preventing chronic diseases linked to diet.
- But food regulations are not a popular solution because many Americans object to government restrictions on personal choice.
- Food regulations designed to prevent chronic disease don't ask Americans to give up their freedom; they ask Americans to see health as a matter of public good.

After you have written a rough draft, a formal outline can help you test and fine-tune the organization of your argument. See C1-d to read an example—Harba's formal outline.

MLA-1c Use sources to inform and support your argument.

The source materials you have gathered can play many different roles and will help you support and develop your argument.

Providing background information or context

Readers need some background information and context to anchor their understanding of your topic. Describing a research study or offering statistics can help readers grasp your topic's significance. Student writer Sophie Harba uses a source to give context for her topic, the benefits of laws designed to prevent chronic disease.

> To give just one example, Marion Nestle, New York University professor of nutrition and public health, notes that "a 1% reduction in intake of saturated fat across the population would prevent more than 30,000 cases of coronary heart disease annually and save more than a billion dollars in health care costs" (7).

Explaining terms or concepts

If readers are unfamiliar with a term or concept, you will want to define or explain it; or if your argument depends on a term with multiple meanings, you will want to explain your use of the term. Quoting or paraphrasing a source can help you define terms and concepts in accessible language. Harba defines the term *refined grains* as part of her claim that the typical American diet is getting less healthy over time.

> A diet that is low in nutritional value and high in sugars, fats, and refined grains—grains that have been processed to increase shelf life but that contain little fiber, iron, and B vitamins—can be damaging over time (United States, Dept. of Agriculture and Dept. of Health and Human Services 36).

Supporting your claims

As you develop your argument, back up your assertions with facts, examples, and other evidence from your research. (See also A4-e.) Harba, for example, uses factual evidence to support her claim that the typical American diet is damaging.

> Michael Pollan, who has written extensively about Americans' unhealthy eating habits, notes that "[t]he Centers for Disease Control estimates that fully three quarters of US health care spending goes to treat chronic diseases, most of which are preventable and linked to diet: heart disease, stroke, type 2 diabetes, and at least a third of all cancers."

Lending authority to your argument

Expert opinion can add credibility to your argument. (See also A4-e.) But don't rely on experts to make your argument for you. State your ideas in your own words and, when appropriate, cite the judgment of an authority in the field to support your position.

> Debates surrounding the government's role in regulating food have a long history in the United States. According to Lorine Goodwin, a food historian, nineteenth-century reformers who sought to purify the food supply were called "fanatics" and "radicals" by critics who argued that consumers should be free to buy and eat what they want (77).

Anticipating and countering objections

Do not ignore sources that contradict your position. Instead, use them to give voice to opposing points of view and to state potential objections to your argument before you counter them (see A-4f). By anticipating her readers' argument that many Americans oppose laws that limit what they eat, Sophie Harba creates an opportunity to counter that objection and build common ground with her readers.

> Why is the public largely resistant to laws that would limit unhealthy choices or penalize those choices with so-called fat taxes? Many consumers and civil rights advocates find such laws to be an unreasonable restriction on individual freedom of choice. As health policy experts Mello and others point out, opposition to food and beverage regulation is similar to the opposition to early tobacco legislation: the public views the issue as one of personal responsibility rather than one requiring government intervention (2602). In other words, if a person eats unhealthy food and becomes ill as a result, that is his or her choice. But those who favor legislation claim that freedom of choice is a myth because of the strong influence of food and beverage industry marketing on consumers' dietary habits.

MLA-2 Citing sources; avoiding plagiarism

In a research paper, you will draw on the work of other writers, and you must document their contributions by citing your sources. Sources are cited for two reasons:

1. to tell readers where your information comes from — so that they can assess its reliability and, if interested, find and read the original source
2. to give credit to the writers from whom you have borrowed words and ideas

You must include a citation when you quote from a source, when you summarize or paraphrase, and when you borrow facts that are not common knowledge. Borrowing another writer's language, sentence structures, or ideas without proper acknowledgment is a form of dishonesty known as *plagiarism*.

The only exception is common knowledge; information that your readers may know or could easily locate in any number of reference sources doesn't need to be cited.

MLA-2a Understand how the MLA system works.

Here, briefly, is how the MLA citation system usually works. (See MLA-4 for more details and model citations.)

1. The source is introduced by a signal phrase that names its author.
2. The material being cited is followed by a page number in parentheses (unless the source is an unpaginated web source).
3. At the end of the paper, a list of works cited (arranged alphabetically by authors' last names or by title if no author is listed) gives complete publication information for the source.

IN-TEXT CITATION

Bioethicist David Resnik emphasizes that such policies, despite their potential to make our society healthier, "open the door to excessive government control over food, which could restrict dietary choices, interfere with cultural, ethnic, and religious traditions, and exacerbate socioeconomic inequalities" (31).

ENTRY IN THE LIST OF WORKS CITED

Resnik, David. "Trans Fat Bans and Human Freedom." *American Journal of Bioethics*, vol. 10, no. 3, Mar. 2010, pp. 27-32.

 LaunchPad ACTIVITIES FOR MLA-2
macmillan learning
7 Exercises, 1 LearningCurve activity

This basic MLA format varies for different types of sources. For a detailed discussion and other models, see MLA-4.

MLA-2b Understand what plagiarism is.

In a research paper, you draw on the work of other writers. To be fair and responsible, you must document their contributions by citing your sources. When you acknowledge and document your sources, you avoid plagiarism, a serious academic offence. (See also R2-c.)

In general, these three acts are considered plagiarism:

1. failing to cite quotations and borrowed ideas
2. failing to enclose borrowed language in quotation marks
3. failing to put summaries and paraphrases in your own words

Definitions of plagiarism may vary; it's a good idea to find out how your school defines academic dishonesty.

MLA-2c Use quotation marks around borrowed language.

To indicate that you are using a source's exact phrases or sentences, you must enclose them in quotation marks unless they have been set off from the text by indenting (see p. 376). To omit the quotation marks is to claim, falsely, that the language is your own, as in the example below. Such an omission is plagiarism even if you have cited the source.

ORIGINAL SOURCE

Although these policies may have a positive impact on human health, they open the door to excessive government control over food, which could restrict dietary choices, interfere with cultural, ethnic, and religious traditions, and exacerbate socioeconomic inequalities.

— David Resnik, "Trans Fat Bans and Human Freedom," p. 31

PLAGIARISM

Bioethicist David Resnik points out that government policies to ban trans fats may have a positive impact on human health, but they open the door to excessive government control over food, which could restrict dietary choices and interfere with cultural, ethnic, and religious traditions (31).

BORROWED LANGUAGE IN QUOTATION MARKS

Bioethicist David Resnik emphasizes that government policies to ban trans fats, despite their potential to make our society healthier, "open the door to excessive government control over food, which could restrict dietary choices" and "interfere with cultural, ethnic, and religious traditions" (31).

MLA-2d Put summaries and paraphrases in your own words.

Summaries and paraphrases are written in your own words. A summary condenses information from a source; a paraphrase uses roughly the same number of words as the original source to convey the information. When you summarize or paraphrase, it is not enough to name the source; you must restate the source's meaning using your own words and sentence structure. (See also R2-c and, if English is not your first language, M6.) Half-copying the author's sentences by using the author's phrases in your own sentences without quotation marks or by plugging synonyms into the author's sentence structure (sometimes called *patchwriting*) is a form of plagiarism.

The first paraphrase of the following source is plagiarized. Even though the source is cited, the paraphrase borrows too much of its language from the original. The highlighted strings of words have been copied exactly (without quotation marks). In addition, the writer has closely echoed the sentence structure of the source, merely substituting some synonyms (*interfere with lifestyle choices* for *constitute paternalistic intervention into lifestyle choices* and *decrease the feeling of personal responsibility* for *enfeeble the notion of personal responsibility*).

ORIGINAL SOURCE

[A]ntiobesity laws encounter strong opposition from some quarters on the grounds that they constitute paternalistic intervention into lifestyle choices and enfeeble the notion of personal responsibility. Such arguments echo those made in the early days of tobacco regulation.

— Michelle M. Mello et al., "Obesity — the
New Frontier of Public
Health Law," p. 2602

PLAGIARISM: UNACCEPTABLE BORROWING

Health policy experts Mello and others argue that antiobesity laws encounter strong opposition from some people because they interfere with lifestyle choices and decrease the feeling of personal responsibility. These arguments mirror those made in the early days of tobacco regulation (2602).

To avoid plagiarizing an author's language, resist the temptation to look at the source while you are summarizing or paraphrasing. After you have read the passage you want to paraphrase, set the source aside. Ask yourself, "What is the author's meaning?" In your own words, state your understanding of the author's ideas. Return to the source and check that you haven't used the author's language or sentence structure or misrepresented the author's ideas. Following these steps will help you avoid plagiarizing the source. When you fully understand another writer's meaning, you can more easily and accurately present those ideas in your own words.

ACCEPTABLE PARAPHRASE

As health policy experts Mello and others point out, opposition to food and beverage regulation is similar to the opposition to early tobacco legislation: the public views the issue as one of personal responsibility rather than one requiring government intervention (2602).

Integrating sources

Quotations, summaries, and paraphrases will help you develop your argument, but they cannot speak for you. You need to find a balance between the words of your sources and your own voice, so that readers always know who is speaking in your paper — you or your source. You can use several strategies to integrate sources into your paper while maintaining your own voice.

- Use sources as concisely as possible so that your own thinking and voice aren't lost (MLA-3a and MLA-3b).
- Use signal phrases to help you avoid dropping quotations into your paper without indicating the boundary between your words and the source's words (MLA-3c).
- Use language that shows readers how each source supports your argument and how the sources relate to one another (MLA-3d).

MLA-3a Summarize and paraphrase effectively.

In your academic writing, keep the emphasis on your ideas and your language; use your own words to summarize and paraphrase sources and to explain your points. Whether you choose to summarize or paraphrase a source depends on your purpose.

Summarizing

When you summarize a source, you express another writer's ideas in your own words, condensing the author's key points and using fewer words than the author.

Be a responsible research writer

Using good citation habits is the best way to avoid plagiarizing sources and to demonstrate your responsibility as a researcher.

1 Cite your sources as you write drafts. Don't wait until your final draft is complete to add citations. Include a citation when you quote from a source, when you summarize or paraphrase, and when you borrow facts that are not common knowledge.

2 Place quotation marks around direct quotations, both in your notes and in your drafts.

3 Check each quotation, summary, and paraphrase against the source to make certain you aren't misrepresenting the source. Also be sure that your language and sentence structure differ from those in the original passage.

4 Provide a full citation in your works cited. It is not sufficient to cite a source only in the body of your paper; you must also provide complete publication information for each source in a list of works cited.

WHEN TO USE A SUMMARY

- When a passage is lengthy and you want to condense a chapter to a paragraph or a paragraph to a sentence
- When you want to state the source's main ideas simply and briefly in your own words
- When you want to compare arguments or ideas from various sources
- When you want to provide readers with an understanding of the source's argument before you respond to it or launch your own argument

Paraphrasing

When you paraphrase, you express an author's ideas in your own words and sentence structure, using approximately the same number of words and details as in the source.

WHEN TO USE A PARAPHRASE

- When the ideas and information are important but the author's exact words are not needed
- When you want to restate the source's ideas in your own words
- When you need to simplify or explain a technical or complicated source
- When you need to reorder a source's ideas

Using sources responsibly: When you use your own words to summarize or paraphrase, the original idea remains the intellectual property of the author, so you must include a citation.

MLA-3b Use quotations effectively.

When you quote a source, you borrow some of the author's exact words and enclose them in quotation marks. Quotation marks show your readers that both the idea and the words belong to the author.

WHEN TO USE QUOTATIONS

- When language is especially vivid or expressive
- When exact wording is needed for technical accuracy
- When it is important to let the debaters of an issue explain their positions in their own words
- When the words of an authority lend weight to an argument
- When the language of a source is the topic of your discussion

Limiting your use of quotations

Keep the emphasis on your own ideas. It is not always necessary to quote full sentences from a source. Often you can integrate words and phrases from a source into your own sentence structure. (For the use of signal phrases in integrating quotations, see MLA-3c.)

> Resnik acknowledges that his argument relies on "slippery slope" thinking, but he insists that "social and political pressures" regarding food regulation make his concerns valid (31).

Using the ellipsis mark and brackets

Two useful marks of punctuation, the ellipsis mark and brackets, allow you to keep quoted material to a minimum and to integrate it smoothly into your text.

THE ELLIPSIS MARK   To condense a quoted passage, you can use the ellipsis mark (three periods, with spaces between) to indicate that you have left words out. What remains must be grammatically complete.

> In Mississippi, legislators passed "a ban on bans—a law that forbids . . . local restrictions on food or drink" (Conly A23).

The writer has omitted the words *municipalities to place* before *local restrictions* to condense the quoted material.

If you want to leave out one or more full sentences, use a period before the three ellipsis dots.

> Legal scholars Gostin and Gostin argue that "individuals have limited willpower to defer immediate gratification for longer-term health benefits. . . . A person understands that high-fat foods or a sedentary lifestyle will cause adverse health effects, or that excessive spending or gambling will cause financial hardship, but it is not always easy to refrain" (217).

Ordinarily, do not use an ellipsis mark at the beginning or at the end of a quotation. Your readers will understand that the quoted material comes from a longer passage, so such marks are not necessary. The only exception occurs when you have dropped words at the end of the final quoted sentence. In such cases, put three ellipsis dots before the closing quotation mark and parenthetical reference.

Using sources responsibly: Make sure omissions and ellipsis marks do not distort the meaning of your source.

BRACKETS Brackets allow you to insert your own words into quoted material to clarify a confusing reference or to keep a sentence grammatical in your context. You also use brackets to indicate that you are changing a letter from capital to lowercase (or vice versa) to fit into your sentence. In the following example, the writer inserted words in brackets to clarify the meaning of *help*.

> Neergaard and Agiesta argue that "a new poll finds people are split on how much the government should do to help [find solutions to the national health crisis]— and most draw the line at attempts to force healthier eating."

To indicate an error such as a misspelling in a quotation, insert the word "sic" in brackets right after the error.

> "While Americans of every race, gender and ethnicity are affected by this disease, diabetes disproportionately effects [sic] minority populations."

Setting off long quotations

When you quote more than four typed lines of prose or more than three lines of poetry, set off the quotation by indenting it one-half inch (1.25 cm) from the left margin.

Long quotations should be introduced by an informative sentence, usually followed by a colon. Quotation marks are unnecessary because the indented format tells readers that the passage is taken word-for-word from the source.

> In response to critics who claim that laws aimed at stopping us from eating whatever we want are an assault on our freedom of choice, Conly offers a persuasive counterargument:
>
>> [L]aws aren't designed for each one of us individually. Some of us can drive safely at 90 miles per hour, but we're bound by the same laws as the people who can't, because individual speeding laws aren't practical. Giving up a little liberty is something we agree to when we agree to live in a democratic society that is governed by laws. (A23)

At the end of an indented quotation, the parenthetical citation goes outside the final mark of punctuation. (When a quotation is run into your text, the opposite is true. See the sample citations on p. 375.)

MLA-3c Use signal phrases to integrate sources.

When you include a paraphrase, summary, or direct quotation of another writer's work in your paper, prepare your readers for it with introductory words called a *signal phrase*. A signal phrase usually names the author of the source,

Using signal phrases in MLA papers

To avoid monotony, try to vary both the language and the placement of your signal phrases.

Model signal phrases

Michael Pollan, who has written extensively about Americans' unhealthy eating habits, argues that "..."

As health policy experts Mello and others point out, "..."

Marion Nestle, New York University professor of nutrition and public health, notes ...

Bioethicist David Resnik acknowledges that his argument ...

In response to critics, Conly offers a persuasive counterargument: "..."

Verbs in signal phrases

acknowledges	comments	endorses	reasons
adds	compares	grants	refutes
admits	confirms	illustrates	rejects
agrees	contends	implies	reports
argues	declares	insists	responds
asserts	denies	notes	suggests
believes	disputes	observes	thinks
claims	emphasizes	points out	writes

provides some context for the source material — such as the author's credentials — and helps readers distinguish your ideas from those of the source.

When you write a signal phrase, choose a verb that is appropriate for the way you are using the source (see MLA-1c). Are you providing background, explaining a concept, supporting a claim, lending authority, or refuting a belief? Write a signal phrase that communicates the specific relationship between the source's idea and another idea (whether it be yours or that of another source). Doing so gives your writing energy and shows that you understand the source's position in the debate.

> Lorine Goodwin, a food historian, ~~says,~~ "..."

(above "says,": *rejects the claim:*)

NOTE: MLA style calls for verbs in the present tense or present perfect tense (*argues* or *has argued*) to introduce source material unless you include a date that specifies the time of the original author's writing.

Marking boundaries

Readers need to move from your words to the words of a source without feeling a jolt. Avoid dropping quotations into the text without warning. Instead, provide clear signal phrases, including at least the author's name, to indicate the boundary between your words and the source's words. (The signal phrase is highlighted in the second example.)

DROPPED QUOTATION

> Laws designed to prevent chronic disease by promoting healthier food and beverage consumption also have potentially enormous benefits. "[A] 1% reduction in intake of saturated fat across the population would prevent more than 30,000 cases of coronary heart disease annually and save more than a billion dollars in health care costs" (Nestle 7).

QUOTATION WITH SIGNAL PHRASE

> Laws designed to prevent chronic disease by promoting healthier food and beverage consumption also have potentially enormous benefits. Marion Nestle, New York University professor of nutrition and public health, notes that "a 1% reduction in intake of saturated fat across the population would prevent more than 30,000 cases of coronary heart disease annually and save more than a billion dollars in health care costs" (7).

Establishing authority

The first time you mention a source, include in the signal phrase the author's title, credentials, or experience to help your readers recognize the source's authority and your own credibility (*ethos*) as a responsible researcher who has located reliable sources. (Signal phrases are highlighted in the next two examples.)

SOURCE WITH NO CREDENTIALS

> Michael Pollan notes that "[t]he Centers for Disease Control estimates that fully three quarters of US health care spending goes to treat chronic diseases, most of which are preventable and linked to diet: heart disease, stroke, type 2 diabetes, and at least a third of all cancers."

SOURCE WITH CREDENTIALS

> Michael Pollan, who has written extensively about Americans' unhealthy eating habits, notes that "[t]he Centers for Disease Control estimates that fully three quarters of US health care spending goes to treat chronic diseases, most of which are preventable and linked to diet: heart disease, stroke, type 2 diabetes, and at least a third of all cancers."

Introducing summaries and paraphrases

Introduce most summaries and paraphrases with a signal phrase that names the author and places the material in the context of your argument. Readers will then understand that everything between the signal phrase and the parenthetical citation summarizes or paraphrases the cited source.

Without the signal phrase (highlighted) in the following example, readers might think that only the quotation at the end is being cited, when in fact the whole paragraph is based on the source.

> To improve public health, advocates such as Bowdoin College philosophy professor Sarah Conly contend that it is the government's duty to prevent people from making harmful choices whenever feasible and whenever public benefits outweigh the costs. In response to critics who claim that laws aimed at stopping us from eating whatever we want are an assault on our freedom of choice, Conly asserts that "laws aren't designed for each one of us individually" (A23).

There are times when a summary or a paraphrase does not require a signal phrase naming the author. When the context makes clear where the cited material begins, you may omit the signal phrase and include the author's last name in parentheses.

Using signal phrases with statistics and other facts

When you cite a statistic or another specific fact, a signal phrase is often not necessary. Readers usually will understand that the citation refers to the statistic or fact (not the whole paragraph).

> Seventy-five percent of Americans are opposed to laws that restrict or put limitations on access to unhealthy foods (Neergaard and Agiesta).

There is nothing wrong, however, with using a signal phrase to introduce a statistic or another fact.

Putting source material in context

Readers should not have to guess why source material appears in your paper. A signal phrase can help you connect your own ideas with those of another writer by clarifying how the source will contribute to your paper (see R3-a).

If you use another writer's words, you must explain how they relate to your argument. Quotations don't speak for themselves; you must create a context for readers. Sandwich each quotation between sentences of your own: Introduce the quotation with a signal phrase, and follow it with interpretive comments that link the quotation to your paper's argument (see also MLA-3d).

QUOTATION WITH EFFECTIVE CONTEXT (QUOTATION SANDWICH)

In response to critics who claim that laws aimed at stopping us from eating whatever we want are an assault on our freedom of choice, Conly offers a persuasive counterargument:

> [L]aws aren't designed for each one of us individually. Some of us can drive safely at 90 miles per hour, but we're bound by the same laws as the people who can't, because individual speeding laws aren't practical. Giving up a little liberty is something we agree to when we agree to live in a democratic society that is governed by laws. (A23)

The student writer sandwiches a quotation between sentences of her own—a signal phrase and an interpretive comment.

As Conly suggests, we need to change our either/or thinking (either we have complete freedom of choice *or* we have government regulations and lose our freedom) and instead need to see health as a matter of public good, not individual liberty.

MLA-3d Synthesize sources.

When you synthesize multiple sources in a research paper, you create a conversation about your research topic. You show readers that your argument is based on your active analysis and integration of ideas, not just a series of quotations and paraphrases. Your synthesis will show how your sources relate to one another; one source may support, extend, or counter the ideas of another. Not every source has to "speak" to another in a research paper, but readers should understand how each source functions in your argument (see R3-a).

Considering how sources relate to your argument

Before you integrate sources and show readers how they relate to one another, consider how each source might contribute to your own argument. As student writer Sophie Harba became more informed about her research topic, she asked herself these questions: *What have I learned from my sources? Which sources might support my ideas or illustrate the points I want to make? What common counterarguments do I need to address to strengthen my position?* She annotated a passage from one of her sources — a nonprofit group's assertion that our choices about food are skewed by marketing messages.

STUDENT NOTES ON A SOURCE

Useful factual information ⟶

The food and beverage industry spends approximately $2 billion per year

↳ marketing to children.   — "Facts on Junk Food"

Could use this to counter the personal choice point in Mello et al.

Placing sources in conversation

You can show readers how the ideas of one source relate to those of another by connecting and analyzing the ideas in your own voice. After all, you've done the research and thought through the issues, so you should control the conversation. Keep the emphasis on your own writing. The thread of your argument should be easy to identify and to understand, with or without your sources.

SAMPLE SYNTHESIS

Student writer Sophie Harba sets up her synthesis with a question.

> Why is the public largely resistant to laws that would limit unhealthy choices or penalize those choices with so-called fat taxes? Many consumers and civil rights advocates find such laws to be an unreasonable restriction on individual freedom of choice. As health

Student writer

A signal phrase indicates how the source contributes to Harba's argument and shows that the idea that follows is not her own.

> policy experts Mello and others point out, opposition to food and beverage regulation is similar to the opposition to early tobacco legislation: the public views the issue as one of personal responsibility rather than one requiring government intervention (2602). In other words, if a

Source 1

Harba interprets a paraphrased source.

> person eats unhealthy food and becomes ill as a result, that is his or her choice. But those who favor legislation claim that freedom of choice is a myth because of the strong influence of food and beverage industry marketing

Student writer

Harba uses a source to support her counterargument.

> on consumers' dietary habits. According to one nonprofit health advocacy group, food and beverage companies spend roughly two billion dollars per year marketing directly to children. As a result, kids see nearly four thousand ads per year encouraging them to eat unhealthy food and drinks ("Facts"). As was the case with antismoking laws passed in recent decades, taxes and legal restrictions on junk food sales could help to counter the strong marketing messages that promote unhealthy products.

Source 2

Student writer

Harba extends the argument and follows it with an interpretive comment.

> The United States has a history of state and local public health laws that have successfully promoted a particular behavior by punishing an undesirable behavior. The decline in tobacco use as a result of antismoking taxes and laws is perhaps the most obvious example. Another example is legislation requiring the use of seat belts, which have significantly reduced fatalities in car crashes.

One government agency reports that seat belt use saved | **Source 3**
an average of more than fourteen thousand lives per year
in the United States between 2000 and 2010 (United
States, Dept. of Transportation, Natl. Highway Traffic
Safety Administration 231). Perhaps seat belt laws have
public support because the cost of wearing a seat belt is | **Student writer**
small, especially when compared with the benefit of
saving fourteen thousand lives per year.

In this synthesis, Harba uses her own analysis to shape the conversation among her sources. She does not simply string quotations together or allow them to overwhelm her writing. She guides her readers through a conversation about a variety of laws that could promote and have promoted public health. She finds points of intersection among her sources, acknowledges the contributions of others in the conversation, and shows readers, in her own voice, how the sources support her argument.

When synthesizing sources, ask yourself the following questions:

- How do your sources address your research question? How do your sources respond to each other's ideas?
- Have you varied the function of sources — to provide background, to explain concepts, to lend authority, and to anticipate counterarguments?
- Do you connect and analyze sources in your own voice?
- Is your own argument easy to identify and to understand, with or without your sources?

Reviewing an MLA paper: Use of sources

Use of quotations

- Have you used quotation marks around quoted material (unless it has been set off from the text)? (See MLA-2c.)
- Have you checked that quoted language is word-for-word accurate? If it is not, do ellipsis marks or brackets indicate the omissions or changes? (See pp. 375–76.)
- Does a clear signal phrase (usually naming the author) prepare readers for each quotation and for the purpose the quotation serves? (See MLA-3c.)
- Does a parenthetical citation follow each quotation? (See MLA-4a.)
- Is each quotation put in context? (See pp. 379–80.)

Reviewing an MLA paper: Use of sources, *continued*

Use of summaries and paraphrases

- Are summaries and paraphrases free of plagiarized wording — not copied or half-copied from the source? (See MLA-2d.)
- Are summaries and paraphrases documented with parenthetical citations? (See MLA-4a.)
- Do readers know where the cited material begins? In other words, does a signal phrase mark the boundary between your words and the summary or paraphrase? (See MLA-3c.)
- Does a signal phrase prepare readers for the purpose the summary or paraphrase has in your argument?

Use of statistics and other facts

- Are statistics and facts (other than common knowledge) documented with parenthetical citations? (See p. 369.)
- If there is no signal phrase, will readers understand exactly which facts are being cited? (See MLA-3c.)

MLA-4 Documenting sources

In English and other humanities classes, you may be asked to use the MLA (Modern Language Association) system for documenting sources, which is set forth in the *MLA Handbook*, 8th edition (MLA, 2016).

MLA recommends in-text citations that refer readers to a list of works cited. A typical in-text citation names the author of the source, often in a signal phrase, and gives a page number in parentheses. At the end of the paper, the list of works cited provides publication information about the source; the list is alphabetized by authors' last names (or by titles for works without authors).

LaunchPad ACTIVITIES FOR MLA-4
macmillan learning
8 Exercises, 7 Video tutorials

There is a direct connection between the in-text citation and the alphabetical listing. In the following example, that connection is highlighted in blue.

IN-TEXT CITATION

Bioethicist David Resnik emphasizes that such policies, despite their potential to make our society healthier, "open the door to excessive government control over food, which could restrict dietary choices, interfere with cultural, ethnic, and religious traditions, and exacerbate socioeconomic inequalities" (31).

ENTRY IN THE LIST OF WORKS CITED

Resnik, David. "Trans Fat Bans and Human Freedom." *The American Journal of Bioethics*, vol. 10, no. 3, Mar. 2010, pp. 27-32.

For a list of works cited that includes this entry, see page 432.

MLA-4a MLA in-text citations

MLA in-text citations are made with a combination of signal phrases and parenthetical references. A signal phrase introduces information taken from a source (a quotation, summary, paraphrase, or fact); usually the signal phrase includes the author's name. The parenthetical reference comes after the cited material, often at the end of the sentence. It includes at least a page number (except for unpaginated sources, such as those found on the web). In the models in MLA-4a, the elements of the in-text citation are highlighted in blue.

IN-TEXT CITATION

Resnik acknowledges that his argument relies on "slippery slope" thinking, but he insists that "social and political pressures" regarding food regulation make his concerns valid (31).

Readers can look up the author's last name in the alphabetized list of works cited, where they will learn the work's title and other publication information. If readers decide to consult the source, the page number will take them straight to the passage that has been cited.

General guidelines for signal phrases and page numbers

Items 1–5 explain how the MLA system usually works for all sources — in print, on the web, in other media, and with or without authors and page numbers. Items 6–27 give variations on the basic guidelines.

1. Author named in a signal phrase   Ordinarily, introduce the material being cited with a signal phrase that includes the author's name. In addition to preparing readers for the source, the signal phrase allows you to keep the parenthetical citation brief.

> According to Lorine Goodwin, a food historian, nineteenth-century reformers who sought to purify the food supply were called "fanatics" and "radicals" by critics who argued that consumers should be free to buy and eat what they want (77).

The signal phrase — *According to Lorine Goodwin* — names the author; the parenthetical citation gives the page number of the book in which the quoted words may be found.

Notice that the period follows the parenthetical citation. When a quotation ends with a question mark or an exclamation point, leave the end punctuation inside the quotation mark and add a period at the end of your sentence, after the parenthetical citation.

> Burgess asks a critical question: "How can we think differently about food labeling?" (51).

2. Author named in parentheses   If you do not give the author's name in a signal phrase, put the last name in parentheses along with the page number (if the source has one). Use no punctuation between the name and the page number: (Moran 351).

> According to a nationwide poll, 75% of Americans are opposed to laws that restrict or put limitations on access to unhealthy foods (Neergaard and Agiesta).

3. Author unknown   If a source has no author, the works cited entry will begin with the title. In your in-text citation, either use the complete title in a signal phrase or use a short form of the title in parentheses. Titles of books and other long works are italicized; titles of articles and other short works are put in quotation marks (see also pp. 424–25).

> As a result, kids see nearly four thousand ads per year encouraging them to eat unhealthy food and drinks ("Facts").

NOTE: If the author is a corporation or a government agency, see items 8 and 17 on pages 387 and 389, respectively.

4. Page number unknown   Do not include the page number if a work lacks page numbers, as is the case with many web sources. Do not use page numbers from a printout from a website. (When the pages of a web source are stable, as in PDF files, supply a page number in your in-text citation.)

> Michael Pollan points out that "cheap food" actually has "significant costs—to the environment, to public health, to the public purse, even to the culture."

If a source has numbered paragraphs or sections, use "par." (or "pars.") or "sec." (or "secs.") in the parentheses: (Smith, par. 4). Notice that a comma follows the author's name.

5. One-page source If the source is one page long, it is a good idea to include the page number; without it readers may not know where your citation ends or, worse, may not realize that you have provided a citation at all.

> **NO PAGE NUMBER IN CITATION**
> Sarah Conly uses John Stuart Mill's "harm principle" to argue that citizens need their government to intervene to prevent them from taking harmful actions—such as driving too fast or buying unhealthy foods—out of ignorance of the harm they can do. But government intervention may overstep in the case of food choices.

> **PAGE NUMBER IN CITATION**
> Sarah Conly uses John Stuart Mill's "harm principle" to argue that citizens need their government to intervene to prevent them from taking harmful actions—such as driving too fast or buying unhealthy foods—out of ignorance of the harm they can do (A23). But government intervention may overstep in the case of food choices.

Variations on the general guidelines

This section describes the MLA guidelines for handling a variety of situations not covered in items 1–5.

6. Two authors Name the authors in a signal phrase, as in the following example, or include their last names in the parenthetical reference: (Gostin and Gostin 214).

> As legal scholars Gostin and Gostin explain, "[I]nterventions that do not pose a truly significant burden on individual liberty" are justified if they "go a long way towards safeguarding the health and well-being of the populace" (214).

7. Three or more authors In a parenthetical citation, give the first author's name followed by "et al." (Latin for "and others"). In a signal phrase, give the first author's name followed by "and others."

> The clinical trials were extended for two years, and only after results were reviewed by an independent panel did the researchers publish their findings (Blaine et al. 35).

> Researchers Blaine and others note that clinical trial results were reviewed by an independent panel (35).

8. Organization as author When the author is a corporation or an organization, name that author either in the signal phrase or in the parenthetical citation. (For a government agency as author, see item 17 on p. 389.)

> The American Diabetes Association estimates that the cost of diagnosed diabetes in the United States in 2012 was $245 billion.

In the list of works cited, the American Diabetes Association is treated as the author and alphabetized under *A*. When you give the organization name in the text, spell out the name; when you use it in parentheses, abbreviate common words in the name: "Assn.," "Dept.," "Natl.," "Soc.," and so on.

> The cost of diagnosed diabetes in the United States in 2012 was estimated at $245 billion (Amer. Diabetes Assn.).

9. Authors with the same last name If your list of works cited includes works by two or more authors with the same last name, include the author's first name in the signal phrase or first initial in the parentheses.

> One approach to the problem is to introduce nutrition literacy at the K-5 level in public schools (E. Chen 15).

10. Two or more works by the same author Mention the title of the work in the signal phrase or include a short version of the title in the parentheses.

> The American Diabetes Association tracks trends in diabetes across age groups. In 2012, more than 200,000 children and adolescents had diabetes ("Fast"). Because of an expected dramatic increase in diabetes in young people over the next forty years, the association encourages "strategies for implementing childhood obesity prevention programs and primary prevention programs for youth at risk of developing type 2 diabetes" ("Number").

Titles of articles and other short works are placed in quotation marks; titles of books and other long works are italicized. (See also pp. 424–25.)

In the rare case when both the author's name and a short title must be given in parentheses, separate them with a comma.

> Researchers have estimated that "the number of youth with type 2 [diabetes] could quadruple and the number with type 1 could triple" by 2050, "with an increasing proportion of youth with diabetes from minority populations" (Amer. Diabetes Assn., "Number").

11. Two or more works in one citation   To cite more than one source in the parentheses, list the authors (or titles) in alphabetical order and separate them with semicolons.

> The prevalence of early-onset Type 2 diabetes has been well documented (Finn 68; Sharma 2037; Whitaker 118).

It may be less distracting to use an information note for multiple citations (see MLA-4c).

12. Repeated citations from the same source   When you are writing about a single work, you do not need to include the author's name each time you quote from or paraphrase the work. After you mention the author's name at the beginning of your paper, you may include just the page number in your parenthetical citations.

> In Susan Glaspell's short story "A Jury of Her Peers," two women accompany their husbands and a county attorney to an isolated house where a farmer named John Wright has been choked to death in his bed with a rope. The chief suspect is Wright's wife, Minnie, who is in jail awaiting trial. The sheriff's wife, Mrs. Peters, has come along to gather some personal items for Minnie, and Mrs. Hale has joined her. Early in the story, Mrs. Hale sympathizes with Minnie and objects to the way the male investigators are "snoopin' round and criticizin'" her kitchen (249). In contrast, Mrs. Peters shows respect for the law, saying that the men are doing "no more than their duty" (249).

In a paper with multiple sources, if you are citing a source more than once in a paragraph, you may omit the author's name after the first mention in the paragraph as long as it is clear that you are still referring to the same source.

13. Encyclopedia or dictionary entry   When an encyclopedia or a dictionary entry does not have an author, it will be alphabetized in the list of works cited under the word or entry that you consulted (see item 26 on p. 407). Either in your text or in your parenthetical citation, mention the word or entry and give a page number on which the entry may be found.

> The word *crocodile* has a complex etymology ("Crocodile" 139).

14. Multivolume work   If your paper cites more than one volume of a multivolume work, indicate in the parentheses the volume you are referring to, followed by a colon and the page number.

> In his studies of gifted children, Terman describes a pattern of accelerated language acquisition (2: 279).

If you cite only one volume of a multivolume work, you will include the volume number in the list of works cited and will not need to include it in the parentheses. (See the second example in item 35 on p. 411.)

15. Entire work   Use the author's name in a signal phrase or a parenthetical citation. There is no need to use a page number.

> Pollan explores the issues surrounding food production and consumption from a
> political angle.

16. Selection in an anthology or a collection   Put the name of the author of the selection (not the editor of the anthology) in the signal phrase or the parentheses.

> In "Love Is a Fallacy," the narrator's logical teachings disintegrate when Polly
> declares that she should date Petey because "[h]e's got a raccoon coat"
> (Shulman 372).

In the list of works cited, the work is alphabetized under *Shulman*, the author of the story, not under the name of the editor of the anthology. (See item 32 on p. 409.)

> Shulman, Max. "Love Is a Fallacy." *Current Issues and Enduring Questions*, edited
> > by Sylvan Barnet and Hugo Bedau, 11th ed., Bedford/St. Martin's, 2017,
> > pp. 365-72.

17. Government document   When a government agency is the author, you will alphabetize it in the list of works cited under the name of the government, such as Canada or United States (see item 61 on p. 421). For this reason, you must name the government as well as the agency in your in-text citation.

> One government agency reports that seat belt use saved an average of more
> than fourteen thousand lives per year in the United States between 2000 and
> 2010 (United States, Dept. of Transportation, Natl. Highway Traffic Safety
> Administration 231).

18. Historical document   For a historical document, such as the Canadian Charter of Rights and Freedoms or the Constitution of the United States, provide the document title, neither italicized nor in quotation marks, along with relevant article and section numbers. In parenthetical citations, use common abbreviations such as "art." and "sec."

> The Charter of Rights and Freedoms guarantees every Canadian "the right to life,
> liberty and security of the person" (sec. 7).

Cite other historical documents as you would any other work, by the first element in the works cited entry (see item 62 on p. 422).

19. Legal source For a legislative act (law) or court case, name the act or case either in a signal phrase or in parentheses. Italicize the names of cases but not the names of acts. (See also items 63 and 64 on p. 422.)

The Youth Criminal Justice Act came into force in 2003.

The 1930 ruling in *Edwards v. Canada (Attorney General)*, informally known in Canada as the Persons Case, acknowledged that women have the same political rights as men.

20. Visual such as a table, a chart, or another graphic To cite a visual that has a figure number in the source, use the abbreviation "fig." and the number in place of a page number in your parenthetical citation: (Manning, fig. 4). If you refer to the figure in your text, spell out the word "figure."

To cite a visual that does not have a figure number in a print source, use the visual's title or a description in your text and cite the author and page number as for any other source.

For a visual not in a print source, identify the visual in your text and then in parentheses use the first element in the works cited entry: the artist's or photographer's name or the title of the work. (See items 56–60 on pp. 420–21.)

Photographs such as *Woman Aircraft Worker* (Bransby) and *Women Welders* (Parks) demonstrate the US government's attempt to document the contributions of women during World War II.

21. Personal communication and social media Cite personal letters, personal interviews, email messages, and social media posts by the name listed in the works cited entry, as you would for any other source. Identify the type of source in your text if you feel it is necessary for clarity. (See items 65–69 on pp. 422–23.)

22. Web source Your in-text citation for a source from the web should follow the same guidelines as for other sources. If the source lacks page numbers but has numbered paragraphs, sections, or divisions, use those numbers with the appropriate abbreviation in your parenthetical citation: "par.," "sec.," "ch.," "pt.," and so on. Do not add such numbers if the source itself does not use them; simply give the author or title in your in-text citation.

Sanjay Gupta, CNN chief medical correspondent, explains that "limited access to fresh, affordable, healthy food" is one of America's most pressing health problems.

23. Indirect source (source quoted in another source) When a writer's or a speaker's quoted words appear in a source written by someone else, begin the parenthetical citation with the abbreviation "qtd. in." (See also item 12 on p. 400.)

In the following example, Gostin and Gostin are the authors of the source given in the works cited list; their work contains a quotation by Beauchamp.

> Public health researcher Dan Beauchamp has said that "public health practices are 'communal in nature, and concerned with the well-being of the community as a whole and not just the well-being of any particular person'" (qtd. in Gostin and Gostin 217).

Literary works and sacred texts

Literary works and sacred texts are usually available in a variety of editions. Your list of works cited will specify which edition you are using, and your in-text citation will usually consist of a page number from the edition you consulted (see item 24). When possible, give enough information — such as book parts, play divisions, or line numbers — so that readers can locate the cited passage in any edition of the work (see items 25–27).

24. Literary work without parts or line numbers Many literary works, such as most short stories and many novels and plays, do not have parts or line numbers. In such cases, simply cite the page number.

> At the end of Kate Chopin's "The Story of an Hour," Mrs. Mallard drops dead upon learning that her husband is alive. In the final irony of the story, doctors report that she has died of a "joy that kills" (25).

25. Verse play or poem For verse plays, give act, scene, and line numbers that can be located in any edition of the work. Use arabic numerals and separate the numbers with periods.

> In Shakespeare's *King Lear*, Gloucester, blinded for suspected treason, learns a profound lesson from his tragic experience: "A man may see how this world goes / with no eyes" (4.2.148-49).

For a poem, cite the part, stanza, and line numbers, if it has them, separated by periods.

> The Green Knight claims to approach King Arthur's court "because the praise of you, prince, is puffed so high, / And your manor and your men are considered so magnificent" (1.12.258-59).

For poems that are not divided into numbered parts or stanzas, use line numbers. For a first reference, use the word "lines": (lines 5-8). Thereafter use just the numbers: (12-13).

26. Novel with numbered divisions When a novel has numbered divisions, put the page number first, followed by a semicolon, and then the book, part, or chapter in which the passage may be found. Use abbreviations such as "bk.," "pt.," and "ch."

> One of Kingsolver's narrators, teenager Rachel, pushes her vocabulary beyond its limits. For example, Rachel complains that being forced to live in the Congo with her missionary family is "a sheer tapestry of justice" because her chances of finding a boyfriend are "dull and void" (117; bk. 2, ch. 10).

27. Sacred text When citing a sacred text such as the Bible or the Qur'an, name the edition you are using in your works cited entry (see item 36 on p. 411). In your parenthetical citation, give the book, chapter, and verse (or their equivalent), separated with periods. Common abbreviations for books of the Bible are acceptable.

> Consider the words of Solomon: "If your enemy is hungry, give him bread to eat; and if he is thirsty, give him water to drink" (*Oxford Annotated Bible*, Prov. 25.21).

The title of a sacred work is italicized when it refers to a specific edition of the work, as in the preceding example. If you refer to the book in a general sense in your text, neither italicize it nor put it in quotation marks (see also the note on p. 301 in section P10-a).

> The Bible and the Qur'an provide allegories that help readers understand how to lead a moral life.

MLA-4b MLA list of works cited

Your list of works cited, which you will place at the end of your paper, guides readers to the sources you have quoted, summarized, and paraphrased. Ask yourself: *What would readers need to know to find this source for themselves?* Usually, you will provide basic information common to most sources, such as author, title, publisher, publication date, and location (page numbers or URL, for example).

Throughout this section of the book, you'll find models organized by type (article, book, website, multimedia source, and so on). But even if you aren't sure exactly what type of source you have (*Is this a blog post or an article?*), you can follow two general principles:

Gather key publication information about the source — the citation elements.

Organize the basic information about the source using what MLA calls "containers."

The author's name and the title of the work are needed for many (though not all) sources and are the first two pieces of information to gather. For the remaining pieces of information, you might find it helpful to think about whether the work is contained within one or more larger works. Some sources are self-contained. Others are nested in larger containers.

☐	Self-contained	a *book*
		a *film*
⊡	One container	an *article* in a scholarly journal
		a *poem* in a collection of poetry
		a *video* posted to YouTube
		a *fact sheet* on a government website
⊡	Two containers	an *article* in a journal within a database (JSTOR, etc.)
		an *episode* from a TV series within a streaming service (Netflix, etc.)

Keep in mind that most sources won't include all of the following pieces of information, so gather only those that are relevant to and available for your source.

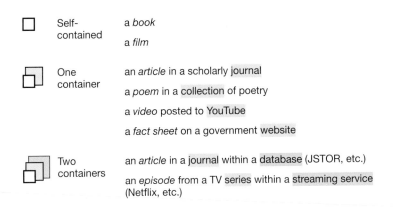

Author.

Title of source.

Title of container,   Title of container 2,

Other contributors,   Other contributors,

Version (or edition),   Version (or edition),

Volume and issue   *If there is a second*   Volume and issue
numbers,   *container, gather the*   →   numbers,
          same information for it
          (if available).

Publisher,   Publisher,

Date,   Date,

Location (page numbers,   Location.
URL, DOI, etc.).

See the following page for examples of works cited entries for a one-container source and a two-container source.

WORKS CITED ENTRY, ONE CONTAINER (SELECTION IN AN ANTHOLOGY)

······························ container 1 ·····················

| author | title of selection | title of collection | contributor |

Eisenberg, Deborah. "Some Other, Better Otto." *New American Stories*, edited by Ben Marcus,

| publisher | year | location (pages) |

Vintage Books, 2015, pp. 94-136.

WORKS CITED ENTRY, TWO CONTAINERS (ARTICLE IN A JOURNAL IN A DATABASE)

| author | title of article | journal title |

Coles, Kimberly Anne. "The Matter of Belief in John Donne's Holy Sonnets." *Renaissance*

·············· container 1 ·············· ········ container 2 ············

| volume, issue | date | location (pages) | database title | location (DOI) |

Quarterly, vol. 68, no. 3, Fall 2015, pp. 899-931. *JSTOR*, doi:10.1086/683855.

Once you've gathered the relevant and available information about a source, you will organize the elements using the list at the bottom of page 393 as your guideline. Note the punctuation after each element in that list. You will find many examples of how elements and containers are combined to create works cited entries on pages 394–423 of this section.

- Directory to MLA works cited models, page 363
- General guidelines for the works cited list, page 396

General guidelines for listing authors

The formatting of authors' names in items 1–12 applies to all sources — books, articles, websites — in print, on the web, or in other media. For more models of specific source types, see items 13–69.

1. Single author

| author: last name first | title (book) |

Marche, Stephen. *The Unmade Bed: The Messy Truth About Men and Women in the 21st Century.*

| publisher | year |

HarperCollins, 2017.

2. Two authors

| first author: last name first | second author: in normal order | title (book) | publisher |

Brennan, Thomas J., and Finbarr O'Reilly. *Shooting Ghosts*. Penguin Random House Canada,

| year |

2017.

3. Three or more authors   Name the first author followed by "et al." (Latin for "and others"). For in-text citations, see item 7 on page 386.

first author: "et al."
last name   for other
first   authors   title (book)   publisher   year

Giltrow, Janet, et al. *Academic Writing: An Introduction*. 2nd ed., Broadview Press, 2009.

4. Organization or company as author

author: organization
name, not abbreviated   title (book)   publisher   year

Human Rights Watch. *World Report of 2015: Events of 2014*. Seven Stories Press, 2015.

Your in-text citation also should treat the organization as the author (see item 8 on p. 387).

5. No author listed

                                   newspaper title
                  article title   (city in brackets)   date   page(s)

"The Unspoken Problem in Pikangikum." *Globe and Mail* [Toronto], 25 Jul. 2017, p. B3.

descriptive
label

Editorial.

                  title of
episode title   TV show   producer network date

"Something's Fishy." *Marketplace*, produced by Greg Sadler, CBC, 2010.

TIP: In web sources, often the author's name is available but is not easy to find (see p. 398). It may appear at the end of a web page, in tiny print, or on another page of the site, such as the home page. Also, an organization or a government may be the author (see items 4 and 61).

General guidelines for the works cited list

In the list of works cited, include only sources that you have quoted, summarized, or paraphrased in your paper. MLA's guidelines apply to a wide variety of sources. You can adapt the guidelines and models in this section to source types you encounter in your research.

Gathering information and organizing entries

The elements needed for a works cited entry are the following:

- The author (if a work has one)
- The title
- The title of the larger work in which the source is located, if it is contained in a larger work (MLA calls the larger work a "container" — a collection, a journal, a magazine, a website, and so on)
- As much of the following information as is available about the source and the container:

      Editor, translator, director, performer
      Version or edition
      Volume and issue numbers
      Publisher
      Date of publication
      Location of the source: page numbers, URL, DOI, and so on

Not all sources will require every element. See pages 392–93 and specific models in this section for more details.

Authors

- Arrange the list alphabetically by authors' last names or by titles for works with no authors.
- For the first author, place the last name first, a comma, and the first name. Put a second author's name in normal order (first name followed by last name). For three or more authors, use "et al." after the first author's name.
- Spell out "editor," "translator," "edited by," and so on.

Titles

- In titles of works, capitalize all words except articles (*a, an, the*), prepositions, coordinating conjunctions, and the *to* in infinitives — unless the word is first or last in the title or subtitle.
- Use quotation marks for titles of articles and other short works. Place single quotation marks around a quoted term or a title of a short work that appears within an article title; italicize a term or title that is normally italicized.
- Italicize titles of books and other long works. If a book title contains another title that is normally italicized, neither italicize the internal title nor place it in quotation marks. If the title within the title is normally put in quotation marks, retain the quotation marks and italicize the entire book title.

General guidelines for the works cited list, *continued*

Publication information

- Do not give the place of publication for a book publisher.
- Use the complete version of publishers' names, except for terms such as "Inc." and "Co."; retain terms such as "Books" and "Press." For university publishers, use "U" and "P" for "University" and "Press."
- For a book, take the name of the publisher from the title page (or from the copyright page if it is not on the title page). For a website, the publisher might be at the bottom of a page or on the "About" page. If a work has two or more publishers, separate the names with slashes.
- If the title of a website and the publisher are the same or similar, give the title of the site but omit the publisher.

Dates

- For a book, give the most recent year found on the title page or the copyright page. For a web source, use the copyright date or the most recent update date. Use the complete date as listed in the source.
- Abbreviate all months except May, June, and July and give the date in inverted form: 13 Mar. 2017.
- If the source has no date, give your date of access at the end: Accessed 24 Feb. 2017.

Page numbers

- For most articles and other short works, give page numbers when they are available, preceded by "pp." (or "p." for only one page).
- Do not use the page numbers from a printout of a web source.
- If a short work does not appear on consecutive pages, give the number of the first page followed by a plus sign: 35+.

URLs and DOIs

- Give a permalink or a DOI (digital object identifier) if a source has one.
- If a source does not have a permalink or a DOI, include the full URL for the source (omitting the protocol, such as http://).
- If a database provides only a URL that is long and complicated and if your readers are not likely to be able to use it to access the source, your instructor may allow you to use the URL for the database home page (such as go.galegroup.com). Check with your instructor.
- For open databases and archives, such as Google Books, give the complete URL for the source. (See item 28b.)
- If a URL or a DOI must be divided across lines, break it before a period or a hyphen or before or after any other mark of punctuation. Do not add a hyphen.

Answer the basic question "Who is the author?"

Problem: Sometimes when you need to cite a source, it's not clear who the author is. This is especially true for sources on the web or other nonprint sources, which may have been created by one person and uploaded by a different person or an organization. Whom do you cite as the author in such a case? How do you determine who *is* the author?

Example: The video "Surfing the Web on the Job" (see below) was uploaded to YouTube by CBSNewsOnline. Is the person or organization who uploads the video the author of the video? Not necessarily.

Surfing the Web on The Job

CBSNewsOnline · 42,491 videos

▶ Subscribe | 85,736

Uploaded on Nov 12, 2009
As the Internet continues to emerge as a critical facet of everyday life, CBS News' Daniel Sieberg reports that companies are cracking down on employees' personal Web use.

Strategy: After you view or listen to the source a few times, ask yourself whether you can tell who is chiefly responsible for creating the content in the source. It could be an organization. It could be an identifiable individual. This video consists entirely of reporting by Daniel Sieberg, so in this case the author is Sieberg.

Citation: To cite the source, you would use the basic MLA guidelines for a video found on the web (item 47).

author:
last name first   title of video   website title   upload information

Harris, Jonny. "Crickets Are the Food of the Future." *YouTube*, uploaded by CBC,

update date   URL

21 Aug. 2017, www.youtube.com/watch?v=jPx7TTPDaNU.

6. Two or more works by the same author First alphabetize the works by title (ignoring the article *A*, *An*, or *The* at the beginning of a title). Use the author's name for the first entry; for subsequent entries, use three hyphens and a period. The three hyphens must stand for exactly the same name as in the first entry.

Shields, Carol. *Jane Austen: A Life*. Penguin, 2005.

---. *The Stone Diaries*. Vintage, 1993.

7. Two or more works by the same group of authors Alphabetize the works by title. Use the authors' names in the proper form for the first entry (see items 2 and 3). Begin subsequent entries with three hyphens and a period. The three hyphens must stand for the same names as in the first entry.

Agha, Hussein, and Robert Malley. "The Arab Counterrevolution." *The New York Review of Books*, 29 Sept. 2011, www.nybooks.com/articles/2011/09/29/arab
-counterrevolution.

---. "This Is Not a Revolution." *The New York Review of Books*, 8 Nov. 2012, www.nybooks
.com/articles/2012/11/08/not-revolution.

8. Editor or translator Begin with the editor's or translator's name. After the name, add "editor" or "translator." Use "editors" or "translators" for more than two (see also items 2 and 3 for how to handle multiple contributors).

first editor:
last name first   second editor:
in normal order   title (book)

Scott, John C., and Raymond E. Jones, editors. *The Harbrace Anthology of Short Fiction*.

publisher year

Nelson, 2010.

9. Author with editor or translator Begin with the name of the author. Place the editor's or translator's name after the title.

author:
last name first   title (book)

Leroux, Georges. *Partita for Glenn Gould: An Inquiry into the Nature of Genius*. Translated

translator:
in normal order   publisher   year

by Donald Winkler, McGill-Queen's UP, 2010.

10. Graphic narrative or other illustrated work If a work has both an author and an illustrator, the order in your citation will depend on which of those persons you emphasize in your paper.

Gaiman, Neil. *The Sandman: Overture*. Illustrated by J. H. William III, DC Comics, 2015.

Wenzel, David, illustrator. *The Hobbit*. By J. R. R. Tolkien, Ballantine Books, 2012.

11. Author using a pseudonym (pen name) or screen name   Give the author's name as it appears in the source (the pseudonym), followed by the author's real name, if available, in parentheses.

Grammar Girl (Mignon Fogarty). "Lewis Carroll: He Loved to Play with Language."

QuickandDirtyTips.com, 21 May 2015, www.quickanddirtytips.com/education/

grammar/lewis-carroll-he-loved-to-play-with-language.

Pauline. Comment on "Is This the End?" *The New York Times*, 25 Nov. 2012,

nyti.ms/1BRUvqQ.

12. Author quoted by another author (indirect source)   If one of your sources uses a quotation from another source and you'd like to use the quotation, provide a works cited entry for the source in which you found the quotation. In your in-text citation, indicate that the quoted words appear in the source (see item 23 on p. 390).

Articles and other short works

- Citation at a glance: Article in an online journal, page 401
- Citation at a glance: Article from a database, page 402

13. Basic format for an article or other short work

a. Print

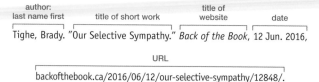

author:
last name first   article title   journal title   volume, issue

Tilman, David. "Food and Health of a Full Earth." *Daedalus*, vol. 144, no. 4,

date   page(s)

Fall 2015, pp. 5-7.

b. Web

author:
last name first   title of short work   title of website   date

Tighe, Brady. "Our Selective Sympathy." *Back of the Book*, 12 Jun. 2016,

URL

backofthebook.ca/2016/06/12/our-selective-sympathy/12848/.

Citation at a glance: Article in an online journal

To cite an article in an online journal in MLA style, include the following elements:

1 Author(s) of article
2 Title and subtitle of article
3 Title of journal
4 Volume and issue numbers

5 Date of publication (including month or season, if any)
6 Page number(s) of article, if given
7 Location of source (DOI, permalink, or URL)

ONLINE JOURNAL ARTICLE

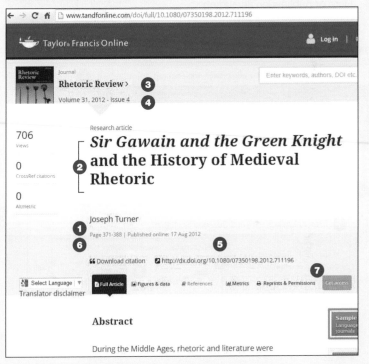

WORKS CITED ENTRY FOR AN ARTICLE IN AN ONLINE JOURNAL

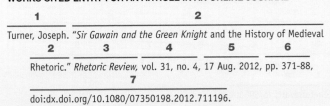

Turner, Joseph. "*Sir Gawain and the Green Knight* and the History of Medieval Rhetoric." *Rhetoric Review,* vol. 31, no. 4, 17 Aug. 2012, pp. 371-88, doi:dx.doi.org/10.1080/07350198.2012.711196.

For more on citing online articles in MLA style, see item 14.

Citation at a glance: Article from a database

To cite an article in a database in MLA style, include the following elements:

1 Author(s) of article
2 Title and subtitle of article
3 Title of journal, magazine, or newspaper
4 Volume and issue numbers (for journal)
5 Date of publication (including month or season, if any)
6 Page number(s) of article, if any
7 Name of database
8 DOI or permalink, if available; otherwise, complete URL or shortened URL of database (see item 13c)

DATABASE RECORD

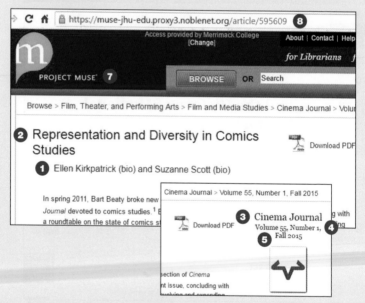

WORKS CITED ENTRY FOR AN ARTICLE FROM A DATABASE

Kirkpatrick, Ellen, and Suzanne Scott. "Representation and Diversity in Comics Studies."

Cinema Journal, vol. 55, no. 1, Fall 2015. *Project Muse*, muse-jhu-edu.proxy3

.noblenet.org/article/595609.

For more on citing articles from a database in MLA style, see items 13 and 14.

13. Basic format for an article or other short work (*cont.*)

c. Database   If a database provides a DOI or a permalink, use that at the end of your citation. If it provides only a URL that is long and complicated and if your readers may not be able to access it, your instructor may allow you to use the URL for the database home page (such as go.galegroup.com). Check with your instructor.

first author:
last name first

second author:
in normal order

article title

Meyer, Michaela D. E., and Megan M. Wood. "Sexuality and Teen Television: Emerging

Adults Respond to Representations of Queer Identity on *Glee.*"

journal title

volume,
issue

date

page(s)

database title

Sexuality and Culture, vol. 17, no. 3, Sept. 2013, pp. 434-48. *Academic OneFile*,

URL

go.galegroup.com/ps/i.do?p=PPGB&sw=w&u=mlin_n_merrcol&v=2.1&id=

GALE%7CA343054749&it=r&asid=c78658b5b509de7c41177489da8e89ce.

14. Article in a journal

a. Print

author: last
name first

article title

McPherson, Kathryn. "Imagining Gerontological Nursing: Canadian Nurses and Eldercare,

journal title

volume,
issue

date

page(s)

1905-70." *Journal of Canadian Studies*, vol. 50, no. 2, Spring 2016, pp. 422-45.

b. Online journal

author:
last name first

article title

journal
title

Butler, Janine. "Where Access Meets Multimodality: The Case of ASL Music Videos." *Kairos*,

volume,
issue

date

URL

vol. 21, no. 1, Fall 2016, kairos.technorhetoric.net/21.1/topoi/butler/index.html.

c. Database

author:
last name first

article title

journal title

Maier, Jessica. "A 'True Likeness': The Renaissance City Portrait." *Renaissance Quarterly*,

volume,
issue

date

page(s)

database
title

DOI

vol. 65, no. 3, Fall 2012, pp. 711-52. *JSTOR*, doi:10.1086/668300.

15. Article in a magazine

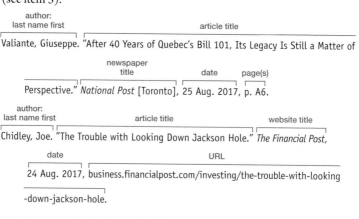

author:
last name first   article title   magazine title   date   page(s)

Bryan, Christy. "Ivory Worship." *National Geographic,* Oct. 2012, pp. 28-61.

author:
last name first   article title   magazine title   date   page(s)

Vick, Karl. "The Stateless Statesman." *Time,* 15 Oct. 2012, pp. 32-37.

author:
last name first   article title   website title   date

Leonard, Andrew. "The Surveillance State High School." *Salon,* 27 Nov. 2012,

URL

www.salon.com/2012/11/27/the_surveillance_state_high_school.

16. Article in a newspaper
If the city of publication is not obvious from the title of the newspaper, include the city in brackets after the newspaper title (see item 5).

author:
last name first   article title

Valiante, Giuseppe. "After 40 Years of Quebec's Bill 101, Its Legacy Is Still a Matter of

newspaper title   date   page(s)

Perspective." *National Post* [Toronto], 25 Aug. 2017, p. A6.

author:
last name first   article title   website title

Chidley, Joe. "The Trouble with Looking Down Jackson Hole." *The Financial Post,*

date   URL

24 Aug. 2017, business.financialpost.com/investing/the-trouble-with-looking

-down-jackson-hole.

17. Abstract
Include the label "Abstract" at the end of the entry (and before any database information).

a. Abstract of an article

Bottomore, Stephen. "The Romance of the Cinematograph." *Film History,* vol. 24, no. 3, July 2012, pp. 341-44. Abstract. *JSTOR,* doi:10.2979/filmhistory.24.3.341.

b. Abstract of a dissertation

Memon, Nadeem Ahmed. *From Protest to Praxis: A History of Islamic Schools in North America.* 2010. University of Toronto, PhD dissertation. Abstract. TSpace Repository, hdl.handle.net/1807/19154.

18. Editorial Cite as a source with no author (see item 5) and use the label "Editorial" at the end (and before any database information).

"Oppose Hate, Don't Amplify It." *Toronto Star*, 21 Aug. 2017, www.thestar.com/opinion/
editorials/2017/08/21/oppose-hate-dont-amplify-it-editorial.html. Editorial.

19. Letter to the editor Use the label "Letter" at the end of the entry (and before any database information). If the letter has no title, place the label directly after the author's name.

Fahey, John A. "Recalling the Cuban Missile Crisis." *The Washington Post*, 28 Oct.
2012, p. A16. Letter. *LexisNexis Library Express*, www.lexisnexis.com/hottopics/
Inpubliclibraryexpress.

20. Comment on an online article For the use of a screen name and a real name (if known), see item 11. After the name, include "Comment on" followed by the title of the article and publication information for the article.

author:
screen name   article title

pablosharkman. Comment on " 'We All Are Implicated': Wendell Berry Laments

website title

a Disconnection from Community and the Land." *The Chronicle of Higher Education,*

date   URL

23 Apr. 2012, chronicle.com/article/In-Jefferson-Lecture-Wendell/131648.

21. Paper or presentation at a conference If the paper or presentation is included in the proceedings of a conference, cite it as a selection in an anthology (see item 32; see also item 38 for proceedings of a conference). If you viewed the presentation live, cite it as a lecture or public address (see item 53).

first author: "et al."
last name first for others   presentation title

Irvine, Yene, et al. "An Analysis of CSB Investigation Reports." Presentation

conference
conference title   information

at 66th Canadian Chemical Engineering Conference, Canadian Society for Chemical

date   URL

Engineers, Quebec City, 16 Oct. 2016, www.cheminst.ca/sites/default/files/pdfs/

Connect/PMS/An%20Analysis%20of%20CSB%20Reports.pdf.

22. Book review Name the reviewer and the title of the review, if any, followed by "Review of" and the title and author of the work reviewed. Add publication information for the publication in which the review appears. If the review has no author and no title, begin with "Review of" and alphabetize the entry by the first principal word in the title of the work reviewed.

Della Subin, Anna. "It Has Burned My Heart." Review of *The Lives of Muhammad*, by
Kecia Ali. *London Review of Books*, 22 Oct. 2015, www.lrb.co.uk/v37/n20/anna
-della-subin/it-has-burned-my-heart.

Spychalski, John C. Review of *American Railroads—Decline and Renaissance in the
Twentieth Century*, by Robert E. Gallamore and John R. Meyer. *Transportation
Journal*, vol. 54, no. 4, Fall 2015, pp. 535-38. *JSTOR*, doi:10.5325/
transportationj.54.4.0535.

23. Film review or other review   Name the reviewer and the title of the review, if any, followed by "Review of" and the title and the writer or director of the work reviewed. Add publication information for the publication in which the review appears. If the review has no author and no title, begin with "Review of" and alphabetize the entry by the first principal word in the title of the work reviewed.

Farquharson, Vanessa. "In Praise of Scrunchy-Faced Women." Review of *Miss Potter*,
directed by Chris Noonan. *National Post*, 12 Jan. 2007, p. E4.

Savage, Phil. "*Fallout 4* Review." Review of *Fallout 4*, by Bethesda Game Studios. *PC
Gamer*, Future Publishing, 8 Nov. 2015, www.pcgamer.com/fallout-4-review.

24. Performance review   Name the reviewer and the title of the review, if any, followed by "Review of" and the title of the work reviewed. After the title, add the author or director of the work, if relevant. Add publication information for the publication in which the review appears. If the review has no author and no title, begin with "Review of" and alphabetize the entry by the first principal word in the title of the work reviewed.

Sulemaan, Ahmed. "Why You Shouldn't Read Adam Grant's *Originals*." Review of *Originals*.
HuffPostCanada, 2 Mar. 2017, www.huffingtonpost.ca/sulemaan-ahmed/adam
-grant-originals_b_9136656.html.

25. Interview   Begin with the person interviewed, followed by the title of the interview (if there is one). If the interview does not have a title, include the word "Interview" after the interviewee's name. If you wish to include the name of the interviewer, put it after the title of the interview.

Weddington, Sarah. "Sarah Weddington: Still Arguing for *Roe*." Interview by Michele
Kort. *Ms.*, Winter 2013, pp. 32-35.

Putin, Vladimir. Interview. By Charlie Rose. *Charlie Rose: The Week*, PBS, 19 June 2015.

Akufo, Rosa. Personal interview. 11 Apr. 2016.

26. Article in a dictionary or an encyclopedia (including a wiki)   List the author of the entry (if there is one), the title of the entry, and publication information for the reference work. Include page numbers for a print source as you would for a selection in a collection (see item 32).

Elliott, Ward E. Y. "Gerrymandering." *The Oxford Companion to the Supreme Court of the United States*, edited by Kermit L. Hall, Oxford UP, 1992, pp. 336-37.

Foot, Richard and Daniel Latouche. "Lévesque, René." *The Canadian Encyclopedia*, 3 Apr. 2015, www.thecanadianencyclopedia.ca/en/article/rene-levesque/.

"House Music." *Wikipedia*, 16 Nov. 2015, en.wikipedia.org/wiki/House_music.

27. Letter in a collection

a. Print   Begin with the writer of the letter, the words "Letter to" and the recipient, and the date of the letter. Add the title of the collection and other publication information. Add the page range at the end.

Grey Owl. Letter to William Deacon. 10 May 1935. *Canada: A Portrait in Letters, 1800-2000*, edited by Charlotte Gray, Anchor-Random, 2004, pp. 362-66.

b. Web   After information about the letter writer, recipient, and date (if known), give the name of the website or archive, italicized; the publisher of the site; and the URL.

Oblinger, Maggie. Letter to Charlie Thomas. 31 Mar. 1895. *Prairie Settlement: Nebraska Photographs and Family Letters, 1862-1912*, Library of Congress / American Memory, memory.loc.gov/cgi-bin/query/r?ammem/ps:@field(DOCID+l306) #l3060001.

Books and other long works

* Citation at a glance: Book, page 408

28. Basic format for a book

a. Print book or e-book   If you have used an e-book, indicate "e-book" or the specific reader (using the abbreviation "ed." for "edition") before the publisher's name.

author: last
name first   book title   publisher   year

Short, Donn. *Am I Safe Here? LGBTQ Teens and Bullying in Schools*. UBC Press, 2017.

Beard, Mary. *SPQR: A History of Ancient Rome*. Nook ed., Liveright Publishing, 2015.

Citation at a glance: Book

To cite an article in an online journal in MLA style, include the following elements:

1. Author(s)
2. Title and subtitle
3. Publisher
4. Year of publication (latest year)

TITLE PAGE

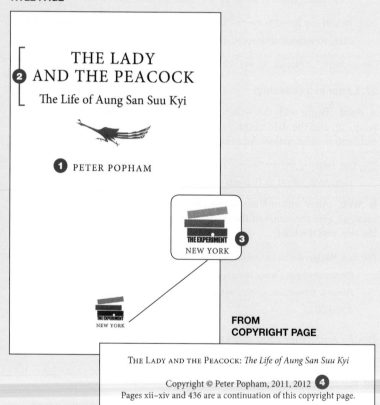

THE LADY
2 AND THE PEACOCK
The Life of Aung San Suu Kyi

1 PETER POPHAM

THE EXPERIMENT **3**
NEW YORK

THE EXPERIMENT
NEW YORK

**FROM
COPYRIGHT PAGE**

THE LADY AND THE PEACOCK: *The Life of Aung San Suu Kyi*

Copyright © Peter Popham, 2011, 2012 **4**
Pages xii–xiv and 436 are a continuation of this copyright page.

WORKS CITED ENTRY FOR A PRINT BOOK

<u>   1   </u>   <u>   2   </u>

Popham, Peter. *The Lady and the Peacock: The Life of Aung San Suu Kyi*.
<u>   3   </u> <u> 4 </u>
The Experiment, 2012.

For more on citing books in MLA style, see items 28–36.

28. Basic format for a book (*cont.*)

b. **Web** Give whatever print publication information is available for the work, followed by the title of the website and the URL.

author: last
name first — book title — translator: in normal order

Piketty, Thomas. *Capital in the Twenty-First Century*. Translated by Arthur Goldhammer,

publisher — year — website title — URL

Harvard UP, 2014. *Google Books*, books.google.com/books?isbn=0674369556.

29. Parts of a book

a. Foreword, introduction, preface, or afterword

author of foreword:
last name first — book part — book title

Bennett, Hal Zina. Foreword. *Shimmering Images: A Handy Little Guide to Writing Memoir*,

author of book:
in normal order — publisher — year — page(s)

by Lisa Dale Norton, St. Martin's Griffin, 2008, pp. xiii-xvi.

Sullivan, John Jeremiah. "The Ill-Defined Plot." Introduction. *The Best American Essays 2014*, edited by Sullivan, Houghton Mifflin Harcourt, 2014, pp. xvii-xxvi.

b. Chapter in a book

Rizga, Kristina. "Mr. Hsu." *Mission High: One School, How Experts Tried to Fail It, and the Students and Teachers Who Made It Triumph*, Nation Books, 2015, pp. 89-114.

30. Book in a language other than English Capitalize the title according to the conventions of the book's language. If your readers are not familiar with the language of the book, include a translation of the title in brackets.

Vargas Llosa, Mario. *El sueño del celta* [*The Dream of the Celt*]. Alfaguara Ediciones, 2010.

31. Entire anthology or collection An anthology is a collection of works on a common theme, often with different authors for the selections and usually with an editor for the entire volume.

editor:
last name first — title of anthology — publisher — year

Marcus, Ben, editor. *New American Stories*. Vintage Books, 2015.

32. One selection from an anthology or a collection

- Citation at a glance: Selection from an anthology or a collection, page 410

author of selection — title of selection — title of anthology — editor(s) of anthology

Rosenblum, Rebecca. "Marriage." *15: Best Canadian Stories*, edited by John Metcalf,

publisher — year — page(s)

Oberon Press, 2015, pp. 59-68.

Citation at a glance: Selection from an anthology or a collection

To cite a selection from an anthology in MLA style, include the following elements:

1. Author(s) of selection
2. Title and subtitle of selection
3. Title and subtitle of anthology
4. Editor(s) of anthology
5. Publisher
6. Year of publication
7. Page number(s) of selection

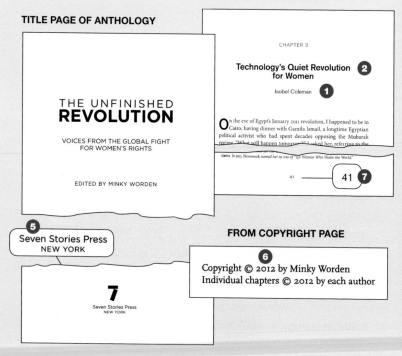

TITLE PAGE OF ANTHOLOGY

FIRST PAGE OF SELECTION

THE UNFINISHED
REVOLUTION

VOICES FROM THE GLOBAL FIGHT
FOR WOMEN'S RIGHTS

EDITED BY MINKY WORDEN

CHAPTER 3

Technology's Quiet Revolution 2
for Women

Isobel Coleman 1

On the eve of Egypt's January 2011 revolution, I happened to be in Cairo, having dinner with Gamila Ismail, a longtime Egyptian political activist who had spent decades opposing the Mubarak regime. "What will happen tomorrow?" I asked her, referring to the

tiative. In 2011, Newsweek named her as one of "150 Women Who Shake the World."

41 ———— 41 7

5
Seven Stories Press
NEW YORK

FROM COPYRIGHT PAGE

6
Copyright © 2012 by Minky Worden
Individual chapters © 2012 by each author

7
Seven Stories Press
NEW YORK

WORKS CITED ENTRY FOR A SELECTION FROM AN ANTHOLOGY

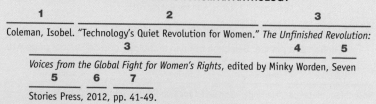

        1   2   3
Coleman, Isobel. "Technology's Quiet Revolution for Women." *The Unfinished Revolution:*
                        3   4   5
    Voices from the Global Fight for Women's Rights, edited by Minky Worden, Seven
        5   6   7
    Stories Press, 2012, pp. 41-49.

For more on citing selections from anthologies in MLA style, see items 31–33.

33. Two or more selections from an anthology or a collection   Provide an entry for the entire anthology (see item 31) and a shortened entry for each selection. Alphabetize the entries by authors' or editors' last names.

author of selection · title of selection · editor(s) of anthology · page(s)

Eisenberg, Deborah. "Some Other, Better Otto." Marcus, pp. 94-136.

editor of anthology · title of anthology · publisher · year

Marcus, Ben, editor. *New American Stories*. Vintage Books, 2015.

author of selection · title of selection · editor(s) of anthology · page(s)

Sayrafiezadeh, Saïd. "Paranoia." Marcus, pp. 3-29.

34. Edition other than the first   If the book has a translator or an editor in addition to the author, give the name of the translator or editor before the edition number (see item 9 for a book with an editor or a translator).

Draper, Dianne and Ann Zimmerman. *Our Environment: A Canadian Perspective*. 5th ed., Nelson Education, 2017.

35. Multivolume work   Include the total number of volumes at the end of the entry, using the abbreviation "vols." If the volumes were published over several years, give the inclusive dates of publication.

author: last name first · book title · editor(s): in normal order · publisher · inclusive dates · total volumes

Stark, Freya. *Letters*. Edited by Lucy Moorehead, Compton Press, 1974-82. 8 vols.

If you cite only one volume in your paper, include the volume number before the publisher and give the date of publication for that volume. After the date, give the total number of volumes.

author: last name first · book title · editor(s): in normal order · volume cited · publisher · date of volume · total volumes

Stark, Freya. *Letters*. Edited by Lucy Moorehead, vol. 5, Compton Press, 1978. 8 vols.

36. Sacred text   Give the title of the edition (taken from the title page), italicized; the editor's or translator's name (if any); and publication information. Add the name of the version, if there is one, before the publisher.

The Oxford Annotated Bible with the Apocrypha. Edited by Herbert G. May and Bruce M. Metzger, Revised Standard Version, Oxford UP, 1965.

The Qur'an: Translation. Translated by Abdullah Yusuf Ali, Tahrike Tarsile Qur'an, 2001.

37. Dissertation

Kidd, Celeste. *Rational Approaches to Learning and Development.* 2013. U of Rochester,
PhD dissertation.

West, Michael. *Enhanced Vascularization of Modular Engineered Tissues Using
Activated Macrophages.* 2016. U of Toronto, Master's thesis. *Theses Canada,*
www.collectionscanada.gc.ca/obj/thesescanada/vol2/OTU/TC-OTU-71707.pdf.

38. Proceedings of a conference   Cite as you would a book, adding the
name, date, and location of the conference after the title.

Sowards, Stacey K., et al., editors. *Across Borders and Environments: Communication
and Environmental Justice in International Contexts.* Proceedings of Eleventh
Biennial Conference on Communication and the Environment, 25-28 June
2011, U of Texas at El Paso, International Environmental Communication
Association, 2012.

Websites and parts of websites

39. An entire website

a. Website with author or editor

author or editor: last name first	title of website	publisher	update date

Railton, Stephen. *Mark Twain in His Times.* Stephen Railton / U of Virginia Library, 2012,

URL

twain.lib.virginia.edu/.

Halsall, Paul, editor. *Internet Modern History Sourcebook.* Fordham U, 4 Nov. 2011,
legacy.fordham.edu/halsall/index.asp.

b. Website with organization as author

organization	title of website

Transparency International. *Transparency International: The Global Coalition against Corruption,*

date   URL

2015, www.transparency.org.

c. Website with no author   Begin with the title of the site. If the site has no
title, begin with a label such as "Home page."

The Newton Project. U of Sussex, 2016, www.newtonproject.sussex.ac.uk/prism
.php?id=1.

___

d. Website with no title Use the label "Home page" or another appropriate description in place of a title.

Bae, Rebecca. Home page. Iowa State U, 2015, www.engl.iastate.edu/rebecca-bae
-directory-page.

40. Work from a website The titles of short works, such as articles or individual web pages, are placed in quotation marks. Titles of long works, such as books and reports, are italicized.

- Citation at a glance: Work from a website, page 414

author: last
name first   title of short work   title of
website

Gallagher, Sean. "The Last Nomads of the Tibetan Plateau." *Pulitzer Center on Crisis*

date   URL

Reporting, 25 Oct. 2012, pulitzercenter.org/reporting/china-glaciers-global

-warming-climate-change-ecosystem-tibetan-plateau-grasslands-nomads.

title of article   title of website

"Social and Historical Context: Vitality." *Arapesh Grammar and Digital Language*

publisher

Archive Project, Institute for Advanced Technology in the Humanities,

URL   access date
for undated site

www.arapesh.org/socio_historical_context_vitality.php. Accessed 22 Mar. 2016.

first author: last   "et al." for
name first   other authors   title of long work

Byndloss, D. Crystal, et al. *In Search of a Match: A Guide for Helping Students Make Informed*

title of   update
website   date   URL

College Choices. Ford Foundation, Apr. 2015, fordfoundcontentthemes.blob.core

.windows.net/media/2607/in_search_of_a_match.pdf.

41. Entire blog Cite a blog as you would an entire website (see item 39).

Akin, David. *David Akin's On the Hill*, 2017, blogs.canoe.com/davidakin/about/.

Citation at a glance: Work from a website

To cite a work from a website in MLA style, include the following elements:

1 Author(s) of work, if any
2 Title and subtitle
3 Title of website
4 Publisher of website (unless it is the same as the title of site)
5 Update date
6 URL of page (or of home page of site)
7 Date of access (if no update date on site)

INTERNAL PAGE FROM A WEBSITE

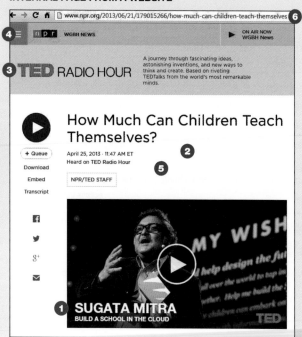

WORKS CITED ENTRY FOR A WORK FROM A WEBSITE

Mitra, Sugata. "How Much Can Children Teach Themselves?" *TED Radio Hour*, NPR,

25 Apr. 2013, www.npr.org/2013/06/21/179015266/how-much-can-children

-teach-themselves.

For more on citing sources from websites in MLA style, see item 40.

414

42. Blog post or comment Cite a blog post or comment as you would a work from a website (see item 40), with the title of the post or comment in quotation marks. If the post or comment has no title, use the label "Blog post" or "Blog comment" (with no quotation marks). Follow with the remaining information as for an entire blog (see item 41). (See item 11 for the use of screen names.)

```
author: last                                              title of
name first              title of blog post                  blog
┌────────┐ ┌──────────────────────────────────────┐  ┌─────────┐
```
Paikin, Steve. "A Simple Request for More Truth in Political Advertising." *The Agenda,*

```
   publisher  update date                    URL
   ┌────────┐ ┌─────────┐ ┌──────────────────────────────────────────┐
```
   TVOntario, 26 Jul. 2017, tvo.org/blog/current-affairs/a-simple-request-for-more-truth

   -in-political-advertising.

```
   author:
screen name      label                 title of blog post
┌──────────┐ ┌──────┐ ┌────────────────────────────────────────────────┐
```
robert_viera. Comment on "A Simple Request for More Truth in Political Advertising."

```
   title of
     blog     publisher       date                    URL
   ┌──────┐ ┌─────────┐ ┌─────────┐ ┌──────────────────────────────────────┐
```
   The Agenda, TVOntario, 26 Jul. 2017, tvo.org/blog/current-affairs/a-simple-request

   -for-more-truth-in-political-advertising.

43. Academic course or department home page Cite as a work from a website (see item 40). For a course home page, begin with the name of the instructor and the title of the course or title of the page, without quotation marks or italics. (Use "Course home page" if there is no other title.) For a department home page, begin with the name of the department and the label "Department home page."

Masiello, Regina. 355:101: Expository Writing. *Rutgers School of Arts and Sciences,* 2016,

   wp.rutgers.edu/courses/55-355101.

Physical Chemistry. Department home page. *University of Toronto,* 2017,

   www.chem.utoronto.ca/research/physical.php.

Audio, visual, and multimedia sources

44. Podcast

```
   author:
last name first           podcast title          website title        publisher
┌────────────┐ ┌──────────────────────────┐ ┌───────────────┐ ┌─────────────────┐
```
Tanner, Laura. "Virtual Reality in 9/11 Fiction." *Literature Lab,* Department of English,

```
                                       URL
   ┌────────┐ ┌──────────────────────────────────────────────────────┐
```
   Brandeis U, www.brandeis.edu/departments/english/literaturelab/tanner.html.

```
        date of access
        for undated site
        ┌──────────────┐
```
   Accessed 14 Feb. 2016.

45. Film Generally, begin the entry with the title, followed by the director and lead performers, as in the first example. If your paper emphasizes one or more people involved with the film, you may begin with those names, as in the second example.

film title   director

Birdman or (The Unexpected Virtue of Ignorance). Directed by Alejandro González Iñárritu,

major performers

performances by Michael Keaton, Emma Stone, Zach Galifianakis, Edward Norton,

             distributor   release date

and Naomi Watts, Fox Searchlight, 2014.

director: last name first   film title   major performers

Scott, Ridley, director. *The Martian.* Performances by Matt Damon, Jessica Chastain,

           distributor   release date

Kristen Wiig, and Kate Mara, Twentieth Century Fox, 2015.

46. Supplementary material accompanying a film   Begin with the title of the supplementary material, in quotation marks, and the names of any important contributors, as for a film. End with information about the film, as in item 45, and about the location of the supplementary material.

"Sweeney's London." Produced by Eric Young. *Sweeney Todd: The Demon Barber of Fleet*

    Street, directed by Tim Burton, DreamWorks, 2007, disc 2.

47. Video or audio from the web   Cite video or audio that you accessed on the web as you would a work from a website (see item 40), with the title of the video or audio in quotation marks.

author: last name first   title of video   website title   upload information   date

Lewis, Paul. "Citizen Journalism." *YouTube,* uploaded by TEDx Talks, 14 May 2011,

URL

    www.youtube.com/watch?v=9AP09_yNbcg.

author: last name first   title of video   website title

Fletcher, Antoine. "The Ancient Art of the Atlatl." *Russell Cave National Monument,*

      narrator   publisher   date

narrated by Brenton Bellomy, National Park Service, 12 Feb. 2014,

URL

    www.nps.gov/media/video/view.htm?id=C92C0D0A-1DD8-B71C-07CBC6E8970CD73F.

author: last name first   title of video   website title   date   URL

Burstein, Julie. "Four Lessons in Creativity." *TED,* Feb. 2012, www.ted.com/talks/julie

    _burstein_4_lessons_in_creativity.

48. Video game   List the developer or author of the game (if any); the title, italicized; the version, if there is one; and the distributor and date of publication. If the game can be played on the web, add information as for a work from a website (see item 40).

Firaxis Games. *Sid Meier's Civilization Revolution*. Take-Two Interactive, 2008.

Edgeworld. Atom Entertainment, 1 May 2012, www.kabam.com/games/edgeworld.

49. Computer software or app   Cite as a video game (see item 48), giving whatever information is available about the version, distributor, and date.

Words with Friends. Version 5.84, Zynga, 2013.

50. Television or radio episode or program   If you are citing an episode of a program, begin with the title of the episode, in quotation marks. Then give the title of the program, italicized; relevant information about the program, such as the writer, director, performers, or narrator; the episode number (if any); the network; and the date of broadcast.

   For a program you accessed on the web, after the information about the program give the network, the original broadcast date, and the URL. If you are citing an entire program (not an episode or a segment) or an episode that has no title, begin your entry with the title of the program, italicized.

title of episode · program title

"Death Inc.: Hidden Camera Investigation of Funeral Homes." *Marketplace*, narrated by

narrator · publisher · date of posting · URL

David Common, CBC, 10 Mar. 2017, www.cbc.ca/marketplace/episodes/2015-2016/

funeral-homes.

51. Transcript   Cite the source (interview, radio or television program, video, and so on), and add the label "Transcript" at the end of the entry.

"How Long Can Florida's Citrus Industry Survive?" *All Things Considered*, narrated by
   Greg Allen, NPR, 27 Nov. 2015, www.npr.org/templates/transcript/transcript
   .php?storyId=457424528. Transcript.

"The Economics of Sleep, Part 1." *Freakonomics Radio*, narrated by Stephen J. Dubner,
   9 July 2015, freakonomics.com/2015/07/09/the-economics-of-sleep-part-1-full
   -transcript. Transcript.

Cite a source reposted from another source

Problem: Some sources that you find online, particularly on blogs or on video-sharing sites, did not originate with the person who uploaded or published the source online. In such a case, how do you give proper credit for the source?

Example: Say you need to cite President John F. Kennedy's inaugural address. You have found a video on YouTube that provides footage of the address (see image). The video was uploaded by PaddyIrishMan2 on October 29, 2006. But clearly, PaddyIrishMan2 is not the author of the video or of the address.

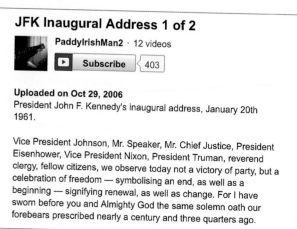

JFK Inaugural Address 1 of 2

PaddyIrishMan2 · 12 videos

▶ Subscribe ⟨ 403

Uploaded on Oct 29, 2006
President John F. Kennedy's inaugural address, January 20th 1961.

Vice President Johnson, Mr. Speaker, Mr. Chief Justice, President Eisenhower, Vice President Nixon, President Truman, reverend clergy, fellow citizens, we observe today not a victory of party, but a celebration of freedom — symbolising an end, as well as a beginning — signifying renewal, as well as change. For I have sworn before you and Almighty God the same solemn oath our forebears prescribed nearly a century and three quarters ago.

Strategy: Start with what you know. The source is a video that you viewed on the web. For this particular video, John F. Kennedy is the speaker and the author of the inaugural address. PaddyIrishMan2 is identified as the person who uploaded the source to YouTube.

Citation: To cite the source, you can follow the basic MLA guidelines for a video found on the web (see item 47).

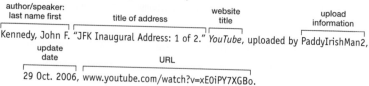

author/speaker: last name first — title of address — website title — upload information

Kennedy, John F. "JFK Inaugural Address: 1 of 2." *YouTube*, uploaded by PaddyIrishMan2,

update date — URL

29 Oct. 2006, www.youtube.com/watch?v=xE0iPY7XGBo.

NOTE: If your work calls for a primary source, you should try to find the original source of the video; a reference librarian can help.

52. Live performance   Begin with the title of the work performed, italicized (unless it is named by form, number, and key). Then give the author or composer of the work; relevant information such as the director, the choreographer, the conductor, or the major performers; the theatre, ballet, or opera company, if any; the theatre and location; and the date of the performance.

The Draft. By Peter Snoad, directed by Diego Arciniegas, Hibernian Hall, Boston,
10 Sept. 2015.

Piano Concerto no. 1. By Frédéric Chopin, conducted by Michael Newnham, performances
by Jan Lisiecki and Symphony New Brunswick, Capitol Theatre, Moncton, 18 Oct.
2010.

53. Lecture or public address   Begin with the speaker's name, the title of the lecture, the sponsoring organization, location, and date. If you viewed the lecture on the web, cite as you would a work from a website (see item 40). Add the label "Address" or "Lecture" at the end if it is not clear from the title.

Tallamy, Douglas. "Bringing Nature Home." Edwards Charitable Foundation, Toronto
Botanical Garden, 27 Oct. 2010. Lecture.

Khosla, Raj. "Precision Agriculture and Global Food Security." *US Department of State:*
Diplomacy in Action, 26 Mar. 2013, www.state.gov/e/stas/series/212172.htm.
Address.

54. Musical score   Begin with the composer's name; the title of the work, italicized (unless it is named by form, number, and key); and the date of composition. For a print source, give the publisher and date. For an online source, give the title of the website; the publisher; the date; and the URL.

Beethoven, Ludwig van. Symphony no. 5 in C Minor, op. 67. 1807. *Center for Computer*
Assisted Research in the Humanities, Stanford U, 2000, scores.ccarh.org/beethoven/
sym/beethoven-sym5-1.pdf.

55. Sound recording   Begin with the name of the person you want to emphasize: the composer, conductor, or performer. For a long work, give the title, italicized (unless it is named by form, number, and key); the names of pertinent artists; and the orchestra and conductor. End with the manufacturer and the date.

Bizet, Georges. *Carmen*. Performances by Jennifer Larmore, Thomas Moser, Angela
Gheorghiu, Samuel Ramey, and Bavarian State Orchestra and Chorus, conducted by
Giuseppe Sinopoli, Warner, 1996.

Voisine, Roch. "Avant de partir." *Best of Roch*, RCA, 2007.

56. Artwork, photograph, or other visual art   Begin with the artist and the title of the work, italicized. If you viewed the original work, give the date of composition followed by a comma and the location. If you viewed the work online, give the date of composition followed by a period and the website title, publisher (if any), and URL. If you viewed the work reproduced in a book, cite as a work in an anthology or a collection (item 32), giving the date of composition after the title. If the medium of composition is not apparent or is important for your work, you may include it at the end (as in the second example).

Bool, Shannon. *The Spinner*. 2015, National Gallery of Canada, Ottawa.

Lindsey, Lindsay Jones. *Fibonacci Spiral*. 2012, University of Alabama, Tuscaloosa. Public
  sculpture.

Clough, Charles. *January Twenty-First*. 1988-89. Joslyn Art Museum, Omaha, www.joslyn
  .org/collections-and-exhibitions/permanent-collections/modern-and-contemporary/
  charles-clough-january-twenty-first.

Hura, Sohrab. *Old Man Lighting a Fire*. 2015. *Magnum Photos*, www.magnumphotos.com/
  C.aspx?VP3=SearchResult&ALID=2K1HRG681B_Q.

Kertész, André. *Meudon*. 1928. *Street Photography: From Atget to Cartier-Bresson*, by
  Clive Scott, Tauris, 2011, p. 61.

57. Visual such as a table, a chart, or another graphic   Cite a visual as you would a short work within a longer work. Add a descriptive label at the end if the type of visual is not clear from the title.

"Brazilian Waxing and Waning: The Economy." *The Economist*, 1 Dec. 2015, www
  .economist.com/blogs/graphicdetail/2015/12/economic-backgrounder. Graph.

"Distribution of Active, Confirmed Measles Cases by Health Region." *Public Health
  Agency of Canada*, 29 Aug. 2016, www.canada.ca/en/public-health/services/
  publications/diseases-conditions/measles-rubella-weekly-monitoring-report-june-
  19-25-2016-week-25.html#f2. Figure.

58. Cartoon   Give the cartoonist's name; the title of the cartoon, if it has one, in quotation marks, or the label "Cartoon" without quotation marks in place of a title; and publication information. Add the label "Cartoon" at the end. Cite an online cartoon as a work from a website (item 40).

MacKay, Graeme. "Inclusive Pier 8 Promenade Concept Design #168." *Hamilton Spectator*,
  25 Aug. 2017, mackaycartoons.net/2017/08/24/friday-august-25-2017/. Cartoon.

59. Advertisement   Name the product or company being advertised and publication information for the source in which the advertisement appears. Add the label "Advertisement" at the end if it is not clear from the title.

AT&T. *National Geographic*, Dec. 2015, p. 14. Advertisement.

Toyota. *The Root*. Slate Group, 28 Nov. 2015, www.theroot.com. Advertisement.

60. Map   Cite a map as you would a short work within a longer work. If the map is published on its own, cite it as a book or another long work. Use the label "Map" at the end if it is not clear from the title or source information.

"Map of Sudan." *Global Citizen*, Citizens for Global Solutions, 2011, globalsolutions.org/ blog/bashir#.VthzNMfi_FI.

"Vote on Secession, 1861." *Perry-Castañeda Library Map Collection*, U of Texas at Austin, 1976, www.lib.utexas.edu/maps/atlas_texas/texas_vote_secession _1861.jpg.

Government and legal documents

61. Government document   Treat the government agency as the author, giving the name of the government followed by the name of the department and the agency, if any. For sources found on the web, follow the model for an entire website (item 39) or for a work from a website (item 40).

government   department   agency (or agencies)

United States, Department of Agriculture, Food and Nutrition Service, Child Nutrition

title of work

Programs. *Eligibility Manual for School Meals: Determining and Verifying Eligibility.*

website title   date   URL

National School Lunch Program, July 2015, www.fns.usda.gov/sites/default/files/ cn/SP40_CACFP18_SFSP20-2015a1.pdf.

Canada, Minister of Aboriginal Affairs and Northern Development. *2015-16 Report on Plans and Priorities*. Minister of Public Works and Government Services Canada, 2015.

62. Historical document   The titles of most historical documents, such as the Canadian Charter of Rights and Freedoms and the US Constitution, are neither italicized nor put in quotation marks.

Constitution Act, 1982. Canadian Charter of Rights and Freedoms, Justice Laws Website, laws-lois.justice.gc.ca/eng/Const/page-15.html.

63. Legislative act (law) Begin with the name of the act, neither italicized nor in quotation marks. Then provide the act's Statutes of Canada volume number and chapter number and its date of enactment.

Personal Information Protection and Electronic Documents Act. SC 2000, ch. 5. 13 Apr. 2000.

64. Court case Name the first plaintiff and the first defendant. Then give the volume, name, and page number of the law report; the court name; the year of the decision; and publication information. Do not italicize the name of the case. (In the text of the paper, the name of the case is italicized; see item 19 on p. 390.)

Arsenault-Cameron v. Prince Edward Island. 1 SCR 3, 2000 SCC 1. *Judgments of the Supreme Court of Canada*, Lexum, scc-csc.lexum.com/scc-csc/scc-csc/en/ item/1762/index.do.

Personal communication and social media

65. Personal letter

Primak, Shoshana. Letter to the author. 6 May 2016.

66. Email message Begin with the writer's name and the subject line. Then write "Received by," followed by the name of the recipient and the date of the message.

Thornbrugh, Caitlin. "Coates Lecture." Received by Rita Anderson, 20 Oct. 2015.

67. Text message

Wiley, Joanna. Message to the author. 4 Apr. 2016.

68. Online discussion list post Begin with the author's name, followed by the title or subject line, in quotation marks (use the label "Online posting," with no quotation marks, if the posting has no title). Then proceed as for a work from a website (see item 40).

Robin, Griffith. "Write for the Reading Teacher." *Developing Digital Literacies*, NCTE, 23 Oct. 2015, ncte.connectedcommunity.org/communities/community-home/ digestviewer/viewthread?GroupId=1693&MID=24520&tab=digestviewer &CommunityKey=628d2ad6-8277-4042-a376-2b370ddceabf.

69. Social media post Begin with the writer's screen name, followed by the real name in parentheses, if both are given. For a tweet, use the entire post as a title, in quotation marks. For other media, give a title if the post has one. If it does not, use the label "Post," without quotation marks, in place of a title. Give the date of the post, the time (if the post specifies one), and the URL.

Curiosity Rover. "Can you see me waving? How to spot #Mars in the night sky: https://youtu.be/hv8hVvJlcJQ." *Twitter*, 5 Nov. 2015, 11:00 a.m., twitter.com/ marscuriosity/status/672859022911889408.

natgeo (National Geographic). Post. *Instagram*, 22 July 2016, www.instagram.com/p/ BIKyGHtDD4W.

MLA-4c MLA information notes (optional)

Researchers who use the MLA system of parenthetical documentation may also use information notes for one of two purposes:

1. to provide additional material that is important but might interrupt the flow of the paper
2. to refer to several sources that support a single point or to provide comments on sources

Information notes may be either footnotes or endnotes. Footnotes appear at the foot of the page; endnotes appear on a separate page at the end of the paper, just before the list of works cited. For either style, the notes are numbered consecutively throughout the paper. The text of the paper contains a raised arabic numeral that corresponds to the number of the note.

TEXT

In the past several years, employees have filed a number of lawsuits against employers because of online monitoring practices.[1]

NOTE

1. For a discussion of federal law applicable to electronic surveillance in the workplace, see Kesan 293.

MLA-5 Manuscript format; sample research paper

The following guidelines are consistent with advice given in the *MLA Handbook*, 8th edition (MLA, 2016), and with typical requirements for student papers. For a sample MLA research paper, see pages 427–32.

LaunchPad macmillan learning

MODEL FOR MLA-5

1 Sample student paper

MLA-5a MLA manuscript format

Formatting the paper

Papers written in MLA style should be formatted as follows.

Font If your instructor does not require a specific font, choose one that is standard and easy to read (such as Times New Roman).

Title and identification MLA does not require a title page. On the first page of your paper, place your name, your instructor's name, the course title, and the date on separate lines against the left margin. Then centre your title. (See p. 427 for a sample first page.)

If your instructor requires a title page, ask for formatting guidelines. A format similar to the one on page 529 may be acceptable.

Page numbers (running head) Put the page number preceded by your last name in the upper right corner of each page, one-half inch (1.25 cm) below the top edge. Use arabic numerals (1, 2, 3, and so on).

Margins, line spacing, and paragraph indents Leave margins of one inch (2.5 cm) on all sides of the page. Left-align the text.

Double-space throughout the paper. Do not add extra space above or below the title of the paper or between paragraphs.

Indent the first line of each paragraph one-half inch (1.25 cm) from the left margin.

Capitalization, italics, and quotation marks In titles of works, capitalize all words except articles (*a, an, the*), prepositions (*to, from, between,* and so on), coordinating conjunctions (*and, but, or, nor, for, so, yet*), and the *to* in infinitives — unless the word is first or last in the title or subtitle. Follow these guidelines in your paper even if the title appears in all capital or all lowercase letters in the source.

In the text of an MLA paper, when a complete sentence follows a colon, lowercase the first word following the colon.

Italicize the titles of books, journals, magazines, and other long works, such as websites. Use quotation marks around the titles of articles, short stories, poems, and other short works.

Long quotations When a quotation is longer than four typed lines of prose or three lines of poetry, set it off from the text by indenting the entire quotation one-half inch (1.25 cm) from the left margin. Double-space the indented quotation and do not add extra space above or below it.

Do not use quotation marks when a quotation has been set off from the text by indenting. See page 431 for an example.

URLs If you need to break a URL at the end of a line in the text of a paper, break it before a period or a hyphen or before or after any other mark of punctuation. Do not add a hyphen. If you will post your project online or submit it electronically and you want your readers to click on your URLs, do not insert any line breaks. For MLA guidelines on dividing URLs in your list of works cited, see page 426.

Headings   MLA neither encourages nor discourages the use of headings and provides no guidelines for their use. If you would like to insert headings in a long essay or research paper, check first with your instructor.

Visuals   MLA classifies visuals as tables and figures (figures include graphs, charts, maps, photographs, and drawings). Label each table with an arabic numeral ("Table 1," "Table 2," and so on) and provide a clear title that identifies the subject. Capitalize as you would the title of an article (see P8-c), but do not use italics or quotation marks. Place the table number and title on separate lines above the table, flush with the left margin.

For a table that you have borrowed or adapted, give the source below the table in a note like the following:

Source: Boris Groysberg and Michael Slind, "Leadership Is a Conversation," *Harvard Business Review*, June 2012, p. 83.

For each figure, place the figure number (using the abbreviation "Fig.") and a caption below the figure, flush left. Capitalize the caption as you would a sentence; include source information following the caption. (When referring to the figure in your paper, use the abbreviation "fig." in parenthetical citations; otherwise spell out the word.) See page 428 for an example of a figure in a paper.

Place visuals in the text, as close as possible to the sentences that relate to them, unless your instructor prefers that visuals appear in an appendix.

Preparing the list of works cited

Begin the list of works cited on a new page at the end of the paper. Centre the title "Works Cited" about one inch (2.5 cm) from the top of the page. Double-space throughout. See pages 99 and 432 for sample lists of works cited.

Alphabetizing the list   Alphabetize the list by the last names of the authors (or editors); if a work has no author or editor, alphabetize by the first word of the title other than *A, An,* or *The.*

If your list includes two or more works by the same author, use the author's name for the first entry only. For subsequent entries, use three hyphens followed by a period. List the titles in alphabetical order. (See items 6 and 7 on p. 399.)

Indenting Do not indent the first line of each works cited entry, but indent any additional lines one-half inch (1.25 cm). This technique highlights the names of the authors, making it easy for readers to scan the alphabetized list. See page 432.

URLs and DOIs If a URL or a DOI in a works cited entry must be divided across lines, break it before a period or a hyphen or before or after any other mark of punctuation. Do not add a hyphen. If you will post your project online or submit it electronically and you want your readers to click on your URLs, do not insert any line breaks.

MLA-5b Sample MLA research paper

On the following pages is a research paper on the topic of the role of government in legislating food choices, written by Sophie Harba, a student in a composition class. Harba's paper is documented with in-text citations and a list of works cited in MLA style. Annotations in the margins of the paper draw your attention to Harba's use of MLA style and her effective writing.

Sophie Harba

Professor Baros-Moon

Engl 1101

30 April 2013

What's for Dinner? Personal Choices vs. Public Health

Should the government enact laws to regulate healthy eating choices? Many Americans would answer an emphatic "No," arguing what and how much we eat should be left to individual choice rather than unreasonable laws. Others might argue that it would be unreasonable for the government not to enact legislation, given the rise of chronic diseases that result from harmful diets. In this debate, both the definition of reasonable regulations and the role of government to legislate food choices are at stake. In the name of public health and safety, state governments have the responsibility to shape health policies and to regulate healthy eating choices, especially since doing so offers a potentially large social benefit for a relatively small cost.

Debates surrounding the government's role in regulating food have a long history in the United States. According to Lorine Goodwin, a food historian, nineteenth-century reformers who sought to purify the food supply were called "fanatics" and "radicals" by critics who argued that consumers should be free to buy and eat what they want (77). Thanks to regulations, though, such as the 1906 federal Pure Food and Drug Act, food, beverages, and medicine are largely free from toxins. In addition, to prevent contamination and the spread of disease, meat and dairy products are now inspected by government agents to ensure that they meet health requirements. Such regulations can be considered reasonable because they protect us from harm with little, if any, noticeable consumer cost. It is not considered an unreasonable infringement on personal choice that contaminated meat or arsenic-laced cough drops are *un*available at our local supermarket. Rather, it is an important government function to stop such harmful items from entering the marketplace.

Even though our food meets current safety standards, there is a need for further regulation. Not all food dangers, for example, arise from obvious toxins like arsenic and *E. coli*. A diet that is low in nutritional value and high in sugars, fats, and refined grains—grains that have been processed

Title is centred.

Opening research question engages readers.

Writer highlights the research conversation.

Thesis answers the research question and presents Harba's main point.

Signal phrase names the author. The parenthetical citation includes a page number.

Historical background provides context.

Harba explains her use of a key term, *reasonable*.

Harba establishes common ground with the reader.

Transition helps readers move from one paragraph to the next.

Marginal annotations indicate MLA-style formatting and effective writing.

Harba 2

Harba uses a graph to illustrate Americans' poor nutritional choices.

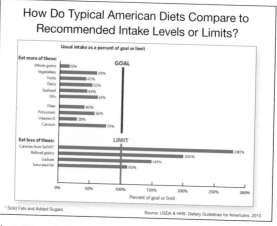

How Do Typical American Diets Compare to Recommended Intake Levels or Limits?

Usual intake as a percent of goal or limit

Eat more of these:
- Whole grains — 15%
- Vegetables — 59%
- Fruits — 42%
- Dairy — 52%
- Seafood — 44%
- Oils — 61%
- Fiber — 40%
- Potassium — 56%
- Vitamin D — 28%
- Calcium — 75%

GOAL

Eat less of these:
- Calories from SoFAS* — 280%
- Refined grains — 200%
- Sodium — 149%
- Saturated fat — 110%

LIMIT

0%   50%   100%   150%   200%   250%   300%
Percent of goal or limit

* Solid Fats and Added Sugars

Source: USDA & HHS: Dietary Guidelines for Americans. 2010

The visual includes a figure number, descriptive caption, and source information.

Fig. 1. This graph shows that Americans consume about three times more fats and sugars and twice as many refined grains as is recommended but only half of the recommended foods (United States, Dept. of Agriculture and Dept. of Health and Human Services, fig. 5-1).

to increase shelf life but that contain little fiber, iron, and B vitamins—can be damaging over time (United States, Dept. of Agriculture and Dept. of Health and Human Services 36). A graph from the government's *Dietary Guidelines for Americans, 2010* provides a visual representation of the American diet and how far off it is from the recommended nutritional standards (see fig. 1).

Michael Pollan, who has written extensively about Americans' unhealthy eating habits, notes that "[t]he Centers for Disease Control estimates that fully three quarters of US health care spending goes to treat chronic diseases, most of which are preventable and linked to diet: heart

No page number is available for this web source.

disease, stroke, type 2 diabetes, and at least a third of all cancers." In fact, the amount of money the United States spends to treat chronic illnesses is increasing so rapidly that the Centers for Disease Control has labeled chronic disease "the public health challenge of the 21st century" (United States, Dept. of Health and Human Services 1). In fighting this epidemic,

Harba sets forth the urgency of her argument.

the primary challenge is not the need to find a cure; the challenge is to prevent chronic diseases from striking in the first place.

Harba 3

Legislation, however, is not a popular solution when it comes to most Americans and the food they eat. According to a nationwide poll, 75% of Americans are opposed to laws that restrict or put limitations on access to unhealthy foods (Neergaard and Agiesta). When New York mayor Michael Bloomberg proposed a regulation in 2012 banning the sale of soft drinks in servings greater than twelve ounces in restaurants and movie theaters, he was ridiculed as "Nanny Bloomberg." In California in 2011, legislators failed to pass a law that would impose a penny-per-ounce tax on soda, which would have funded obesity prevention programs. And in Mississippi, legislators passed "a ban on bans—a law that forbids . . . local restrictions on food or drink" (Conly A23).

Why is the public largely resistant to laws that would limit unhealthy choices or penalize those choices with so-called fat taxes? Many consumers and civil rights advocates find such laws to be an unreasonable restriction on individual freedom of choice. As health policy experts Mello and others point out, opposition to food and beverage regulation is similar to the opposition to early tobacco legislation: the public views the issue as one of personal responsibility rather than one requiring government intervention (2602). In other words, if a person eats unhealthy food and becomes ill as a result, that is his or her choice. But those who favor legislation claim that freedom of choice is a myth because of the strong influence of food and beverage industry marketing on consumers' dietary habits. According to one nonprofit health advocacy group, food and beverage companies spend roughly two billion dollars per year marketing directly to children. As a result, kids see nearly four thousand ads per year encouraging them to eat unhealthy food and drinks ("Facts"). As was the case with antismoking laws passed in recent decades, taxes and legal restrictions on junk food sales could help to counter the strong marketing messages that promote unhealthy products.

The United States has a history of state and local public health laws that have successfully promoted a particular behavior by punishing an undesirable behavior. The decline in tobacco use as a result of antismoking taxes and laws is perhaps the most obvious example. Another example is legislation requiring the use of seat belts, which have significantly reduced fatalities in car crashes. One government agency reports that seat belt

Harba treats both sides fairly.

Harba anticipates objections to her idea. She counters opposing views and provides support for her argument.

An analogy extends Harba's argument.

use saved an average of more than fourteen thousand lives per year in the United States between 2000 and 2010 (United States, Dept. of Transportation, Natl. Highway Traffic Safety Administration 231). Perhaps seat belt laws have public support because the cost of wearing a seat belt is small, especially when compared with the benefit of saving fourteen thousand lives per year.

Laws designed to prevent chronic disease by promoting healthier food and beverage consumption also have potentially enormous benefits. To give just one example, Marion Nestle, New York University professor of nutrition and public health, notes that "a 1% reduction in intake of saturated fat across the population would prevent more than 30,000 cases of coronary heart disease annually and save more than a billion dollars in health care costs" (7). Few would argue that saving lives and dollars is not an enormous benefit. But three-quarters of Americans say they would object to the costs needed to achieve this benefit—the regulations needed to reduce saturated fat intake.

Why do so many Americans believe there is a degree of personal choice lost when regulations such as taxes, bans, or portion limits on unhealthy foods are proposed? Some critics of anti-junk-food laws believe that even if state and local laws were successful in curbing chronic diseases, they would still be unacceptable. Bioethicist David Resnik emphasizes that such policies, despite their potential to make our society healthier, "open the door to excessive government control over food, which could restrict dietary choices, interfere with cultural, ethnic, and religious traditions, and exacerbate socioeconomic inequalities" (31). Resnik acknowledges that his argument relies on "slippery slope" thinking, but he insists that "social and political pressures" regarding food regulation make his concerns valid (31). Yet the social and political pressures that Resnik cites are really just the desire to improve public health, and limiting access to unhealthy, artificial ingredients seems a small price to pay. As legal scholars L. O. Gostin and K. G. Gostin explain, "[I]nterventions that do not pose a truly significant burden on individual liberty" are justified if they "go a long way towards safeguarding the health and well-being of the populace" (214).

To improve public health, advocates such as Bowdoin College philosophy professor Sarah Conly contend that it is the government's

Harba introduces a direct quotation with a signal phrase and follows with a comment that shows readers why she chose to use the source.

Harba acknowledges critics and counterarguments.

Including the source's credentials makes Harba more credible.

Harba 5

duty to prevent people from making harmful choices whenever feasible and whenever public benefits outweigh the costs. In response to critics who claim that laws aimed at stopping us from eating whatever we want are an assault on our freedom of choice, Conly offers a persuasive counterargument:

> [L]aws aren't designed for each one of us individually. Some of us can drive safely at 90 miles per hour, but we're bound by the same laws as the people who can't, because individual speeding laws aren't practical. Giving up a little liberty is something we agree to when we agree to live in a democratic society that is governed by laws. (A23)

As Conly suggests, we need to change our either/or thinking (either we have complete freedom of choice *or* we have government regulations and lose our freedom) and instead need to see health as a matter of public good, not individual liberty. Proposals such as Mayor Bloomberg's that seek to limit portions of unhealthy beverages aren't about giving up liberty; they are about asking individuals to choose substantial public health benefits at a very small cost.

Despite arguments in favor of regulating unhealthy food as a means to improve public health, public opposition has stood in the way of legislation. Americans freely eat as much unhealthy food as they want, and manufacturers and sellers of these foods have nearly unlimited freedom to promote such products and drive increased consumption, without any requirements to warn the public of potential hazards. Yet mounting scientific evidence points to unhealthy food as a significant contributing factor to chronic disease, which we know is straining our health care system, decreasing Americans' quality of life, and leading to unnecessary premature deaths. Americans must consider whether to allow the costly trend of rising chronic disease to continue in the name of personal choice or whether to support the regulatory changes and public health policies that will reverse that trend.

Long quotation is introduced with a signal phrase naming the author.

Long quotation is set off from the text. Quotation marks are omitted.

Long quotation is followed with comments that connect the source to Harba's argument.

Conclusion sums up Harba's argument and provides closure.

Harba 6

Works Cited

Conly, Sarah. "Three Cheers for the Nanny State." *The New York Times*, 25 Mar. 2013, p. A23.

"The Facts on Junk Food Marketing and Kids." *Prevention Institute*, www.preventioninstitute.org/focus-areas/supporting-healthy-food-a-activity/supporting-healthy-food-and-activity-environments-advocacy/get-involved-were-not-buying-it/735-were-not-buying-it-the-facts-on-junk-food-marketing-and-kids.html. Accessed 21 Apr. 2013.

Goodwin, Lorine Swainston. *The Pure Food, Drink, and Drug Crusaders, 1879-1914*. McFarland, 2006.

Gostin, L. O., and K. G. Gostin. "A Broader Liberty: J. S. Mill, Paternalism, and the Public's Health." *Public Health*, vol. 123, no. 3, 2009, pp. 214-21, doi:10.1016/j.puhe.2008.12.024.

Mello, Michelle M., et al. "Obesity—the New Frontier of Public Health Law." *The New England Journal of Medicine*, vol. 354, no. 24, 2006, pp. 2601-10, www.nejm.org/doi/pdf/10.1056/NEJMhpr060227.

Neergaard, Lauran, and Jennifer Agiesta. "Obesity's a Crisis but We Want Our Junk Food, Poll Shows." *The Huffington Post*, 4 Jan. 2013, www.huffingtonpost.com/2013/01/04/obesity-junk-food-government-intervention-poll_n_2410376.html.

Nestle, Marion. *Food Politics: How the Food Industry Influences Nutrition and Health*. U of California P, 2013.

Pollan, Michael. "The Food Movement, Rising." *The New York Review of Books*, 10 June 2010, www.nybooks.com/articles/2010/06/10/food-movement-rising.

Resnik, David. "Trans Fat Bans and Human Freedom." *The American Journal of Bioethics*, vol. 10, no. 3, Mar. 2010, pp. 27-32.

United States, Department of Agriculture and Department of Health and Human Services. *Dietary Guidelines for Americans, 2010*, health.gov/dietaryguidelines/dga2010/dietaryguidelines2010.pdf.

United States, Department of Health and Human Services, Centers for Disease Control and Prevention. *The Power of Prevention*. National Center for Chronic Disease Prevention and Health Promotion, 2009, www.cdc.gov/chronicdisease/pdf/2009-Power-of-Prevention.pdf.

United States, Department of Transportation, National Highway Traffic Safety Administration. *Traffic Safety Facts 2010: A Compilation of*

APA
CMS

APA and CMS Papers

What is expected of me when I write in psychology and other social sciences?

I have a research paper to write in history. How do the numbers and notes work?

How is APA formatting different from MLA formatting?

See APA-1 through APA-3

See APA-5

See CMS-3 and CMS-4

APA CMS APA and CMS Papers

Directory to APA in-text citation models

Directory to APA reference list models

Directory to CMS-style notes and bibliography entries is on page 495.

Directory to APA reference list models, *continued*

This tabbed section shows how to document sources in APA style for the social sciences and fields such as nursing and business, and in CMS (*Chicago*) style for history and some humanities classes. It also includes discipline-specific advice on three important topics: supporting a thesis, citing sources and avoiding plagiarism, and integrating sources.

NOTE: For advice on finding and evaluating sources and on managing information in courses across the disciplines, see the tabbed section R, Researching.

APA Papers

Most instructors in the social sciences and some instructors in other disciplines will ask you to document your sources with the American Psychological Association (APA) system of in-text citations and references described in APA-4. When writing an APA-style paper that draws on sources, you face three main challenges: (1) supporting a thesis, (2) citing your sources and avoiding plagiarism, and (3) integrating source material effectively.

Examples in this section are drawn from one student's research for a review of the literature on technology's role in the shift to student-centred learning. April Wang's paper appears on pages 483–94.

 APA-1 Supporting a thesis

Most research assignments ask you to form a thesis, or main idea, and to support that thesis with well-organized evidence. In a paper reviewing the literature on a topic, the thesis analyzes the conclusions drawn by a variety of researchers.

APA-1a Form a working thesis.

Once you have read a range of sources, considered your issue from different perspectives, and chosen an entry point in the research conversation (see R1-b), you are ready to form a working thesis: a one-sentence (or occasionally a two-sentence) statement of your central idea. (See also C1-c.) The working thesis expresses more than your opinion; it expresses your informed, reasoned answer to your research question — a question about which people might disagree. As you learn more about your subject, your ideas may change, and you

 LaunchPad ACTIVITIES FOR APA-1
macmillan learning
2 Exercises

can revise your thesis as you draft. Here, for example, is a research question posed by April Wang, a student in an education class, followed by her thesis in response.

RESEARCH QUESTION

Can educational technology improve student learning and solve the problem of teacher shortages?

WORKING THESIS

Educational technology can help solve teacher shortages by shifting the focus from teachers to students.

The thesis usually appears at the end of the introductory paragraph. To read April Wang's thesis in the context of her introduction, see page 485.

See page 366 for guidelines for testing your working thesis statement.

APA-1b Organize your ideas.

The American Psychological Association encourages the use of headings to help readers follow the organization of a paper. For an original research report, the major headings often follow a standard model: "Method," "Results," "Discussion." The introduction does not have a heading; it consists of the material between the title of the paper and the first heading.

For a literature review, headings will vary. Student writer April Wang used three questions to focus her research (see her final paper in APA-5b); the questions then became headings in her paper:

In what ways is student-centred learning effective?

Can educational technology help students drive their own learning?

How can public schools effectively combine teacher talent and educational technology?

APA-1c Use sources to inform and support your argument.

The source materials you have gathered can play many different roles and will help you support and develop your argument.

Providing background information or context

Readers need some background information and context to anchor their understanding of your topic. Describing a research study or offering facts and statistics, as student writer April Wang does, can help readers grasp your topic's significance.

> In the United States, most public school systems are struggling with teacher shortages, which are projected to worsen as the number of applicants to education schools decreases (Donitsa-Schmidt & Zuzovsky, 2014, p. 420). Citing federal data, *The New York Times* reported a 30% drop in "people entering teacher preparation programs" between 2010 and 2014 (Rich, 2015).

Explaining terms or concepts

If readers are unfamiliar with a term or concept important to your topic, you will want to define or explain it; or if your argument depends on a term with multiple meanings, you will want to explain your use of the term. Quoting or paraphrasing a source can help you define terms and concepts in accessible language. April Wang uses a source to define a key concept, student-centred learning.

> According to the International Society for Technology in Education (2016), "Student-centered learning moves students from passive receivers of information to active participants in their own discovery process."

Supporting your claims

As you draft, make sure to back up your assertions with facts, examples, and other evidence from your research (see also A4-e). April Wang, for example, uses one source's findings to support her claim that a combination of teachers and educational technology can promote student-centred learning.

> Many schools have already effectively paired a reduced faculty with educational technology to support successful student-centered learning. For example, Watson (2008) offered a case study of the Cincinnati Public Schools Virtual High School, which brought students together in a physical school building to work with an assortment of online learning programs. Although there were only 10 certified teachers in the building, students were able to engage in highly individualized instruction according to their own needs, strengths, and learning styles, using the 10 teachers as support (p. 7).

Lending authority to your argument

Expert opinion can add credibility to your argument (see also A4-e). But don't rely on experts to make your points for you. State your ideas in your own words and, when appropriate, cite the judgment of an authority in the field to support your position.

> Horn and Staker (2011) concluded that the chief benefit of technological learning was that it could adapt to the individual student in a way that whole-class delivery by a single teacher could not. Their study examined various schools where technology enabled student-centered learning.

Anticipating and countering alternative interpretations

Do not ignore sources that contradict your position. Instead, use them to state potential objections to your argument before you counter them (see A4-f). Readers often have objections in mind already, whether or not they agree with you. Wang uses a source to acknowledge that some teachers oppose student instruction driven by technology.

> Some researchers have expressed doubt that schools are ready for student-centered learning—or any type of instruction—that is driven by technology. In a recent survey conducted by the Nellie Mae Education Foundation, Moeller and Reitzes (2011) reported not only that many teachers lacked confidence in their ability to incorporate technology in the classroom but that 43% of polled high school students said that they lacked confidence in their technological proficiency going into college and careers.

APA-2 Citing sources; avoiding plagiarism

In a research paper, you will draw on the work of other researchers and writers, and you must document their contributions by citing your sources. Sources are cited for two reasons:

1. to tell readers where your information comes from — so that they can assess its reliability and, if interested, find and read the original source
2. to give credit to the writers from whom you have borrowed words and ideas

You must cite anything you borrow from a source, including direct quotations; statistics and other facts; visuals such as tables and graphs; and summaries and paraphrases. Borrowing without proper acknowledgment is a form of dishonesty known as *plagiarism*. The only exception is common knowledge — information that your readers may know or could easily locate in any number of reference sources.

APA-2a Understand how the APA system works.

The American Psychological Association recommends an author-date system of citation. The following describes that system.

1. The source is introduced by a signal phrase that includes the last name of the author followed by the date of publication in parentheses.
2. The material being cited is followed by a page number in parentheses (unless the source is unpaginated).
3. At the end of the paper, an alphabetized list of references gives complete publication information for the source.

IN-TEXT CITATION

Bell (2010) reported that students engaged in this kind of learning performed better on both project-based assessments and standardized tests (pp. 39-40).

ENTRY IN THE LIST OF REFERENCES

Bell, S. (2010). Project-based learning for the 21st century: Skills for the future. *The Clearing House, 83*(2), 39-43.

This basic APA format varies for different types of sources. For a detailed discussion and other models, see APA-4.

APA-2b Understand what plagiarism is.

In a research paper, you draw on the work of other writers. To be fair and responsible, you must document their contributions by citing your sources. When you acknowledge and document your sources, you avoid plagiarism, a serious academic offence.

Three different acts are considered plagiarism:

1. failing to cite quotations and borrowed ideas
2. failing to enclose borrowed language in quotation marks
3. failing to put summaries and paraphrases in your own words

Definitions of plagiarism may vary; it's a good idea to find out how your school defines and addresses academic dishonesty.

APA-2c Use quotation marks around borrowed language.

To indicate that you are using a source's exact phrases or sentences, you must enclose them in quotation marks unless they have been set off from the text by indenting (see p. 446). To omit the quotation marks is to claim — falsely — that the language is your own. Such an omission is plagiarism even if you have cited the source.

ORIGINAL SOURCE

Student-centered learning, or student centeredness, is a model which puts the student in the center of the learning process.

— Z. Çubukçu, "Teachers' Evaluation of Student-Centered Learning Environments" (2012), p. 50

PLAGIARISM

According to Çubukçu (2012), student-centered learning . . . is a model which puts the student in the centre of the learning process (p. 50).

The student writer has cited the source, Çubukçu; however, the writer has not put quotation marks around the definition of *student-centered learning*, which is taken word-for-word from the source.

BORROWED LANGUAGE IN QUOTATION MARKS

According to Çubukçu (2012), "student-centered learning . . . is a model which puts the student in the center of the learning process" (p. 50).

NOTE: Quotation marks are not used when quoted sentences are set off from the text by indenting (see p. 446).

APA-2d Put summaries and paraphrases in your own words.

Summaries and paraphrases are written in your own words. A summary condenses information; a paraphrase conveys the information using roughly the same number of words as in the original source.

When you summarize or paraphrase, it is not enough to name the source; you must present the source's meaning using your own words and sentence structure. (See also R2-c.) You commit plagiarism if you patchwrite — half-copy the author's sentences, either by mixing the author's phrases with your own without using quotation marks or by plugging your own synonyms into the author's sentence structure.

The following paraphrases are plagiarized — even though the source is cited — because their language or sentence structure is too close to that of the source.

ORIGINAL SOURCE

Student-centered teaching focuses on the student. Decision-making, organization and content are determined for most by taking individual students' needs and interests into consideration. Student-centered teaching provides opportunities to develop students' skills of transferring knowledge to other situations, triggering retention, and adapting a high motivation for learning.

— Z. Çubukçu, "Teachers' Evaluation of Student-Centered Learning Environments" (2012), p. 52

UNACCEPTABLE BORROWING OF PHRASES

According to Çubukçu (2012), student-centered teaching takes into account the needs and interests of each student, making it possible to foster students' skills of transferring knowledge to new situations and triggering retention (p. 52).

UNACCEPTABLE BORROWING OF STRUCTURE

According to Çubukçu (2012), this new model of teaching centers on the student. The material and flow of the course are chosen by considering the students' individual requirements. Student-centered teaching gives a chance for students to develop useful, transferable skills, ensuring they'll remember material and stay motivated (p. 52).

To avoid plagiarizing an author's language, resist the temptation to look at the source while you are summarizing or paraphrasing. After you have read the passage you want to paraphrase, set the source aside. Ask yourself, "What is the author's meaning?" In your own words, state your understanding of the author's basic point. Return to the source and check that you haven't used the author's language or sentence structure or misrepresented the author's ideas. When you fully understand another writer's meaning, you can more easily and accurately present those ideas in your own words.

ACCEPTABLE PARAPHRASE

Çubukçu's (2012) research has documented the numerous benefits of student-centered teaching in putting the student at the center of teaching and learning. When students are given the option of deciding what they learn and how they learn, they are motivated to apply their learning to new settings and to retain the content of their learning (p. 52).

APA-3 Integrating sources

Summaries, paraphrases, quotations, and data will help you support your argument, but they cannot speak for you. You can use several strategies to integrate information from sources into your paper while maintaining your own voice.

APA-3a Summarize and paraphrase effectively.

In your academic writing, keep the emphasis on your ideas and your language; use your own words to summarize and to paraphrase your sources and to explain your points. How you choose to use a source — as summary or paraphrase — depends on your purpose.

Summarizing

When you summarize a source, you express another writer's ideas in your own words, condensing the author's key points and using fewer words than the author. Even though a summary is in your own words, the original ideas remain the intellectual property of the author, so you must include a citation. Summarizing allows you to state the source's main idea simply before you respond to or counter it.

See "When to use a summary" (p. 374) for more advice.

Paraphrasing

When you paraphrase, you express an author's ideas in your own words, using approximately the same number of words and details as in the source. Even though the words are your own, the original ideas are the author's intellectual property, so you must give a citation. Paraphrasing allows you to capture a source's ideas but perhaps simplify or reorder them.

See "When to use a paraphrase" (p. 374) for more advice.

APA-3b Use quotations effectively.

When you quote a source, you borrow some of the author's exact words and enclose them in quotation marks. Quotation marks show your readers that both the idea and the words belong to the author.

See "When to use quotations" (p. 374) for more advice.

 LaunchPad **ACTIVITIES FOR APA-3**
macmillan learning
7 Exercises

Limiting your use of quotations

Although it is tempting to insert many quotations in your paper and to use your own words only for connecting passages, do not quote excessively. It is almost impossible to integrate numerous long quotations smoothly into your own text.

It is not always necessary to quote full sentences from a source. You can often integrate language from a source into your own sentence structure.

> Citing federal data, *The New York Times* reported a 30% drop in "people entering teacher preparation programs" between 2010 and 2014 (Rich, 2015).

> Bell (2010) has argued that the chief benefit of student-centered learning is that it can connect students with "real-world tasks," thus making learning more engaging as well as more comprehensive.

Using the ellipsis mark

To condense a quoted passage, you can use the ellipsis mark (three periods, with spaces between) to indicate that you have omitted words. What remains must be grammatically complete.

> Demski (2012) noted that "personalized learning . . . acknowledges and accommodates the range of abilities, prior experiences, needs, and interests of each student" (p. 33).

The writer has omitted the phrase *a student-centered teaching and learning model that* from the source.

If you leave out one or more full sentences, use a period before the three ellipsis dots.

> According to Demski (2012), "In any personalized learning model, the student—not the teacher—is the central figure. . . . Personalized learning may finally allow individualization and differentiation to actually happen in the classroom" (p. 34).

Ordinarily, do not use an ellipsis mark at the beginning or at the end of a quotation. Readers will understand that you have taken the quoted material from a longer passage. The only exception occurs when you feel it is necessary, for clarity, to indicate that your quotation begins or ends in the middle of a sentence.

Using sources responsibly: Make sure omissions and ellipsis marks do not distort the meaning of your source.

Using brackets

Brackets allow you to insert your own words into quoted material to clarify a confusing reference or to keep a sentence grammatical in the context of your own writing.

> Demski's (2012) research confirms that "implement[ing] a true personalized learning model on a national level" is difficult for a number of reasons (p. 36).

To indicate an error such as a misspelling in a quotation, insert [*sic*], italicized and with brackets around it, right after the error. (See P6-b.)

Setting off long quotations

When you quote forty or more words from a source, set off the quotation by indenting it one-half inch (1.25 cm) from the left margin. Use the normal right margin and do not single-space the quotation.

Long quotations should be introduced by an informative sentence, usually followed by a colon. Quotation marks are unnecessary because the indented format tells readers that the passage is taken word-for-word from the source.

> According to Svokos (2015), College and Education Fellow for *The Huffington Post*, some educational technology resources entertain students while supporting student-centered learning:
>
> > GlassLab, a nonprofit that was launched with grants from the Bill & Melinda Gates and MacArthur Foundations, creates educational games that are now being used in more than 6,000 classrooms across the country. Some of the company's games are education versions of existing ones—for example, its first release was SimCity EDU—while others are originals. Teachers get real-time updates on students' progress as well as suggestions on what topics students need to spend more time on.

For a source with page numbers (unlike the example, which is a web source), the parenthetical citation with a page number goes outside the final mark of punctuation. (When a quotation is run into your text, the opposite is true. See the sample citations on p. 445.)

APA-3c Use signal phrases to integrate sources.

Whenever you include a paraphrase, summary, or direct quotation of another writer's work in your paper, prepare your readers for it with a signal phrase. A signal phrase usually names the author of the source, gives the publication year in parentheses, and often provides some context. It is generally acceptable in APA style to call authors by their last name only, even on a first mention. If your paper refers to two authors with the same last name, use initials as well.

When you write a signal phrase, choose a verb that is appropriate for the way you are using the source (see APA-1c). Are you providing background, explaining a concept, supporting a claim, lending authority, or refuting an argument? See the chart on page 449 for a list of verbs commonly used in signal phrases.

NOTE: APA requires using verbs in the past tense or present perfect tense (*explained* or *has explained*) to introduce source material. Use the present tense only for discussing the applications or effects of your own results (*the data suggest*) or knowledge that has been clearly established (*researchers agree*).

Marking boundaries

Readers need to move from your words to the words of a source without feeling a jolt. Avoid dropping direct quotations into your text without warning. Instead, provide clear signal phrases, including at least the author's name and the year of publication. A signal phrase marks the boundary between source material and your own words and can also tell readers why a source is worth quoting. (The signal phrase is highlighted in the second example.)

DROPPED QUOTATION

Many educators have been intrigued by the concept of blended learning but have been unsure how to define it. "Blended learning is a formal education program in which a student learns at least in part through online delivery of content and instruction with some element of student control over time, place, and pace" (Horn & Staker, 2011, p. 4).

QUOTATION WITH SIGNAL PHRASE

Many educators have been intrigued by the concept of blended learning but have been unsure how to define it. As Horn and Staker (2011) have argued, "Blended learning is a formal education program in which a student learns at least in part through online delivery of content and instruction with some element of student control over time, place, and pace" (p. 4).

Using signal phrases with summaries and paraphrases

As with quotations, you should introduce most summaries and paraphrases with a signal phrase that mentions the author and the year and places the material in the context of your own writing. Readers will then understand where the summary or paraphrase begins.

Without the signal phrase (highlighted) in the following example, readers might think that only the last sentence is being cited, when in fact the whole paragraph is based on the source.

> Watson (2008) reported that for American postsecondary students, technology is integral to their academic lives. Nearly three-quarters own their own laptops, and 83% have used a course management system for an online component of a class. Watson pointed out that online and blended learning models are even more widespread outside of the United States (p. 15).

There are times, however, when a summary or a paraphrase does not require a signal phrase naming the author. When the context makes clear where the cited material begins, you may omit the signal phrase and include the author's name and the year in parentheses.

Integrating statistics and other data

When you cite a statistic or other data, a signal phrase is often not necessary. In most cases, readers will understand that the citation refers to the data (not the whole paragraph).

> Of polled high school students, 43% said that they lacked confidence in their technological proficiency going into college and careers (Moeller & Reitzes, 2011).

There is nothing wrong, however, with using a signal phrase to introduce a statistic or other data.

Putting source material in context

Readers should not have to guess why source material appears in your paper; you must put the source in context. If you use another writer's words, you must explain how they relate to your point. It's a good idea to sandwich a quotation between sentences of your own, introducing it with a signal phrase and following it with interpretive comments that link the quotation to your paper's argument. (See also APA-3d.)

QUOTATION WITH EFFECTIVE CONTEXT

> According to the International Society for Technology in Education (2016), "Student-centered learning moves students from passive receivers of information to active participants in their own discovery process. What students learn, how they learn it and how their learning is assessed are all driven by each individual student's needs and abilities." The results of student-centered learning have been positive, not only for academic achievement but also for student self-esteem. In this model of instruction, the teacher acts as a facilitator, and the students actively participate in the process of learning and teaching.

Using signal phrases in APA papers

To avoid monotony, try to vary both the language and the placement of your signal phrases.

Model signal phrases

In the words of Mitra (2013), "..."

As Bell (2010) has noted, "..."

Donitsa-Schmidt and Zuzovsky (2014) pointed out that "..."

"...," claimed Çubukçu (2012).

"...," explained Demski (2012), "..."

Horn and Staker (2011) have offered a compelling argument for this view: "..."

Moeller and Reitzes (2011) answered objections with the following analysis: "..."

Verbs in signal phrases

admitted	contended	reasoned
agreed	declared	refuted
argued	denied	rejected
asserted	emphasized	reported
believed	insisted	responded
claimed	noted	suggested
compared	observed	thought
confirmed	pointed out	wrote

APA-3d Synthesize sources.

When you synthesize multiple sources in a research paper, you create a conversation about your research topic. You show readers how the ideas of one source relate to those of another by connecting and analyzing the ideas in the context of your argument. Keep the emphasis on your own writing. The thread of your argument should be easy to identify and to understand, with or without your sources. A sample synthesis appears on page 450.

SAMPLE SYNTHESIS

Student writer April Wang begins with a claim that needs support.	It is clear that educational technology will continue to play a role in student and school performance. — *Student writer*
A signal phrase indicates how the source contributes to Wang's paper and shows that the ideas that follow are not her own.	Horn and Staker (2011) acknowledged that they focused on programs in which integration of educational technology led to improved student performance. In other schools, technological learning is simply distance learning—watching a remote teacher—and not student-centered learning that allows students to partner with teachers to develop enriching learning experiences. — *Source 1*
	That said, many educators seem convinced that educational technology has the potential to help them transition from traditional teacher-driven learning to student-centered learning. — *Student writer*
Wang extends the argument and sets up two additional sources.	All four schools in the Stanford study heavily relied on technology (Friedlaender et al., 2014). — *Source 2* And indeed, Demski (2012) argued that technology is not supplemental but instead is "central" to student-centered learning (p. 33). — *Source 3*
Wang closes the paragraph by interpreting the source and connecting it to her claim.	Rather than turning to a teacher as the source of information, students are sent to investigate solutions to problems by searching online, e-mailing experts, collaborating with one another in a wiki space, or completing online practice. Rather than turning to a teacher for the answer to a question, students are driven to perform—driven to use technology to find those answers themselves. — *Student writer*

In this synthesis, Wang uses her own analyses to shape the conversation among her sources. She does not simply string quotations and statistics together or allow her sources to overwhelm her writing. The final sentence, written in her own voice, gives her an opportunity to explain to readers how her sources support and extend her argument.

When synthesizing sources, ask yourself these questions:

- How do your sources address your research question?
- How do your sources respond to each other's ideas?
- Have you varied the functions of sources — to provide background, explain concepts, lend authority, and anticipate counterarguments? Do your signal phrases indicate these functions?
- Do you connect and analyze sources in your own voice?
- Is your own argument easy to identify and to understand, with or without your sources?

APA-4 Documenting sources

In most social science classes, you will be asked to use the APA system for documenting sources, which is set forth in the *Publication Manual of the American Psychological Association*, 6th ed. (Washington, DC: APA, 2010).

APA recommends in-text citations that refer readers to a list of references. An in-text citation gives the author of the source (often in a signal phrase), the year of publication, and often a page number in parentheses. At the end of the paper, a list of references provides publication information about the source; the list is alphabetized by authors' last names (or by titles for works with no authors). The direct link between the in-text citation and the entry in the reference list is highlighted in the following example.

IN-TEXT CITATION

Bell (2010) reported that students engaged in this kind of learning performed better on both project-based assessments and standardized tests (pp. 39-40).

ENTRY IN THE LIST OF REFERENCES

Bell, S. (2010). Project-based learning for the 21st century: Skills for the future. *The Clearing House, 83*(2), 39-43.

For a reference list that includes this entry, see page 493.

APA-4a APA in-text citations

APA's in-text citations provide the author's last name and the year of publication, usually before the cited material, and a page number in parentheses directly after the cited material. In the following models, the elements of the in-text citation are highlighted.

NOTE: APA style requires the use of the past tense or the present perfect tense in signal phrases introducing cited material: *Smith (2012) reported, Smith (2012) has argued.* (See also p. 447.)

1. Basic format for a quotation Ordinarily, introduce the quotation with a signal phrase that includes the author's last name followed by the year of publication in parentheses. Put the page number (preceded by "p.," or "pp." for more than one page) in parentheses after the quotation. For sources from the web without page numbers, see item 12a on page 454.

> Çubukçu (2012) argued that for a student-centered approach to work, students must maintain "ownership for their goals and activities" (p. 64).

If the author is not named in the signal phrase, place the author's name, the year, and the page number in parentheses after the quotation: (Çubukçu, 2012, p. 64). (See items 6 and 12 for citing sources that lack authors; item 12 also explains how to handle sources without dates or page numbers.)

NOTE: Do not include a month in an in-text citation, even if the entry in the reference list includes the month.

2. Basic format for a summary or a paraphrase   As for a quotation (see item 1), include the author's last name and the year either in a signal phrase introducing the material or in parentheses following it. Use a page number, if one is available, following the cited material. For sources from the web without page numbers, see item 12a on page 454.

> Watson (2008) offered a case study of the Cincinnati Public Schools Virtual High School, in which students were able to engage in highly individualized instruction according to their own needs, strengths, and learning styles, using 10 teachers as support (p. 7).

> The Cincinnati Public Schools Virtual High School brought students together to engage in highly individualized instruction according to their own needs, strengths, and learning styles, using 10 teachers as support (Watson, 2008, p. 7).

3. Work with two authors   Name both authors in the signal phrase or in parentheses each time you cite the work. In the parentheses, use "&" between the authors' names; in the signal phrase, use "and."

> According to Donitsa-Schmidt and Zuzovsky (2014), "demographic growth in the school population" can lead to teacher shortages (p. 426).

> In the United States, most public school systems are struggling with teacher shortages, which are projected to worsen as the number of applicants to education schools decreases (Donitsa-Schmidt & Zuzovsky, 2014, p. 420).

4. Work with three to five authors   Identify all authors in the signal phrase or in parentheses the first time you cite the source.

> In 2013, Harper, Findlen, Ibori, and Wenz studied teachers' perceptions of project-based learning (PBL) before and after participating in a PBL pilot program.

In subsequent citations, use the first author's name followed by "et al." in either the signal phrase or the parentheses.

> Surprisingly, Harper et al. (2013) advised school administrators "not to jump into project-based pedagogy without training and feedback."

5. Work with six or more authors Use the first author's name followed by "et al." in the signal phrase or in parentheses.

> Hermann et al. (2012) tracked 42 students over a three-year period to look closely at the performance of students in the laptop program (p. 49).

6. Work with unknown author If the author is unknown, mention the work's title in the signal phrase or give the first word or two of the title in the parentheses. Titles of short works such as articles are put in quotation marks; titles of long works such as books and reports are italicized.

> Collaboration increases significantly among students who own or have regular access to a laptop ("Tech Seeds," 2015).

NOTE: In the rare case when "Anonymous" is specified as the author, treat it as if it were a real name: (Anonymous, 2011). In the list of references, also use the name Anonymous as author.

7. Organization as author If the author is an organization or a government agency, name the organization in the signal phrase or in the parentheses the first time you cite the source.

> According to the International Society for Technology in Education (2016), "Student-centered learning moves students from passive receivers of information to active participants in their own discovery process."

If the organization has a familiar abbreviation, you may include it in brackets the first time you cite the source and use the abbreviation alone in later citations.

FIRST CITATION	(Canadian Institute for Health Information [CIHI], 2017)
LATER CITATIONS	(CIHI, 2017)

8. Authors with the same last name To avoid confusion if your reference list includes two or more authors with the same last name, use initials with the last names in your in-text citations.

> Research by E. Smith (1989) revealed that . . .

> One 2012 study contradicted . . . (R. Smith, p. 234).

9. Two or more works by the same author in the same year In your reference list, you will use lowercase letters ("a," "b," and so on) with the year to order the entries (see item 8 on p. 461). Use those same letters with the year in the in-text citation.

> Research by Durgin (2013b) has yielded new findings about the role of smartphones in the classroom.

10. Two or more works in the same parentheses Put the works in the same order that they appear in the reference list, separated with semicolons: (Nazer, 2015; Serrao et al., 2014).

11. Multiple citations to the same work in one paragraph If you give the author's name in the text of your paper (not in parentheses) and you mention that source again in the text of the same paragraph, give only the author's name, not the date, in the later citation. If any subsequent reference in the same paragraph is in parentheses, include both the author and the date in the parentheses.

> Principal J. Patrice said, "You have to be able to reach students where they are instead of making them come to you. If you don't, you'll lose them" (personal communication, April 10, 2006). Patrice expressed her desire to see all students get something out of their educational experience. This feeling is common among members of Waverly's faculty. With such a positive view of student potential, it is no wonder that 97% of Waverly High School graduates go on to a four-year university (Patrice, 2006).

12. Web source Cite sources from the web as you would cite any other source, giving the author and the year when they are available.

> Atkinson (2011) found that children who spent at least four hours a day engaged in online activities in an academic environment were less likely to want to play video games or watch TV after school.

Usually a page number is not available; occasionally a web source will lack an author or a date (see 12a, 12b, and 12c).

a. No page numbers When a web source lacks stable numbered pages, you may include a paragraph number or a heading to help readers locate the passage being cited.

If the source has numbered paragraphs, use the paragraph number preceded by the abbreviation "para." (or "paras." for more than one paragraph): (Hall, 2012, para. 5). If the source has no numbered paragraphs but contains headings, cite the appropriate heading in parentheses.

> Crush and Jayasingh (2015) pointed out that several other school districts in low-income areas had "jump-started their distance learning initiatives with available grant funds" ("Funding Change," para. 6).

b. Unknown author If no author is named in the source, mention the title of the source in a signal phrase or give the first word or two of the title in parentheses (see also item 6). (If an organization serves as the author, see item 7.)

> A student's IEP may, in fact, recommend the use of mobile technology ("Considerations," 2012).

c. Unknown date When the source does not give a date, use the abbreviation "n.d." (for "no date").

> Administrators believe 1-to-1 programs boost learner engagement (Magnus, n.d.).

13. An entire website If you are citing an entire website, not an internal page or a section, give the URL in the text of your paper but do not include it in the reference list.

> The Berkeley Center for Teaching and Learning website (https://teaching.berkeley.edu/) shares ideas for using mobile technology in the classroom.

14. Multivolume work If you have used more than one volume from a multivolume work, add the volume number in parentheses with the page number.

> Banford (2013) has demonstrated steady increases in performance since the program began a decade ago (Vol. 2, p. 135).

15. Personal communication Interviews that you conduct, memos, letters, email messages, social media posts, and similar communications that would be difficult for your readers to retrieve should be cited in the text only, not in the reference list. (Use the first initial with the last name either in your text sentence or in parentheses.)

> One of Yim's colleagues, who has studied the effect of social media on children's academic progress, has contended that the benefits of this technology for children under 12 years old are few (F. Johnson, personal communication, October 20, 2013).

16. Course materials Cite lecture notes from your instructor or your own class notes as personal communication (see item 15). If your instructor's material contains publication information, cite as you would the appropriate source. See also item 60 on page 478.

17. Part of a source (chapter, figure) To cite a specific part of a source, such as a whole chapter or a figure or table, identify the element in parentheses. Don't abbreviate terms such as "Figure," "Chapter," and "Section"; "page" is abbreviated "p." (or "pp." for more than one page).

> The data support the finding that peer relationships are difficult to replicate in a completely online environment (Hanniman, 2010, Figure 8-3, p. 345).

18. Indirect source (source quoted in another source) When a writer's or a speaker's quoted words appear in a source written by someone else, begin the parenthetical citation with the words "as cited in." In the following example, Demski is the author of the source in the reference list; that source contains a quotation by Cator.

> Karen Cator, director of the U.S. Department of Education's Office of Educational Technology, calls technology "the essence" of a personalized learning environment (as cited in Demski, 2012, p. 34).

19. Sacred or classical text Identify the text, the version or edition you used, and the relevant part (chapter, verse, line). It is not necessary to include the source in the reference list.

> Peace activists have long cited the biblical prophet's vision of a world without war: "And they shall beat their swords into plowshares, and their spears into pruning hooks; nation shall not lift up sword against nation, neither shall they learn war any more" (Isaiah 2:4 Revised Standard Version).

APA-4b APA list of references

As you gather sources for an assignment, you will likely find sources in print, on the web, and in other places. The information you will need for the reference list at the end of your paper will differ slightly for some sources, but the main principles apply to all sources: You should identify an author, a creator, or a producer whenever possible; give a title; and provide the date on which the source was produced. Some sources will require page numbers; some will require a publisher; and some will require retrieval information.

- General guidelines for the reference list, page 458

Section APA-4b provides specific requirements for and examples of many of the sources you are likely to encounter. When you cite sources, your goals are to show that the sources you've used are reliable and relevant to your work, to provide your readers with enough information so that they can find your sources easily, and to provide that information in a consistent way according to APA conventions.

In the list of references, include only sources that you have quoted, summarized, or paraphrased in your paper.

General guidelines for listing authors

The formatting of authors' names in items 1–11 applies to all sources in print and on the web — books, articles, websites, and so on. For more models of specific source types, see items 12–63.

1. Single author

author:
last name   year
+ initial(s)   (book)   title (book)   place of
                                                                    publication publisher

Yman, D. M. (2017). *Fearless photographer: Nature.* Toronto, ON: Nelson.

2. Two to seven authors List up to seven authors by last names followed by initials. Use an ampersand (&) before the name of the last author. (See items 3–5 on pp. 452–53 for citing works with multiple authors in the text of your paper.)

all authors: year
last name + initial(s) (book)   title (book)

Berg, M., & Seeber, B. (2016). *The slow professor: Challenging the culture of speed in the*

                place of
                publication   publisher

academy. Toronto, ON: University of Toronto Press.

                        all authors: year
                        last name + initial(s)   (journal)   title (article)

Hurtley, F., Roberts, L., Ray, L. B., Purnell, B. A., & Ash, C. (2014). Putting off the

                journal
                title   volume   page(s)   DOI

inevitable. *Science, 350,* 1180-1181. doi:10.1126/science.aad3267

3. Eight or more authors List the first six authors followed by three ellipsis dots and the last author's name.

Datta, S. J., Khumnoon, C., Lee, Z. H., Moon, W. K., Docao, S., Nguyen,

T. H., . . . Yoon, K. B. (2015). CO_2 capture from humid flue gases and humid

atmosphere using a microporous coppersilicate. *Science, 350,* 302-306.

doi:10.1126/science.aab1680

General guidelines for the reference list

In APA style, the alphabetical list of works cited, which appears at the end of the paper, is titled "References."

Authors and dates

- Alphabetize entries in the list of references by authors' last names; if a work has no author, alphabetize it by its title.
- For all authors' names, put the last name first, followed by a comma; use initials for the first and middle names.
- With two or more authors, use an ampersand (&) before the last author's name. Separate the names with commas. Include names for up to seven authors; if there are eight or more authors, give the first six authors, three ellipsis dots, and the last author.
- If the author is a company or an organization, give the name in normal order.
- Put the date of publication immediately after the first element of the citation. Enclose the date in parentheses, followed by a period (outside the parentheses).
- Use the date as given in the publication. Generally, give the year for books and journals; the year and month for monthly magazines; and the year, month, and day for weekly magazines and for newspapers. Use the season when a publication gives the season. For sources on the web, use the date of posting, if it is available.

Titles

- Italicize the titles and subtitles of books, journals, and other long works. If a book title contains another book title or an article title, do not italicize the internal title and do not put quotation marks around it.
- Use no italics or quotation marks for the titles of articles. If an article title contains another article title or a term usually placed in quotation marks, use quotation marks around the internal title or term. If it contains a title or term usually italicized, place the title or term in italics.
- For books and articles, capitalize only the first word of the title and subtitle and all proper nouns.
- For the titles of journals, magazines, and newspapers, capitalize all words of four letters or more (and all nouns, pronouns, verbs, adjectives, and adverbs of any length).

General guidelines for the reference list, *continued*

Place of publication and publisher (books)

- Take the information from the title page and copyright page. If more than one place of publication is listed, use only the first.
- Give the city and province or territory for Canadian cities. Use postal abbreviations for provinces and territories.
- Give the city and state for all US cities. Use postal abbreviations for all states.
- Give the city and country for cities outside Canada and the United States. Do not abbreviate the country.
- Do not give a province, territory, or state if the publisher's name includes it (Edmonton: University of Alberta Press, for example).
- In publishers' names, omit terms such as "Company" (or "Co.") and "Inc." but keep "Books" and "Press." Omit first names or initials (Norton, not W. W. Norton, for example).
- If the publisher is the same as the author, use the word "Author" in the publisher position.

Volume, issue, and page numbers (articles)

- For a journal or a magazine, give only the volume number if the publication is paginated continuously through each volume; give the volume and issue numbers if each issue begins on page 1.
- Italicize the volume number and put the issue number, not italicized, in parentheses.
- For daily and weekly newspapers, use "p." or "pp." before page numbers (if any). For journals and magazines, do not add "p." or "pp."
- When an article appears on consecutive pages, provide the range of pages. When an article does not appear on consecutive pages, give all page numbers: A1, A17.

URLs, DOIs, and other retrieval information

- For articles and books from the web, use the DOI (digital object identifier) if the source has one, and do not give a URL. If a source does not have a DOI, give the URL.
- Use a retrieval date for a web source only if the content is likely to change. Most of the examples in APA-4b do not show a retrieval date because the content of the sources is stable. If you are unsure about whether to use a retrieval date, include the date or consult your instructor.

4. Organization as author

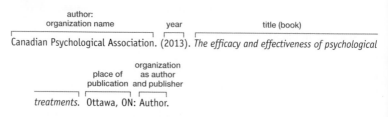

author:
organization name   year   title (book)

Canadian Psychological Association. (2013). *The efficacy and effectiveness of psychological*

place of publication | organization as author and publisher

treatments. Ottawa, ON: Author.

5. Unknown author   Begin the entry with the work's title.

title (article) | year + month + day (weekly publication) | magazine title | volume, issue | page(s)

The rise of the sharing economy. (2013, March 9). *The Economist, 406*(8826), 14.

title (book) | edition | year | place of publication | publisher

The Canadian almanac & directory (171st ed.). (2018). Toronto, ON: Grey House.

6. Author using a pseudonym (pen name) or screen name   Use the author's real name, if known, and give the pseudonym or screen name in brackets exactly as it appears in the source. If only the screen name is known, begin with that name and do not use brackets. (See also items 42 and 63 on citing screen names in social media.)

screen name | year + month + day (daily publication) | title of original article

BasicInstinct. (2015, December 4). Re: U.S. economy added 211,000 jobs in

label

November; unemployment rate holds at 5 percent [Comment].
title of publication   URL for web publication

The Washington Post. Retrieved from http://washingtonpost.com/

7. Two or more works by the same author   Use the author's name for all entries. List the entries by year, the earliest first.

MacGregor, R. (2013). *A life in the bush: Lessons from my father.* Toronto, ON: Random House Canada.

MacGregor, R. (2017). *Original highways: Travelling the great rivers of Canada.* Toronto, ON: Random House Canada

8. Two or more works by the same author in the same year   List the works alphabetically by title. In the parentheses, following the year add "a," "b," and so on. Use these same letters when giving the year in the in-text citation. (See also p. 482 and item 9 on p. 454.)

Brym, R. (2016a). After postmaterialism: An essay on China, Russia and the United
    States. *Canadian Journal of Sociology, 41*(2), 195-211.

Brym, R. (2016b). Ronald Inglehart's comment on "After postmaterialism": A reply.
    Canadian Journal of Sociology, 41(2), 223-227.

9. Editor   Begin with the name of the editor or editors; place the abbreviation "Ed." (or "Eds." for more than one editor) in parentheses following the name. (See item 10 for a work with both an author and an editor.)

all editors:
last name + initial(s)   year   title (book)

Rohleder, P., & Lyons, A. (Eds.). (2014). *Qualitative research in clinical and health*
                    place of
                    publication   publisher
psychology. New York, NY: Palgrave.

10. Author and editor   Begin with the name of the author, followed by the name of the editor and the abbreviation "Ed." in parentheses. For a book with an author and two or more editors, use the abbreviation "Ed." after each editor's name: Gray, W., & Jones, P. (Ed.), & Smith, A. (Ed.).

author   editor   year   title (book)

James, W., & Pelikan, J. (Ed.). (2009). *The varieties of religious experience.*
    place of   original
    publication   publisher   publication information
New York, NY: Library of America. (Original work published 1902)

11. Translator   Begin with the name of the author. After the title, in parentheses place the name of the translator (in normal order) and the abbreviation "Trans." (for "Translator"). Add the original date of publication at the end of the entry.

author   year   title (book)

Murakami, H. (2014). *Colorless Tsukuru Tazaki and his years of pilgrimage*
                    place of   original
    translator   publication   publisher   publication information
(P. Gabriel, Trans.). Cambridge, England: Knopf. (Original work published 2013)

Articles and other short works

- Citation at a glance: Online article in a journal or magazine, page 464
- Citation at a glance: Article from a database, page 465

12. Article in a journal   If an article from the web or a database has no DOI, include the URL for the journal's home page.

a. Print

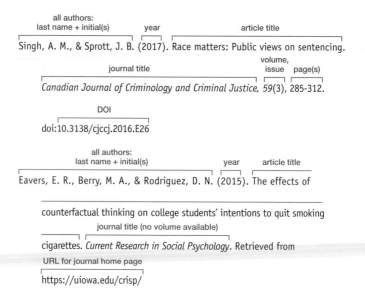

authors: last name + initial(s) year article title

French, R., & Oreopoulos, P. (2017). Applying behavioural economics to public policy in

volume,
journal title issue page(s)

Canada. *Canadian Journal of Economics, 50*(3), 599-635.

b. Web

all authors:
last name + initial(s) year article title

Singh, A. M., & Sprott, J. B. (2017). Race matters: Public views on sentencing.

volume,
journal title issue page(s)

Canadian Journal of Criminology and Criminal Justice, 59(3), 285-312.

DOI

doi:10.3138/cjccj.2016.E26

all authors:
last name + initial(s) year article title

Eavers, E. R., Berry, M. A., & Rodriguez, D. N. (2015). The effects of

counterfactual thinking on college students' intentions to quit smoking

journal title (no volume available)

cigarettes. *Current Research in Social Psychology*. Retrieved from

URL for journal home page

https://uiowa.edu/crisp/

c. Database

author year article title

Lyons, M. (2015). Writing up: How the weak wrote to the powerful. *Journal of*

volume,
journal title issue page(s) DOI

Social History, 49(2), 317-330. doi:10.1093/jsh/shv038

13. Article in a magazine   If an article from the web or a database has no DOI, use the URL for the magazine's home page.

a. Print

| author | year + month (monthly magazine) | article title | magazine title | volume, issue | page(s) |

Paris, W. (2015, March/April). The new survivors. *Psychology Today, 48*(2), 66-73, 82.

b. Web

| author | date of posting (when available) | article title |

Root, F. (2017, April/May). Why the North Pole matters: An important history of

| magazine title |

challenges and global fascination. *Canadian Geographic.* Retrieved from

| URL for home page |

https://www.canadiangeographic.ca

c. Database

| author | year + month + day (weekly magazine) | article title | magazine title | volume, issue |

Thompson, M. (2015, December 3). Sending women to war. *Time, 186*(24),

| page(s) | URL for magazine home page |

52-55. Retrieved from http://time.com/

14. Article in a newspaper

a. Print

| author | year + month + day | article title |

Saul, S. (2015, December 6). Colleges pile renovation costs onto the plates of

| newspaper title | page(s) |

students. *The New York Times,* pp. 1, 18.

b. Web

| author | year + month + day | article title |

Chan, C. (2017, September 4). New Vancouver chat app aims to get people talking.

| newspaper title | URL for home page |

Vancouver Sun. Retrieved from http://vancouversun.com

Citation at a glance: Online article in a journal or magazine

To cite an online article in a journal or magazine in APA style, include the following elements:

1 Author(s)
2 Year of publication for journal; complete date for magazine
3 Title and subtitle of article
4 Name of journal or magazine

5 Volume number; issue number, if required (see p. 459)
6 DOI (digital object identifier), if article has one; otherwise, URL for journal's or magazine's home page

ONLINE ARTICLE

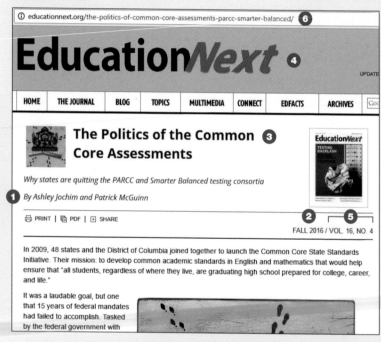

REFERENCE LIST ENTRY FOR AN ONLINE ARTICLE IN A JOURNAL OR MAGAZINE

       1   2   3

Jochim, A., & McGuinn, P. (2016, Fall). The politics of the Common Core assessments.
       4   5   6

Education Next, 16(4). Retrieved from educationnext.org/

For more on citing online articles in APA style, see items 12–14.

Citation at a glance: Article from a database

To cite an article from a database in APA style, include the following elements:

1 Author(s)
2 Year of publication for journal; complete date for magazine or newspaper
3 Title and subtitle of article
4 Name of periodical
5 Volume number; issue number, if required (see p. 459)
6 Page number(s)
7 DOI (digital object identifier), if available; otherwise, URL for periodical's home page

DATABASE RECORD

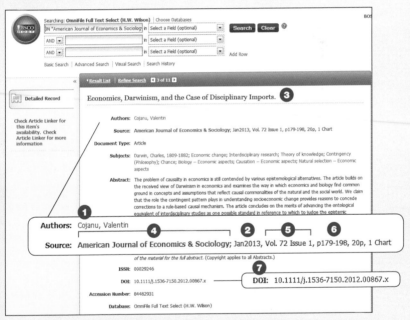

REFERENCE LIST ENTRY FOR AN ARTICLE FROM A DATABASE

1   2   3   4

Cojanu, V. (2013). Economics, Darwinism, and the case of disciplinary imports. *American*

             4   5   6   7

Journal of Economics & Sociology, 72, 179–198. doi:10.1111/j.1536-7150.2012

  7

.00867.x

For more on citing articles from a database in APA style, see items 12–14.

15. Abstract   Add the label "Abstract," in brackets, after the title.

a. Abstract of a journal article

Muanda, F. T., Sheehy, O., & Bérard, A. (2017). Use of antibiotics during pregnancy and
risk of spontaneous abortion [Abstract]. *Canadian Medical Association Journal, 189,*
E625–E633. Retrieved from http://www.cmaj.ca/content/189/17/E625.abstract

b. Abstract of a paper

Dicristo, G. (2017). Mechanisms of refinement of cortical GABAergic circuits [Abstract].
Paper presented at the Canadian Neuroscience Meeting 2017, Montreal, QC.
Retrieved from http://can-acn.org/documents/2017/CAN2017AbstractBooklet.pdf

16. Supplemental material   If an article on the web contains supplemental material that is not part of the main article, cite the material as you would an article and add the label "Supplemental material" in brackets following the title.

Hansen, J. D., & Reich, J. (2015). Democratizing education? Examining access and usage
patterns in massive open online courses [Supplemental material]. *Science, 350*(6265),
1245-1248. doi:10.1126/science.290.5494.1148

17. Letter to the editor   Insert the words "Letter to the editor" in brackets after the title of the letter. If the letter has no title, use the bracketed words as the title (as in the following example).

Kingston, S. (2017, September 5). [Letter to the editor]. *Globe and Mail.* Retrieved from
https://theglobeandmail.com/opinion/letters/sept-5-math-back-to-school
-plus-other-letters-to-the-editor/article36149806/

18. Editorial or other unsigned article

Getting aid with debt [Editorial]. (2018, September 5). *Chronicle Herald.* Retrieved from
http://thechronicleherald.ca/

19. Newsletter article   Cite as you would an article in a magazine, giving whatever publication information is available (volume, issue, page numbers, and so on).

Scrivener, L. (n.d.). Why is the minimum wage issue important for food justice
advocates? *Food Workers—Food Justice, 15.* Retrieved from http://www
.thedatabank.com/dpg/199/pm.asp?nav=1&ID=41429

20. Review   If the review has no author or title, use the description in brackets as the title.

author   year
of review   (journal)   book title
Chernus, L. A. (2014). [Review of the book *Therapist in mourning: From the faraway*
                                                              volume,
                        book author(s)   journal title issue page(s)
       nearby, by A. J. Adelman & K. J. Malawista]. *Psychotherapy, 51*(3), 464-465.

              DOI
     doi:10.1037/a0036509

              year + month + day
author   (online magazine)   review title
Romney, J. (2016, November 10). Film of the week: *Arrival* [Review of
                        year
              film title (film)   magazine title
       the motion picture *Arrival*, 2016]. *Film Comment*. Retrieved from

              URL
     http://www.filmcomment.com/

21. Published interview

Al-Jeraisy, H. (2016, January 8). An interview with a female Saudi councillor [Interview
       by Z. M. Beddoes]. *The Economist*. Retrieved from http://www.economist.com/

22. Article in a dictionary or an encyclopedia (including a wiki)

a. Print   See also item 28 on citing one volume in a multivolume work.

Konijn, E. A. (2015). Health communication. In W. Donsbach (Ed.), *The concise
       encyclopedia of communication* (Vol. 1, pp. 240-242). Malden, MA: Blackwell.

b. Web

Actor-network theory (ANT). (2011, February 22). In *STS wiki*. Retrieved December 10,
       2015, from http://www.stswiki.org/index.php?title=Actor-network_theory_(ANT)

23. Comment on an online article   If the writer's real name and screen name are both given, put the real name first, followed by the screen name in brackets. Before the title, use "Re" and a colon. Add "Comment" in brackets following the title.

Good Points. (2017, September 7). Re: Nunavut schools face a dark future [Comment].
       Nunatsiaq News. Retrieved from http://www.nunatsiaqonline.ca

24. Testimony before a legislative body

Goodman, J. (2013, June 27). *Addressing the neglected diseases treatment gap*. Testimony
before the Subcommittee on Africa, Global Health, Global Human Rights, and
International Organizations of the U.S. House of Representatives Committee on
Foreign Affairs. Retrieved from http://www.hhs.gov/asl/testify/2013/06/4484.html

Books and other long works

- Citation at a glance: Book, page 469

25. Basic format for a book

a. Print

author(s):
last name
+ initial(s)   year   book title   place of publication   publisher

Smith, B. (2016). *The valiant Nellie McClung.* Surrey, BC: Heritage House

b. Web (or online library)   Give the URL for the home page of the website or the online library.

author(s) or editor(s)   year   book title

Ansari, S., & Martin, V. (Eds.). (2014). *Women, religion, and culture in Iran.*
URL
Retrieved from http://books.google.com/

c. E-book   Give the version in brackets after the title ("Kindle version," "Nook version," and so on). Include the DOI or, if a DOI is not available, the URL for the home page of the site from which you downloaded the book.

Wolf, D. A., & Folbre, N. (Eds.). (2012). *Universal coverage of long-term care
in the United States* [Adobe Digital Editions version]. Retrieved from
https://www.russellsage.org/

d. Database   Give the URL for the database.

Bertz, N. (2015). *Diaspora and nation in the Indian Ocean: Transnational histories of race
and urban space in Tanzania.* Retrieved from http://muse.jhu.edu/

Citation at a glance: Book

To cite a print book in APA style, include the following elements:

1 Author(s)
2 Year of publication
3 Title and subtitle
4 Place of publication
5 Publisher

TITLE PAGE

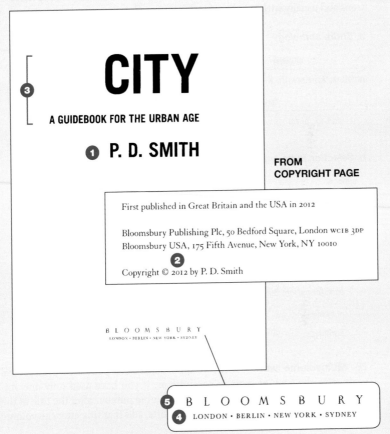

CITY

A GUIDEBOOK FOR THE URBAN AGE

1 P. D. SMITH

FROM COPYRIGHT PAGE

First published in Great Britain and the USA in 2012

Bloomsbury Publishing Plc, 50 Bedford Square, London WC1B 3DP
Bloomsbury USA, 175 Fifth Avenue, New York, NY 10010

2

Copyright © 2012 by P. D. Smith

B L O O M S B U R Y
LONDON · BERLIN · NEW YORK · SYDNEY

5 4 B L O O M S B U R Y
LONDON · BERLIN · NEW YORK · SYDNEY

REFERENCE LIST ENTRY FOR A PRINT BOOK

1	2	3	4	5

Smith, P. D. (2012). *City: A guidebook for the urban age*. London, England: Bloomsbury.

For more on citing books in APA style, see items 25–32.

26. Edition other than the first   Include the edition number (abbreviated) in parentheses after the title.

Harvey, P. (2013). *An introduction to Buddhism: Teachings, history, and practices*
(2nd ed.). Cambridge, England: Cambridge University Press.

27. Selection in an anthology or a collection   An anthology is a collection of works on a common theme, often with different authors for the selections and usually with an editor for the entire volume.

a. Entire anthology

editor(s)
year
Amelina, A., Horvath, K., & Meeus, B. (Eds.). (2016). *An anthology of migration*
title of anthology
place of
publication   publisher
and social transformation: European perspectives. Cham, Switzerland: Springer.

b. Selection in an anthology

author of
selection   year   title of selection
Abdou, L. H. (2016). The Europeanization of immigration policies. In A. Amelina,
editors of anthology   title of anthology
K. Horvath, & B. Meeus (Eds.), *An anthology of migration and social*
page numbers   place of
of selection   publication
transformation: European perspectives (pp. 105-119). Cham, Switzerland:
publisher
Springer.

28. Multivolume work   If the volumes have been published over several years, give the span of years in parentheses. If you have used only one volume of a multivolume work, indicate the volume number after the title of the complete work; if the volume has its own title, add that title after the volume number.

a. All volumes

Khalakdina, M. (2008-2011). *Human development in the Indian context: A socio-cultural*
focus (Vols. 1-2). New Delhi, India: Sage.

b. One volume, with title

Palmer, S., & Gyllensten, K. (Eds.). (2015). *Psychological stress, resilience, and wellbeing: Vol. 2. The measurement of stress*. London, England: Sage.

29. Introduction, preface, foreword, or afterword

Bloomberg, M. (2014). Foreword. In S. Goldsmith & S. Crawford, *The responsive city: Engaging communities through data-smart governing* (pp. v-vi). San Francisco, CA: Jossey-Bass.

30. Dictionary or other reference work

Leong, F. T. L. (Ed.). (2008). *Encyclopedia of counseling* (Vols. 1-4). Thousand Oaks, CA: Sage.

31. Republished book

Dickner, N. (2009). *Nikolski* (L. Lederhendler, Trans.). Toronto, ON: Vintage Canada. (Original work published 2005)

32. Book in a language other than English   Place the English translation, not italicized, in brackets.

Carminati, G. G., & Méndez, A. (2012). *Étapes de vie, étapes de soins* [Stages of life, stages of care]. Chêne-Bourg, Switzerland: Médecine & Hygiène.

33. Dissertation

a. Published

Moore, C. L. (2016). *Stress and oppression: Identifying possible protective factors for African American men* (Doctoral dissertation). Available from ProQuest Dissertations and Theses database. (AAT 3717844)

b. Unpublished

Morcos, S. M. (2015). *From Cairo to California: A journey through the lives and roles of Coptic women from Egypt to the diaspora* (Unpublished doctoral dissertation). Claremont Graduate University, Claremont, CA.

34. Conference proceedings

Shermer, T. C. (2016). *Proceedings of the 28th Canadian Conference on Computational Geometry*. Retrieved from http://cccg.ca/proceedings/2016/proceedings2016.pdf

35. Government document If the document has a number, place the number in parentheses after the title.

Statistics Canada. (2017). *Insights on Canadian society* (Catalogue No. 75-006-X). Retrieved from http://www.statcan.gc.ca/pub/75-006-x/75-006-x2017001-eng.htm

36. Report from a private organization If the publisher and the author are the same, begin with the publisher. For a print source, use "Author" as the publisher at the end of the entry (see item 4 on p. 460); for an online source, give the URL. If the report has a number, put it in parentheses following the title.

Ford Foundation International Fellowships Program. (2014, September). *Linking higher education and social change*. Retrieved from http://fordifp.net/portals/0 /IFP%20PDF/IFP%20Final%20Publication.pdf

37. Legal source The title of a court case is italicized in an in-text citation, but it is not italicized in the reference list.

Ritchie v. Canada (Attorney General), 2017 FCA 114. Retrieved from CanLII website: http://canlii.ca/t/h40qt

38. Sacred or classical text It is not necessary to list sacred works such as the Bible or the Qur'an or classical Greek and Roman works (such as the *Odyssey*) in your reference list. See item 19 on page 456 for how to cite these sources in the text of your paper.

Websites and parts of websites

- Citation at a glance: Section in a web document, page 474

39. Entire website Do not include an entire website in the reference list. Give the URL in parentheses when you mention it in the text of your paper. (See item 13 on p. 455.)

40. Document from a website List as many of the following elements as are available: author's name, publication date (or "n.d." if there is no date), title (in italics), publisher (if any), and URL. If the publisher is known and is not named as the author, include the publisher in your retrieval statement.

Badrunnesha, M., & Kwauk, C. (2015, December). *Improving the quality of girls' education in madrasa in Bangladesh*. Retrieved from Brookings Institution website: http://www.brookings.edu/research/papers/2015/12/05-bangladesh -girls-education-madrasa-badrunnesha

Indigenous and Northern Affairs Canada. (2017). *About Jordan's principle*. Retrieved from https://www.aadnc-aandc.gc.ca/eng/1334329827982/1334329861879

41. Section in a web document Cite as you would a chapter in a book or a selection in an anthology (see item 27b).

Pew Research Center. (2015, October 22). About the 2012 Current Population Survey. In *Self-employed workers and job creation*. Retrieved from http:// www.pewsocialtrends.org/2015/10/22/three-in-ten-u-s-jobs-are-held-by-the -self-employed-and-the-workers-they-hire

42. Blog post If the writer's real name and screen name are both given, put the real name first, followed by the screen name in brackets. Add the date of the post (or "n.d." if the post is undated). Place the label "Blog post" in brackets following the title of the post. If there is no title, use the bracketed material as the title. End with the URL for the post.

Costandi, M. (2015, April 9). Why brain scans aren't always what they seem [Blog post]. Retrieved from http://www.theguardian.com/science/neurophilosophy/2015 /apr/09/bold-assumptions-fmri

43. Blog comment Cite as a blog post, but add "Re" and a colon before the title of the original post and the label "Blog comment" in brackets.

mkt42. (2015, November 9). Re: Big data and the logic of consumerism [Blog comment]. Retrieved from https://www.insidehighered.com/blogs/library-babel-fish/big-data -and-logic-consumerism

Citation at a glance: Section in a web document

To cite a section in a web document in APA style, include the following elements:

1 Author(s)
2 Date of publication or most recent update ("n.d." if there is no date)
3 Title of section

4 Title of document
5 Publisher of website (if not named as author)
6 URL of section

WEB DOCUMENT CONTENTS PAGE

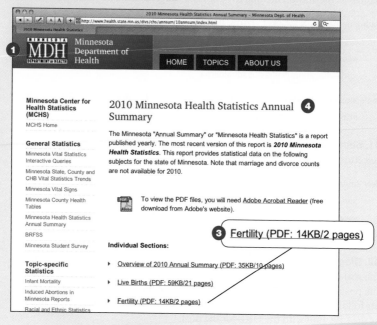

Minnesota Center for Health Statistics (MCHS)
MCHS Home

General Statistics
Minnesota Vital Statistics Interactive Queries
Minnesota State, County and CHB Vital Statistics Trends
Minnesota Vital Signs
Minnesota County Health Tables
Minnesota Health Statistics Annual Summary
BRFSS
Minnesota Student Survey

Topic-specific Statistics
Infant Mortality
Induced Abortions in Minnesota Reports
Racial and Ethnic Statistics

2010 Minnesota Health Statistics Annual Summary

The Minnesota "Annual Summary" or "Minnesota Health Statistics" is a report published yearly. The most recent version of this report is *2010 Minnesota Health Statistics*. This report provides statistical data on the following subjects for the state of Minnesota. Note that marriage and divorce counts are not available for 2010.

To view the PDF files, you will need Adobe Acrobat Reader (free download from Adobe's website).

3 Fertility (PDF: 14KB/2 pages)

Individual Sections:
▸ Overview of 2010 Annual Summary (PDF: 35KB/10 pages)
▸ Live Births (PDF: 59KB/21 pages)
▸ Fertility (PDF: 14KB/2 pages)

6 http://www.health.state.mn.us/divs/chs/annsum/10annsum/Fertility2010.pdf

ON-SCREEN VIEW OF DOCUMENT

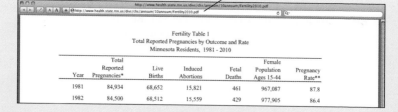

Fertility Table 1
Total Reported Pregnancies by Outcome and Rate
Minnesota Residents, 1981 - 2010

Year	Total Reported Pregnancies*	Live Births	Induced Abortions	Fetal Deaths	Female Population Ages 15-44	Pregnancy Rate**
1981	84,934	68,652	15,821	461	967,087	87.8
1982	84,500	68,512	15,559	429	977,905	86.4

REFERENCE LIST ENTRY FOR A SECTION IN A WEB DOCUMENT

    1   **2**   **3**   **4**

Minnesota Department of Health. (n.d.). Fertility. In *2010 Minnesota health statistics*
      4   **6**

    annual summary. Retrieved from http://www.health.state.mn.us/divs/chs
                      6

    /annsum/10annsum/Fertility2010.pdf

For more on citing documents from websites in APA style, see items 40 and 41.

Audio, visual, and multimedia sources

44. Podcast

Ekstrom, A. (2015, March). *The moral bias behind your search results* [Video podcast].
    Retrieved from TED on http://itunes.apple.com/

Abumrad, J., & Krulwich, R. (2015, August 30). *Remembering Oliver Sacks* [Audio
    podcast]. Retrieved from http://www.radiolab.org/

45. Video or audio on the web

Moffit, M., & Brown, G. (2017, July 6). *Are drugs good for you?* [Video file]. Retrieved
    from https://www.youtube.com/watch?v=I7AiQzedfxg

Bever, T., Piattelli-Palmarini, M., Hammond, M., Barss, A., & Bergesen, A. (2012,
    February 2). *A basic introduction to Chomsky's linguistics* [Audio file]. Retrieved
    from University of Arizona, College of Social & Behavioral Sciences, Department of
    Linguistics website: http://linguistics.arizona.edu/node/711

46. Transcript of an audio or a video file

Glass, I. (2015, April 24). *The incredible rarity of changing your mind* [Transcript of audio
    file No. 555]. In *This American life*. Retrieved from http://www.thisamericanlife.org/

47. Film (DVD, BD, or other format)
Give the director, producer, and other relevant contributors, followed by the year of the film's release and the title. In brackets, add a description of the medium: "Motion picture," "Video file," "DVD," "BD," and so on. For a motion picture or a DVD or BD, add the location where the film was made and the studio. If you retrieved the film from the web or used a streaming service, give the URL for the home page.

Cooper, S. (Director). (2015). *Black mass* [Motion picture]. Burbank, CA: Warner Bros.

Ross, G. (Director and Writer), & Collins, S. (Writer). (2012). *The hunger games*
    [Video file]. Retrieved from http://netflix.com/

475

48. Television or radio series or episode

Hawkins, N. (Producer). (2010). *Allen Gregg in conversation* [Television series]. Toronto, ON: TVO.

Hirsch, L. (Producer). (2015). ISIS in Afghanistan [Television series episode]. In M. Smith (Executive producer), *Frontline*. Retrieved from http://www.wgbh.org/

49. Music recording

Chibalonza, A. Jubilee. (2012). On *African voices* [CD]. Merenberg, Germany: ZYX Music.

African voices [CD]. (2012). Merenberg, Germany: ZYX Music.

50. Lecture, speech, or address

King, R. (2010, March 5). *From Manitoba to Matisse*. Lecture at the Winnipeg Art Gallery, Winnipeg, MB.

51. Data set or graphic representation of data (graph, chart, table)
Give information about the type of source in brackets following the title. If there is no title, give a brief description of the content of the source in brackets in place of the title. If the item is numbered in the source, indicate the number in parentheses after the title. If the graphic appears within a larger document, do not italicize the title of the graphic.

Statistics Canada. (2017, August 3). *Variance and bias* [Chart]. Retrieved from http://www.statcan.gc.ca/eng/dai/btd/variance_bias

Gallup. (2015). *Gallup worldwide research data collected from 2005-2015* [Data set]. Retrieved from http://www.gallup.com/services/177797/country-data-set-details.aspx

52. Mobile application software (app)
Begin with the developer of the app, if known (as in the second example). Add the label "Mobile application software" in brackets after the title of the program.

Instagram 7.12 [Mobile application software]. (2015). Retrieved from http://itunes.apple.com/

Quora, Inc. (2015). Quora 2.2.6 [Mobile application software]. Retrieved from http://play.google.com/

53. Video game   Begin with the creator of the video game, if known. Add the label "Video game" in brackets after the title of the program. If the game can be played on the web or was downloaded from the web, give the URL instead of publication information.

Big Blue Bubble. (2012). My singing monsters [Video game.] London, ON: Big Blue
    Bubble. Android.

Atom Entertainment. (2012). Edgeworld [Video game]. Retrieved from http://www
    .addictinggames.com/

54. Map

Ukraine [Map]. (2015). Retrieved from the University of Texas at Austin Perry-Castañeda
    Library Map Collection website: https://www.lib.utexas.edu/maps/ukraine.html

Syria: Mapping the conflict [Map]. (2015, July). Retrieved from http://www
    .bbc.com/news/world-middle-east-22798391

55. Advertisement

VMware [Advertisement]. (2012, September). *Harvard Business Review, 90*(9), 27.

56. Work of art or photograph

Van Halm, R. (2013). *Reversal* [Painting]. National Gallery of Canada, Ottawa, ON.

Whitten, J. (2015). *Soul map* [Painting]. Retrieved from http://www.walkerart.org/

Sabogal, J. (2015). *Los hijos of the revolution* [Outdoor mural]. San Francisco, CA.

57. Brochure or fact sheet

Ryerson University. (2017). *Manage your stress* [Brochure]. Retreived from
    http://www.ryerson.ca/healthandwellness/counselling/About/CSDC_Brochure/

World Health Organization. (2015, December). *Food safety* (No. 399) [Fact sheet].
    Retrieved from http://www.who.int/mediacentre/factsheets/fs399/en/

58. Press release

Urban Institute. (2012, October 11). Two studies address health policy on campaign trail
    [Press release]. Retrieved from http://www.urban.org/publications/901537.html

59. Presentation slides

Perry, M. (2015, September). *Eras in epidemiology* [Presentation slides]. Retrieved from
    http://acepidemiology.org/content/2015-presentation-slides

60. Lecture notes or other course materials Cite materials that your instructor has posted on the web as you would a web document or a section in a web document (see item 40 or 41). Cite other material from your instructor as personal communication in the text of your paper (see items 15 and 16 on p. 455).

Blum, R. (2011). Neurodevelopment in the first decade of life [Lecture notes and audio file]. In R. Blum & L. M. Blum, *Child health and development*. Retrieved from http://ocw.jhsph.edu/index.cfm/go/viewCourse/course/childhealth/coursePage /lectureNotes/

Personal communication and social media

61. Email Email messages, letters, and other personal communication are not included in the list of references. (See item 15 on p. 455 for citing these sources in the text of your paper.)

62. Online posting If an online posting is not archived, cite it as a personal communication in the text of your paper and do not include it in the list of references. If the posting is archived, give the URL and the name of the discussion list if it is not part of the URL.

McKinney, J. (2006, December 19). Adult education-healthcare partnerships [Electronic mailing list message]. Retrieved from http://www.nifl.gov/pipermail/healthliteracy /2006/000524.html

63. Social media post Use the author's real name, if it is given, and put the screen name in brackets. If only the screen name is known, begin with that name, not in brackets. Add the date of posting in parentheses (use "n.d." if the post has no date). For the title, include the entire post or a caption (up to forty words); use a description of the post if there is no title or caption. After the title, add a label such as "Tweet," "Facebook status update," or "Photograph" in brackets. Include the URL for the post. Provide a retrieval date only if the content is undated. Cite personal media posts that are not accessible to all readers as personal communication in the text of your paper (see item 15 on p. 455).

National Science Foundation. (2015, December 8). Simulation shows key to building powerful magnetic fields 1.usa.gov/1TZUiJ6 #supernovas #supercomputers [Tweet]. Retrieved from https://twitter.com/NSF/status/674352440582545413

U.S. Department of Education. (2015, December 10). We're watching President Obama sign the Every Student Succeeds Act [Facebook status update]. Retrieved from http://www.facebook.com/ED.gov/

APA-5 Manuscript format; sample research paper

The guidelines in this section are consistent with advice given in the *Publication Manual of the American Psychological Association*, 6th ed. (Washington, DC: APA, 2010), and with typical requirements for undergraduate papers.

APA-5a APA manuscript format

Formatting the paper

The guidelines on pages 479–81 in this section describe APA's recommendations for formatting the text of your paper. For guidelines on preparing the reference list, see pages 481–82.

Font If your instructor does not require a specific font, use one that is standard and easy to read (such as Times New Roman).

Title page Begin at the top left, with the words "Running head," followed by a colon and the title of your paper (shortened to no more than fifty characters) in all capital letters. Put the page number 1 at the right margin.

About halfway down the page, on separate lines, centre the full title of your paper, your name, and your school's name. At the bottom of the page, you may add the heading "Author Note," centred, followed by a brief paragraph that lists specific information about the course or department or provides acknowledgments or contact information. See page 483 for a sample title page.

Page numbers and running head Number all pages with arabic numerals (1, 2, 3, and so on) in the upper right corner one-half inch (1.25 cm) from the top of the page. At the left margin on the same line as the page number, type a running head consisting of the title of the paper (shortened to no more than fifty characters) in all capital letters. On the title page only, include the words "Running head" followed by a colon before the title. See pages 483–94.

Margins, line spacing, and paragraph indents Use margins of one inch (2.5 cm) on all sides of the page. Left-align the text.

Double-space throughout the paper. Indent the first line of each paragraph one-half inch (1.25 cm).

Capitalization, italics, and quotation marks In headings and in titles of works that appear in the text of the paper, capitalize all words of four letters or

LaunchPad macmillan learning **MODEL FOR APA-5**
1 Sample student paper

more (and all nouns, pronouns, verbs, adjectives, and adverbs of any length). Capitalize the first word following a colon if the word begins a complete sentence.

In the body of your paper, italicize the titles of books, journals, magazines, and other long works, such as websites. Use quotation marks around the titles of articles, short stories, and other short works.

NOTE: APA has different requirements for titles in the reference list. See page 482.

Long quotations   When a quotation is forty or more words, set it off from the text by indenting it one-half inch (1.25 cm) from the left margin. Double-space the quotation. Do not use quotation marks around it. (See p. 489 for an example. See also p. 446 for more information about integrating long quotations.)

Footnotes   To insert a footnote number in the text of your paper, place the number, raised above the line, immediately following any mark of punctuation except a dash. At the bottom of the page, begin the note with a one-half-inch (1.25 cm) indent and the superscript number corresponding to the number in the text. Insert an extra double-spaced line between the last line of text on the page and the footnote. Double-space the footnote.

Abstract and keywords   An abstract is a 150-to-250-word paragraph that provides readers with a quick overview of your essay. It should express your main idea and your key points; it might also briefly suggest any implications or applications of the research you discuss in the paper.

If your instructor requires one, include an abstract on a new page after the title page. Centre the word "Abstract" (in regular font, not boldface) one inch (2.5 cm) from the top of the page. Double-space the abstract and do not indent the first line.

An optional list of keywords follows the abstract; the keywords help readers search for a published paper on the web or in a database. On the line following the abstract, begin with the word "Keywords," italicized and indented one-half inch (1.25 cm), followed by a colon. Then list important words related to your paper. Check with your instructor for requirements in your course. (See p. 484 for an example of an abstract.)

Headings   Although headings are not always necessary, their use is encouraged in the social sciences. For most undergraduate papers, one level of heading is usually sufficient. (See pp. 486–92.)

First-level headings are centred and boldface. In research papers and laboratory reports, the major headings are "Method," "Results," and "Discussion." In other types of papers, the major headings should be informative and concise, conveying the structure of the paper. (The headings "Abstract" and "References" are not boldface.)

Second-level headings are left-aligned and boldface. Third-level headings are indented and boldface, followed by a period and the text on the same line.

In first- and second-level headings, capitalize the first and last words and all words of four or more letters (and nouns, pronouns, verbs, adjectives, and adverbs of any length). In third-level headings, capitalize only the first word, any proper nouns, and the first word after a colon.

First-Level Heading Centred

Second-Level Heading Aligned Left

Third-level heading indented. Text immediately follows.

Visuals (tables and figures)   APA classifies visuals as tables and figures. Tables display complex data in an efficient, easily understood way. Figures include graphs, charts, drawings, and photographs.

Label each table with an arabic numeral (Table 1, Table 2, and so on) and provide a clear title. Place the label and title on separate lines above the table, left-aligned and double-spaced. Type the table number in regular font; italicize the table title. (See a sample table on p. 487.)

If you have used data from an outside source or have taken or adapted the table from a source, give the source information in a note below the table. Begin with the word "Note," italicized and followed by a period. If any data in the table require an explanatory footnote, use a superscript lowercase letter in the table and in a footnote following the source note. Double-space source notes and footnotes; do not indent the first line of each note.

For each figure, place the figure number and a caption below the figure, left-aligned and double-spaced. Begin with the word "Figure" and an arabic numeral, both italicized, followed by a period. Place the caption, not italicized, on the same line. If you have taken or adapted the figure from an outside source, give the source information immediately following the caption. Use the term "From" or "Adapted from" before the source information.

In the text of your paper, discuss the most significant features of each visual. Place the visual as close as possible to the sentences that relate to it unless your instructor prefers that visuals appear in an appendix.

Preparing the list of references

Begin your list of references on a new page at the end of the paper. Centre the title "References" one inch (2.5 cm) from the top of the page. Double-space throughout. For a sample reference list, see pages 493–94.

Indenting entries   Type the first line of each entry at the left margin and indent any additional lines one-half inch (1.25 cm).

Alphabetizing the list   Alphabetize the reference list by the last names of the authors (or editors) or by the first word of an organization name (if the author is an organization). When a work has no author or editor, alphabetize by the first word of the title other than *A*, *An*, or *The*.

  If your list includes two or more works by the same author, arrange the entries by year, the earliest first. If your list includes two or more works by the same author in the same year, arrange the works alphabetically by title. Add the letters "a," "b," and so on within the parentheses after the year. For journal articles, use only the year and the letter: (2012a). For articles in magazines and newspapers, use the full date and the letter in the reference list: (2012a, July 7); use only the year and the letter in the in-text citation.

Authors' names   Invert all authors' names and use initials instead of first names. Separate the names with commas. For two to seven authors, use an ampersand (&) before the last author's name. For eight or more authors, give the first six authors, three ellipsis dots, and the last author (see item 3 on p. 457).

Titles of books and articles   In the reference list, italicize the titles and subtitles of books. Do not italicize or use quotation marks around the titles of articles. For both books and articles, capitalize only the first word of the title and subtitle (and all proper nouns). Capitalize names of journals, magazines, and newspapers as you would capitalize them normally (see P8-c).

Abbreviations for page numbers   Abbreviations for "page" and "pages" ("p." and "pp.") are used before page numbers of newspaper articles and selections in anthologies (see item 14 on p. 463 and item 27 on p. 470). Do not use "p." or "pp." before page numbers of articles in journals and magazines (see items 12 and 13 on pp. 462–63).

Breaking a URL or DOI   When a URL or a DOI (digital object identifier) must be divided, break it after a double slash or before any other mark of punctuation. Do not insert a hyphen; do not add a period at the end. If you will post your project online or submit it electronically and you want to include live URLs for readers to click on, do not insert any line breaks.

APA-5b Sample APA research paper

On the following pages is a research paper on the use of educational technology in the shift to student-centred learning, written by April Wang, a student in an education class. Wang's assignment was to write a literature review paper documented with APA-style citations and references.

Running head: TECHNOLOGY AND STUDENT-CENTERED LEARNING   1

A running head consists of a title (shortened to no more than fifty characters) in all capital letters. On the title page, it is preceded by the label "Running head." Page numbers appear in the upper right corner.

Technology and the Shift From Teacher-Delivered
to Student-Centered Learning:
A Review of the Literature
April Bo Wang
Glen County Community College

Full title, writer's name, and school name are centred halfway down the page.

Author Note
This paper was prepared for Education 107, taught by Professor
Gomez.

An author's note lists specific information about the course or department and can provide acknowledgments and contact information.

Marginal annotations indicate APA-style formatting and effective writing.

Abstract appears on a separate page. Heading is centred and not boldface.

Abstract

In recent decades, instructors and administrators have viewed student-centered learning as a promising pedagogical practice that offers both the hope of increasing academic performance and a solution for teacher shortages. Differing from the traditional model of instruction in which a teacher delivers content from the front of a classroom, student-centered learning puts the students at the center of teaching and learning. Students set their own learning goals, select appropriate resources, and progress at their own pace. Student-centered learning has produced both positive results and increases in students' self-esteem. Given the recent proliferation of technology in classrooms, school districts are poised for success in making the shift to student-centered learning. The question for district leaders, however, is how to effectively balance existing teacher talent with educational technology.

Keywords: digital learning, student-centered learning, personalized learning, education technology, transmissive, blended

Keywords (optional) help readers search for a paper on the web or in a database.

Technology and the Shift From Teacher-Delivered
to Student-Centered Learning:
A Review of the Literature

In the United States, most public school systems are struggling with teacher shortages, which are projected to worsen as the number of applicants to education schools decreases (Donitsa-Schmidt & Zuzovsky, 2014, p. 420). Citing federal data, *The New York Times* reported a 30% drop in "people entering teacher preparation programs" between 2010 and 2014 (Rich, 2015). Especially in science and math fields, the teacher shortage is projected to escalate in the next 10 years (Hutchison, 2012). In recent decades, instructors and administrators have viewed the practice of student-centered learning as one promising solution. Unlike traditional teacher-delivered (also called "transmissive") instruction, student-centered learning allows students to help direct their own education by setting their own goals and selecting appropriate resources for achieving those goals. Though student-centered learning might once have been viewed as an experimental solution in understaffed schools, it is gaining credibility as an effective pedagogical practice. What is also gaining momentum is the idea that technology might play a significant role in fostering student-centered learning. This literature review will examine three key questions:

1. In what ways is student-centered learning effective?
2. Can educational technology help students drive their own learning?
3. How can public schools effectively combine teacher talent and educational technology?

In the face of mounting teacher shortages, public schools should embrace educational technology that promotes student-centered learning in order to help all students become engaged and successful learners.

In What Ways Is Student-Centered Learning Effective?

According to the International Society for Technology in Education (2016), "Student-centered learning moves students from passive receivers of information to active participants in their own discovery process. What students learn, how they learn it, and how their learning is assessed are all driven by each individual student's needs and abilities." The results

Source provides background information and context.

Wang sets up her organization by posing three questions.

Wang states her thesis.

Headings, centred and boldface, help readers follow the organization.

Wang uses a source to define the key term *student-centered learning*.

of student-centered learning have been positive, not only for academic achievement but also for student self-esteem. In this model of instruction, the teacher acts as a facilitator, and the students actively participate in the process of learning and teaching. With guidance, students decide on the learning goals most pertinent to themselves, they devise a learning plan that will most likely help them achieve those goals, they direct themselves in carrying out that learning plan, and they assess how much they learned (Çubukçu, 2012). The major differences between student-centered learning and instructor-centered learning are summarized in Table 1.

Bell (2010) has argued that the chief benefit of student-centered learning is that it can connect students with "real-world tasks," thus making learning more engaging as well as more comprehensive. For example, Bell observed a group of middle-school students who wanted to build a social justice monument for their school. They researched social justice issues, selected several to focus on, and then designed a three-dimensional playground to represent those issues. In doing so, they achieved learning goals in the areas of social studies, physics, and mathematics and practiced research and teamwork. Bell reported that students engaged in this kind of learning performed better on both project-based assessments and standardized tests (pp. 39-40).

A Stanford study came to a similar conclusion; researchers examined four schools that had moved from teacher-driven instruction to student-centered learning (Friedlaender, Burns, Lewis-Charp, Cook-Harvey, & Darling-Hammond, 2014). The study focused on students from a mix of racial, cultural, and socioeconomic backgrounds, with varying levels of English-language proficiency. The researchers predicted that this mix of students, representing differing levels of academic ability, would benefit from a student-centered approach. Through interviews, surveys, and classroom observations, the researchers identified key characteristics of the new student-centered learning environments at the four schools:

- teachers who prioritized building relationships with students
- support structures for teachers to improve and collaborate on instruction
- a shift in classroom activity from lectures and tests to projects and performance-based assessments (pp. 5-7)

Because the author (Çubukçu) is not named in the signal phrase, the name and the date appear in parentheses.

When the author's name and year of publication are given in a signal phrase, only the page number or numbers, if available, are needed in parentheses at the end of the source material.

Wang summarizes an important article, providing parenthetical citations even for a summary.

TECHNOLOGY AND STUDENT-CENTERED LEARNING   5

Table 1

Comparison of Two Approaches to Teaching and Learning

Teaching and learning period	Instructor-centered approach	Student-centered approach
Before class	• Instructor prepares a lecture/instruction on a new topic. • Students complete homework on the previous topic.	• Students read and view new material, practice new concepts, and prepare questions ahead of class. • Instructor views student questions and practice and identifies learning opportunities.
During class	• Instructor delivers new material in a lecture or prepared discussion. • Students—unprepared—listen, watch, take notes, and try to follow along with the new material.	• Students lead discussions of the new material or practice applying the concepts or skills in an active environment. • Instructor answers student questions and provides immediate feedback.
After class	• Instructor grades homework and gives feedback about the previous lesson. • Students work independently to practice or apply the new concepts.	• Students apply the concepts/skills to more complex tasks, some of their own choosing, individually and in groups. • Instructor posts additional resources to help students.

Note. Adapted from "The Flipped Class Demystified," n.d., retrieved from New York University website: https://www.nyu.edu/faculty /teaching-and-learning-resources/instructional-technology-support /instructional-design-assessment/flipped-classes/the-flipped-class -demystified.html.

> Wang creates a table to compare and contrast two key concepts for her readers.

After the schools designed their curriculum to be personalized to individual students rather than standardized across a diverse student body and to be inclusive of skills such as persistence as well as traditional academic skills, students outperformed peers on state tests and increased their rates of high school and college graduation (Friedlaender et al., 2014, p. 3).

Can Educational Technology Help Students Drive Their Own Learning?

When students engage in self-directed learning, they rely less on teachers to deliver information and require less face-to-face time with teachers. For content delivery, many school districts have begun to use educational technology resources that, in recent years, have become more available, more affordable, and easier to use. For the purposes of this paper, the term "educational technology resources" encompasses the following: distance learning, by which students learn from a remote instructor online; other online education programming such as slide shows and video or audio lectures; interactive online activities, such as quizzing or games; and the use of computers, tablets, smartphones, SMART Boards, or other such devices for coursework.

Much like student-centered learning, the use of educational technology began in many places as a temporary measure to keep classes running despite teacher shortages. A Horn and Staker study (2011) examined the major patterns over time for students who subscribed to distance learning, for example. A decade ago, students who enrolled in distance learning often fell into one of the following categories: They lived in a rural community that had no alternative for learning; they attended a school where there were not enough qualified teachers to teach certain subjects; or they were homeschooled or homebound. But faced with tighter budgets, teacher shortages, increasingly diverse student populations, and rigorous state standards, schools recognized the need and the potential for distance learning across the board.

As the teacher shortage has intensified, educational technology resources have become more tailored to student needs and more affordable. Pens that convert handwritten notes to digital text and

---

When this article was first cited, all authors were named. In subsequent citations of a work with three to five authors, "et al." is used after the first author's name.

Wang develops her thesis.

In a signal phrase, the word "and" links the names of two authors; the date is given in parentheses.

organize them, backpacks that charge electronic devices, and apps that create audiovisual flash cards are just a few of the more recent innovations. According to Svokos (2015), College and Education Fellow for *The Huffington Post*, some educational technology resources entertain students while supporting student-centered learning:

> GlassLab, a nonprofit that was launched with grants from the Bill & Melinda Gates and MacArthur Foundations, creates educational games that are now being used in more than 6,000 classrooms across the country. Some of the company's games are education versions of existing ones—for example, its first release was SimCity EDU—while others are originals. Teachers get real-time updates on students' progress as well as suggestions on what topics students need to spend more time on.

Many of the companies behind these products offer institutional discounts to schools where such devices are used widely by students and teachers.

Horn and Staker (2011) concluded that the chief benefit of technological learning was that it could adapt to the individual student in a way that whole-class delivery by a single teacher could not. Their study examined various schools where technology enabled student-centered learning. For example, Carpe Diem High School in Yuma, Arizona, hired only six certified subject teachers and then outfitted its classrooms with 280 computers connected to online learning programs. The programs included software that offered "continual feedback, assessment, and incremental victory in a way that a face-to-face teacher with a class of 30 students never could. After each win, students continue to move forward at their own pace" (p. 9). Students alternated between personalized 55-minute courses online and 55-minute courses with one of the six teachers. The academic outcomes were promising. Carpe Diem ranked first in its county for student math and reading scores. Similarly, Rocketship Education, a charter network that serves low-income, predominantly Latino students, created a digital learning lab, reducing the need to hire more teachers. Rocketship's academic scores ranked in the top 15 of all California low-income public schools.

A quotation longer than forty words is indented without quotation marks.

Wang uses her own analysis to shape the conversation among her sources in this synthesis paragraph.

It is clear that educational technology will continue to play a role in student and school performance. Horn and Staker (2011) acknowledged that they focused on programs in which integration of educational technology led to improved student performance. In other schools, technological learning is simply distance learning—watching a remote teacher—and not student-centered learning that allows students to partner with teachers to develop enriching learning experiences. That said, many educators seem convinced that educational technology has the potential to help them transition from traditional teacher-driven learning to student-centered learning. All four schools in the Stanford study heavily relied on technology (Friedlaender et al., 2014). And indeed, Demski (2012) argued that technology is not supplemental but instead is "central" to student-centered learning (p. 33). Rather than turning to a teacher as the source of information, students are sent to investigate solutions to problems by searching online, e-mailing experts, collaborating with one another in a wiki space, or completing online practice. Rather than turning to a teacher for the answer to a question, students are driven to perform—driven to use technology to find those answers themselves.

How Can Public Schools Effectively Combine Teacher Talent and Educational Technology?

Some researchers have expressed doubt that schools are ready for student-centered learning—or any type of instruction—that is driven by technology. In a recent survey conducted by the Nellie Mae Education Foundation, Moeller and Reitzes (2011) reported not only that many teachers lacked confidence in their ability to incorporate technology in the classroom but that 43% of polled high school students said that they lacked confidence in their technological proficiency going into college and careers. The study concluded that technology alone would not improve learning environments. Yet others argued that students adapt quickly to even unfamiliar technology and use it to further their own learning. For example, Mitra (2013) caught the attention of the education world with his study of how to educate students in the slums of India. He installed an Internet-accessible

Wang uses a source to introduce a counterposition.

computer in a wall in a New Delhi urban slum and left it there with no instructions. Over a few months, many of the children had learned how to use the computer, how to access information over the Internet, how to interpret information, and how to communicate this information to one another. Mitra's experiment was "not about making learning happen. [It was] about letting it happen." He concluded that in the absence of teachers, even in developing countries less inundated by technology, a tool that allowed access to an organized database of knowledge (such as a search engine) was sufficient to provide students with a rewarding learning experience.

Brackets indicate Wang's change in the quoted material.

According to the Stanford study, however, the presence of teachers is still crucial (Friedlaender et al., 2014). Their roles will simply change from distributors of knowledge to facilitators and supporters of self-directed student-centered learning. The researchers asserted that teacher education and professional development programs can no longer prepare their teachers in a single instructional mode, such as teacher-delivered learning; they must instead equip teachers with a wide repertoire of skills to support a wide variety of student learning experiences. The Stanford study argued that since teachers would be partnering with students to shape the learning experience, rather than designing and delivering a curriculum on their own, the main job of a teacher would become relationship building. The teacher would establish a relationship with each student so that the teacher could support whatever learning the student pursues.

Many schools have already effectively paired a reduced faculty with educational technology to support successful student-centered learning. For example, Watson (2008) offered a case study of the Cincinnati Public Schools Virtual High School, which brought students together in a physical school building to work with an assortment of online learning programs. Although there were only 10 certified teachers in the building, students were able to engage in highly individualized instruction according to their own needs, strengths, and learning styles, using the 10 teachers as support (p. 7). Commonwealth Connections Academy (CCA), a public school in Pennsylvania, also brings students into a physical

TECHNOLOGY AND STUDENT-CENTERED LEARNING 10

school building to engage in digital curriculum. However, rather than having students identify their own learning goals and design their own curriculum around those goals, CCA uses educational technology as an assessment tool to identify areas of student weakness. It then partners students with teachers to address those areas (pp. 8-9).

Conclusion

The conclusion is objective in tone and presents answers to Wang's three organizational questions.

Public education faces the opportunity for a shift from the model of teacher-delivered instruction that has characterized American public schools since their foundation to a student-centered learning model. Not only has student-centered learning proved effective in improving student academic and developmental outcomes, but it can also synchronize with technological learning for widespread adaptability across schools. Because it relies on student direction rather than an established curriculum, student-centered learning supported by educational technology can adapt to the different needs of individual students and a variety of learning environments—urban and rural, well funded and underfunded. Similarly, when student-centered learning relies on technology rather than a corps of uniformly trained teachers, it holds promise for schools that would otherwise suffer from a lack of human or financial resources.

References

Bell, S. (2010). Project-based learning for the 21st century: Skills for the future. *The Clearing House, 83*(2), 39-43.

Çubukçu, Z. (2012). Teachers' evaluation of student-centered learning environments. *Education, 133*(1), 49-66.

Demski, J. (2012, January). This time it's personal. *THE Journal (Technological Horizons in Education), 39*(1), 32-36.

Donitsa-Schmidt, S., & Zuzovsky, R. (2014). Teacher supply and demand: The school level perspective. *American Journal of Educational Research, 2*(6), 420-429.

Friedlaender, D., Burns, D., Lewis-Charp, H., Cook-Harvey, C. M., & Darling-Hammond, L. (2014). Student-centered schools: Closing the opportunity gap [Research brief]. Retrieved from Stanford Center for Opportunity Policy in Education website: https://edpolicy.stanford .edu/sites/default/files/scope-pub-student-centered-research-brief.pdf

Horn, M. B., & Staker, H. (2011). The rise of K-12 blended learning. Retrieved from Innosight Institute website: http://www .christenseninstitute.org/wp-content/uploads/2013/04/The -rise-of-K-12-blended-learning.pdf

Hutchison, L. F. (2012). Addressing the STEM teacher shortage in American schools: Ways to recruit and retain effective STEM teachers. *Action in Teacher Education, 34*(5/6), 541-550.

International Society for Technology in Education. (2016). *Student-centered learning*. Retrieved from http://www.iste.org/standards/essential -conditions/student-centered-learning

Mitra, S. (2013, February). *Build a school in the cloud* [Video file]. Retrieved from https://www.ted.com/talks/sugata_mitra_build_a_school_in _the_cloud?language=en

Moeller, B., & Reitzes, T. (2011, July). Integrating technology with student- centered learning. Retrieved from Nellie Mae Education Foundation website: http://www.nmefoundation.org/research/personalization /integrating-technology-with-student-centered-learn

Rich, M. (2015, August 9). Teacher shortages spur a nationwide hiring scramble (credentials optional). *The New York Times*. Retrieved from http://www.nytimes.com/

List of references begins on a new page. Heading is centred and not boldface.

List is alphabetized by authors' last names. All authors' names are inverted.

The first line of an entry is at the left margin; subsequent lines indent 1/2" (or 1.25 cm).

Double-spacing is used throughout.

TECHNOLOGY AND STUDENT-CENTERED LEARNING 12

Svokos, A. (2015, May 7). 5 innovations from the past decade that
    aim to change the American classroom [Blog post]. Retrieved from
    http://www.huffingtonpost.com/2015/05/07/technology-changes
    -classrooms_n_7190910.html

Watson, J. (2008, January). *Blended learning: The convergence of online
    and face-to-face education*. Retrieved from North American Council
    for Online Learning website: http://www.inacol.org/wp-content
    /uploads/2015/02/NACOL_PP-BlendedLearning-lr.pdf

Directory to CMS-style notes and bibliography entries

CMS (*Chicago*) Papers

Most history instructors and some humanities instructors require you to document sources with footnotes or endnotes based on *The Chicago Manual of Style*, 17th ed. (Chicago: University of Chicago Press, 2017).

You face three main challenges when you write a paper that draws on sources: (1) supporting a thesis, (2) citing your sources and avoiding plagiarism, and (3) integrating quotations and other source material.

Examples in this section appear in CMS (*Chicago*) style and are drawn from one student's research on the Fort Pillow massacre, which occurred during the American Civil War. Sample pages from Ned Bishop's paper are on pages 529–34.

CMS-1 Supporting a thesis

Most assignments based on reading or research — such as those assigned in history or other humanities classes — ask you to form a thesis, or main idea, and to support that thesis with well-organized evidence.

CMS-1a Form a working thesis.

Once you have read a variety of sources, considered your issue from different perspectives, and chosen an entry point in the research conversation (see R1-b), you are ready to form a working thesis: a one-sentence (or occasionally a two-sentence) statement of your central idea. (See also C1-c.) Because it is a working, or tentative, thesis, you can remain flexible and revise it as your ideas develop. Ultimately, the thesis will express not just your opinion but your informed, reasoned answer to your research question (see R1-b). Here, for example, are student writer Ned Bishop's research question and working thesis statement.

> **RESEARCH QUESTION**
>
> To what extent was Confederate Major General Nathan Bedford Forrest responsible for the massacre of Union troops at Fort Pillow?

> **WORKING THESIS**
>
> By encouraging racism among his troops, Nathan Bedford Forrest was directly responsible for the massacre of Union troops at Fort Pillow.

Notice that the thesis expresses a view on a debatable issue — an issue about which intelligent, well-meaning people might disagree. The writer's job is to persuade such readers that this view is worth taking seriously. To read Ned Bishop's thesis in the context of his introduction, see page 530.

 LaunchPad ACTIVITIES FOR CMS-1
macmillan learning
2 Exercises

CMS-1b Organize your ideas.

The body of your paper will consist of evidence in support of your thesis. It will be useful to sketch an informal plan that helps you begin to organize your ideas. Ned Bishop, for example, used a simple outline to structure his ideas. In the paper, the points in the outline became headings that help readers follow his line of argument.

> What happened at Fort Pillow?
>
> Did Forrest order the massacre?
>
> Can Forrest be held responsible for the massacre?

CMS-1c Use sources to inform and support your argument.

Used thoughtfully, your source materials will make your argument more complex and convincing for readers. Sources can support your thesis by playing several different roles.

Providing background information or context

You can use facts and statistics to support generalizations or to establish the importance of your topic, as student writer Ned Bishop does near the beginning his paper.

> Fort Pillow, Tennessee, which sat on a bluff overlooking the Mississippi River, had been held by the Union for two years. It was garrisoned by 580 men, 292 of them from United States Colored Heavy and Light Artillery regiments, 285 from the white Thirteenth Tennessee Cavalry. Nathan Bedford Forrest commanded about 1,500 troops.[1]

Explaining terms or concepts

If readers are unlikely to be familiar with a word, a phrase, or an idea important to your topic, you must explain it for them. Quoting or paraphrasing a source can help you define terms and concepts clearly and concisely.

> The Civil War practice of giving no quarter to an enemy — in other words, "denying [an enemy] the right of survival" — defied Lincoln's mandate for humane and merciful treatment of prisoners.[9]

Supporting your claims

As you draft, make sure to back up your assertions with facts, examples, and other evidence from your research (see also A4-e). Ned Bishop, for example, uses an eyewitness report of the racially motivated violence perpetrated by Nathan Bedford Forrest's troops.

> The slaughter at Fort Pillow was no doubt driven in large part by racial hatred. . . . A Southern reporter traveling with Forrest makes clear that the discrimination was deliberate: "Our troops maddened by the excitement, shot down the ret[r]eating Yankees, and not until they had attained t[h]e water's edge and turned to beg for mercy, did any prisoners fall in [t]o our hands — Thus the whites received quarter, but the negroes were shown no mercy."[19]

Lending authority to your argument

Expert opinion can give weight to your argument (see also A4-e). But don't rely on experts to make your argument for you. Construct your argument in your own words and, when appropriate, cite the judgment of an authority in the field for support.

> Fort Pillow is not the only instance of a massacre or threatened massacre of black soldiers by troops under Forrest's command. Biographer Brian Steel Wills points out that at Brice's Cross Roads in June 1864, "black soldiers suffered inordinately" as Forrest looked the other way and Confederate soldiers deliberately sought out those they termed "the damned negroes."[21]

Anticipating and countering alternative interpretations

Do not ignore sources that seem contrary to your position or that offer arguments different from your own. Instead, use them to give voice to opposing points of view and alternative interpretations before you counter them (see A4-f). Your readers will often have opposing points of view in mind already, whether or not they agree with you. Ned Bishop, for example, presents conflicting evidence to acknowledge that some readers may give Nathan Bedford Forrest credit for stopping the massacre. In doing so, Bishop creates an opportunity to counter their objections and persuade those readers that Forrest can be held accountable.

> Hurst suggests that the temperamental Forrest "may have ragingly ordered a massacre and even intended to carry it out — until he rode inside the fort and viewed the horrifying result" and ordered it stopped.[15] While this is an intriguing interpretation of events, even Hurst would probably admit that it is merely speculation.

CMS-2 Citing sources; avoiding plagiarism

In a research paper, you will draw on the work of other writers, and you must document their contributions by citing your sources. Sources are cited for two reasons:

1. to tell readers where your information comes from — so that they can assess its reliability and, if interested, find and read the original source
2. to give credit to the writers from whom you have borrowed words and ideas

You must cite anything you borrow from a source, including direct quotations; statistics and other specific facts; visuals such as tables, graphs, and diagrams; and any ideas you present in a summary or paraphrase. Borrowing another writer's language, sentence structures, or ideas without proper acknowledgment is a form of dishonesty known as *plagiarism*. The only exception is common knowledge — information that your readers may know or could easily locate in any number of reference sources.

CMS-2a Use the CMS (*Chicago*) system for citing sources.

CMS citations consist of superscript numbers in the text of the paper that refer readers to notes with corresponding numbers either at the foot of the page (footnotes) or at the end of the paper (endnotes).

TEXT

Governor John Andrew was not allowed to recruit black soldiers from out of state. "Ostensibly," writes Peter Burchard, "no recruiting was done outside Massachusetts, but it was an open secret that Andrew's agents were working far and wide."[1]

NOTE

1. Peter Burchard, *One Gallant Rush: Robert Gould Shaw and His Brave Black Regiment* (New York: St. Martin's, 1965), 85.

For detailed advice on using CMS-style notes, see CMS-4. When you use footnotes or endnotes, you will usually need to provide a bibliography as well.

BIBLIOGRAPHY ENTRY

Burchard, Peter. *One Gallant Rush: Robert Gould Shaw and His Brave Black Regiment.* New York: St. Martin's, 1965.

 LaunchPad macmillan learning **ACTIVITIES FOR CMS-2**
7 Exercises

CMS-2b Understand what plagiarism is.

Your research paper is a collaboration between you and your sources. To be fair and ethical, you must acknowledge your debt to the writers of those sources. Failure to do so is a form of academic dishonesty known as *plagiarism*.

Three different acts are generally considered plagiarism: (1) failing to cite quotations and borrowed ideas, (2) failing to enclose borrowed language in quotation marks, and (3) failing to put summaries and paraphrases in your own words. Definitions of plagiarism may vary; it's a good idea to find out how your school defines and addresses academic dishonesty.

CMS-2c Use quotation marks around borrowed language.

To indicate that you are using a source's exact phrases or sentences, you must enclose them in quotation marks unless they have been set off from the text by indenting (see p. 504). To omit the quotation marks is to claim — falsely — that the language is your own. Such an omission is plagiarism even if you have cited the source.

ORIGINAL SOURCE

For many Southerners it was psychologically impossible to see a black man bearing arms as anything but an incipient slave uprising complete with arson, murder, pillage, and rapine.

— Dudley Taylor Cornish, *The Sable Arm*, p. 158

PLAGIARISM

According to Civil War historian Dudley Taylor Cornish, for many Southerners it was psychologically impossible to see a black man bearing arms as anything but an incipient slave uprising complete with arson, murder, pillage, and rapine.[2]

BORROWED LANGUAGE IN QUOTATION MARKS

According to Civil War historian Dudley Taylor Cornish, "For many Southerners it was psychologically impossible to see a black man bearing arms as anything but an incipient slave uprising complete with arson, murder, pillage, and rapine."[2]

NOTE: Long quotations are set off from the text by indenting and do not need quotation marks (see the example on p. 504).

CMS-2d Put summaries and paraphrases in your own words.

Summaries and paraphrases are written in your own words. A summary condenses information; a paraphrase conveys the information using roughly the same number of words as in the original source. When you summarize or paraphrase, it is not enough to name the source; you must present the source's meaning using your own language and sentence structure. (See also R2-c.)

You commit plagiarism if you *patchwrite* — half-copy the author's sentences, either by mixing the author's phrases with your own without using quotation marks or by plugging your own synonyms into the author's sentence structure.

The first paraphrase of the following source is plagiarized — even though the source is cited — because too much of its language is borrowed from the original. The highlighted strings of words have been copied exactly (without quotation marks). In addition, the writer has closely followed the sentence structure of the original source, merely making a few substitutions (such as *Fifty percent* for *Half* and *angered and perhaps frightened* for *enraged and perhaps terrified*).

ORIGINAL SOURCE

Half of the force holding Fort Pillow were Negroes, former slaves now enrolled in the Union Army. Toward them Forrest's troops had the fierce, bitter animosity of men who had been educated to regard the colored race as inferior and who for the first time had encountered that race armed and fighting against white men. The sight enraged and perhaps terrified many of the Confederates and aroused in them the ugly spirit of a lynching mob.
— Albert Castel, "The Fort Pillow Massacre," pp. 46–47

PLAGIARISM: UNACCEPTABLE BORROWING

Albert Castel suggests that much of the brutality at Fort Pillow can be traced to racial attitudes. Fifty percent of the troops holding Fort Pillow were Negroes, former slaves who had joined the Union Army. Toward them Forrest's soldiers displayed the savage hatred of men who had been taught the inferiority of blacks and who for the first time had confronted them armed and fighting against white men. The vision angered and perhaps frightened the Confederates and aroused in them the ugly spirit of a lynching mob.[3]

To avoid plagiarizing an author's language, resist the temptation to look at the source while you are summarizing or paraphrasing. After you have read the passage you want to paraphrase, set the source aside. Ask yourself, "What is the author's meaning?" In your own words, state your understanding of the author's basic point. Return to the source and check that you haven't used the author's language or sentence structure or misrepresented the author's ideas. Following these steps will help you avoid plagiarizing the source. When you fully understand another writer's meaning, you can more easily and accurately present those ideas in your own words.

ACCEPTABLE PARAPHRASE

Albert Castel suggests that much of the brutality at Fort Pillow can be traced to racial attitudes. Nearly half of the Union troops were blacks, men whom the Confederates had been raised to consider their inferiors. The shock and perhaps fear of facing armed ex-slaves in battle for the first time may well have unleashed the fury that led to the massacre.[3]

CMS-3 Integrating sources

Quotations, summaries, paraphrases, and facts will support your argument, but they cannot speak for you. You can use several strategies to integrate information from research sources into your paper while maintaining your own voice.

CMS-3a Use quotations appropriately.

Keep the emphasis on your ideas; use your own words to summarize and to paraphrase your sources and to explain your points. Sometimes, however, quotations can be the most effective way to integrate a source.

WHEN TO USE QUOTATIONS

- When language is especially vivid or expressive
- When exact wording is needed for technical accuracy
- When it is important to let the debaters of an issue explain their positions in their own words
- When the words of an authority lend weight to an argument
- When the language of a source is the topic of your discussion (as in an analysis or interpretation)

Limiting your use of quotations

Although it is tempting to insert many quotations in your paper and to use your own words only for connecting passages, do not quote excessively. It is almost impossible to integrate numerous quotations smoothly into your own text.

It is not always necessary to quote full sentences from a source. To reduce your reliance on the words of others, you can often integrate language from a source into your own sentence structure.

> As Hurst has pointed out, until "an outcry erupted in the Northern press," even the Confederates did not deny that there had been a massacre at Fort Pillow.[4]

> Union surgeon Dr. Charles Fitch testified that after he was in custody, he "saw" Confederate soldiers "kill every negro that made his appearance dressed in Federal uniform."[20]

Using the ellipsis mark

To condense a quoted passage, you can use the ellipsis mark (three periods, with spaces between) to indicate that you have left words out. What remains must be grammatically complete.

> Union surgeon Fitch's testimony that all women and children had been evacuated from Fort Pillow before the attack conflicts with Forrest's report: "We captured . . . about 40 negro women and children."[6]

The writer has omitted several words not relevant to the issue at hand: *164 Federals, 75 negro troops, and.*

When you want to leave out one or more full sentences, use a period before the three ellipsis dots. For an example, see the long quotation on page 504.

Ordinarily, do not use an ellipsis mark at the beginning or at the end of a quotation. Readers will understand that you have taken the quoted material from a longer passage, so such marks are not necessary. The only exception occurs when you have dropped words at the end of the final quoted sentence. In such cases, put three ellipsis dots before the closing quotation mark.

Using sources responsibly: Make sure omissions and ellipsis marks do not distort the meaning of your source.

Using brackets

Brackets allow you to insert your own words into quoted material to explain a confusing reference or to keep a sentence grammatical in the context of your own writing.

> According to Albert Castel, "It can be reasonably argued that he [Forrest] was justified in believing that the approaching steamships intended to aid the garrison [at Fort Pillow]."[7]

NOTE: Use the word *sic*, italicized and in brackets, to indicate that an error in a quoted sentence appears in the original source. (An example appears on page 504.) Do not overuse *sic* to call attention to errors in a source. Sometimes paraphrasing is a better option. (See p. 286.)

Setting off long quotations

CMS style allows you some flexibility in deciding whether to set off a long quotation or run it into your text. For emphasis, you may want to set off a quotation of more than four or five typed lines of text; almost certainly you should set off quotations of ten or more lines. To set off a quotation, indent it one-half inch (1.25 cm) from the left margin and use the normal right margin. Double-space the indented quotation.

Long quotations should be introduced by an informative sentence, usually followed by a colon. Quotation marks are unnecessary because the indented format tells readers that the passage is taken word-for-word from the source.

> In a letter home, Confederate officer Achilles V. Clark recounted what happened at Fort Pillow:
>
> > Words cannot describe the scene. The poor deluded negroes would run up to our men fall upon their knees and with uplifted hands scream for mercy but they were ordered to their feet and then shot down. The whitte [*sic*] men fared but little better. . . . I with several others tried to stop the butchery and at one time had partially succeeded, but Gen. Forrest ordered them shot down like dogs, and the carnage continued.[8]

CMS-3b Use signal phrases to integrate sources.

Whenever you include a paraphrase, summary, or direct quotation of another writer's work in your paper, prepare your readers for it with a *signal phrase*. A signal phrase names the author of the source and often provides some context for the source material.

When you write a signal phrase, choose a verb that is appropriate for the way you are using the source (see CMS-1c). Are you providing background, explaining a concept, supporting a claim, lending authority, or refuting an argument? By choosing an appropriate verb, you can make your source's role clear. See the chart on page 506 for a list of verbs commonly used in signal phrases.

Note that CMS style calls for verbs in the present tense or present perfect tense (*points out* or *has pointed out*) to introduce source material unless you include a date that specifies the time of the original author's writing.

The first time you mention an author, use the full name: *Shelby Foote argues. . . .* When you refer to the author again, you may use the last name only: *Foote raises an important question.*

Marking boundaries

Readers should be able to move from your own words to the words of a source without feeling a jolt. Avoid dropping quotations into your text without warning. Instead, provide clear signal phrases, usually including the author's name, to indicate the boundary between your words and the source's words. (The signal phrase is highlighted in the second example.)

DROPPED QUOTATION

Not surprisingly, those testifying on the Union and Confederate sides recalled events at Fort Pillow quite differently. Unionists claimed that their troops had abandoned their arms and were in full retreat. "The Confederates, however, all agreed that the Union troops retreated to the river with arms in their hands."[9]

QUOTATION WITH SIGNAL PHRASE

Not surprisingly, those testifying on the Union and Confederate sides recalled events at Fort Pillow quite differently. Unionists claimed that their troops had abandoned their arms and were in full retreat. "The Confederates, however," writes historian Albert Castel, "all agreed that the Union troops retreated to the river with arms in their hands."[9]

Using signal phrases with summaries and paraphrases

As with quotations, you should introduce most summaries and paraphrases with a signal phrase that mentions the author and places the material in the context of your own writing. Readers will then understand where the summary or paraphrase begins.

Without the signal phrase (highlighted) in the following example, readers might think that only the last sentence is being cited, when in fact the whole paragraph is based on the source.

According to Jack Hurst, official Confederate policy was that black soldiers were to be treated as runaway slaves; in addition, the Confederate Congress decreed that white Union officers commanding black troops be killed. Confederate Lieutenant General Kirby Smith went one step further, declaring that he would kill all captured black troops. Smith's policy never met with strong opposition from the Richmond government.[10]

Integrating statistics and other facts

When you are citing a statistic or another specific fact, a signal phrase is often not necessary. In most cases, readers will understand that the citation refers to the statistic or fact (not the whole paragraph).

Of 295 white troops garrisoned at Fort Pillow, 168 were taken prisoner. Black troops fared worse, with only 58 of 262 captured and most of the rest presumably killed or wounded.[12]

There is nothing wrong, however, with using a signal phrase to introduce a statistic or another fact.

Shelby Foote notes that of 295 white troops garrisoned at Fort Pillow, 168 were taken prisoner but that black troops fared worse, with only 58 of 262 captured and most of the rest presumably killed or wounded.[12]

Using signal phrases in CMS papers

To avoid monotony, try to vary both the language and the placement of your signal phrases.

Model signal phrases

In the words of historian James M. McPherson, "..."[1]

As Dudley Taylor Cornish has argued, "..."[2]

In a letter to his wife, a Confederate soldier who witnessed the massacre wrote that "..."[3]

"...," claims Benjamin Quarles.[4]

"...," writes Albert Castel, "..."[5]

Shelby Foote offers an intriguing interpretation: "..."[6]

Verbs in signal phrases

admits	compares	insists	rejects
agrees	confirms	notes	reports
argues	contends	observes	responds
asserts	declares	points out	suggests
believes	denies	reasons	thinks
claims	emphasizes	refutes	writes

Putting source material in context

Readers should not have to guess why source material appears in your paper. A signal phrase can help you make the connection between your own ideas and those of another writer by setting up how a source will contribute to your paper (see R3).

If you use another writer's words, you must explain how they relate to your point. It's a good idea to embed a quotation between sentences of your own. In addition to introducing it with a signal phrase, follow it with interpretive comments that link the source material to your paper's argument.

QUOTATION WITH EFFECTIVE CONTEXT

In a respected biography of Nathan Bedford Forrest, Hurst suggests that the temperamental Forrest "may have ragingly ordered a massacre and even intended to carry it out—until he rode inside the fort and viewed the horrifying result" and ordered it stopped.[11] While this is an intriguing interpretation of events, even Hurst would probably admit that it is merely speculation.

NOTE: When you bring other sources into a conversation about your research topic, you are synthesizing. For more on synthesis, see MLA-3d.

CMS-4 Documenting sources

In history and some other humanities courses, you may be asked to use the documentation system of *The Chicago Manual of Style*, 17th ed. (Chicago: University of Chicago Press, 2017). In CMS style, superscript numbers (like this[1]) in the text of the paper refer readers to notes with corresponding numbers either at the foot of the page (footnotes) or at the end of the paper (endnotes). A bibliography is often required as well; it appears at the end of the paper and gives publication information for all the works cited in the notes.

TEXT

As Jack Hurst points out and Forrest must have known, in this twenty-minute battle, "Federals running for their lives had little time to concern themselves with a flag."[6]

FOOTNOTE OR ENDNOTE

6. Jack Hurst, *Nathan Bedford Forrest: A Biography* (New York: Knopf, 1993), 174.

BIBLIOGRAPHY ENTRY

Hurst, Jack. *Nathan Bedford Forrest: A Biography*. New York: Knopf, 1993.

CMS-4a First and later notes for a source

The first time you cite a source, the note should include publication information for that work as well as the page number for the passage you are citing.

1. Peter Burchard, *One Gallant Rush: Robert Gould Shaw and His Brave Black Regiment* (New York: St. Martin's, 1965), 85.

For later references to a source you have already cited, you may simply give the author's last name, a short form of the title, and the page or pages cited. A short form of the title of a book or another long work is italicized; a short form of the title of an article or another short work is put in quotation marks.

4. Burchard, *One Gallant Rush*, 31.

When you have two notes in a row from the same source, give the author's last name and the page or pages cited.

6. Jack Hurst, *Nathan Bedford Forrest: A Biography* (New York: Knopf, 1993), 174.

7. Hurst, 182.

 LaunchPad ACTIVITIES FOR CMS-4
macmillan learning 9 Exercises

CMS-4b CMS-style bibliography

A bibliography at the end of your paper lists the works you have cited in your notes; it may also include works you consulted but did not cite. See pages 527–28 for how to construct the list; see page 534 for a sample bibliography.

NOTE: If you include a bibliography, *The Chicago Manual of Style* suggests that you shorten all notes, including the first reference to a source, as described at the bottom of page 507. Check with your instructor, however, to see whether using an abbreviated note for a first reference to a source is acceptable.

CMS-4c Model notes and bibliography entries

The following models are consistent with guidelines in *The Chicago Manual of Style*, 17th ed. For each type of source, a model note appears first, followed by a model bibliography entry. The note shows the format you should use when citing a source for the first time. For subsequent, or later, citations of a source, use shortened notes (see p. 507).

Some sources on the web, typically periodical articles, use a permanent locator called a digital object identifier (DOI). Use the DOI, when it is available, in place of a URL in your citations.

When a URL or a DOI must break across lines, do not insert a hyphen or break at a hyphen if the URL or DOI contains one. Instead, break after a colon or a double slash or before any other mark of punctuation.

General guidelines for listing authors

1. One author

1. Thomas King, *The Inconvenient Indian: A Curious Account of Native People in North America* (Toronto: Doubleday Canada, 2012), 35.

King, Thomas. *The Inconvenient Indian: A Curious Account of Native People in North America*. Toronto: Doubleday Canada, 2012.

2. Two or three authors
For a work with two or three authors, give all authors' names in both the note and the bibliography entry.

2. Gabriel Filippi with Brett Popplewell, *The Escapist: Cheating Death on the World's Highest Mountains* (Toronto: HarperCollins Canada, 2016), 73.

Filippi, Gabriel, with Brett Popplewell. *The Escapist: Cheating Death on the World's Highest Mountains*. Toronto: HarperCollins Canada, 2016.

3. Four or more authors For a work with four or more authors, in the note give the first author's name followed by "et al." (for "and others"); in the bibliography entry, list all authors' names.

3. Lynn Hunt et al., *The Making of the West: Peoples and Cultures*, 5th ed. (Boston: Bedford/St. Martin's, 2015), 541.

Hunt, Lynn, Thomas R. Martin, Barbara H. Rosenwein, and Bonnie G. Smith. *The Making of the West: Peoples and Cultures*. 5th ed. Boston: Bedford/St. Martin's, 2015.

4. Organization as author

4. Policy Horizons Canada, *The Future of Asia* (Ottawa: Her Majesty the Queen in Right of Canada, 2014), 13.

Policy Horizons Canada. *The Future of Asia*. Ottawa: Her Majesty the Queen in Right of Canada, 2014.

5. Unknown author

5. *The Men's League Handbook on Women's Suffrage* (London, 1912), 23.

The Men's League Handbook on Women's Suffrage. London, 1912.

6. Multiple works by the same author In the bibliography, arrange the entries alphabetically by title. Use six hyphens in place of the author's name in the second and subsequent entries.

Clarke, Tony. *Getting to Zero: Canada Confronts Global Warming*. Toronto: Lorimer, 2017.

------. *Tar Sands Showdown: Canada and the New Politics of Oil in an Age of Climate Change*. Toronto: Lorimer, 2008.

7. Editor

7. Jodi Lee Aoki, ed., *Revisiting "Our Forest Home": The Immigrant Letters of Frances Stewart* (Toronto: Dundurn Press, 2011), 45.

Aoki, Jodi Lee, ed. *Revisiting "Our Forest Home": The Immigrant Letters of Frances Stewart*. Toronto: Dundurn Press, 2011.

8. Editor with author

8. Susan Sontag, *As Consciousness Is Harnessed to Flesh: Journals and Notebooks, 1964-1980*, ed. David Rieff (New York: Farrar, Straus and Giroux, 2012), 265.

Sontag, Susan. *As Consciousness Is Harnessed to Flesh: Journals and Notebooks, 1964-1980*. Edited by David Rieff. New York: Farrar, Straus and Giroux, 2012.

9. Translator with author

9. Karin Wieland, *Dietrich and Riefenstahl: Hollywood, Berlin, and a Century in Two Lives*, trans. Shelley Frisch (New York: Liveright, 2015), 52.

Wieland, Karin. *Dietrich and Riefenstahl: Hollywood, Berlin, and a Century in Two Lives*. Translated by Shelley Frisch. New York: Liveright, 2015.

Books and other long works

- Citation at a glance: Book, page 511

10. Basic format for a book

a. Print

10. Tony Robinson-Smith, *The Dragon Run: Two Canadians, Ten Bhutanese, One Stray Dog* (Edmonton: University of Alberta Press, 2017), 63.

Robinson-Smith, Tony. *The Dragon Run: Two Canadians, Ten Bhutanese, One Stray Dog.* Edmonton: University of Alberta Press, 2017.

b. E-book

10. Atul Gawande, *Being Mortal: Medicine and What Matters in the End* (New York: Metropolitan, 2014), chap. 3, NOOK.

Gawande, Atul. *Being Mortal: Medicine and What Matters in the End.* New York: Metropolitan, 2014. NOOK.

c. Web (or online library)

10. Charles Hursthouse, *New Zealand, or Zealandia, the Britain of the South* (1857; Hathi Trust Digital Library, n.d.), 2:356, http://catalog.hathitrust.org /Record/006536666.

Hursthouse, Charles. *New Zealand, or Zealandia, the Britain of the South.* 2 vols. 1857. Hathi Trust Digital Library, n.d. http://catalog.hathitrust .org/Record/006536666.

11. Edition other than the first

11. Judy Root Aulette and Judith Wittner, *Gendered Worlds*, 3rd ed. (Oxford: Oxford University Press, 2015), 86.

Aulette, Judy Root, and Judith Wittner. *Gendered Worlds.* 3rd ed. Oxford: Oxford University Press, 2015.

12. Volume in a multivolume work   If each volume has its own title, give the volume title first, followed by the volume number and the title of the entire work, as in the following examples. If the volumes do not have individual titles, give the volume and page number in the note (for example, 2:356) and the total number of volumes in the bibliography entry (see item 10c).

12. Robert A. Caro, *The Years of Lyndon Johnson,* vol 4, *The Passage of Power* (New York: Knopf, 2012), 198.

Caro, Robert A. *The Passage of Power.* Vol. 4 of *The Years of Lyndon Johnson.* New York: Knopf, 2012.

13. Work in an anthology or a collection

13. Heather O'Neil, "A Story Without Words," in *Finding the Words: Writers on Inspiration, Desire, War, Celebrity, Exile, and Breaking the Rules,* ed. Jared Bland (Toronto: McClelland & Stewart, 2011), 9.

O'Neil, Heather. "A Story Without Words." In *Finding the Words: Writers on Inspiration, Desire, War, Celebrity, Exile, and Breaking the Rules,* edited by Jared Bland, 7-21. Toronto: McClelland & Stewart, 2011.

Citation at a glance: Book

To cite a print book in CMS style, include the following elements:

1   Author(s)
2   Title and subtitle
3   City of publication

4   Publisher
5   Year of publication
6   Page number(s) cited
    (for notes)

TITLE PAGE

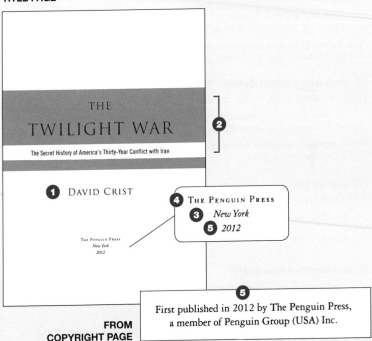

THE
TWILIGHT WAR
The Secret History of America's Thirty-Year Conflict with Iran

1 DAVID CRIST

THE PENGUIN PRESS
New York
2012

4 THE PENGUIN PRESS
3 New York
5 2012

5
First published in 2012 by The Penguin Press,
a member of Penguin Group (USA) Inc.

**FROM
COPYRIGHT PAGE**

NOTE

    1   **2**

1. David Crist, *The Twilight War: The Secret History of America's Thirty-Year Conflict*

   2   **3**   **4**   **5** **6**

with Iran (New York: Penguin Press, 2012), 354.

BIBLIOGRAPHY

  1   **2**

Crist, David. *The Twilight War: The Secret History of America's Thirty-Year Conflict with*

     2   **3**   **4**   **5**

Iran. New York: Penguin Press, 2012.

For more on citing books in CMS style, see items 10–17.

14. Introduction, preface, foreword, or afterword

14. Diane Brown, foreword to *Out of Concealment: Female Supernatural Beings of Haida Gwaii,* by Terri-Lynn Williams-Davidson (Surrey, BC: Heritage Press, 2017), xiii.

Brown, Diane. Foreword to *Out of Concealment: Female Supernatural Beings of Haida Gwaii,* by Terri-Lynn Williams-Davidson, xii-xix. Surrey, BC: Heritage Press, 2017.

15. Republished book

15. Arthur M. Okun, *Equality and Efficiency: The Big Tradeoff* (1975; repr., Washington, DC: Brookings Institution Press, 2015), 26.

Okun, Arthur M. *Equality and Efficiency: The Big Tradeoff.* 1975. Reprint, Washington, DC: Brookings Institution Press, 2015.

16. Book with a title in its title   Use quotation marks around any title, whether a long or a short work, within an italicized title.

16. Noel Merino, ed., *Wilderness Adventure in Jon Krakauer's "Into the Wild"* (Detroit, MI: Greenhaven Press, 2015), 47.

Merino, Noel, ed. *Wilderness Adventure in Jon Krakauer's "Into the Wild."* Detroit, MI: Greenhaven Press, 2015.

17. Sacred text   Sacred texts such as the Bible are usually not included in the bibliography.

17. Matt. 20:4-9 (Revised Standard Version).

17. Qur'an 18:1-3.

18. Government document

18. Canada House of Commons, Standing Committee on Natural Resources, *De-Risking the Adoption of Clean Technology in Canada's Natural Resources Sector,* 42nd Parl., 1st sess. (Ottawa: Parliament of Canada, 2017), 26.

Canada House of Commons. Standing Committee on Natural Resources. *De-Risking the Adoption of Clean Technology in Canada's Natural Resources Sector,* 42nd Parl., 1st sess. Ottawa: Parliament of Canada, 2017.

19. Published proceedings of a conference   Cite as a book, adding the location and dates of the conference after the title.

19. Patrícia Dias da Silva and Artur de Matos Alves, eds., *Proceedings of the Technology and Emerging Media (TEM) Interest Group of the Canadian Communication Association,* University of Ottawa, June 3-5, 2016 (Ottawa: Canadian Communication Association, 2017), 12.

Dias da Silva, Patrícia, and Artur de Matos Alves, eds. *Proceedings of the Technology and Emerging Media (TEM) Interest Group of the Canadian Communication Association.* University of Ottawa, June 3-5, 2016. Ottawa: Canadian Communication Association, 2017.

20. Source quoted in another source (a secondary source) Sometimes you will want to use a quotation from one source that you have found in another source. In your note and bibliography entry, cite whatever information is available about the original source of the quotation, including a page number. Then add the words "quoted in" and give publication information for the source in which you found the words. In the following examples, author John Matteson quotes the words of Thomas Wentworth Higginson. Matteson's book includes a note with information about the Higginson book.

20. Thomas Wentworth Higginson, *Margaret Fuller Ossoli* (Boston: Houghton Mifflin, 1890), 11, quoted in John Matteson, *The Lives of Margaret Fuller* (New York: Norton, 2012), 7.

Higginson, Thomas Wentworth. *Margaret Fuller Ossoli*. Boston: Houghton Mifflin, 1890, 11. Quoted in John Matteson, *The Lives of Margaret Fuller* (New York: Norton, 2012), 7.

Articles and other short works

- Citation at a glance: Article in an online journal, page 514
- Citation at a glance: Article from a database, page 516

NOTE ON PAGE NUMBERS: For print articles, give a page number in a note and a page range in the bibliography entry. For articles on the web and in databases, if the source gives only a beginning page, do not give a page number in your note, but use a plus sign after the beginning page number in the bibliography entry: 21+. If a source has no page numbers but has headings or numbered paragraphs, you may use those locators in a note.

NOTE ON DATABASES: For articles in databases, at the end of the note and bibliography entry give one of the following pieces of information, in this order of preference: a DOI for the article; *or* a "stable" or "persistent" URL for the article; *or* the name of the database. (The DOI consists of the prefix https://doi.org/ followed by the DOI identifier or locator found in the source. See item 21b for an example.)

21. Article in a journal Include the volume and issue numbers (if the journal has them) and the date.

a. Print

21. Kevin Huhn, "Scaling vs. Growing Your Business," *Canadian Business Journal* 10, no. 9 (2017): 26.

Huhn, Kevin. "Scaling vs. Growing Your Business." *Canadian Business Journal* 10, no. 9 (2017): 26-33.

Citation at a glance: Article in an online journal

To cite an article in an online journal or magazine in CMS style, include the following elements:

1. Author(s)
2. Title and subtitle of article
3. Title of journal
4. Volume and issue numbers
5. Year of publication
6. Page number(s) cited (for notes); page range of article (for bibliography), if available
7. DOI, if article has one; otherwise, URL for article

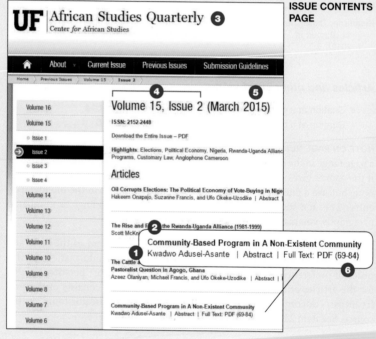

ISSUE CONTENTS PAGE

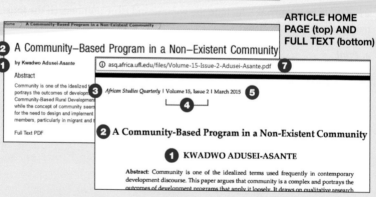

ARTICLE HOME PAGE (top) AND FULL TEXT (bottom)

1   2

1. Kwadwo Adusei-Asante, "A Community-Based Program in a Non-Existent

2   3   4   5 6   7

Community," *African Studies Quarterly* 15, no. 2 (2015): 72, http://asq.africa.ufl.edu

7

/files/Volume-15-Issue-2-Adusei-Asante.pdf.

BIBLIOGRAPHY

1   2

Adusei-Asante, Kwadwo. "A Community-Based Program in a Non-Existent Community."

3   4   5   6   7

   African Studies Quarterly 15, no. 2 (2015): 69-84. http://asq.africa.ufl.edu

7

   /files/Volume-15-Issue-2-Adusei-Asante.pdf.

For more on citing articles in CMS style, see items 21–23.

21. Article in a journal *(cont.)*

b. Web   Give the complete DOI if the article has one; if there is no DOI, give the URL for the article.

   21. Anne-Lise François, "Flower Fisting," *Postmodern Culture* 22, no. 1 (2011), https://doi.org/10.1353/pmc.2012.0004.

François, Anne-Lise. "Flower Fisting." *Postmodern Culture* 22, no. 1 (2011). https://doi.org/10.1353/pmc.2012.0004.

c. Database   For more on citing page numbers and database information, see the notes on page 513.

   21. Estelle Joubert, "Performing Sovereignty, Sounding Autonomy: Political Representation in the Operas of Maria Antonia of Saxony," *Music and Letters* 96, no. 3 (2015): 345, https://muse.jhu.edu/article/597807.

Joubert, Estelle. "Performing Sovereignty, Sounding Autonomy: Political Representation in the Operas of Maria Antonia of Saxony." *Music and Letters* 96, no. 3 (2015): 344-89. https://muse.jhu.edu/article/597807.

22. Article in a magazine   Give the month and year for a monthly publication; give the month, day, and year for a weekly publication. (For more on citing page numbers and database information, see the notes on p. 513.)

a. Print

   22. Alexandra Fuller, "Haiti on Its Own Terms," *National Geographic*, December 2015, 112.

Fuller, Alexandra. "Haiti on Its Own Terms." *National Geographic*, December 2015, 98-118.

Citation at a glance: Article from a database

To cite an article from a database in CMS style, include the following elements:

1. Author(s)
2. Title and subtitle of article
3. Title of journal
4. Volume and issue numbers
5. Year of publication

6. Page number(s) cited (for notes, if available); page range of article (for bibliography), if given
7. DOI; *or* "stable" or "persistent" URL for article; *or* database name

ISSUE CONTENTS PAGE

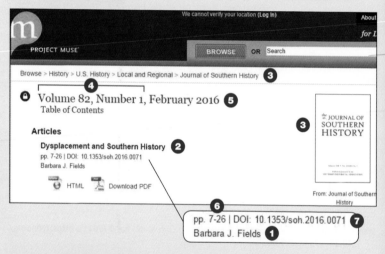

ARTICLE FIRST PAGE

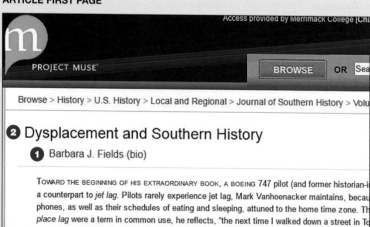

1. Barbara J. Fields, "Dysplacement and Southern History," *Journal of Southern History* 82, no. 1 (2016): 22, https://doi.org/10.1353/soh.2016.0071.

BIBLIOGRAPHY

Fields, Barbara J. "Dysplacement and Southern History." *Journal of Southern History* 82, no. 1 (2016): 7-26. https://doi.org/10.1353/soh.2016.0071.

For more on citing articles from databases in CMS style, see items 21–23.

22. Article in a magazine (*cont.*)

b. Web

22. Alan Lightman, "What Came before the Big Bang?," *Harper's*, January 2016, http://harpers.org/archive/2016/01/what-came-before-the-big-bang.

Lightman, Alan. "What Came before the Big Bang?" *Harper's*, January 2016. http://harpers.org/archive/2016/01/what-came-before-the-big-bang.

c. Database

22. Ron Rosenbaum, "The Last Renaissance Man," *Smithsonian*, November 2012, 40, OmniFile Full Text Select.

Rosenbaum, Ron. "The Last Renaissance Man." *Smithsonian*, November 2012, 39-44. OmniFile Full Text Select.

23. Article in a newspaper   Page numbers are not necessary; a section letter or number, if available, is sufficient. (For more on citing page numbers and database information, see the notes on p. 513.)

a. Print

23. Alex MacPherson, "Cameco's Gender Diversity Figures 'Disappointing,' Its Vice President Says," *StarPhoenix*, August 21, 2017, sec. B.

MacPherson, Alex. "Cameco's Gender Diversity Figures 'Disappointing,' Its Vice President Says." *StarPhoenix*, August 21, 2017, sec. B.

b. Web Include the complete URL for the article. Omit page numbers, even if the source provides them.

23. Ian Bickis, "Farmers Turn to Specialized Forecasting in Face of Rising Extreme Weather Threat," *Brandon Sun,* August 11, 2017, https://www.brandonsun.com/national /breaking-news/farmers-turn-to-specialized-forecasting-in-face-of-rising-extreme -weather-threat-439889593.html.

Bickis, Ian. "Farmers Turn to Specialized Forecasting in Face of Rising Extreme Weather Threat." *Brandon Sun,* August 11, 2017, https://www.brandonsun.com/national /breaking-news/farmers-turn-to-specialized-forecasting-in-face-of-rising-extreme -weather-threat-439889593.html.

c. Database For more on citing page numbers and database information, see the notes on page 513.

23. "Safe in Sioux City at Last: Union Pacific Succeeds in Securing Trackage from the St. Paul Road," *Omaha Daily Herald,* May 16, 1889, America's Historical Newspapers.

"Safe in Sioux City at Last: Union Pacific Succeeds in Securing Trackage from the St. Paul Road." *Omaha Daily Herald,* May 16, 1889. America's Historical Newspapers.

24. Unsigned newspaper article See item 23. In the note, begin with the title of the article. In the bibliography entry, begin with the title of the newspaper.

24. "Dear First Year Me," *Brunswickan,* September 8, 2017, http://thebruns.ca /2017/09/06/dear-first-year-me/.

Brunswickan. "Dear First Year Me." September 8, 2017. http://thebruns.ca/2017/09/06 /dear-first-year-me/.

25. Article with a title in its title Use italics for titles of long works such as books and for terms that are normally italicized. Use single quotation marks for titles of short works and terms that would otherwise be placed in double quotation marks.

25. Julia Hudson-Richards, "'Women Want to Work': Shifting Ideologies of Women's Work in Franco's Spain, 1939-1962," *Journal of Women's History* 27, no. 2 (2015): 91.

Hudson-Richards, Julia. "'Women Want to Work': Shifting Ideologies of Women's Work in Franco's Spain, 1939-1962." *Journal of Women's History* 27, no. 2 (2015): 87-109.

26. Review If the review has a title, provide it immediately following the author of the review.

26. Philip Zozzaro, review of *Among the Ruins: The Decline and Fall of the Roman Catholic Church,* by Paul L. Williams, *San Francisco Book Review,* October 1, 2017, https://sanfranciscobookreview.com/product/among-the-ruins-the-decline-and-fall-of -the-roman-catholic-church/.

Zozzaro, Philip. Review of *Among the Ruins: The Decline and Fall of the Roman Catholic Church,* by Paul L. Williams. *San Francisco Book Review,* October 1, 2017. https:// sanfranciscobookreview.com/product/among-the-ruins-the-decline-and-fall-of-the -roman-catholic-church/.

27. Letter to the editor   Do not use the letter's title, even if the publication gives one.

27. Fredric Rolando, letter to the editor, *Economist*, December 5, 2015, http://www.economist.com/.

Rolando, Fredric. Letter to the editor. *Economist*, December 5, 2015. http://www
.economist.com/.

28. Article in a dictionary or an encyclopedia (including a wiki)   Reference works such as encyclopedias do not require publication information and are usually not included in the bibliography. The abbreviation "s.v." is for the Latin *sub verbo* ("under the word").

28. *Encyclopaedia Britannica*, 15th ed. (2010), s.v. "Red River Rebellion."

28. Wikipedia, s.v. "Tommy Douglas," last modified August 25, 2017, https://en.wikipedia.org/wiki/Tommy_Douglas.

28. Bryan A. Garner, *Garner's Modern American Usage*, 4th ed. (Oxford: Oxford University Press, 2016), s.v. "brideprice."

Garner, Bryan A. *Garner's Modern American Usage*. 4th ed. Oxford: Oxford University
Press, 2016.

29. Letter in a published collection   If the letter writer's name is part of the book title, begin the note with only the last name but begin the bibliography entry with the full name.

- Citation at a glance: Letter in a published collection, **page 520**

29. Langton to William Langton, June 27, 1837, in *A Gentlewoman in Upper Canada: The Journals, Letters, and Art of Anne Langton,* ed. Barbara Williams (Toronto: University of Toronto Press, 2008), 127.

Langton, Anne. *A Gentlewoman in Upper Canada: The Journals, Letters, and Art of Anne
Langton*. Edited by Barbara Williams. Toronto: University of Toronto Press, 2008.

Web sources

For most websites, include an author if a site has one, the title of the site, the sponsor, the date of publication or the modified (update) date, and the site's complete URL. Do not italicize a website title unless the site is an online book, blog, or periodical. Use quotation marks for the titles of sections or pages in a website. If a site does not have a date of publication or a modified date, give the date you accessed the site ("accessed January 3, 2013").

30. An entire website

30. Aulavik National Park of Canada (website), Parks Canada, last modified April 5, 2017, http://www.pc.gc.ca/eng/pn-np/nt/aulavik/index.aspx.

Parks Canada. Aulavik National Park of Canada (website). Last modified April 5, 2017.
http://www.pc.gc.ca/eng/pn-np/nt/aulavik/index.aspx.

Citation at a glance: Letter in a published collection

To cite a letter in a published collection in CMS style, include the following elements:

1. Author of letter
2. Recipient of letter
3. Date of letter
4. Title of collection
5. Editor of collection
6. City of publication
7. Publisher
8. Year of publication
9. Page number(s) cited (for notes)

TITLE PAGE OF BOOK

Selected Letters of
① Langston Hughes ④

EDITED BY ARNOLD RAMPERSAD
AND DAVID ROESSEL
⑤

with Christa Fratantoro

⑦ ALFRED A. KNOPF   New York ⑥
⑧ 2015

FROM COPYRIGHT PAGE (top) AND LETTER (bottom)

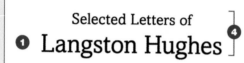

⑧ Copyright © 2015 by The Estate of Langston Hughes
Additional material copyright © 2015 by Arnold Rampersad

All rights reserved. Published in the United States by Alfred A. Knopf, a division of Random House LLC, New York, and distributed in Canada by Random House of Canada Limited, Toronto, Penguin Random House companies.
www.aaknopf.com

⑨ 344   SELECTED LETTERS OF LANGSTON HUGHES

② TO RICHARD WRIGHT   [TLS]

August 11, 1957 ③

Dear Dick:

Sometime ago, Knopf forwarded to me your request to use the last four lines of LET AMERICA BE AMERICA AGAIN in your book of four lectures.* I am happy to grant you permission to use these lines.

NOTE

1   2   3   4

    1. Hughes to Richard Wright, August 11, 1957, in *Selected Letters of Langston*

4   5   6   7

Hughes, ed. Arnold Rampersad, David Roessel, and Christa Fratantoro (New York: Knopf,

8   9

2015), 344-45.

BIBLIOGRAPHY

1   4   5

Hughes, Langston. *Selected Letters of Langston Hughes*. Edited by Arnold Rampersad,

         5   6   7   8

    David Roessel, and Christa Fratantoro. New York: Knopf, 2015.

For another citation of a letter in CMS style, see item 29.

31. Work from a website

- Citation at a glance: Primary source from a website, page 522

    31. Alexios Mantzarlis, "How TV Fact-Checked Spain's Final Debate," Poynter, last modified December 15, 2015, https://www.poynter.org/news/how-tv-fact-checked -spains-final-debate.

Mantzarlis, Alexios. "How TV Fact-Checked Spain's Final Debate." Poynter, last modified
    December 15, 2015. https://www.poynter.org/news/how-tv-fact-checked-spains
    -final-debate.

32. Blog post   Treat as a work from a website (see item 31), but italicize the name of the blog. Insert "blog" in parentheses after the name if the word *blog* is not part of the name. If the blog is part of a larger site (such as a newspaper's or an organization's site), add the title of the site after the blog title.

    32. Gregory LeFever, "Skull Fraud 'Created' the Brontosaurus," *Ancient Tides* (blog), December 16, 2012, http://ancient-tides.blogspot.com/2012/12/skull-fraud-created -brontosaurus.html.

LeFever, Gregory. "Skull Fraud 'Created' the Brontosaurus." *Ancient Tides* (blog). http://
    ancient-tides.blogspot.com/2012/12/skull-fraud-created-brontosaurus.html.

33. Comment on a blog post

    33. OllyPye, December 12, 2015, comment on Graham Readfern, "Paris Agreement a Victory for Climate Change and Ultimate Defeat for Fossil Fuels," *Planet Oz* (blog), *Guardian*, http://www.theguardian.com/environment/planet-oz/2015/dec/12/paris -agreement-a-victory-for-climate-science-and-ultimate-defeat-for-fossil -fuels#comments-64993862.

OllyPye. December 12, 2015. Comment on Graham Readfern, "Paris Agreement a Victory
    for Climate Change and the Ultimate Defeat for Fossil Fuels." *Planet Oz* (blog).
    Guardian. http://www.theguardian.com/environment/planet-oz/2015/dec/12
    /paris-agreement-a-victory-for-climate-science-and-ultimate-defeat-for-fossil
    -fuels#comments-64993862.

Citation at a glance: Primary source from a website

To cite a primary source (or any other document) from a website in CMS style, include as many of the following elements as are available:

1 Author(s)

2 Title of document

3 Title of site

4 Sponsor of site

5 Publication date or modified date; date of access (if no publication date)

6 URL of document page

WEBSITE HOME PAGE

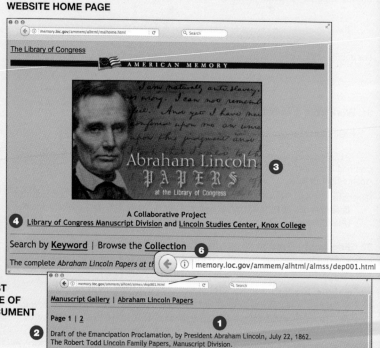

FIRST PAGE OF DOCUMENT

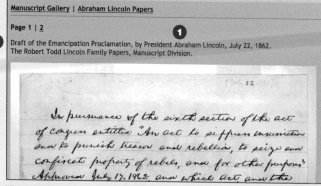

Library of Congress

1. Abraham Lincoln, "Draft of the Emancipation Proclamation," Abraham Lincoln Papers at the Library of Congress, Library of Congress Manuscript Division and Lincoln Studies Center, Knox College, accessed February 4, 2017, http://memory.loc.gov/ammem/alhtml/almss/dep001.html.

BIBLIOGRAPHY

Lincoln, Abraham. "Draft of the Emancipation Proclamation." Abraham Lincoln Papers at the Library of Congress. Library of Congress Manuscript Division and Lincoln Studies Center, Knox College. Accessed February 4, 2017. http://memory.loc.gov/ammem/alhtml/almss/dep001.html.

For more on citing documents from websites in CMS style, see item 31.

Audio, visual, and multimedia sources

34. Podcast Treat as a work from a website (see item 31), including the following, if available: the author, speaker, or host; title of the episode; an identifying number, if any; date of release or upload; title of the podcast (italicized); sponsor or database; time stamp; and complete URL.

34. Toyin Falola, "Creativity and Decolonization: Nigerian Cultures and African Epistemologies," November 17, 2015, episode 96 in *Africa Past and Present*, African Online Digital Library, podcast, MP3 audio, 43:44, http://afripod.aodl.org/2015/11/afripod-96/.

Falola, Toyin. "Creativity and Decolonization: Nigerian Cultures and African Epistemologies." Episode 96, November 17, 2015. *Africa Past and Present*. African Online Digital Library. Podcast, MP3 audio, 43:44. http://afripod.aodl.org/2015/11/afripod-96/.

35. Online audio or video Cite as a work from a website (see item 31). If the source is downloadable, identify the format or medium before the URL.

35. Will Potter, "The Secret US Prisons You've Never Heard of Before," November 9, 2015, TED Talks, video, 14:56, https://www.youtube.com/watch?v=xuAAPsiD768.

Potter, Will. "The Secret US Prisons You've Never Heard of Before." TED Talks, November 9, 2015. Video, 14:56. https://www.youtube.com/watch?v=xuAAPsiD768.

36. Published or broadcast interview

36. Ta-Nehisi Coates, interview by James Bennet, *Atlantic,* October 16, 2015, http://www.theatlantic.com/video/index/410815/in-conversation-with-ta-nehisi-coates/.

Coates, Ta-Nehisi. Interview by James Bennet. *Atlantic,* October 16, 2015. http://www .theatlantic.com/video/index/410815/in-conversation-with-ta-nehisi-coates/.

36. Vladimir Putin, interview by Charlie Rose, *Charlie Rose Show,* WGBH, Boston, June 19, 2015.

Putin, Vladimir. Interview by Charlie Rose. *Charlie Rose Show.* WGBH, Boston, June 19, 2015.

37. Film (DVD, BD, or other format).   Include both the date of original release and the date of release for the format being cited.

37. *Brooklyn,* dir. by John Crowley (2015; Los Angeles, CA: Fox Searchlight Pictures, 2016), DVD.

Crowley, John, dir. *Brooklyn.* 2015; Los Angeles, CA: Fox Searchlight Pictures, 2016. DVD.

38. Sound recording

38. Gustav Holst, *The Planets,* Royal Philharmonic Orchestra, conducted by André Previn, recorded April 14-15, 1986, Telarc 80133, 1986, compact disc.

Holst, Gustav. *The Planets.* Royal Philharmonic Orchestra. Conducted by André Previn. Recorded April 14-15, 1986. Telarc 80133, 1986, compact disc.

38. "Work," MP3 audio, track 4 on Rihanna, *Anti,* Roc Nation, 2016.

Rihanna. "Work." *Anti.* Roc Nation, 2016, MP3 audio.

39. Musical score or composition

39. Antonio Vivaldi, *L'Estro armonico,* op. 3, ed. Eleanor Selfridge-Field (Mineola, NY: Dover, 1999).

Vivaldi, Antonio. *L'Estro armonico,* op. 3. Edited by Eleanor Selfridge-Field. Mineola, NY: Dover, 1999.

40. Work of art

40. Robert Davidson, *Eagles,* 1991, gouache and watercolour on paper, Vancouver Art Gallery, Vancouver, BC.

Davidson, Robert. *Eagles.* 1991. Gouache and watercolour on paper. Vancouver Art Gallery, Vancouver, BC.

41. Performance

41. Wendy Wasserstein, *The Heidi Chronicles,* dir. Vivienne Benesch, Trinity Repertory Company, Providence, RI, December 3, 2015.

Wasserstein, Wendy. *The Heidi Chronicles.* Directed by Vivienne Benesch. Trinity Repertory Company, Providence, RI, December 3, 2015.

Personal communication and social media

42. Personal communication   Personal communications are not included in the bibliography.

> 42. Sara Lehman, email message to author, August 13, 2015.

43. Online posting or email   If an online posting has been archived, include a URL. Emails that are not part of an online discussion are treated as personal communication (see item 42). Online postings and emails are not included in the bibliography.

> 43. Bart Dale, reply to "Which country made best science/technology contribution?," Historum General History Forums, December 15, 2015, http://historum.com/general-history/46089-country-made-best-science-technology-contribution-16.html.

44. Social media post

> 44. Canadian Space Agency (@agencespatialecanadienne), "A fascinating picture of Jupiter's south pole," Instagram photo, November 7, 2017, https://www.instagram.com/p/BbMOZq9AC-a/?hl=en&taken-by=canadianspaceagency.

> Canadian Space Agency. "A fascinating picture of Jupiter's south pole." Instagram photo, November 7, 2017. https://www.instagram.com/p/BbMOZq9AC-a/?hl=en&taken-by=canadianspaceagency.

CMS-5 Manuscript format; sample pages

The following guidelines for formatting a CMS-style paper and preparing its endnotes and bibliography are based on *The Chicago Manual of Style*, 17th ed. (Chicago: University of Chicago Press, 2017). For pages from a sample paper, see CMS-5b.

CMS-5a   CMS (*Chicago*) manuscript format

Formatting the paper

The guidelines on pages 525–27 describe recommendations for formatting the text of your paper. For guidelines on preparing the endnotes, see page 527, and for preparing the bibliography, see pages 527–28.

Font   If your instructor does not require a specific font, choose one that is standard and easy to read (such as Times New Roman).

LaunchPad   **MODEL FOR CMS-5**
macmillan learning   1 Sample student paper

Title page   Include the full title of your paper, your name, the course title, the instructor's name, and the date. See page 529 for a sample title page.

Pagination   Using arabic numerals, number the pages in the upper right corner. Do not number the title page but count it in the manuscript numbering; that is, the first page of the text will be numbered 2. Depending on your instructor's preference, you may also use a short title or your last name before the page numbers to help identify pages.

Margins, line spacing, and paragraph indents   Leave margins of at least one inch (2.5 cm) at the top, bottom, and sides of the page. Double-space the body of the paper, including long quotations that have been set off from the text. (For line spacing in notes and the bibliography, see pp. 527–28.) Left-align the text.

Indent the first line of each paragraph one-half inch (1.25 cm) from the left margin.

Capitalization, italics, and quotation marks   In titles of works, capitalize all words except articles (*a, an, the*), prepositions (*at, from, between*, and so on), coordinating conjunctions (*and, but, or, nor, for, so, yet*), and *to* and *as* — unless the word is first or last in the title or subtitle. Follow these guidelines in your paper even if the title is styled differently in the source.

Lowercase the first word following a colon even if the word begins a complete sentence. When the colon introduces a series of sentences or questions, capitalize the first word in all sentences in the series, including the first.

Italicize the titles of books and other long works. Use quotation marks around the titles of periodical articles, short stories, poems, and other short works.

Long quotations   You can choose to set off a long quotation of five to ten typed lines by indenting the entire quotation one-half inch (1.25 cm) from the left margin. (Always set off quotations of ten or more lines.) Double-space the quotation; do not use quotation marks and do not add extra space above or below it. (See p. 530 for a long quotation in the text of a paper; see also pp. 503–4.)

Visuals   CMS classifies visuals as tables and figures (graphs, drawings, photographs, maps, and charts). Keep visuals as simple as possible.

Label each table with an arabic numeral (Table 1, Table 2, and so on) and provide a clear title that identifies the table's subject. The label and the title should appear on separate lines above the table, left-aligned. For a table that you have borrowed or adapted, give its source in a note like this one, below the table:

Source: Edna Bonacich and Richard P. Appelbaum, *Behind the Label* (Berkeley: University of California Press, 2000), 145.

For each figure, place a label and a caption below the figure, left-aligned. The label and caption need not appear on separate lines. The word "Figure" may be abbreviated to "Fig."

In the text of your paper, discuss the most significant features of each visual. Place visuals as close as possible to the sentences that relate to them unless your instructor prefers that visuals appear in an appendix.

URLs and DOIs   When a URL or a DOI (digital object identifier) must break across lines, do not insert a hyphen or break at a hyphen. Instead, break after a colon or a double slash or before any other mark of punctuation. If you will post your project online or submit it electronically and you want to include live URLs for readers to click on, do not insert any line breaks.

Headings   CMS does not provide guidelines for the use of headings in student papers. If you would like to insert headings in a long essay or research paper, check first with your instructor. See pages 530–32 for typical placement and formatting of headings in a CMS-style paper.

Preparing the endnotes

Begin the endnotes on a new page at the end of the paper. Centre the title "Notes" about one inch (2.5 cm) from the top of the page, and number the pages consecutively with the rest of the paper. See page 533 for an example.

Indenting and numbering   Indent the first line of each note one-half inch (1.25 cm) from the left margin; do not indent additional lines in the note. Begin the note with the arabic numeral that corresponds to the number in the text. Put a period after the number.

Line spacing   Single-space each note and double-space between notes (unless your instructor prefers double-spacing throughout).

Preparing the bibliography

Typically, the notes in CMS-style papers are followed by a bibliography, an alphabetically arranged list of all the works cited or consulted. Centre the title "Bibliography" about one inch (2.5 cm) from the top of the page. Number bibliography pages consecutively with the rest of the paper. See page 534 for a sample bibliography.

Alphabetizing the list   Alphabetize the bibliography by the last names of the authors (or editors); when a work has no author or editor, alphabetize it by the first word of the title other than *A, An,* or *The.*

If your list includes two or more works by the same author, arrange the entries alphabetically by title. Then use six hyphens instead of the author's name in all entries after the first. (See item 6 on p. 509.)

Indenting and line spacing   Begin each entry at the left margin, and indent any additional lines one-half inch (1.25 cm). Single-space each entry and double-space between entries (unless your instructor prefers double-spacing throughout).

CMS-5b Sample pages from a CMS-style research paper

Following are pages from a research paper by Ned Bishop, a student in a history class. Bishop used CMS-style endnotes, bibliography, and manuscript format.

The Massacre at Fort Pillow:
Holding Nathan Bedford Forrest Accountable

Ned Bishop

History 214
Professor Citro
March 22, 2012

Title of paper.

Writer's name.

Title of course,
instructor's name,
and date.

Marginal annotations indicate CMS-style formatting and effective writing.

Bishop 2

Although Northern newspapers of the time no doubt exaggerated some of the Confederate atrocities at Fort Pillow, most modern sources agree that a massacre of Union troops took place there on April 12, 1864. It seems clear that Union soldiers, particularly black soldiers, were killed after they had stopped fighting or had surrendered or were being held prisoner. Less clear is the role played by Major General Nathan Bedford Forrest in leading his troops. Although we will never know whether Forrest directly ordered the massacre, evidence suggests that he was responsible for it.

Thesis asserts Bishop's main point.

What happened at Fort Pillow?

Headings, centred, help readers follow the organization.

Fort Pillow, Tennessee, which sat on a bluff overlooking the Mississippi River, had been held by the Union for two years. It was garrisoned by 580 men, 292 of them from United States Colored Heavy and Light Artillery regiments, 285 from the white Thirteenth Tennessee Cavalry. Nathan Bedford Forrest commanded about 1,500 troops.[1]

Statistics are cited with an endnote.

The Confederates attacked Fort Pillow on April 12, 1864, and had virtually surrounded the fort by the time Forrest arrived on the battlefield. At 3:30 p.m., Forrest demanded the surrender of the Union forces, sending in a message of the sort he had used before: "The conduct of the officers and men garrisoning Fort Pillow has been such as to entitle them to being treated as prisoners of war. . . . Should my demand be refused, I cannot be responsible for the fate of your command."[2] Union Major William Bradford, who had replaced Major Booth, killed earlier by sharpshooters, asked for an hour to consider the demand. Forrest, worried that vessels in the river were bringing in more troops, "shortened the time to twenty minutes."[3] Bradford refused to surrender, and Forrest quickly ordered the attack.

Quotation is cited with an endnote.

The Confederates charged to the fort, scaled the parapet, and fired on the forces within. Victory came quickly, with the Union forces running toward the river or surrendering. Shelby Foote describes the scene like this:

Long quotation is set off from text by indenting. Quotation marks are omitted.

> Some kept going, right on into the river, where a number drowned and the swimmers became targets for marksmen on the bluff. Others, dropping their guns in terror, ran back toward the Confederates with their hands up, and of these some were spared as prisoners, while others were shot down in the act of surrender.[4]

In his own official report, Forrest makes no mention of the massacre. He does make much of the fact that the Union flag was not lowered by the Union forces, saying that if his own men had not taken down the flag, "few, if any, would have survived unhurt another volley."[5] However, as Jack Hurst points out and Forrest must have known, in this twenty-minute battle, "Federals running for their lives had little time to concern themselves with a flag."[6]

> Bishop uses a primary source as well as secondary sources.

> Quotation is introduced with a signal phrase.

The federal congressional report on Fort Pillow, which charged the Confederates with appalling atrocities, was strongly criticized by Southerners. Respected writer Shelby Foote, while agreeing that the report was "largely" fabrication, points out that the "casualty figures . . . indicated strongly that unnecessary killing had occurred."[7] In an important article, John Cimprich and Robert C. Mainfort Jr. argue that the most trustworthy evidence is that written within about ten days of the battle, before word of the congressional hearings circulated and Southerners realized the extent of Northern outrage. The article reprints a group of letters and newspaper sources written before April 22 and thus "untainted by the political overtones the controversy later assumed."[8] Cimprich and Mainfort conclude that these sources "support the case for the occurrence of a massacre" but that Forrest's role remains "clouded" because of inconsistencies in testimony.[9]

> Bishop draws attention to an article that reprints primary sources.

Did Forrest order the massacre?

We will never really know whether Forrest directly ordered the massacre, but it seems unlikely. True, Confederate soldier Achilles Clark, who had no reason to lie, wrote to his sisters that "I with several others tried to stop the butchery . . . but Gen. Forrest ordered them [Negro and white Union troops] shot down like dogs, and the carnage continued."[10] But it is not clear whether Clark heard Forrest giving the orders or was just reporting hearsay. Many Confederates had been shouting "No quarter! No quarter!" and, as Shelby Foote points out, these shouts were "thought by some to be at Forrest's command."[11] A Union soldier, Jacob Thompson, claimed to have seen Forrest order the killing, but when asked to describe the six-foot-two general, he called him "a little bit of a man."[12]

> Topic sentence states the main idea for this section.

> Writer presents a balanced view of the evidence.

Perhaps the most convincing evidence that Forrest did not order the massacre is that he tried to stop it once it had begun. Historian Albert Castel quotes several eyewitnesses on both the Union and

Confederate sides as saying that Forrest ordered his men to stop firing.[13] In a letter to his wife three days after the battle, Confederate soldier Samuel Caldwell wrote that "if General Forrest had not run between our men & the Yanks with his pistol and sabre drawn not a man would have been spared."[14]

In a respected biography of Nathan Bedford Forrest, Hurst suggests that the temperamental Forrest "may have ragingly ordered a massacre and even intended to carry it out—until he rode inside the fort and viewed the horrifying result" and ordered it stopped.[15] While this is an intriguing interpretation of events, even Hurst would probably admit that it is merely speculation.

Can Forrest be held responsible for the massacre?

Topic sentence for this section reinforces the thesis.

Even assuming that Forrest did not order the massacre, he can still be held accountable for it. That is because he created an atmosphere ripe for the possibility of atrocities and did nothing to ensure that it wouldn't happen. Throughout his career Forrest repeatedly threatened "no quarter," particularly with respect to black soldiers, so Confederate troops had good reason to think that in massacring the enemy they were carrying out his orders. As Hurst writes, "About all he had to do to produce a massacre was issue no order against one."[16] Dudley Taylor Cornish agrees:

> It has been asserted again and again that Forrest did not order a massacre. He did not need to. He had sought to terrify the Fort Pillow garrison by a threat of no quarter, as he had done at Union City and at Paducah in the days just before he turned on Pillow. If his men did enter the fort shouting "Give them no quarter; kill them; kill them; it is General Forrest's orders," he should not have been surprised.[17]

The slaughter at Fort Pillow was no doubt driven in large part by racial hatred. Numbers alone suggest this: of 295 white troops, 168 were taken prisoner, but of 262 black troops, only 58 were taken into custody, with the rest either dead or too badly wounded to walk.[18] A Southern reporter traveling with Forrest makes clear that the discrimination was deliberate: "Our troops maddened by the excitement, shot down the ret[r]eating Yankees, and not until they had attained t[h]e water's edge and turned to beg for mercy, did any prisoners fall in [t]o our hands—Thus the whites received quarter, but the negroes were shown no mercy."[19]

Notes begin on a new page.

Notes

1. John Cimprich and Robert C. Mainfort Jr., eds., "Fort Pillow Revisited: New Evidence about an Old Controversy," *Civil War History* 28, no. 4 (1982): 293-94.

First line of each note is indented ½" (1.25 cm). Note number is followed by a period. Authors' names are not inverted.

2. Quoted in Brian Steel Wills, *A Battle from the Start: The Life of Nathan Bedford Forrest* (New York: HarperCollins, 1992), 182.

3. Quoted in Wills, 183.

4. Shelby Foote, *The Civil War, a Narrative: Red River to Appomattox* (New York: Vintage, 1986), 110.

Notes are single-spaced, with double-spacing between notes. (Some instructors may prefer double-spacing throughout.)

5. Nathan Bedford Forrest, "Report of Maj. Gen. Nathan B. Forrest, C.S. Army, Commanding Cavalry, of the Capture of Fort Pillow," Shotgun's Home of the American Civil War, accessed March 6, 2012, http://www.civilwarhome.com/forrest.htm.

6. Jack Hurst, *Nathan Bedford Forrest: A Biography* (New York: Knopf, 1993), 174.

7. Foote, *Civil War*, 111.

8. Cimprich and Mainfort, "Fort Pillow," 295.

Last names and title refer to an earlier note by the same authors.

9. Cimprich and Mainfort, 295.

10. Cimprich and Mainfort, 295.

11. Foote, *Civil War*, 110.

12. Quoted in Wills, *Battle from the Start*, 187.

Writer cites an indirect source: words quoted in another source.

13. Albert Castel, "The Fort Pillow Massacre: A Fresh Examination of the Evidence," *Civil War History* 4, no. 1 (1958): 44-45.

14. Cimprich and Mainfort, "Fort Pillow," 300.

15. Hurst, *Nathan Bedford Forrest*, 177.

16. Hurst, 177.

17. Dudley Taylor Cornish, *The Sable Arm: Black Troops in the Union Army, 1861-1865* (Lawrence: University Press of Kansas, 1987), 175.

18. Foote, *Civil War*, 111.

19. Cimprich and Mainfort, "Fort Pillow," 304.

20. Quoted in Wills, *Battle from the Start*, 189.

21. Quoted in Wills, 215.

22. Quoted in Hurst, *Nathan Bedford Forrest*, 177.

23. Quoted in James M. McPherson, *Battle Cry of Freedom: The Civil War Era* (New York: Oxford University Press, 1988), 402.

24. Hurst, *Nathan Bedford Forrest*, 74.

25. Quoted in Foote, *Civil War*, 106.

Bibliography begins on a new page.

Entries are alphabetized by authors' last names.

First line of entry is at left margin; additional lines are indented ½" (1.25 cm).

Entries are single-spaced, with double-spacing between entries. (Some instructors may prefer double-spacing throughout.)

Bibliography

Castel, Albert. "The Fort Pillow Massacre: A Fresh Examination of the Evidence." *Civil War History* 4, no. 1 (1958): 37-50.

Cimprich, John, and Robert C. Mainfort Jr., eds. "Fort Pillow Revisited: New Evidence about an Old Controversy." *Civil War History* 28, no. 4 (1982): 293-306.

Cornish, Dudley Taylor. *The Sable Arm: Black Troops in the Union Army, 1861-1865.* Lawrence: University Press of Kansas, 1987.

Foote, Shelby. *The Civil War, a Narrative: Red River to Appomattox.* New York: Vintage, 1986.

Forrest, Nathan Bedford. "Report of Maj. Gen. Nathan B. Forrest, C.S. Army, Commanding Cavalry, of the Capture of Fort Pillow." Shotgun's Home of the American Civil War. Accessed March 6, 2012. http://www.civilwarhome .com/forrest.htm.

Hurst, Jack. *Nathan Bedford Forrest: A Biography.* New York: Knopf, 1993.

McPherson, James M. *Battle Cry of Freedom: The Civil War Era.* New York: Oxford University Press, 1988.

Wills, Brian Steel. *A Battle from the Start: The Life of Nathan Bedford Forrest.* New York: HarperCollins, 1992.

L

Writing about Literature

How can I come up with a good interpretation of a poem or story?

I put someone else's analysis of a poem into my own words. Is that plagiarism?

If I'm writing about a story written forty years ago, should I use past tense?

See L1-b

See L4-b

See L6

Writing about Literature

All good writing about literature attempts to answer a question about the text:

- How does street language function in Gwendolyn Brooks's "We Real Cool"?
- What does George Orwell's "Shooting an Elephant" imply about the role the British played in colonial India?
- Why does Margaret Atwood make so many biblical allusions in *The Handmaid's Tale*?
- What purpose does nature serve in Pablo Neruda's poem "If You Forget Me," and how does memory correspond to the natural world?

The goal of a literature analysis should be to answer such questions with a meaningful and persuasive interpretation.

L1 Reading to form an interpretation

L1-a Get involved in the work; be an active reader.

Responding to literature starts with becoming an engaged and active reader. Read the work through once, closely and carefully. What is it telling you? Asking you? Trying to make you feel? With these questions in mind, go back and read it a second time. If the work provides an introduction and footnotes, read them carefully; they often contain key information. Use the dictionary to look up unfamiliar words or words with connotations that may influence the work's meaning.

Rereading is a central part of the process of developing an analysis. You should read short works a few times, first to get an overall impression and then again to focus on meaningful details. With longer works, such as novels or plays, read the most important chapters or scenes more than once while keeping in mind the work as a whole.

As you read and reread, interact with the work by posing questions and looking for possible answers. The chart that begins on page 540 suggests some questions about literature that may help you become a more engaged, active reader.

Annotating the work

Annotating the work — interacting with the text by taking notes — is a way to
focus your reading, capture your responses, and prepare for a class discussion.
The first time you read the work through, you may want to indicate passages
you find especially significant or puzzling. On rereading, pay particular attention to those passages, and jot down your ideas and reactions in a notebook or
(if you own the text) on the pages. As you annotate, you can try out ideas and
develop your questions and perspectives about the work.

Here is one student's annotation of a poem by Shakespeare.

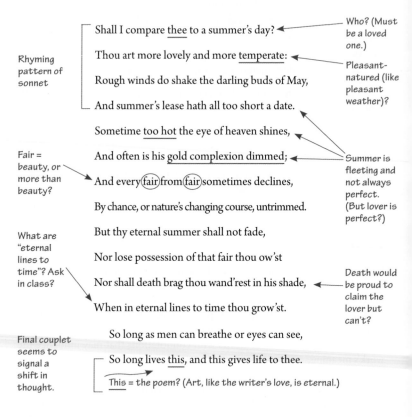

Rhyming pattern of sonnet

Shall I compare <u>thee</u> to a summer's day? — *Who? (Must be a loved one.)*

Thou art more lovely and more <u>temperate:</u> — *Pleasant-natured (like pleasant weather)?*

Rough winds do shake the darling buds of May,

And summer's lease hath all too short a date.

Sometime <u>too hot the eye of heaven shines,</u>

Fair = beauty, or more than beauty?

And often is his <u>gold complexion dimmed;</u> — *Summer is fleeting and not always perfect. (But lover is perfect?)*

And every (fair) from (fair) sometimes declines,

By chance, or nature's changing course, untrimmed.

What are "eternal lines to time"? Ask in class?

But thy eternal summer shall not fade,

Nor lose possession of that fair thou ow'st

Nor shall death brag thou wand'rest in his shade, — *Death would be proud to claim the lover but can't?*

When in eternal lines to time thou grow'st.

Final couplet seems to signal a shift in thought.

So long as men can breathe or eyes can see,

So long lives <u>this,</u> and this gives life to thee.

<u>This</u> = the poem? (Art, like the writer's love, is eternal.)

Taking notes

Note taking is also a key part of rereading a work of literature. In your notes
you can try out ideas and develop your perspective on the work. Here are a
student's notes on a short story, "The Chrysanthemums," by John Steinbeck.
Notice that some of these notes pose questions for further thought.

Note taking on a literary work

Notes on "The Chrysanthemums"

Elisa's gardening clothes—"clodhopper" shoes and a dress "covered by a big corduroy apron"—not very feminine

The words "strong," "strength," "power," and "powerful" pop up in connection with Elisa and her gardening. Why?

Conversation with pots-and-pans repairman about growing chrysanthemums is sexually charged.

Is she attracted to the repairman or just his way of life? Envies his freedom to sleep outdoors in his wagon: "I wish women could do such things."

What do chrysanthemums symbolize? Beauty? Femininity? Source of pride? Strength? All of these?

Elisa sees chrysanthemums tossed into a ditch. Disillusion?

Discussing the work

Understanding literature can be a social experience, and class discussions often lead to interesting insights about a literary work, perhaps by calling attention to details that you missed on a first reading. Discussions don't always need to occur face-to-face. In many classes, they happen online in discussion forums, chatrooms, blogs, or wikis.

L1-b Form an interpretation.

After rereading, taking notes, and discussing the work, you are ready to start forming an interpretation — your understanding of the meaning of details in the work. At this stage, try to focus on one aspect of the work. Look through your notes for recurring questions and insights.

Focusing on a central issue

In writing an analysis of literature, you will focus on a central issue. Your job is not to say everything about the work that can possibly be said. It is to develop a sustained, in-depth interpretation that illuminates the work in

Questions to ask about literature

Questions about technique

Plot: What conflicts drive the plot? Are they internal (within a character) or external (between characters or between a character and a force)? How are conflicts resolved? Why do events happen in a particular order?

Setting: Does the setting (time and place) create an atmosphere, give insight into a character, suggest symbolic meaning, or hint at the theme?

Character: What seems to motivate the central characters? Do any characters change significantly? If so, what have they learned from their experiences? Do contrasts between characters highlight important themes?

Point of view: Does the point of view — the perspective from which the story is narrated or the poem is spoken — influence our understanding of events? Does the narration reveal the character traits of the speaker, or does the speaker merely observe others?

Theme: Does the work have an overall theme (a central insight about people or a truth about life, for example)? If so, how do details in the work serve to illuminate this theme?

Language: Does language — such as formal or informal, standard or dialect, ordinary or poetic — reveal the character of speakers? How do metaphors, similes, and sensory images contribute to the work? How do recurring images enrich the work and hint at its meaning?

Questions about social context

Historical context: What does the work reveal about — or how was it shaped by — the time and place in which it was written? Does the work appear to promote or undermine a philosophy that was popular in its time, such as social Darwinism in the late nineteenth century or feminism in the mid-twentieth century?

Class: How does social class shape or influence characters' choices and actions? How does class affect the way characters view — or are viewed by — others?

Race and culture: Are any characters portrayed as being caught between cultures: between a traditional and an emerging culture, for example? Are any characters engaged in a conflict with society because of their race or ethnic background? Does the work celebrate a specific culture and its traditions?

> ## Questions to ask about literature, *continued*
>
> **Gender:** Are any characters' choices limited because of gender? What are the power relationships between the sexes, and do these change during the course of the work? Do any characters resist the gender roles assigned to them? Do other characters choose to conform to those roles?
>
> **Archetypes (or universal types):** Does a character, an image, or a plot fit a pattern — a type — that has been repeated in stories throughout history and across cultures? (For example, nearly every culture has stories about heroes, quests, redemption, and revenge.) How is an archetypal character, image, or plot line similar to or different from others like it?

some specific way. For example, you may think that *The Great Gatsby* is interesting because it contains a story of unrequited love set against a backdrop of luxurious houses and gritty New York City. But to develop this general response into an interpretation, you will have to find a focus. For example, you might address the ways in which the dual settings of the story — the ritzy West Egg and the squalor of the Valley of Ashes — mirror the disillusionment that Gatsby and Nick experience in the novel. Or you might look at how being an outsider motivates both George and Myrtle Wilson.

Asking questions that lead to an interpretation

Good interpretations generally arise from good questions. What is it about the work that puzzles or intrigues you? What do you want to know more about? By asking yourself such questions, you will push yourself to move beyond your first impressions to deeper insights.

In writing an analysis, you might answer questions about literary techniques, such as the author's handling of plot, setting, or character. Or you could respond to questions about social context as well — what a work reveals about the time and culture in which it was written. Both kinds of questions are included in the chart that begins on page 540.

Often you will find yourself writing about both technique and social context. For example, Margaret Peel, a student who wrote about Langston Hughes's poem "Ballad of the Landlord" (see p. 557), addressed the following question, which touches on both language and race:

> How does the poem's language—through its four voices—dramatize the experience of a black man in a society dominated by whites?

In your introduction, you will usually announce your interpretation in a one- or two-sentence thesis. The thesis answers the central question that you posed. Here, for example, is Margaret Peel's two-sentence thesis:

> Langston Hughes's "Ballad of the Landlord" is narrated through four voices, each with its own perspective on the poem's action. These opposing voices—of a tenant, a landlord, the police, and the press—dramatize a black man's experience in a society dominated by whites.

L2 Planning the paper

L2-a Draft a thesis.

A thesis, which often appears in the introduction, announces an essay's main point. When planning your paper, it is helpful to have a working or preliminary thesis in mind. This preliminary thesis will likely change as you draft.

In a literature analysis, your thesis will answer the central question that you have asked about the work. When drafting your thesis, aim for a strong, assertive summary of your interpretation. Below, for example, are two successful thesis statements taken from student essays, together with the central question each student had posed.

QUESTION

What role does mental illness play in Ophelia's character in *Hamlet*, and how does her illness affect Hamlet himself?

THESIS

Through her slow unraveling and eventual suicide, Ophelia acts as a catalyst for the actions of the main character in William Shakespeare's *Hamlet*.

QUESTION

What is the significance of the explorer Robert Walton in Mary Shelley's novel *Frankenstein*?

THESIS

Through the character of Walton, Shelley suggests that the most profound and useful sort of knowledge is not a knowledge of nature's secrets but a knowledge of the limits of knowledge itself.

As in other postsecondary writing, the thesis of a literature paper should not be too factual, too broad, or too vague. For an essay on Mark Twain's *Huckleberry Finn*, the first three examples would all make weak thesis statements.

TOO FACTUAL

As a runaway slave, Jim is in danger from the law.

TOO BROAD

In *Huckleberry Finn*, Twain criticizes mid-nineteenth-century American society.

TOO VAGUE

Huckleberry Finn is Twain's most exciting work.

The following thesis statement is sharply focused and presents a central idea that requires discussion and support. It connects a general point (that Twain objects to empty piety) to those specific aspects of the novel the paper will address (Huck's status as narrator, Huck's comments on religion).

ACCEPTABLE THESIS

Because Huckleberry Finn is a naive narrator, his comments on conventional religion function ironically at every turn, allowing Twain to poke fun at empty piety.

L2-b Sketch an outline.

Your thesis may strongly suggest a method of organization, in which case you will have little difficulty jotting down your essay's key points. Consider, for example, the following informal outline, based on a thesis that leads naturally to a four-part organization.

Thesis: Langston Hughes's "Ballad of the Landlord" is narrated through four voices, each with its own perspective on the poem's action. These opposing voices—of a tenant, a landlord, the police, and the press—dramatize a black man's experience in a society dominated by whites.

—The tenant's complaints rise to anger; tenant threatens violence.

—The landlord calls the police; repetition in his response shows his fear.

—The voice of the law is punctuated in sharp sounds.

—The voice of the press as shown in newspaper headlines dehumanizes the tenant.

If your thesis does not by itself suggest a method of organization, turn to your notes and begin putting them into categories that relate to the thesis. For example, one student who was writing about Euripides's play *Medea* constructed a formal outline from her notes (see next page).

Thesis: Although Medea professes great love for her children, Euripides gives us reason to doubt her sincerity: Medea does not hesitate to use the children as weapons in her bloody battle with Jason, and from the outset she displays little real concern for their fate.

I. From the beginning of the play, Medea is a less than ideal mother.
   A. Her first words about the children are hostile.
   B. Her first actions suggest indifference.
II. In three scenes Medea appears to be a loving mother, but in each of these scenes we have reason to doubt her sincerity.
III. Throughout the play, as Medea plots her revenge, her overriding concern is not her children but her reputation.
   A. Fearing ridicule, she is proud of her reputation as one who can "help her friends and hurt her enemies."
   B. Her obsession with reputation may stem from the Greek view of reputation as a means to immortality.
IV. After she kills her children, Medea reveals her real concern.
   A. She shows no remorse.
   B. She revels in Jason's agony over their death.

Whether to use a formal or an informal outline is usually a matter of personal preference. For most purposes, you will probably find that an informal outline is sufficient, perhaps even preferable.

L3 Writing the paper

L3-a Draft an introduction that announces your interpretation.

The introduction to a literature analysis is usually one paragraph long. In most cases, you will want to begin the paragraph with a few sentences that provide context for your thesis and to end it with a thesis that sums up your interpretation. You may also want to note the question or issue that motivated your interpretation. In this way, you will help your readers understand not only what your idea or thesis *is* but also why it *matters*.

The following is an introductory paragraph announcing a student's interpretation of one aspect of the novel *Frankenstein*; the thesis is highlighted.

In Mary Shelley's novel *Frankenstein*, Walton's ambition as an explorer, to find a passage to the North Pole, mirrors Frankenstein's ambition as a scientist, to discover and master the secret of life. But where Frankenstein is ultimately destroyed by his quest for knowledge, Walton turns back from his quest when he learns of Frankenstein's fate. Walton's story might seem unimportant, but paired with Frankenstein's, it keeps us from missing one of the novel's most important themes. Through the character of Walton, Shelley suggests that the most profound and useful sort of knowledge is not a knowledge of nature's secrets but a knowledge of the limits of knowledge itself.

L3-b Support your interpretation with evidence from the work; avoid simple plot summary.

Your thesis and preliminary outline will point you toward details in the work relevant to your interpretation. As you begin drafting the body of your paper, make good use of those details.

Supporting your interpretation

As a rule, each paragraph in the body of your paper should focus on some aspect of your overall interpretation and should include a topic sentence that states the main idea of the paragraph. The rest of the paragraph should present details and perhaps quotations from the work that back up your interpretation. In the following paragraph, which develops part of the outline sketched on page 543, the topic sentence comes first. It describes the first voice in Langston Hughes's "Ballad of the Landlord," that of the black tenant.

> The main voice in the poem is that of the tenant, who, as the last line tells us, is black. The tenant is characterized by his informal, nonstandard speech. He uses slang ("Ten Bucks"), contracted words (*'member, more'n*), and nonstandard grammar ("These steps is broken down"). This colloquial English suggests the tenant's separation from the world of convention, represented by the formal voices of the police and the press, which appear later in the poem.

Notice that the writer has quoted from the poem to lend both flavour and substance to her interpretation. Notice too that the writer is *interpreting* the language of the poem: She is not merely summarizing the poem.

Avoiding simple plot summary

In a literature paper, relying heavily on plot summary can cause you to avoid interpretation. Resist this temptation by paying attention to your topic sentences.

DRAFT: A TOPIC SENTENCE THAT LEADS TO PLOT SUMMARY

As they drift down the river on a raft, Huck and the runaway slave Jim have many philosophical discussions.

REVISED: A TOPIC SENTENCE THAT ANNOUNCES AN INTERPRETATION

The theme of dawning moral awareness is reinforced by the many philosophical discussions between Huck and Jim, the runaway slave, as they drift down the river on a raft.

Remember that readers are interested in your ideas about a work — the questions you ask and the details you find significant. To avoid plot summary, keep the following strategies in mind as you write.

- When you write for an academic audience, you can assume that readers have read the work. You need to include some summary as background, but the emphasis should be on your ideas and your interpretation.

- Pose questions that lead to an interpretation or a judgment of the work rather than to a summary. The questions in the chart that begins on page 540 can help steer you away from summary and toward interpretation.

- Organize your paper in a way that brings out the relationship among your ideas, rather than organizing it according to the work's sequence of events.

L4 Observing the conventions of literature papers

The academic discipline of English literature has certain conventions, or standard practices, that scholars in the field use when writing about literature. If you follow these conventions, you will enhance your credibility and enable your readers to focus more easily on your ideas.

L4-a Refer to authors, titles, and characters according to convention.

The first time you refer to the author of a literary work or of a secondary source such as a critical essay, use the author's full name: *Virginia Woolf is known for her experimental novels.* In subsequent references, you may use the last name only: *Woolf's early work was largely overlooked.* As a rule, do not use personal titles such as *Mr.* or *Ms.* or *Dr.* when referring to authors.

When you mention the title of a short story, an essay, or a short or medium-length poem, put the title in quotation marks.

"The Progress of Love," by Alice Munro

"Coming Home Again," by Chang-rae Lee

Italicize the titles of novels, nonfiction books, plays, and long poems.

I Know Why the Caged Bird Sings, by Maya Angelou

M. Butterfly, by David Henry Hwang

Howl, by Allen Ginsberg

Refer to each character by the name most often used for him or her in the work. If, for instance, a character's name is Lambert Strether and he is always referred to as "Strether," do not call him "Lambert" or "Mr. Strether." Similarly, write "Lady Macbeth," not "Mrs. Macbeth."

L4-b Use the present tense to describe fictional events.

Because fictional events have not actually occurred in the past, the convention is to describe them in the present tense. Until you become used to this convention, you may find yourself shifting between present and past tense. As you revise your draft, make sure that you have used the present tense consistently.

INCONSISTENT USE OF TENSES

Octavia <u>demands</u> blind obedience from James and from all of her children. When James and Ty <u>caught</u> two redbirds in their trap, they <u>wanted</u> to play with them; Octavia, however, <u>had</u> other plans for the birds (89-90).

CONSISTENT USE OF THE PRESENT TENSE

Octavia <u>demands</u> blind obedience from James and from all of her children. When James and Ty <u>catch</u> two redbirds in their trap, they <u>want</u> to play with them; Octavia, however, <u>has</u> other plans for the birds (89-90).

NOTE: When integrating quotations from the work into your own text, you will need to be alert to the problem of shifting tenses. See L5-c.

L4-c Use MLA style to format passages quoted from the work.

Unless your instructor suggests otherwise, use MLA (Modern Language Association) style for formatting passages quoted from literary works.

MLA style usually requires that you name the author of the work quoted and give a page number for the exact location of the passage in the work. When writing about nonfiction articles and books, introduce a quotation with a signal phrase naming the author (*John Smith points out that "..."*) or place the author's name with the page number in parentheses at the end of the quoted passage: *"..." for all time (Smith 22).*

When writing about a single work of fiction, however, you do not need to include the author's name each time you quote from the work. You will mention the author's name in the introduction to your paper. Then, when you are quoting from the work, you may include just the page number in parentheses following the quotation (see p. 551). You can still use the author's name in a signal phrase to highlight the author's role or technique, but you are not required to do so. (See L5-a.)

Additional MLA guidelines for handling citations in the text of your paper appear in L5.

L5 Integrating quotations from the text

Integrating quotations from a literary text can lend vivid support to your argument, but keep most quotations fairly short. You can use long quotations to present extended passages you will discuss at length, but use them sparingly. Excessive use of long quotations may interrupt the flow of your interpretation, making your paper more difficult to read and understand.

L5-a Do not confuse the work's author with a narrator, speaker, or character.

When introducing quotations from a literary work, make sure that you don't confuse the author with the narrator of a story, the speaker of a poem, or a character in a story or play. Instead of naming the author, you can refer to the narrator or speaker — or to the work itself.

INAPPROPRIATE

Poet Andrew Marvell describes his fear of death like this: "But at my back I always hear / Time's wingèd chariot hurrying near" (21-22).

APPROPRIATE

Addressing his beloved in an attempt to win her sexual favors, the speaker of the poem argues that death gives them no time to waste: "But at my back I always hear / Time's wingèd chariot hurrying near" (21-22).

APPROPRIATE

The poem "To His Coy Mistress" says as much about fleeting time and death as it does about sexual passion. Its most powerful lines are "But at my back I always hear / Time's wingèd chariot hurrying near" (21-22).

L5-b Provide context for quotations.

When you quote the words of a narrator, speaker, or character in a literary work, you should name who is speaking and provide a context for the quoted words. In the following examples, the quoted language is from Tennessee Williams's play *The Glass Menagerie* and Shirley Jackson's short story "The Lottery."

> Laura is so completely under Amanda's spell that when urged to make a wish on the moon, she asks, "What shall I wish for, Mother?" (1.5.140).

> When a neighbour suggests that the lottery should be abandoned, Old Man Warner responds, "There's *always* been a lottery" (284).

L5-c As you integrate quotations, avoid shifts in tense.

Because it is conventional to write about literature in the present tense (see L4-b) and because literary works often use other tenses, you will need to exercise some care when weaving quotations into your own writing. One student's first draft of a paper on Nadine Gordimer's short story "Friday's Footprint" included the following awkward sentence, in which the present-tense main verb *sees* is followed by the past-tense verb *blushed* in the quotation.

TENSE SHIFT

When Rita sees Johnny's relaxed attitude, "she blushed, like a wave of illness" (159).

When revising, the writer considered two ways to avoid the distracting shift from present to past tense: to paraphrase the reference to Rita's blushing and reduce the length of the quotation or to change the verb in the quotation to the present tense, using brackets to indicate the change.

REVISION 1

When Rita sees Johnny's relaxed attitude, she is overcome with embarrassment, "like a wave of illness" (159).

REVISION 2

When Rita sees Johnny's relaxed attitude, "she blushe[s], like a wave of illness" (159).

L5-d To indicate changes in a quotation, use brackets and the ellipsis mark.

Two marks of punctuation, square brackets and the ellipsis mark (three spaced periods), show readers that you have modified a quoted passage in some way.

Brackets are used for additions, as in the following example from an essay on Khaled Hosseini's novel *A Thousand Splendid Suns*.

Laila, fearful, confides in Tariq: "It's the whistling, the damn whistling [of the rockets], I hate more than anything" (156).

Because some readers might not understand the meaning of *whistling* out of context, the writer has supplied a clarification in brackets. Brackets are also used to change words or letters to keep a quoted sentence grammatical in your context, as in the last example in L5-c, or to change a capital letter to lowercase or vice versa, as on page 554.

The ellipsis mark is used to indicate omissions. In the following example from a paper on Tim O'Brien's "How to Tell a True War Story," the writer has omitted some words from the original in order to keep the quoted passage brief.

O'Brien warns his readers bluntly that they should not seek noble themes in war stories: "If at the end of a war story you feel uplifted, . . . then you have been made the victim of a very old and terrible lie" (347).

If you want to omit one or more full sentences from a quotation, use a period before the three ellipsis dots.

O'Brien regards war as fundamentally immoral: "A true war story is never moral. . . . If a story seems moral, do not believe it" (347).

Usually you do not need an ellipsis mark at the beginning or at the end of a quotation. If you have dropped words at the end of the final quoted sentence, put three ellipsis dots before the closing quotation mark and parenthetical reference, as in the example on page 554.

L5-e Enclose embedded quotations in single quotation marks.

In writing about literature, you may sometimes want to use a quotation with another quotation embedded in it — when you are quoting dialogue in a novel, for example. In such cases, set off the main quotation with double quotation marks, as you usually would, and set off the embedded quotation with single quotation marks. The following example from a student paper quotes lines from Amy Tan's novel *The Hundred Secret Senses*.

> Early in the novel the narrator's half sister Kwan sees—or thinks she sees—ghosts: "'Libby-ah,' she'll say to me. 'Guess who I see yesterday, you guess.' And I don't have to guess that she's talking about someone dead" (3).

L5-f Use MLA style to cite passages from the work.

MLA guidelines for citing quotations differ somewhat for short stories or novels, poems, and plays.

Short stories or novels

To cite a passage from a short story or a novel, use a page number in parentheses after the quoted words.

> The narrator of Madeleine Thien's "Simple Recipes" remembers a conversation with her mother in which the mother described guilt as something one could "shrink" and "compress." After a time, according to the mother, "you can blow it off your body like a speck of dirt" (12).

When a quotation from a work of fiction takes up four or fewer typed lines, put it in quotation marks and run it into the text of your essay, as in the two previous examples. When a quotation is five lines or longer, set it off from the text by indenting one-half inch (1.25 cm) from the left margin; when you set a quotation off from the text, do not use quotation marks. Put the parenthetical citation after the final mark of punctuation.

> Sister's tale begins with "I," and she makes every event revolve around herself, even her sister's marriage:
>
>> I was getting along fine with Mama, Papa-Daddy and Uncle Rondo until my sister Stella-Rondo just separated from her husband and came back home again. Mr. Whitaker! Of course I went with Mr. Whitaker first, when he first appeared here in China Grove, taking "Pose Yourself" photos, and Stella-Rondo broke us up. (46)

Poems

To cite lines from a poem, use line numbers in parentheses at the end of the quotation. For the first reference, use the word "lines": (lines 1–2). Thereafter use just the numbers: (12–13).

> The opening lines of Lewis Carroll's "The Aged Aged Man" strike a conversational tone: "I'll tell thee everything I can; / There's little to relate." (lines 1-2).

Enclose quotations of three or fewer lines of poetry in quotation marks within your text, and indicate line breaks with a slash, as in the example just given.

When you quote four or more lines of poetry, set the quotation off from the text by indenting one-half inch (1.25 cm), and omit the quotation marks. Put the line numbers in parentheses after the final mark of punctuation.

> In the first stanza of his poem "London," William Blake argues that the city's inhabitants are physically marked with their own suffering:
>
>> I wander thro' each charter'd street,
>> Near where the charter'd Thames does flow.
>> And mark in every face I meet
>> Marks of weakness, marks of woe. (lines 1-4)

NOTE: If any line of the poem takes up more than one line of your paper, carry the extra words to the next line of the paper and indent them an additional one-quarter inch (0.5 cm). Alternatively, you may indent the entire poem a little less than one-half inch (1.25 cm) to fit the long line.

Plays

To cite lines from a play, include the act number, scene number, and line numbers (as many of these as are available) in parentheses at the end of the quotation. Separate the numbers with periods, and use arabic numerals (1, 2, 3) unless your instructor prefers roman numerals.

> Nora shakes her head at her husband: "You have never loved me. You have only
> thought it pleasant to be in love with me" (3.1.601-02).

If no act, scene, or line numbers are available, use a page number.

When a quotation from a play takes up four or fewer typed lines in your paper and is spoken by only one character, put quotation marks around it and run it into the text of your essay, as in the previous example. If the quotation consists of two or three lines from a verse play, use a slash for line breaks, as for poetry (see p. 552). When a quotation by a single character in a play is five typed lines or longer (or more than three lines in a verse play), treat it like a passage from a short story or a novel (see p. 552): Indent it one-half inch (1.25 cm) from the left margin and omit the quotation marks. Include the citation in parentheses after the final mark of punctuation.

> Speaking to Electra, Clytemnestra complains about the sexual double standard that
> has allowed her husband to justify sacrificing her other daughter, Iphigenia, to the
> gods. She asks what would have happened if Menelaus, and not his wife Helen,
> had been seized by the Trojans:
>
>> If Menelaus had been raped from home on the sly, should I have
>> had to kill Orestes so my sister's husband could be rescued? You
>> think your father would have borne it? He would have killed me.
>> Then why was it fair for him to kill what belonged to me and not
>> be killed? (1041-45)

When quoting dialogue between two or more characters in a play, set the quotation off from the text. Type each character's name in all capital letters at a one-half-inch (1.25 cm) indent from the left margin. Indent subsequent lines under the character's name an additional one-quarter inch (0.5 cm).

> In the opening act of *Translations*, Friel pointedly contrasts the monolingual
> Captain Lancey with the multilingual Irish:
>
>> HUGH. . . . [Lancey] then explained that he does not speak Irish. Latin? I
>>> asked. None. Greek? Not a syllable. He speaks—on his own admission—
>>> only English; and to his credit he seemed suitably verecund—James?
>> JIMMY. *Verecundus*—humble.
>> HUGH. Indeed—he voiced some surprise that we did not speak his language.
>>> (act 1)

L6 Using secondary sources

Many literature papers rely entirely on primary sources — the literary work or works under discussion. You document such papers with MLA in-text citations as explained in L5-f. If a list of works cited is required, it will consist of the literary work or works (see L6-a).

In addition to relying on primary sources, some literature papers draw on secondary sources: essays of literary criticism, a biography or an autobiography of the author, or histories of the era in which the work was written. When you use secondary sources, you must document them with MLA in-text citations and a list of works cited as explained in L6-a. (For an example of a paper that uses secondary sources, see pp. 560–64.)

Keep in mind that even when you use secondary sources, your main goal should be to develop and communicate your own understanding and interpretation of the literary work.

L6-a Use MLA style to document secondary sources.

Most literature papers use the documentation system recommended by the Modern Language Association (MLA), as set forth in the *MLA Handbook*, 8th edition (MLA, 2016).

MLA recommends in-text citations that refer readers to a list of works cited. An in-text citation names the author, often in a signal phrase, and gives the page number in parentheses. At the end of the paper, a list of works cited provides publication information about the sources used in the paper.

MLA IN-TEXT CITATION

Finding Butler's science fiction novel *Xenogenesis* more hopeful than *Frankenstein*, Theodora Goss and John Paul Riquelme note that "[h]uman and creature never bridge their differences in Shelley's narrative, but in Butler's they do . . ." (437).

The signal phrase names the authors of the secondary source; the number in parentheses is the page on which the quoted words appear.

The in-text citation is used in combination with a list of works cited at the end of the paper. Anyone interested in knowing additional information about the source can consult the list of works cited. Here, for example, is the works cited entry for the work referred to in the sample in-text citation.

ENTRY IN THE LIST OF WORKS CITED

Goss, Theodora, and John Paul Riquelme. "From Superhuman to Posthuman: The Gothic Technological Imaginary in Mary Shelley's *Frankenstein* and Octavia Butler's *Xenogenesis*." *Modern Fiction Studies*, vol. 53, no. 3, 2007, pp. 434-59.

L6-b Avoid plagiarism.

The rules about plagiarism are the same for literature papers as for other academic and research writing. To be fair and ethical, you must acknowledge your responsibility to the writers of any sources you use. If you don't, you commit plagiarism, a serious academic offence.

In general, three different acts are considered plagiarism: (1) failing to cite quotations and borrowed ideas, (2) failing to enclose borrowed language in quotation marks, and (3) failing to put summaries and paraphrases in your own words.

If another critic's work suggested an interpretation or if someone else's research clarified a point, it is your responsibility to cite the source (see L6-a). In addition, you must place any borrowed language in quotation marks. In the following example, the plagiarized words are underlined.

ORIGINAL SOURCE

Here again Glaspell's story reflects a larger truth about the lives of rural women. Their isolation induced madness in many. The rate of insanity in rural areas, especially for women, was a much-discussed subject in the second half of the nineteenth century.

— Elaine Hedges, "Small Things Reconsidered: 'A Jury of Her Peers,'" p. 59

PLAGIARISM

Glaspell may or may not want us to believe that Minnie Wright's murder of her husband is an insane act, but Minnie's loneliness and isolation certainly could have driven her mad. As Elaine Hedges notes, the rate of insanity in rural areas, especially for women, was a much-discussed subject in the second half of the nineteenth century (59).

BORROWED LANGUAGE IN QUOTATION MARKS

Glaspell may or may not want us to believe that Minnie Wright's murder of her husband is an insane act, but Minnie's loneliness and isolation certainly could have driven her mad. As Elaine Hedges notes, "The rate of insanity in rural areas, especially for women, was a much-discussed subject in the second half of the nineteenth century" (59).

Sometimes writers plagiarize unintentionally because they have difficulty paraphrasing a source's ideas. In the first paraphrase of the following source, the writer has copied the underlined words (without quotation marks) and followed the sentence structure of the source too closely, merely plugging in synonyms (*prowess* for *skill*, *respect* for *esteem*, and so on).

ORIGINAL SOURCE

Mothers [in the late nineteenth century] were advised to teach their daughters to make small, exact stitches, not only for durability but as a way of instilling habits of patience, neatness, and diligence. But such stitches also became a badge of one's needlework skill, a source of self-esteem and of status, through the recognition and admiration of other women.

— Elaine Hedges, "Small Things Reconsidered:
'A Jury of Her Peers,'" p. 62

PLAGIARISM: UNACCEPTABLE BORROWING

One of the final clues in the story, the irregular stitching in Minnie's quilt patches, connects immediately with Mrs. Hale and Mrs. Peters. In the late nineteenth century, explains Elaine Hedges, small, exact stitches were valued not only for their durability. They became a badge of one's prowess with the needle, a source of self-respect and of prestige, through the recognition and approval of other women (62).

ACCEPTABLE PARAPHRASE

One of the final clues in the story, the irregular stitching in Minnie's quilt patches, connects immediately with Mrs. Hale and Mrs. Peters. In the late nineteenth century, explains Elaine Hedges, precise needlework was valued for more than its strength. It was a source of pride to women, a way of gaining status in the community of other women (62).

Although the acceptable version uses a few words found in the original source, it does not borrow entire phrases without quotation marks or closely mimic the structure of the original. To write an acceptable paraphrase, resist the temptation to look at the source while you write; instead, write from memory. When you write from memory, you are more likely to use your own words. Ask yourself, "What is the author's meaning?" and then state your understanding of the author's basic point in your own words.

L7 Sample papers

Following are two sample essays that analyze literary works. The first (Peel) has no secondary sources. The second (Larson) uses secondary sources.

Peel 1

Margaret Peel

Professor Lin

English 102

20 April 2015

Opposing Voices in "Ballad of the Landlord"

Langston Hughes's "Ballad of the Landlord" is narrated through
four voices, each with its own perspective on the poem's action. These
opposing voices—of a tenant, a landlord, the police, and the press—
dramatize a black man's experience in a society dominated by whites.

> Thesis states Peel's main idea.

The main voice in the poem is that of the tenant, who, as the
last line tells us, is black. The tenant is characterized by his informal,
nonstandard speech. He uses slang ("Ten Bucks"), contracted words
(*'member, more'n*), and nonstandard grammar ("These steps is broken
down"). This colloquial English suggests the tenant's separation from the
world of convention, represented by the formal voices of the police and
the press, which appear later in the poem.

> Details from the poem illustrate Peel's point.

Although the tenant uses nonstandard English, his argument is
organized and logical. He begins with a reasonable complaint and a
gentle reminder that the complaint is already a week old: "My roof
has sprung a leak. / Don't you 'member I told you about it / Way last
week?" (lines 2-4). In the second stanza, he appeals diplomatically to the
landlord's self-interest: "These steps is broken down. / When you come up
yourself / It's a wonder you don't fall down" (6-8). In the third stanza,
when the landlord has responded to his complaints with a demand for rent
money, the tenant becomes more forceful, but his voice is still reasonable:
"Ten Bucks you say is due? / Well, that's Ten Bucks more'n I'll pay you / Till
you fix this house up new" (10-12).

> The first citation for lines of the poem includes the word "lines." Subsequent citations from the poem are cited with line numbers alone.

The fourth stanza marks a shift in the tone of the argument. At this
point the tenant responds more emotionally, in reaction to the landlord's
threats to evict him. By the fifth stanza, the tenant has unleashed his
anger: "Um-huh! You talking high and mighty" (17). Hughes uses an
exclamation point for the first time; the tenant is raising his voice at
last. As the argument gets more heated, the tenant finally resorts to the
language of violence: "You ain't gonna be able to say a word / If I land
my fist on you" (19-20).

> Topic sentence focuses on an interpretation.

Marginal annotations indicate MLA-style formatting and effective writing.

Peel 2

Transition
prepares readers
for the next topic.

These are the last words the tenant speaks in the poem. Perhaps Hughes wants to show how black people who threaten violence are silenced. When a new voice is introduced—the landlord's—the poem shifts to a frantic tone:

> Police! Police!
>
> Come and get this man!
>
> He's trying to ruin the government
>
> And overturn the land! (21-24)

This response is clearly an overreaction to a small threat. Instead of dealing with the tenant directly, the landlord shouts for the police. His hysterical voice—marked by repetitions and punctuated with exclamation points—reveals his disproportionate fear and outrage. And his conclusions are equally excessive: this black man, he claims, is out to "ruin the government" and "overturn the land." Although the landlord's overreaction is humorous, it is sinister as well, because the landlord knows that, no matter how excessive his claims are, he has the police and the law on his side.

Peel interprets
the landlord's
response.

Peel shows how
meter and rhyme
support the
poem's meaning.

In line 25, the regular meter and rhyme of the poem break down, perhaps showing how an arrest disrupts everyday life. The "voice" in lines 25-29 has two parts: the clanging sound of the police ("Copper's whistle! / Patrol bell!") and, in sharp contrast, the unemotional, factual tone of a police report ("Arrest. / Precinct Station. / Iron cell.").

Peel sums up
her interpretation.

The last voice in the poem is the voice of the press, represented in newspaper headlines: "MAN THREATENS LANDLORD / TENANT HELD NO BAIL / JUDGE GIVES NEGRO 90 DAYS IN COUNTY JAIL" (31-33). Meter and rhyme return here, as if to show that once the tenant is arrested, life can go on as usual. The language of the press, like that of the police, is cold and distant, and it gives the tenant less and less status. In line 31, he is a "man"; in line 32, he has been demoted to a "tenant"; and in line 33, he has become a "Negro," or just another statistic.

By using four opposing voices in "Ballad of the Landlord," Hughes effectively dramatizes different views of minority assertiveness. To the tenant, assertiveness is informal and natural, as his language shows; to the landlord, it is a dangerous threat, as his hysterical response suggests. The police response is, like the language that describes it, short and

Peel 3

sharp. Finally, the press's view of events, represented by the headlines, is distant and unsympathetic.

By the end of the poem, we understand the predicament of the black man. Exploited by the landlord, politically oppressed by those who think he's out "to ruin the government," physically restrained by the police and the judicial system, and denied his individuality by the press, he is saved only by his own sense of humour. The very title of the poem suggests his—and Hughes's—sense of humor. The tenant is singing a *ballad* to his oppressors, but this ballad is no love song. It portrays the oppressors, through their own voices, in an unflattering light: the landlord as cowardly and ridiculous, the police and press as dull and soulless. The tenant may lack political power, but he speaks with vitality, and no one can say he lacks dignity or the spirit to survive.

Peel concludes with an analysis of the poem's political significance.

Larson 1

Dan Larson

Professor Duncan

English 102

17 April 2013

The Transformation of Mrs. Peters:

An Analysis of "A Jury of Her Peers"

The opening lines name the story and establish context.

In Susan Glaspell's 1917 short story "A Jury of Her Peers," two women accompany their husbands and a county attorney to an isolated house where a farmer named John Wright has been choked to death in his bed with a rope. The chief suspect is Wright's wife, Minnie, who is in jail awaiting trial. The sheriff's wife, Mrs. Peters, has come along to gather some personal items for Minnie, and Mrs. Hale has joined her. Early in the story, Mrs. Hale sympathizes with Minnie and objects to the way the male investigators are "snoopin' round and criticizin'" her kitchen (249). In contrast, Mrs. Peters shows respect for the law, saying that the men are doing "no more than their duty" (249). By the end of the story, however, Mrs. Peters has joined Mrs. Hale in a conspiracy of silence, lied to the men, and committed a crime—hiding key evidence. What causes this dramatic change?

Present tense is used to describe details from the story.

Quotations from the story are cited with page numbers in parentheses.

The opening paragraph ends with Larson's research question.

One critic, Leonard Mustazza, argues that Mrs. Hale recruits Mrs. Peters "as a fellow 'juror' in the case, moving the sheriff's wife away from her sympathy for her husband's position and towards identification with the accused wom[a]n" (494). While this is true, Mrs. Peters also reaches insights on her own. Her observations in the kitchen lead her to understand Minnie's grim and lonely plight as the wife of an abusive farmer, and her identification with both Minnie and Mrs. Hale is strengthened as the men conducting the investigation trivialize the lives of women.

The thesis asserts Larson's main point.

The first evidence that Mrs. Peters reaches understanding on her own surfaces in the following passage:

A long quotation is set off by indenting; no quotation marks are needed; ellipsis dots indicate a sentence omitted from the source.

> The sheriff's wife had looked from the stove to the sink—
> to the pail of water which had been carried in from
> outside. . . . That look of seeing into things, of seeing
> through a thing to something else, was in the eyes of the sheriff's
> wife now. (251-52)

Larson 2

Something about the stove, the sink, and the pail of water connects with her own experience, giving Mrs. Peters a glimpse into the life of Minnie Wright. The details resonate with meaning.

Social historian Elaine Hedges argues that such details, which evoke the drudgery of a farm woman's work, would not have been lost on Glaspell's readers in 1917. Hedges tells us what the pail and the stove, along with another detail from the story—a dirty towel on a roller—would have meant to women of the time. Laundry was a dreaded all-day affair. Water had to be pumped, hauled, and boiled; then the wash was rubbed, rinsed, wrung through a wringer, carried outside, and hung on a line to dry. "What the women see, beyond the pail and the stove," writes Hedges, "are the hours of work it took Minnie to produce that one clean towel" (56).

On her own, Mrs. Peters discovers clues about the motive for the murder. Her curiosity leads her to pick up a sewing basket filled with quilt pieces and then to notice something strange: a sudden row of badly sewn stitches. "What do you suppose she was so—nervous about?" asks Mrs. Peters (252). A short time later, Mrs. Peters spots another clue, an empty birdcage. Again she observes details on her own, in this case a broken door and hinge, suggesting that the cage has been roughly handled.

In addition to noticing details, both women draw conclusions from them and speculate on their significance. When Mrs. Hale finds the dead canary beneath a quilt patch, for example, the women conclude that its neck has been wrung and understand who must have wrung it.

As the women speculate on the significance of the dead canary, each connects the bird with her own experience. Mrs. Hale knows that Minnie once sang in the church choir, an activity that Mr. Wright put a stop to, just as he put a stop to the bird's singing. Also, as a farmer's wife, Mrs. Hale understands the desolation and loneliness of life on the prairie. She sees that the bird was both a thing of beauty and a companion. "If there had been years and years of—nothing, then a bird to sing to you," says Mrs. Hale, "it would be awful—still—after the bird was still" (256). To Mrs. Peters, the stillness of the canary evokes memories of the time when she and her husband homesteaded in the northern plains. "I know what stillness is," she says, as she recalls the death of her first child, with no one around to console her (256).

Larson summarizes ideas from a secondary source and then quotes from that source; he names the author in a signal phrase and gives a page number in parentheses.

Topic sentences present Larson's interpretation.

Details from the story provide evidence for the interpretation.

Larson 3

Elaine Hedges has written movingly of the isolation that women experienced on late-nineteenth- and early-twentieth-century farms of the West and Midwest:

> Women themselves reported that it was not unusual to spend five months in a log cabin without seeing another woman . . . or to spend one and a half years after arriving before being able to take a trip to town. . . . (54)

To combat loneliness and monotony, says Hedges, many women bought canaries and hung the cages outside their sod huts. The canaries provided music and colour, a "spot of beauty" that "might spell the difference between sanity and madness" (60).

Mrs. Peters and Mrs. Hale understand—and Glaspell's readers in 1917 would have understood—what the killing of the bird means to Minnie. For Mrs. Peters, in fact, the act has a special significance. When she was a child, a boy axed her kitten to death and, as she says, "If they hadn't held me back I would have . . . hurt him" (256). She has little difficulty comprehending Minnie's murderous rage, for she has felt it herself.

Although Mrs. Peters's growing empathy for Minnie stems largely from her observations, it is also prompted by her negative reaction to the patronizing comments of the male investigators. At several points in the story, her body language reveals her feelings. For example, when Mr. Hale remarks that "women are used to worrying over trifles," both women move closer together and remain silent. When the county attorney asks, "for all their worries, what would we do without the ladies?" the women do not speak, nor do they "unbend" (248). The fact that the women respond in exactly the same way reveals the extent to which they are bonding.

Both women are annoyed at the way in which the men criticize and trivialize the world of women. The men question the difficulty of women's work. For example, when the county attorney points to the dirty towel on the rack as evidence that Minnie wasn't much of a housekeeper, Mrs. Hale replies, "There's a great deal of work to be done on a farm" (248). Even the importance of women's work is questioned. The men kid the women for trying to decide if Minnie was going to quilt or knot patches together for a quilt and laugh about such trivial concerns. Those very

---

Ellipsis dots indicate omitted words within the sentence and at the end of the sentence.

Transition serves as a bridge from one section of the paper to the next.

Larson 4

quilts, of course, kept the men warm at night and cost them nothing
beyond the price of thread.

The men also question the women's wisdom and intelligence. For
example, when the county attorney tells the women to keep their eyes out
for clues, Mr. Hale replies, "But would the women know a clue if they did
come upon it?" (249). The women's response is to stand motionless and
silent. The irony is that the men don't see the household clues that are
right in front of them.

By the end of the story, Mrs. Peters has been so transformed that
she risks lying to the men. When the county attorney walks into the
kitchen and notices the birdcage the women have found, he asks about the
whereabouts of the bird. Mrs. Hale replies, "We think the cat got it" (255),
even though she knows from Mrs. Peters that Minnie was afraid of cats
and would not have owned one. Instead of correcting the lie, Mrs. Peters
elaborates on it, saying of cats, "They're superstitious, you know; they
leave" (255). Clearly Mrs. Hale is willing to risk lying because she is
confident that Mrs. Peters won't contradict her.

> Larson gives
> evidence that
> Mrs. Peters
> has been
> transformed.

The Mrs. Peters character may have been based on a real sheriff's
wife. Seventeen years before writing "A Jury of Her Peers," Susan Glaspell
covered a murder case for the *Des Moines Daily News*. A farmer's wife,
Margaret Hossack, was accused of murdering her sleeping husband with
two axe blows to the head. In one of her newspaper reports, Glaspell wrote
that the sheriff's wife sat next to Mrs. Hossack and "frequently applied her
handkerchief to her eyes" (qtd. in Ben-Zvi 30).

> Larson draws
> on a secondary
> source that gives
> background on
> Glaspell's life.

We do not know from the short story the ultimate fate of Minnie
Wright, but Margaret Hossack, whose case inspired the story, was found
guilty, though the case was later thrown out by the Iowa Supreme Court.
However, as Linda Ben-Zvi points out, the women's guilt or innocence is
not the issue:

> Whether Margaret Hossack or Minnie Wright committed
> murder is moot; what is incontrovertible is the brutality
> of their lives, the lack of options they had to redress
> grievances or to escape abusive husbands, and the
> complete disregard of their plight by the courts and by
> society. (38)

Larson 5

These are the issues that Susan Glaspell wished to stress in "A Jury of Her Peers."

These are also the issues that Mrs. Peters comes to understand as the story unfolds, with her understanding deepening as she identifies with Minnie and Mrs. Hale and is repulsed by male attitudes. Her transformation becomes complete when the men joke that she is "married to the law" and she responds by violating the law: hiding key evidence, the dead canary.

Larson 6

Works Cited

Ben-Zvi, Linda. "'Murder, She Wrote': The Genesis of Susan Glaspell's *Trifles*." *Susan Glaspell: Essays on Her Theater and Fiction*, edited by Ben-Zvi, U of Michigan P, 1995, pp. 19-48. Originally published in *Theatre Journal*, vol. 44, no. 2, May 1992, pp. 141-62.

Glaspell, Susan. "A Jury of Her Peers." *Literature and Its Writers: An Introduction to Fiction, Poetry, and Drama*, edited by Ann Charters and Samuel Charters, 6th ed., Bedford/St. Martin's, 2013, pp. 243-58.

Hedges, Elaine. "Small Things Reconsidered: 'A Jury of Her Peers.'" *Susan Glaspell: Essays on Her Theater and Fiction*, edited by Linda Ben-Zvi, U of Michigan P, 1995, pp. 49-69.

Mustazza, Leonard. "Generic Translation and Thematic Shift in Susan Glaspell's *Trifles* and 'A Jury of Her Peers.'" *Studies in Short Fiction*, vol. 26, no. 4, Fall 1989, pp. 489-96.

Index

Index

In addition to giving you page numbers, this index shows you which tabbed section to flip to. For example, the entry "*a* vs. *an*" directs you to section **W** (Word Choice), page 141, and to section **M** (Multilingual Writers and ESL Topics), page 234. Just flip to the appropriate tabbed section and then track down the exact pages you need.

Multilingual/ESL Menu

A complete section for multilingual writers:

ESL and Academic English notes in other sections:

Revision Symbols

Letter-number codes refer to sections of this book.

abbr	faulty abbreviation		p	error in punctuation
adj	misuse of adjective **G4**		ʼ	comma **P1**
add	add needed word **S2**		no ,	no comma **P2**
adv	misuse of adverb **G4**		;	semicolon **P3**
agr	faulty agreement **G1, G3-a**		:	colon **P3**
appr	inappropriate language **W4**		ʼ	apostrophe **P4**
art	article **M2**		" "	quotation marks **P5**
awk	awkward		. ?	period, question mark **P6**
cap	capital letter **P8**		!	exclamation point **P6**
case	error in case **G3-c, G3-d**		— ( )	dash, parentheses **P6**
cliché	cliché **W5-e**		[ ] . . .	brackets, ellipsis mark **P6**
coh	coherence **C5-d**		/	slash **P6**
coord	faulty coordination **S6-c**		pass	ineffective passive **W3**
cs	comma splice **G6**		pn agr	pronoun agreement **G3-a**
dev	inadequate development **C5-b**		proof	proofreading problem **C3-d**
dm	dangling modifier **S3-e**		ref	error in pronoun reference **G3-b**
-ed	error in -*ed* ending **G2-d**		run-on	run-on sentence **G6**
emph	emphasis **S6**		-s	error in -*s* ending **G2-c**
ESL	ESL grammar **M1, M2, M3, M4, M5**		sexist	sexist language **W4-f**
exact	inexact language **W5**		shift	distracting shift **S4**
frag	sentence fragment **G5**		sl	slang **W4-d**
fs	fused sentence **G6**		sp	misspelled word **P7**
gl/us	see glossary of usage **W1**		sub	faulty subordination **S6-d**
hyph	error in use of hyphen **P7**		sv agr	subject-verb agreement **G1, G2-c**
idiom	idiom **W5-d**		t	error in verb tense **G2-f**
ic	incomplete construction **S2**		trans	transition needed **C5-d**
irreg	error in irregular verb **G2-a**		usage	see glossary of usage **W1**
ital	italics **P10**		v	voice **W3**
jarg	jargon **W4-a**		var	sentence variety **S6-b, S6-c, S7**
lc	lowercase letter **P8**		vb	verb error **G2**
mix	mixed construction **S5**		w	wordy **W2**
mm	misplaced modifier **S3-b**		//	faulty parallelism **S1**
mood	error in mood **G2-g**		^	insert
nonst	nonstandard usage **W4-c**		×	obvious error
num	error in use of number **P9**		#	insert space
om	omitted word **S2**		◡	close up space
¶	new paragraph **C5**			

Detailed Menu